DETROIT STUDIES IN MUSIC BIBLIOGRAPHY
GENERAL EDITOR   BRUNO NETTL   UNIVERSITY OF ILLINOIS AT URBANA-CHAMPAIGN

anal

DETROIT STUDIES IN MUSIC BIBLIOGRAPHY NUMBER FORTY-SEVEN

MUSICAL INSTRUMENT COLLECTIONS
CATALOGUES AND COGNATE LITERATURE

JAMES COOVER

INFORMATION COORDINATORS 1981 DETROIT

Copyright © 1981 by James Coover

Printed and bound in the United States of America
Published by
Information Coordinators, Inc., 1435-37 Randolph Street, Detroit, Michigan 48226

Book design and incidental artwork by Vincent Kibildis

Library of Congress Cataloging in Publication Data

Coover, James, 1925-
    Musical instrument collections.
    (Detroit studies in music bibliography ;
47)
    Includes indexes.
    1. Musical instruments—Catalogs and
collections—Bibliography. I. Title.
II. Series.
ML 155.C63   016.78191'074   81-19901
ISBN 0-89990-013-5   AACR2

AU

CONTENTS

PREFACE

Scope. When this project began many years ago it was loosely aimed at organizing the catalogues of three different kinds of musical instrument collections: 1) those in institutions like the Brussels Conservatoire or the Vienna Kunsthistorisches Museum; 2) those shown in exhibitions like that at the South Kensington Museum in 1872[1] or at the Internationale Ausstellung in Vienna in 1892; and 3) those in private hands like the collections of Paul de Wit, Wilhelm Heyer, and Canon Galpin.[2]

Over the years the search turned up far more, of course, than just catalogues and inventories. Masses of cognate literature accumulated—historical notices, articles about choice items in various collections, summaries of institutions' and collectors' holdings, visitors' guides, reviews of important catalogues, and related publications. These all seemed important and have been included in this book. Other kinds of material sought admission and were denied: biographical works about collectors, curators and compilers of catalogues; trade lists and catalogues from manufacturers;[3] and histories of the collections. Biographical materials are readily available elsewhere, and histories seem unnecessary for they are usually contained in the literature which is cited here. Though there is more disagreement among the writers of those "histories" than one might expect, this is not the place to explain those differences. A few brief historical notes have been included to explain the arrangement of materials under certain entries (e.g., the Kunsthistorisches Museum, Vienna) or to call attention to some provocative questions (e.g., see under CORBETT in Section II). Information about current addresses of museums, their hours, facilities, services and staff has been

---

[1] Organized by Carl Engel, it was the first devoted solely to musical instruments.

[2] A vast amount of literature about private collections of books and scores was accumulated during the same period, and a complementary bibliography of that material is forthcoming.

[3] Literature about their products in expositions and about their own permanent historical collections, however, has been included.

left to a number of handy, recently-published directories, such as those by Adelmann, Lichtenwanger, Brody and Brook, and Jenkins.[4]

Though not at the outset seen as part of the scope of this work, there was no way finally to resist including the literature about regional, national, and international expositions. As early as 1818, the exposition in Paris included musical instruments; the reports and catalogues of those since then—many of them prepared by writers such as Fétis and Berlioz—tell us much about organology and a great deal about the musical marketplace. Perhaps this literature is of less historical interest now than that about museums, exhibitions, and private collections, but if it is made more readily available it should grow in importance.[5]

Many kinds of information were finally brought together in this bibliography and its organization became a problem. Obviously, the literature about institutional collections and exhibits was separable from that about personal collections, but it was not so easy to decide what to do with lesser expositions, "salons," "foires," "Messe," and the literature about them. They have been allowed to rest, a little uneasily perhaps, among the institutional entries in Section I. Most of the large expositions up to 1977 have been included, but the coverage of these smaller, local and national trade fairs ends at about 1940; after that date information about them is readily available and the contents of the shows of less historical interest.

Establishing a separate section for the literature about private collections (Section II) raised the sometimes insoluble problem of deciding just when a collection should be considered "private." Do the inventories of and literature about Ferdinand de Medici's sixteenth-century "Guardaroba," for example, belong under his name in Section II, or under the collection's present abode, the Conservatorio in Florence, in Section I? In most cases, it was decided to keep the information under the collector's name up to the date when it became part of an institution's holdings, a date sometimes difficult to establish. For obvious reasons deliberate exceptions were made for the Ambras, Ruhelust, and Este collections (private for decades under their various counts and dukes), and they are entered under the Vienna Kunsthistorisches Museum in Section I. Occasionally, in such cases, the form chosen for an entry accords with that in the scholarly literature instead of that prescribed by library cataloguing codes, but abundant cross references and a detailed General Index ought to lead readers to what they want.

Two Appendices and a supplemental index are included as a complement to that General Index—and for whatever historical purpose they may serve on their own. The first

---

[4] After entries for a number of museums in Section I, alphanumeric sigla are employed to refer users to specific places in one of these directories. Sigla used are A, BB, J, and L, and complete citations for them will be found in the list on page 17.

[5] Almost as this book goes to press, a serious study of one kind of musical instrument shown at several important trade fairs has appeared, E. J. Shillitoe's "Violin Making at the Great Exhibitions," in *The Strad* 89 (1979): 911-17, 1011-15, 1125-39; 90 (1979): 125-28, 197-200, 358-62. The expositions covered are: Paris, 1827, 1834, 1839, 1844, 1849; London, 1851; Paris, 1855; London, 1862. Shillitoe utilizes many of the official catalogues and reports from those shows along with standard reference tools.

Appendix lists inventories of collections, private and public, up to 1825 (a wholly arbitrary date without organological significance). The second identifies exhibitions and expositions by their place and title up to 1977.

Some catalogues of private collections in Section II comprise what seem to be relatively small groups of instruments, some so small perhaps as to scarcely deserve being called a "collection." A decision was made, however, to err on the side of being too inclusive rather than exclusive, with the hope that users of the list would be tolerant and make their own decisions if necessary. Value of the instruments consigned to a sale was one criterion for inclusion in this Section II, age another. Some small groups in sales before 1825 have been cited as collections though a group of similar size and value sold after 1850 may have been left out.

A sampling of sales of properties belonging to unnamed collectors commences Section II, a sampling, by date, and by no means exhaustive. Included are a few sales of noteworthy contents, several early nineteenth-century sales, and a smattering of the hundreds of Puttick & Simpson auction catalogues issued between 1846 and 1971 which —though the consignors were not identified—were sufficiently important to attract notice in the journal literature of the time. [6]

Format—Section I. The citations beneath each entry in Section I are divided into three *categories.* Because some decisions about where to place a citation were unavoidably subjective, or even conjectural if the item could not be examined, users may disagree with some of the assignments.

The first category (unmarked) includes, in general, the most important materials—a catalogue or other useful list of an institution's holdings, and in some case, prose works standing in lieu of a true catalogue or list.

The second category (marked by the symbol *"Literature"*) includes article and books that describe and discuss the collections or parts of them.

The third category (marked by the symbol *"General"*) encompasses museum and exposition guides, descriptions and reports—usually official— containing sections dealing with musical instruments.

Within the three categories all citations are arranged chronologically. Only the first and second are appropriate for, and used in, Section II.

Locations are supplied for most items cited in the bibliography that were especially difficult to find. Codes used are those of the *National Union Catalog* and the *Répertoire International des Bibliothèques Musicales* (with some modifications and additions; see pages 29-30). No such information is offered for journals as there are other tools for locating them.

---

[6] A history of the firm on which the author is at work will include chronological listings of all of the auctions that included musical instruments (in whatever numbers); those devoted to music scores, manuscripts, and books about music; and those devoted to music publishers' copyrights, plates, stock, good-will, and other paraphernalia.

Abbreviations for secondary sources have been kept to a minimum, but for a number of them that are repeatedly cited (with an asterisk, e.g. Lugt*), as well as some journals, standard sigla have been used and these, with their tags, appear in the list on pages 17-27.

Format—Section II. *Entries* for private collections are often a problem; it is not always certain that the instruments in a catalogue belonged to the individual(s) named on the title page. Some of the attributions here are doubtless erroneous, therefore; others—in cases where the title page does not identify the collector—have been identified through dealers' records, manuscript annotations in catalogues belonging to persons who attended the sales, and various secondary sources such as Lugt*. Catalogues of sales of the properties of more than one instrument collector are entered here only once (with appropriate cross references from the others' names) and generally under the collector whose properties seem to be the most important. Order of names on title pages was mostly ignored.

Ellipses have been used abundantly in an effort to make exceedingly complex title pages as informative but brief as possible. Most of the Dutch and English title pages are voluminous, composed of dozens of lines, each in a different typeface, and though the entries here may seem long, they are in many cases severely shortened in order to eliminate other items in the sales such as "preserved birds," "dead and living farm stock," "sulphur impressions," "genteel furniture," "two ricks of hay," "a capital mangle," and some "capital goosefeather beds."

No lengthy *imprints* are given for most catalogues, and for those from Christie and Puttick & Simpson, not even the place of publication; that should be understood to be London. It should also be understood that the Christie catalogues presently shelved in the muniments room at Christie's in London all include the names of buyers and prices fetched in Ms. as do the Puttick & Simpson catalogues at the British Library. For catalogues from other dealers this feature, if present, is specifically noted beneath each citation.

Annotations occasionally point out interesting aspects and unusual contents, but the lack of such a comment must not be construed to indicate a lack of worth. In travel and correspondence attempting to identify catalogues of unusual interest, there was not always time or circumstance permitting close study. To facilitate—perhaps stimulate—close study of auction catalogues is one purpose of this publication.

Forbears. This work builds on forbears, of course, a long line of them.[7] It attempts to collate the information they presented, verify it, correct it where necessary,[8] assemble a

---

[7] One of the most helpful that compiled by Mr. Michael Wilson of the Victoria & Albert Museum Library (see citation, LV&A*, p. 24). He has been helpful to this compiler through extensive correspondence as well.

[8] Several incorrect datings for one of the SAVOYE catalogues (see item **2272**) typify the problem: Bricqueville* thought it to be 1887, Lambertini* 1880, Weckerlin* 1862, though the title page of the copy at NRU(Rs) clearly states "15 mai 1882." And the Nottebohm *Katalog* of the Gesellschaft der Musikfreunde collection (see item **1542**), cited from Schlesinger*, does not exist, according to Gesellschaft.

complete citation for each reference, standardize the bibliographical format, group the citations as rationally as possible, and add explanations where they seem useful. Many citations gleaned from secondary sources other than those listed were subjected to the same rigors.

But the work is far from done. Despite the seeming wealth of information about such famed collections as the Ambras and Medici, for example, more careful studies need to be undertaken, especially comparative studies of early collections, their contents, their inventories,[9] the makers of the instruments,[10] and their actual employment. The present-day whereabouts of many early private collections (like CORBETT's mentioned above) remains to be established. The organological and historical importance of the instruments shown in some of the more lavish national and international expositions has received slight attention.[11] New *gesamt* catalogues of some of the "monumental" collections—even those catalogued earlier by Mahillon, Bierdimpfl, Schlosser, Chouquet/Pillaut, and others—would be estimable aids to modern researchers. The catalogues of several important collections badly need to be re-done in standard terminology within established classification systems, providing more scientific, organological data.[12]

The search for addenda to this bibliography needs to continue. Hundreds of museum and exposition catalogues, reports, and guides remain to be examined, but they are scattered and difficult to locate. Most major national libraries possess but a small percentage of those which have been published—as a quick glance at the appropriate section in any national bibliography, such as Kayser's *Bücher-Lexikon,* reveals. The same kind of examination must be given the hundreds of volumes of musical and non-musical journals to which this compiler has not had access. Auction catalogues, literally by the thousands, need to be scrutinized; they are generally difficult to find, some impossible. Unfortunately many libraries have treated them, even large runs of them, as "ephemera," allowing them to deteriorate, to be lost or misplaced. In some cases they have been casually discarded. They do not appear in most libraries' card or printed catalogues. The so-called "comprehensive" national bibliographies have routinely ignored them. Scholars have been slow to recognize their value. While those from the major firm of Sotheby are now available on microfilm (in the U.S. from the Center of Research Libraries), most English sale catalogues cannot be so readily studied. Auction catalogues from Christie, Musgrave, White, and others—even those

---

[9] For example, Anthony Baines' "Two Cassel Inventories," *GSJ* 4 (1951): 31-34.

[10] An exemplary recent study is that by Maurice Byrne of instruments made by Rafi in Settala's seventeenth-century collection (see item **2302**).

[11] The Jury reports and other articles written by such luminaries as Fétis, La Fage, and Pontécoulant about the instruments shown at the international exposition in Paris in 1855, for example, appear to have been mostly neglected by scholars. The documents have not been easy to locate, but they deserve serious review and re-assessment, as do the materials exhibited. Shillitoe's series of articles (*op. cit.*) is a beginning, but only a beginning.

[12] Interesting progress is being made towards a universal, standardized cataloguing form for musical instruments by the Comité International des Musées et Collections. See the recent proposal by Denise Perret, "Fiche organologique," *CIMCIM (IAMIC) Newsletter* 3/4 (1975/76): 29-34 plus 2 folded forms.

conveniently listed for musicians by A. H. King in the Appendix to his *Some British Collectors of Music*—are found in the United States more through luck than planning. Those from German, French, and other continental dealers are still more fugitive. The basic, first task of discovering what exists to be scrutinized and evaluated can be irksome indeed. Serendipity plays a very large role.[13]

Aside from King's list (restricted to music collections—no instruments), only four large, important aids have been published: Frits Lugt's extraordinary *Répertoire* (see "Sources," p. 24), a union list of some 58,000 auction catalogues containing *objets d'art* (and musical instruments); the list of *English Book Sales, 1676-1900* in the British Museum that Munby and Coral's works will supercede; the unique, comprehensive catalogues of the Vereeniging ter Bervordering van de Belangen des Boekhandels in Amsterdam (one of the handful of institutions which—like the Grolier Club in New York City, and to their great credit—has treated such catalogues as something other than ephemera); the *Internationale Bibliographie der Antiquariats-, Auktions- und Kunstkataloge* begun in 1965 by Gerhard Loh; and the recently announced microfiche edition of some 20,000 *Catalogs of the Art Exhibition Catalog Collection of the Arts Library, University of California at Santa Barbara.*

Some handwritten inventories and indexes exist but must be consulted *in situ,* as for example, the extensive index to sale catalogues of autographs prepared by Gabriel Austin at the Grolier Club, the Newberry Library's card inventory of sale catalogues with cryptic indication of their contents, or the Rijksbureau voor kunsthistorische Dokumentatie's copious indexes to catalogues issued since the publication of Lugt's *Répertoire.* The amount of information needing continual control and identification is almost inestimable.

Though much remains to be found and added to this bibliography, it, like all others, must be stopped. But stopping the first phase starts the second. I will be grateful to those who have access to materials that I was unable to examine and who are willing to furnish addenda and corrigenda for some future supplement.

---

[13] See Lenore Coral's more extensive comments about the sad state of affairs in the "Introduction" to her and A. N. L. Munby's recently-published *British Book Sale Catalogues, 1676-1800; A Union List* ([London]: Mansell, 1977). Her planned union list of nineteenth-century catalogues may alleviate some of the problems.

ACKNOWLEDGMENTS

Many persons with access to materials I could not see have been very generous with their time and expertise. Without their help this work would be far less dependable than it is. None of its shortcomings, of course, is their responsibility.

The libraries and staffs in charge of numerous collections in which some of this work was done deserve my profound gratitude. The Grolier Club and its Director, Mr. Robert Nikirk, could not have been more helpful to me and my assistant during several visits. A week spent at the Vereeniging ter Bervordering van de Belangen des Boekhandels in Amsterdam, and another at the Gemeentemuseum library in The Hague, were each remarkably productive and pleasurable. To the Director of the Bibliotheek at the Vereeniging, Dr. G. J. Brouwer, and his colleague Dr. F. van den Bosch I am deeply indebted for their help before, during, and after my visit. The staff in the rich collections at the Rijksbureau voor kunsthistorische Dokumentatie in The Hague also assisted me before, during, and after my visit. Access to some very early catalogues was provided by staff members of the Rijksprentenkabinet of the Rijksmuseum in Amsterdam on a fine Saturday afternoon when, I am certain, they would rather have been outside. J. P. Claxton Stevens of Christie's in London answered many questions and supplied me with many Xeroxes before giving me access to the firm's catalogues in their muniments room. Mrs. A. Loewenberg, assistant to the owner of Otto Haas Antiquariat, Mr. Albi Rosenthal, found invaluable information for me—on the spur of the moment—about Liepmannssohn and Haas catalogues and extended unusually gracious hospitality. I am very much in debt to the many persons at the British Library for their help and encouragement extending over a number of years, most recently to Mr. Oliver W. Neighbour's staff, especially Mr. Malcolm Turner for answers to some difficult questions, and to the Book Delivery Service in the General Reading Room under its supervisor, Mr. R. F. Sutton, whose staff, for several weeks, escorted me back and forth to the sale catalogues in the stacks. Colleagues in the Special Collections at both the Newberry Library and at the University of Chicago were equally considerate.

The Sibley Music Library at the Eastman School of Music (and its Associate Director, Mr. Charles Lindahl), as well as the Library of Congress Music Division (and in particular, Ms. Barbara Henry), and the Rare Book Section of the Research Division of the New York Public Library's Music Division, under its head, Ms. Susan Sommer, were helpful and understanding as I leafed through many of their fragile journals and catalogues. Patiently they also answered my telephone and written requests for verifications and collations, and "just one more Xerox copy." I must also thank Mr. and Mrs. Harrison Horblit of Ridgefield, Connecticut for giving me the chance to examine his collection of Puttick & Simpson catalogues (formerly those of the famous Sir Thomas Phillipps). And finally, to Ms. Lenore Coral I am indebted for timely suggestions, citations, and other information.

Though an efficient and sympathetic Interlibrary Loan Service is a *sine qua non* of most humanistic research nowadays, and though that service is often taken for granted, I do not want that at the State University of New York in Buffalo, under the guidance of Ms. Helen Kroll, to go unextolled. Despite all of the problems I loaded upon them, they usually delivered what I needed, no matter how long it took, and I am very grateful to them.

To two of my colleagues in the Music Library at that same university, Ms. Carol June Bradley and Ms. Gudrun Kilburn, I am also obligated. The former's incisive editorial skills helped at several stages of the project, and she wisely and repeatedly called my attention to pestiferous problems which I kept hoping would just go away. Ms. Kilburn unravelled a distressing amount of opaque foreign-language prose to bring some order out of the seemingly infinite number of Herzogs and Erzherzogs whose lives affected this bibliography.

To others whose contributions, mostly via the mails, cannot be fully specified, my thanks. Each problem you helped to solve was, without your help, probably insoluble, and each solution was important:

Claude Abravanel, Director of the AMLI Music Library, Rubin Academy
    of Music, Jerusalem
Hugh Amory, Houghton Library, Harvard University
Dr. Alf Annegarn, Librarian, Instituut voor muziekwetenschap,
    Rijksuniversiteit, Utrecht
Dr. Otto Biba, Gesellschaft der Musikfreunde, Vienna
Ruth Bleecker, Curator of Music, Boston Public Library
François Borel, Musée d'ethnographie, Ville de Neuchâtel, Switzerland
J. E. Bridgewater, Curator, Abbey House Museum, Leeds (U.K.)
Rudolf Bruhin, Arbeitsgemeinschaft für schweizerische Orgeldenkmalpflege,
    Basel
Frank C. Campbell, Chief of the Music Division, Library and Museum
    of the Performing Arts, New York City
H. P. Corin, Mill House, St. Keyne, Lisheard, Cornwall
Margaret Crum, Bodleian Library, Oxford University
P. M. Doran, Book Library, Courtauld Institute of Art, London

Rudolf E. O. Ekkart, Keeper, Rijksmuseum Meermanno-Westreenianum,
    The Hague
Dena J. Epstein, Assistant Music Librarian, University of Chicago
Wolfgang Freitag, Fine Arts Library, Harvard University
Laila Garpe, Lending Department, Kungliga Biblioteket, Stockholm
Dr. C. J. J. von Gleich, Head of the Music Department, Gemeentemuseum,
    The Hague
Herbert K. Goodkind, of Goodkind and Chapman Violins, Larchmont,
    New York
Dr. R. Heilinger, Katalogabteilung, Österreichische Nationalbibliothek,
    Vienna
Dr. H. Henkel, Direktor, Musikinstrumenten-Museum, Karl-Marx
    Universität, Leipzig
Alfred B. Kuhn, Music Library, Yale University
Hans Lassen, Director, Købstadmuseet "Den gamle by," Aarhus
A. Märker, Bibliothek, Historisches Museum, Frankfurt a.M.
René de Maeyer, Curator, Instrumentenmuseum, Koninklijk Muziek-
    conservatorium van Brussel
Ralph Malbon, City Librarian, Liverpool
Jean E. O'Leary, Musical Instrument Department, Sotheby Parke Bernet,
    New York City
João Oliveira da Costa, Biblioteca Nacional de Lisboa
E. W. Quinn, Chief Science Librarian, John Crerar Library, Chicago
Paul Raspe, Library of the Conservatoire Royal de Musique, Brussels
Albi Rosenthal, Otto Haas Antiquariat, London
Dr. Arthur Simon, Musikethnologische Abteilung, Museum für Völkerkunde,
    Berlin
Caroline T. Spicer, Reference Dept., Olin Library, Cornell University
E. Stollar, Phillips (firm), auctioneers, London
Richard Usborne, Custodian, Fenton House, Hampstead, London
Dr. F. Vandenhole, Librarian, Head of the Documentation Department,
    Centrale Bibliotheek, Rijksuniversiteit, Ghent
Barbara F. Veloz, Reference Librarian, Smithsonian Institution Libraries,
    Washington, D.C.
Laurence Vittes, Theodore Front Music Literature, Beverly Hills, California
Simone Wallon, Conservateur, Bibliothèque Nationale, Paris
Graham Wells, Assistant Director, Musical Instrument Department,
    Sotheby Parke Bernet, London
Michael I. Wilson, Research Assistant, The Library, Victoria & Albert
    Museum, London
Prof. Emilia Zanetti, Librarian, Biblioteca musicale governativa del
    Conservatorio de musica "S. Cecilia," Rome

AUTHORITIES, SECONDARY SOURCES, AND JOURNALS
WITH SIGLA EMPLOYED IN THE BIBLIOGRAPHY

A   Adelmann, Marianne. *Musical Europe; An Illustrated Guide.* New York: Paddington Press, [1974].

AfMW   *Archiv für Musikwissenschaft.* Trossingen [etc.] : 1918-

Altenburg, Wilhelm. "Die Instrumentensammlung der South Kensington Museum und ihre Katalog," *ZfI* 21 (1900/1901): 518.

————. "Unmassgeblicke Bemerkungen über Instrumentensammlungen und die Nachbildung alter Originalstücke," *ZfI* 34 (1913/14): 369-71, 412-14.

American Association of Museums. *A Bibliography of Museums and Museum Work.* Compiled by Ralphe Clifton Smith. Washington: 1928.

AMIS   American Musical Instrument Society. *Newsletter.* 1975- .

BB   Brody, Elaine and Claire Brook. *Music Guide to Great Britain.* New York: Dodd, Mead, 1975.

————. *Music Guide to Belgium, Luxembourg, Holland, and Switzerland.* New York: Dodd, Mead, 1977.

BdMS   *Bibliographie des Musikschrifttums.* Frankfurt a.M.: 1936- .

Bibliographie der fremd-sprachigen Zeitschriftenliteratur. (Internationale Bibliographie der Zeitschriftenliteratur, Abt. B.) Gautzsch b. Leipzig: 1911-64.

BdZL   *Bibliographie der deutschen Zeitschriftenliteratur.* (Internationale Bibliographie der Zeitschriftenliteratur, Abt. A.) Gautzsch b. Leipzig: 1896-1964.

Bergmans, Paul. "De l'interét qu'il aurait à dresser un inventaire général des instruments de musique." In Fédération archéologique et histoire de Belgique, *Annales du XXIe congrès,* Tome II, pp. 666-73. Liège: Imp. Liègoise, 1909.

BM/BM-S   British Museum. Department of Printed Books. *General Catalogue of Printed Books,* 1881-1955. *Supplements,* 1956-1970. London.

BM Sales   British Museum. Department of Printed Books. *List of Catalogues of English Book Sales, 1676-1900.* London: British Museum, 1915.

British Museum. Department of Printed Books. *Subject Index of the Modern Works Added to the Library . . .* 1881-1960. Reprint ed. London: H. Pordes, 1966.

BN   Paris. Bibliothèque nationale. *Catalogue général des livres imprimés.* Paris: 1900- .

BNI   *Bibliografia nazionale italiana.* Firenze: 1958- .

Boalch   Boalch, Donald H. *Makers of the Harpsichord and Clavichord, 1440 to 1840.* 2nd ed. Oxford: 1974.

Bobillier   Brenet, Michel, pseudo. "Bibliographie des bibliographies musicales," *L'Année musicale* (1913). Separate reprint. New York: Da Capo, 1971.

BPL   Boston. Public Library. *Dictionary Catalog of the Music Collection.* Boston: G. K. Hall, 1972.

Bricq   Bricqueville, Eugène de. "Les collections d'instruments de musique aux XVIe, XVIIe et XVIIIe siècles." In his *Un coin de la curiosité. Les anciens instruments de musique.* Paris: Librarie de l'Art, 1895.

—————. *Les ventes d'instruments de musique au XVIIIe siècle.* Paris: Fischbacher, 1908.

Brinkmans   *Brinkman's catalogus van boeken.* Amsterdam: 1883-93; Leiden: 1903- .

British National Bibliography. London: 1950- .

BrCA   Brussels. Conservatoire royal de musique. Musée instrumental. *Annuaire.* Bruxelles: 1877- .

      See no. 736 in Fellinger, p. 20.

Bruni, A. *Un inventaire sous la Terreur; état des instruments de musique relevé chez les Emigrés et condamnés. . . .* Paris: George Chamerot, 1890.

      Some of Bruni's inventories are reprinted in *GSJ* 6 (1953): 83-94. See also Russell, Raymond. *The Harpsichord and Clavier,* 1959. Appendix 7, pp. 152-54.

Carse, Adam von Ahn. *Musical Wind Instruments.* [Reprint.] New York: Da Capo, 1965.

Clapp, Jane. *Museum Publications,* vol. 1. New York: Scarecrow Press, 1962.

Comettant, Oscar. "La musique aux diverses expositions," *Le Menestrel* 51 (1884/85): 204-5.

Crane, Frederick. *Extant Medieval Musical Instruments. A Provisional Catalogue by Types.* Iowa City: Iowa University Press, [1972] .

DaSML   Davidsson, Aake. *Bibliografi över Svensk musiklitteratur, 1800-1945.* Uppsala: 1948. Supplements, 1945- . In *Svensk tidskrift för musikforskning.*

DBH   *Deutsche Bibliographie; Halbjahres-verzeichnis.* Frankfurt a.M.: Büch-handler-Vereinigung, 1951- .

DBV   *Deutsches Bücherverzeichnis der Jahre 1911-40.* Leipzig: 1915-43.

DIbZ   *Deutsche Instrumentenbau-Zeitung,* 1899/1900-1943.
See no. 1474 in Fellinger, p. 20.

Donington, Robert. *The Instruments of Music.* [3rd ed.] London:
Methuen, [1962].

Dreyer, Otto. "Die grossen Sammlungen alter Musikinstrumente um
die Jahrhundertwende und ihre Begründer," *Glareana,* vol. 13
(1963). Also in *Schweizerische Blasmusik-Zeitung,* vol. 54 (1965).

Duckles   Duckles, Vincent. *Music Reference and Research Materials.* 3rd ed.
New York: Free Press, [1974].

EngCat   *English Catalogue of Books,* 1801- . London: 1864-1901; 1906-66.

Emsheimer   Emsheimer, Ernest, ed. *Handbuch der europäischen Volksmusikinstrumente.* Leipzig: Deutscher Verlag für Musik, 1967- .

Engel, Carl. "Collections of Musical Instruments." In his *Musical
Myths and Facts,* vol. 1, pp. 32-73. London: Novello; New York:
J. L. Peters, 1876.

Fellinger   Fellinger, Imogen. *Verzeichnis der Musikzeitschriften des 19. Jahrhunderts.* Regensburg: Bosse, 1968.

Fétis   Brussels. Bibliothèque royale de Belgique. *Catalogue de la bibliothèque
de F. J. Fétis, acquise par l'état belge.* Reprint ed. Bologna: Forni,
[1969].

Florence. Biblioteca nazionale centrale. *Catalogo cumulativo 1886-1957
del Bollettino dell pubblicazione italiane.* Firenze: 1886-1957.

FoMRHI   Fellowship of Makers and Restorers of Historical Instruments. *Bulletin,*
1957- .

Fryklund, Lars Axel Daniel. *Svenska musikinstrument i utlandska
samlingar.* Ms., 18 lvs., Stockholm, Musikhistoriska Museet.

Gai   Florence. Conservatorio di musica Luigi Cherubini. Museo. *Gli
strumenti musicali della corte medicea e il Museo.* Edited by
Vinicio Gai. Firenze: 1969.

Galpin, Francis William. *A Textbook of European Musical Instruments.* New York: De Graff, [1956, c1937].

Gaspari   Bologna. Liceo musicale. *Catalogo* di Gaetano Gaspari [and] Federico Parisini. Bologna: 1890-1943.

"Geschichte der gewerblichen Ausstellungen. Original-Uebersetzung aus dem 'Melbourner Argus' . . . von L. Lange," *ZfI* 1 (1880/81): 87-88, 97, 170-71, 185-87.

GFaM   Dreyer, Otto. "Literatur-Verzeichnis aufgestellt im 1965," *Glareana,* vol. 14 (1965); " . . . im Januar 1970," *ibid.,* vol. 19 (1970).

Glareana; Nachrichten der Gesellschaft der Freunde alter Musikinstrumente. Freienbach: 1951- .

Langwill, Lyndesay G. "Instruments, Collections of." In *Grove's Dictionary of Music and Musicians.* Edited by Eric Blom. 5th ed. New York: 1954; Supplement, 1961.

GSJ   *Galpin Society Journal.* [Cambridge?] : 1948- .

Halfpenny, Eric. "A National Collection of Instruments of Music," *Musical Times* (April 1946), pp. 105-7.

————. "Collections of Musical Instruments." In *Hinrichsen's Musical Year Book,* Vols. IV-V, pp. 413-19. London: Hinrichsen Edition, Ltd., 1948.

Harvard University. Peabody Museum of Archaeology and Ethnology. Library. *Catalogue.* . . . Boston: 1963-71.

Heyer   Heyer, Wilhelm. *Musikhistorisches Museums von W. Heyer in Cöln. Katalog von Georg Kinsky.* Leipzig: Breitkopf & Härtel, 1910-16.

HH   [Refers to the collection of Puttick & Simpson catalogs, 1846-72, in the library of Mr. Harrison Horblit, Ridgefield, Conn., formerly the property of Sir Thomas Phillipps (n&p).]

Hiestand   Hiestand-Schnellmann, Josef. "Rückblick auf 25 Jahre GEFAM," *Glareana* 26, no. 3/4 (1977): lvs. 50-58.

Hirsch   British Museum. Department of Printed Books. Hirsch Music Library. *Books in the Hirsch Library.* London: Museum, 1959.

Hirt   Hirt, Franz Josef. *Meisterwerke des Klavierbaus. Geschichte des Saitenklavieres von 1440 bis 1880.* Olten: Ure Graf Verlag, 1955.

Hofmeister, Friedrich. *Handbuch der musikalischen Litteratur.* Leipzig: 1844- .

Hutschenruyter   Hutschenruyter, Wouter. *Bijdrage tot de bibliographie der muziek-literatur.* . . . Zeist: [prive-uitgaff] , 1941-43.

"Instrumentensammlungen." In *Riemann Musik Lexikon.* 12th ed. *Sachteil,* pp. 405-6. Mainz: B. Schott's Söhne, 1967.

International Society for Music Education. *International Directory of Music Education Institutions.* . . . [Paris] : UNESCO, [1968].

J/Jenkins   Jenkins, Jean L., ed. *International Directory of Musical Instrument Collections.* Buren: Knuf, 1977.

JdMM   *Jahresverzeichnis der deutschen Musikalien und Musikschriften.* Leipzig: 1852- .

JbP   *Jahrbuch der Musikbibliothek Peters.* Leipzig: 1895-1940. See no. 1257 in Fellinger, p. 20.

KaY   Kayser, Christian Gottlob. *Vollständiges Bücher-Lexikon, 1750-1910.* Leipzig: 1834-1911.

King   King, Alexander Hyatt. *Some British Collectors of Music.* Cambridge: University Press, 1963.

Kinsky, Georg. "Musikinstrumentensammlungen in Vergangenheit und Gegenwart," *JbP* 27 (1920): [47] -60.

————. "Neue Katalog von Instrumentensammlungen [Breslau (Epstein), Hamburg (Schröder), Salzburg (Geiringer), Claudius (Skjerne)] ," *ZfMW* 16 (1934): 435-38.

Kinsky   Kinsky, Georg. "Randnoten zum Katalog des neuen Wiener Instru-mentenmuseums," *ZfMW* 4 (1921): 162-68.

KmJ *Kirchenmusikalisches Jahrbuch.* Regensburg, 1886- .
See no. 1018 in Fellinger, p. 20.

Koltypina Moscow. Publichnaĩa biblioteka. *Spravochnaĩa literatura po muzyke
. . . 1773-1962.* [Sost. Galina Borisovna Koltypina.] Moskva:
Kniga, 1964.

Kunst, Jaap. *Hindoe-Javaansche muziek-instrumenten.* . . . Weltevreden:
G. Kolff, [1927].

L Music Library Association. *A Survey of Musical Instrument Collections
in the United States and Canada.* . . . William Lichtenwanger,
chairman & compiler. [Chapel Hill, North Carolina] : 1974.

Lambertini Lambertini, Michel' Angelo. *Bibliophilie musicale. Les bibliothèques
(1924) portugais . . . Ed. abregée.* Viseu: Andrade, 1924.

Lambertini ———. *As coleções d'instrumentos musicos.* Lisboa: Annuario
(1913) Commerico, 1913.

LC-NUC *1. Library of Congress and National Union Catalog. Author Lists,
1942-62.* Detroit: 1969.
2. National Union Catalog, Pre-1956 Imprints. London: Mansell, 1968- .
3. National Union Catalog: A Cumulative Author List. Washington, D.C.:
1953- .

Leeuwen Boomkamp, Carel van. *The Carel van Leeuwen Boomkamp
Collection of Musical Instruments. Descriptive Catalogue.*
Amsterdam: Knuf, 1971.

Lehmann, Johannes. "Beiträge zur Musikinstrumente-Forschung.
Literatur-Übersicht. Saiteninstrumente - Flöten," *Abhandlung
zur Anthropologie, Ethnologie und Urgeschichte* (Frankfurt a.M.)
2 (1925): 113-25, pls. 19-20.

Loh, Gerhard. *Internationale Bibliographie der Antiquariats-, Auktions-
und Kunstkataloge . . .* 1960/61- . Leipzig: 1965- .

Lorenz Lorenz, O. H. *Catalogue général de la librairie francaise.* Paris: 1867-1945.

Lütg Lütgendorff, Willibald Leo. *Geigen und Lautenmacher.* . . . [5th & 6th
rev. ed., Frankfurt, 1922.] Reprint ed. Nendeln: Kraus, 1968.

Lugt	Lugt, Frits. *Répertoire des catalogues de ventes publiques intéressant l'art ou la curiosité. . . .* La Haye: Martinus Nijhoff, 1938. 3 vols.
Luithlen	Vienna. Kunsthistorisches Museum. Sammlung alter Musikinstrumente. *Katalog der Sammlung . . .* Einleitung: Victor Luithlen. Wien: the Museum, 1966- .
LV&A	Victoria and Albert Museum, London. National Art Library. *Musical Instruments: A List of Books and Articles in. . . .* Compiled by Michael I. Wilson. [London]: 1976.
	Marie, Sister Stephen. "Historical Collections (Keyboard Instruments)," *Diapason* 60 (1969): 11-12.
Marr	Marr, Robert A. *Musical History as Shown in the International Exhibition of Music and the Drama, Vienna 1892.* London: W. Reeves, 1893.
	Maze-Sencier, Alphonse. *Le livre des collectionneurs . . . Les ébénistes. Les ciseleurs-bronziers. . . .* Paris: Renouard, 1885. Musical instruments: pp. 375-86.
MfM	*Monatshefte für Musikgeschichte.* Liepzig: 1884-1905. See no. 609 in Fellinger, p. 20.
MGG	Berner, Alfred. "Instrumentensammlungen." In *Die Musik in Geschichte und Gegenwart,* vol. 6, cols. 1295-1310. Kassel, 1949- .
Michalowski	Michalowski, K. *Bibliografia polskiego pismiennictwa muzycznego.* [Cracow: c1955.]
	Milan. Conservatorio di musical Giuseppe Verdi. Biblioteca. *Catalogo della biblioteca.* Dir. da Guglielmo Barblan. Firenze: Olschki, 1972- .
Miller	Miller, Dayton Clarence. *Catalogue of Books and Literary Material Relating to the Flute and Other Musical Instruments. . . .* Cleveland: privately printed, 1935.
M & I	*Musique et instruments.* Paris: 1911- . See no. 2086 in Fellinger, p. 20.

MIuP	*Musikinstrument (und Phono)*. Neu-Isenburg: 1952-55; Frankfurt a.M.: 1956- .
MLAN	Music Library Association. *Notes*. Washington, D.C.: 1934- . [In most issues of second series: "Publications Received."]
MT	*Musical Times*. London: 1844- . See no. 223 in Fellinger, p. 20.
Nef	Nef, Karl. *Bibliographie der schweizerischen Schriften über Musik und Volksgesang*. (Bibliographie der schweizer. Landeskunde, vol. 6.) Bern: K. J. Wyss, 1908.
NNMM	New York, N.Y. Metropolitan Museum of Art. Library. *Library Catalog*. Boston: G. K. Hall, 1960.
NN(NYp)	New York, N.Y. Public Library. Music Division. *Dictionary Catalog of the Music Division*. Boston: G. K. Hall, 1964- [and *Supplements*] . New York, N.Y. Public Library. Slavonic Division. *Dictionary Catalog of the Slavonic Division*. Boston: G. K. Hall, 1959.
NZfM	*Neue Zeitschrift für Musik*. Leipzig: 1834- . See no. 120 in Fellinger, p. 20.
P&S Index	See explanation, p. 262.
PaG	Pagliaini, A. *Catalogo generale della libreria italiana dall'anno 1847 a tutto il 1899*. Milano: 1901-5.
Palau	Palau y Dulcet, Antonio. *Manuel del librero hispano-americano*. 2nd ed. Barcelona: 1948-73.
Reeves	Reeves, Harold, antiquariat. *Catalogue No. 73. Books on Musical Instruments, Their History, Development and Technique . . . Catalogues and Printed Descriptions of Collections of Musical Instruments and of Public and Private Libraries of Music*. London: 1927.
RILM	*Répertoire internationale de littérature musicale (RILM Abstracts)*. Edited by Barry Brook. New York: 1967- .

RINDL-1   Rindlisbacher, Hilde. "Musikinstrumentenmacher auf Industrie- und Gewerbeausstellung in der Schweiz im 19. Jahrhundert (ohne Klavier- und Orgelbauer)," *Glareana* 18, no. 2 (1969): lvs. 2-19.

RINDL-2   ———. *Verzeichnis der in der 'Glareana' 1951/52-1971 erschienenen Artikel.* Zürich: [n.d.].

Ripin, Edwin M. *Keyboard Instruments: Studies in Keyboard Organology, 1500-1800.* 2nd rev. enl. ed. New York: Dover, 1977.

RMI   *Rivista musicale italiana.* Turin/Florence: 1894- .
See no. 1277 in Fellinger, p. 20.

Rouget   Rouget, Hébert. "Ventes d'instruments de musique à l'Hôtel Drouot," *Revue musicale* (Paris) 6 (1906): 58, 215-16, 361-62.

Rühlmann, Julius. "Über Museen oder Sammlungen musikalischer Instrumente," *NZfM* 62 (1866): 285.

Russell   Russell, Raymond. "Origins of the Collection." In Victoria & Albert Museum, London. *Catalogue of Musical Instruments,* vol. 1, pp. xv-xvii. London: H.M.S.O., 1968.

Ruth-Sommer, Hermann. *Alte Musikinstrumente; ein Leitfaden für Sammler.* 2. erw. Aufl. Berlin: Schmidt & Co., 1920.

Sachs, Curt. *La signification, la tâche et la technique muséographique des collections d'instruments de musique.* [Paris] : Office international des musées, [1934]. Extract from *Mouseion* 8 (1934): 153-84.

Saunders, B. J. "Some Famous Violin Collections," *Violin Times* 2 (1894/95): 122-23.

Scheurleer   Scheurleer, Daniel Francois. *Catalogue van de Muziek-werken en de Boeken over Muziek.* . . . 3. uitg. 's-Gravenhage: 1923-25.

Schlesinger   Schlesinger, Kathleen. *A Bibliography of Musical Instruments and Archaeology.* . . . London: W. Reeves, 1912.

———. "A Bibliography of Music and Archaeology." In her *Instruments of the Modern Orchestra.* . . . London: W. Reeves, 1910.

Schlosser   Vienna. Kunsthistorisches Museum. Sammlung alter Musikinstrumente. *Die Sammlung alter Musikinstrumente; beschreibendes Verzeichnis,* von Julius Schlosser. Wien: Schroll, 1920. Reprint ed. Hildesheim /New York: Olms, 1974.

SiMG   *Sammelbände der internationalen Musik-Gesellschaft.* Leipzig: 1899/ 1900-1913/14.

              See no. 1505 in Fellinger, p. 20.

              Thibaut, G. "Les collections privées de livres et d'instruments de musique d'autrefois et d'aujourd'hui," *Fontes artis musicae* 6 (1959): 55-67.

Torri   Torri, Luigi. "La costruzione ed i costruttori degli istrumenti ad arco. Bibliografia liutistica," *RMI* 14 (1907): 40-82.

              Second edition issued separately, Padova: Zanibon, [1920].

Valdrighi   Valdrighi, Luigi Francesco. *Musurgiana. . . .* Modena: Soc. Tipogr. Soliani; Tipogr. Vincenzi, 1881-94.

Vannes   Vannes, René. *Dictionnaire universel des luthiers.* 2. éd. Paris: Fisch-bacher, [1951-59].

VfMW   *Vierteljahrsschrift für Musikwissenschaft.* Leipzig: 1885-94.

              See no. 1005 in Fellinger, p. 20.

Waterman   Waterman, Richard, [and others]. "Bibliography of Asiatic Musics," Music Library Association, *Notes,* 2nd ser. Vol. V, no. 1- Vol. VIII, no. 2 (December 1947-March 1951).

Weckerlin   Weckerlin, Jean Baptiste Theodore. *Katalog der Musikbibliothek.* Leipzig: C. G. Boerner, [1910].

ZfI   *Zeitschrfit für Instrumentenbau.* 1, 1880/81 - 63, 1942/43. Hrsg. von Paul de Wit. Leipzig: 1880-1943. [See also under WIT, Paul de in Section II.]

ZfMW   *Zeitschrift für Musikwissenschaft.* Leipzig: 1918-35.

ZiMG   *Zeitschrift der internationalen Musik-Gesellschaft.* Leipzig: 1899/1900- 1913/14.

              See no. 1514 in Fellinger, p. 20.

ZiMG-Schau "Zeitschriftenschau." In issues of *ZiMG* (above).

LIBRARY SIGLA AND ABBREVIATIONS

Sigla used to indicate locations of copies of works cited throughout this work are:
1) for European libraries and museums, RISM codes;
2) for U. S. locations, National Union Catalog codes followed,
in curves, by the RISM code, in most cases without the "U. S." prefix.
Codes for various archives and museums not in the RISM listing
have been invented following RISM principles. They are listed below.

LIBRARY SIGLA

A-Wak	Akademie der bildenden Künste, Vienna
A-Wal	Graphische Sammlung Albertina, Vienna
B-Abm	Bibliothèque municipale, Antwerp
B-Bmr	Bibliothèque des Musées Royaux des Beaux-Arts, Brussels
F-Paa	Bibliothèque d'Art et d'Archéologie de l'Université, Paris
F-Pb	Bibliothèque de l'École des Beaux-Arts, Paris
F-Pe	Cabinet des Estampes, Bibliothèque Nationale, Paris
GB-Lc	Christie's, London
GB-Lcia	Courtauld Institute of Art, London
NL-Ag	Gemeente Archief, Amsterdam
NL-Ak	Kunsthistorisch Instituut der Universiteit, Amsterdam
NL-Apk	Pretenkabinet, Rijksmuseum, Amsterdam
NL-Avb	Vereeniging ter Bervordering van de Belangen des Boekhandels, Amsterdam

NL-DHga	Gemeente Archief, The Hague
NL-DHrk	Rijksbureau voor Kunsthistorische Dokumentatie, The Hague
NL-Hg	Gemeente Archief, Haarlem
NL-Rbm	Bibliothek der Gemeente, Rotterdam
NL-Rga	Gemeente Archief, Rotterdam
US-NYfrick	Frick Art Reference Library, New York City
US-Rihh	Collection of Harrison Horblit

ABBREVIATIONS

ca.	*circa,* about, approximately
cf.	*confer,* compare
col.	column
ed.	edition; editor
enl.	enlarged
fasc.	fascicle
fig.	figure
ibid.	*ibidem,* in the same place
illus.	illustrated, illustration
lvs.	leaves
n & p	Indicates sale catalogue cited includes names of buyers and prices fetched
n.d.	no date
n.p.	no place; no publisher
n.s.	new series
no.	number
op. cit.	*opere citato,* in the work cited
p.	page
pl.	Indicates inclusion of a plate or plates
pt.	part
q.v.	*quod vide,* which see
s.d.	*sine die,* without setting a day for reconvening
ser.	series
vol.	volume

SECTION I

INSTITUTIONS AND EXPOSITIONS

An asterisk attached to a name or siglum in the notes
following a citation, e.g., Scheurleer* *in item no.* **19**, *attributes information*
to a Secondary Source or Authority listed on pages 17-27.
An asterisk attached to a name or siglum followed by volume and page number,
e.g., Duckles* 3:1566 *in item no.* **75**, *indicates where additional information may be found.*
Alphanumeric sigla at the end of some entries, e.g., J32 *at the end*
of entry AARHUS, *indicates directories that provide addresses, hours, facilities,*
and other information about the institution. Further explanation, page 8.

AARHUS (Denmark). KØBSTADSMUSEET "DEN GAMLE BY" (J32)

1 Nyrop-Christensen, Henrik. *Klaverer i "Den Gamle By."* Aarhus: [the Museet], 1966. 26 pp., 14 illus.

> Offprint from the museum's yearbook (1965), pp. 73-99.

ABERDEEN (Scotland). UNIVERSITY. ANTHROPOLOGICAL MUSEUM (J135, A344, BB172)

General

2 *Illustrated Catalogue of the . . . Museum,* by R. W. Reid. (Aberdeen. University. *Studies,* no. 55.) Aberdeen: University Press, 1912. viii, 357 pp.

> Instruments throughout: British Isles, pp. 435, 588, 655; India, pp. 130-31; Malaya, pp. 283-88; W. Africa, pp. 3, 46-49, 127-37, 198, 269; etc.

AISNE (France). DÉPARTEMENT

3 Fleury, Éduard. *Les instruments de musique sur les monuments du moyen âge du département de l'Aisne.* (Antiquités et monuments du département de l'Aisne. *Annuaire,* 1882.) Paris: 1882. 84 pp.

> Copies at CU (BEu), ICJ, DLC (Wc).

ALTENBURG (Germany). LANDESAUSSTELLUNG, 1886

Literature

4   Anger, Walter. "Die Musikinstrumente auf der Landesausstellung," *ZfI* 6 (1885/ 86): 454-56.

AMBRAS, SCHLOSS. *See* VIENNA. KUNSTHISTORISCHES MUSEUM

AMSTERDAM (Netherlands). COLONIAL-AUSSTELLUNG. *See* AMSTERDAM (Netherlands). INTERNATIONALE KOLONIALE EN UITVOERHANDEL-TENTOONSTELLING, 1883

AMSTERDAM (Netherlands). INTERNATIONAL CULTURAL CENTRE

5   *Catalogue. Exhibition of String Instruments of the Low Countries Arranged to Commemorate the Visit of the International Society of Violin and Bow Makers . . . July 1955.* Amsterdam: 1955. [2] pp.
Copy at NL-DHgm.

AMSTERDAM (Netherlands). INTERNATIONALE AUSSTELLUNG "KLANK EN BEELD," 1932

Literature

6   [Reports on musical instrument exhibits], *ZfI* 52 (1931/32): 203-4, 247.

AMSTERDAM (Netherlands). INTERNATIONALE KOLONIALE EN UITVOERHANDEL-TENTOONSTELLING, 1883

Literature

7   "Hier und dort auf der Colonial-Ausstellung. Musikalische Instrumente," *ZfI* 3 (1882/83): 354-56.

8   [List of exhibitors and notes], *ZfI* 3 (1882/83): 319-21, 322, 396.

9   "Bericht des Herrn Commerzienrath Ernst Kaps in Dresden an das Reichskanzler-amt zu Berlin [plus list of exhibitors and prizes]," *ZfI* 3 (1882/83): 363-66.

10   Wit, Paul de. "Umschau unter dem in Amsterdam ausgestellten Streich- und Blasinstrumenten," *ZfI* 3 (1882/83): 366-67, 387-88, 416-18.

11   "Die französischen und deutschen Pianos auf der Ausstellung zu Amsterdam [translated from *Le Voltaire* (Paris)] ," *ZfI* 3 (1882/83): 403-6.

12   "Exposition internationale d'Amsterdam. Récompenses décernées aux exposants dans la classe 33," *L'echo musical* 15 (1883): 220-22, 258-59.

13   "Die Claviere auf der Colonial-Ausstellung," *ZfI* 4 (1883/84): 5, 7-8, 13-15, 25-27, 37-38, 49-50, 61-62, 64.

14   Mahillon, Victor. "Officieller Bericht über die Musikinstrumente auf der Colonial-Ausstellung," *ZfI* 4 (1883/84): 435-36, 447-48; 5 (1884/85): 1-2, 3, 13-14, 25-26.

15   Mahillon, Victor. "Exposition d'Amsterdam 1883. Section belge. Rapport sur les instruments de musique [publié par la Commission royale de Belgique] . Groupe IV - Class 33," *L'echo musical* 16 (1884): 217-19, 229-31, 229-31 [N.B.: repeated pagination, issues 20 and 21] , 241-42, 252-54, 265-68, 277-78.

16   Soufleto, Charles. "Studien an den Pianos und Harmoniums auf der Weltausstellung," *ZfI* 4 (1883/84): 85-88. [A report to the Chambre Syndicale des Fabricants de Pianos, Paris.]

17   [List of Belgian exhibitors] , *ZfI* 5 (1884/85): 235.

AMSTERDAM (Netherlands). INTERNATIONALE TENTOONSTELLING VAN HOTEL-OCH REIZEWEZEN, 1895

Literature

18   Allgäuer, W. G. C. "Die Klaviere auf der Weltausstellung für Hotel- und Reisewesen in Amsterdam," *ZfI* 15 (1894/95): 787-89, 815-16, 925-26.

AMSTERDAM (Netherlands). NEDERLANDSE TOONKUNSTENAARS-VEREENIGING

19   *Catalogus der nationale Tentoonstelling van muziek-instrumenten, boeken, muziekwerken der Nederlanders . . . Uitgeschreven . . . van haar vijf-en-twintig jarig bestaan, 1875-1900.* [Amsterdam: 1900.]

        Cited from Scheurleer*; not examined.

AMSTERDAM (Netherlands). RIJKSMUSEUM [N.B.: These musical instrument collections (which include that of J. C. Boers, added 1899) have been housed since 1951 at the **HAGUE, GEMEENTEMUSEUM**, q.v. See also J95.]

20   *Muziekinstrumenten uit het Rijksmuseum te Amsterdam, 9.-Oct.-24. Nov. 1952.* [Exhibition catalogue.] 's-Gravenhage: Dienst voor schone Kunsten, Gemeentemuseum, 1952. 36 pp.

       Cited from *BdMS** 1952-53; not examined.

Literature

21   Milligan, S. van. "Wat moet er met de oude muziek-instrumenten in ons Rijksmuseum geschieden?" *Caecilia en de muziek* 62 (1905): 281-87.

22   Langwill, L. G. "Musikinstrumenten-Sammlung des Rijks-museum Amsterdam, ausgestellt im Gemeentemuseum in Den Haag, 1952," *Glareana*, vol. 2, no. 2 (1953). 160 items.

ANN ARBOR, MICHIGAN (USA). UNIVERSITY. STEARNS COLLECTION OF MUSICAL INSTRUMENTS (L241)

23   *Catalogue of the Stearns Collection of Musical Instruments, by Albert A. Stanley.* Ann Arbor: University of Michigan, 1918. 260 pp.

24   *Catalogue of the Stearns Collection of Musical Instruments, by Albert A. Stanley.* 2nd ed. Ann Arbor: University of Michigan, 1921. 276 pp.

       Duckles* 3:1564.

Literature

25   Stanley, Albert A. "Die Stearn'sche Sammlung musikalischer Instrumente in der Michigan-Universität zu Ann Arbor," *DiBZ*, vol. 2, no. 14 (1900/1901).

26   "Stearns Collections Includes 1,500 Old Sometimes Rare, Musical Instruments," *Univ. of Michigan, University Record*, vol. 17 (May 1962).

27   *The Stearns Collection of Musical Instruments.* Ann Arbor: School of Music, [1965]. 11 pp., illus. [Originally published in *Journal of the Viola da Gamba Society of America*, vol. 2 (1965).]

28   "The Stearns Collection of Musical Instruments," *Univ. of Michigan, Director of Research Development and Administration, Research News*, vol. 24, nos. 1 & 2 (July/August 1973). 19 pp.

29   "The Stearns Collection of Musical Instruments," *American Musical Instrument Society Newsletter* 3, no. 1 (1974): 1-3. illus.

30 Smith, Bruce Mitchell. *The Chordophones of Western Civilization in the Stearns Collection . . . An Historical and Organological Study.* Ph.D. dissertation, University of Michigan, 197-. With different title, *Two Hundred Forty-One Chordophones in the Stearns Collection,* at NL-DHgm. xix, 792 pp.

31 Barnes, John. "The 'Giusti' Harpsichord in the Stearns Collection," *FoMRHI,* no. 13 (October 1978), p. 44.

ANTWERP (Belgium) — General

Literature

32 Lambrechts-Douillez, Jeanine. "Collections of Musical Instruments in Antwerp." In *Music, Libraries and Instruments,* pp. 128-31. London: Hinrichsen, 1961; mostly about the Vleeshuis.

ANTWERP (Belgium). EXPOSITION INTERNATIONALE, 1930

33 *Catalogue tom 2. (Sculpture - Orfèvrerie civile et religieuse - musique - dentelles.)* Bruxelles: 1930. xiii, 143 pp.

> Hirsch* no. 319; copies in U.S. not located.

34 *Exposition d'art flamand ancien, Anvers 1930. Livre d'art - musique.* [A catalogue.] Anvers: [1930].

> Hirsch* no. 318; copies in U.S. not located.

General

35 *Guide officiel.* Bruxelles: "Mirax," [1930].

> "La musique," pp. 239-42. Copy at NPV (POvc).

ANTWERP (Belgium). EXPOSITION INTERNATIONALE, COLONIALE, MARITIME ET DE L'ART FLAMAND, 1930. *See above* EXPOSITION INTERNATIONALE, 1930

ANTWERP (Belgium). EXPOSITION UNIVERSELLE, 1885

Literature

36 Moreno, H. "Exposition d'Anvers; récompenses," *Le Menestrel* 51 (1884/85): 290-92.

37 "Exposition universelle d'Anvers. Liste des récompenses. Instruments de musique," *L'echo musical* 17 (1885): 194-95, 208-9.

ANTWERP (Belgium). EXPOSITION UNIVERSELLE, 1885 *continued*

Literature

38 "Prämiirungen van Antwerpen," *ZfI* 5 (1884/85): 399-400, 402, 428, 439.

39 "Die Musikinstrumente auf der Ausstellung von Antwerp," *ZfI* 6 (1885/86): 1, 3, 13-14.

General

40 *Catalogue officiel général.* Tome 1- . Anvers: E. Stockmans & Co., [1885-].
    Copy at NN (NYp).

41 *Illustrirter Führer durch die 1885 Weltausstellung, von R. Corneli.* Antwerpen: 1885.
    Copy at MH (CA).

ANTWERP (Belgium). EXPOSITION UNIVERSELLE, 1893

Literature

42 "Die Welt-Ausstellung van Antwerpen," *ZfI* 14 (1893/94): 267, 510 & 519, 578 & 587, 604, 735, 750 (jury), 776, 799-800, 825-26, 828-29 (prizes), 882-23. illus.

43 Schiedmayer, Adolf. "Bericht über die Antwerpener Ausstellung an die Mitglieder des Vereins deutscher Pianofabrikanten," *ZfI* 14 (1893/94): 799-800.

ANTWERP (Belgium). MUSÉE STEEN [N.B.: In the 1950's this became a maritime museum and the musical instruments were transferred to the Vleeshuis.]

44 Génard, Pierre Marie. "Instruments de musique." In *Catalogue du musée . . . 4. éd.,* pp. 187-90. Anvers: Veuve de Backer, 1894.
    Copy at DLC (Wc). Thirty-six items belonging to this collection are also listed by Bergmans* in his *Inventaire général.*

ANTWERP (Belgium). MUSEUM PLANTIN MORETUS (J16)

General

45 *Catalogue . . .* par Max Rooses. Anvers: Buschmann, 1881.
    According to Jenkins* instruments are included. Many other editions through 1965 (see *National Union Catalogue*); none examined.

ANTWERP (Belgium). MUSEUM VLEESHUIS (J17)

46   *Muziekinstrumenten.* (Its *Catalogus* 5.) Antwerpen: [the Museum, n.d., 1956?].
      35 pp., 12 pp., illus. At head of title: Stad Antwerpen. Oudheidkundige Musea.

   Copies at MiDA, MH (CA).

47   Lambrechts-Douillez, Jeanine, et al. *Muziekinstrumenten van het K. Vlaams
      Konservatorium.* (Its *Catalogus* 5, [2nd ed.].) Antwerpen: Goovaerts, 1967.
      47 pp., xxvii pls.

   A collection loaned to the Vleeshuis by the conservatory. Copies
   at IaU (IOu) and ICU (Cu) have publisher: Deurne, [1967].

48   Ligtvoet, A. W. "Aanwisten van de Muziekinstrumenten-verzameling in het
      Museum," *Mens en melodie* 22 (1967): 362-65. illus.

   About the collection from the conservatory.

Literature

49   Lambrechts-Douillez, Jeanine. "Verzameling Muziekinstrumenten te Antwerpen."
      In *Vereeniging voor Muziekgeschiedenis Jaarboek* (1959), pp. 119-25.

50   Lambrechts-Douillez, Jeanine. "Een contrabas blokfluit in het Museum Vleeshuis,"
      Miscellanea Jozef Duverger, pp. 907-19. Ghent: 1968.

51   Lambrechts-Douillez, Jeanine. *Antwerpse klavicimbels in het Museum.* Antwerp:
      1970. 24 pp., illus.

ANTWERP (Belgium). RUCKERS GENOOTSCHAP

52   Lambrechts-Douillez, Jeanine. "Documents Dealing with the Ruckers Family."
      In *Keyboard Instruments; Studies in Keyboard Organology,* edited by E. M. Ripin,
      pp. 39-43. Edinburgh: University Press, 1971. Reprint ed. New York: Dover, 1977.

   Discusses several inventories of Ruckers' productions.

53   Lambrechts-Douillez, Jeanine. "Catalogus Ruckers: Documentation en Instruments
      [Exhibition, Antwerp, 1974]," *Brussels Museum of Musical Instruments Bulletin*
      4 (1974): 65-70. illus.

ARLES (France). MUSEON ARLATEN (J36)

Literature

54   Benoit, Fernand. *Le museon Arlaten.* (Its *Memoranda.*) Paris: H. Laurens, 1945.
      64 pp., 48 pls.

   Jenkins* notes instrument collection.
   Citation from LoR*; not examined.

ARNHEM (Netherlands). GEMEENTEMUSEUM

55   *Luister van het orgel. [Catalogus van de tentoonstelling gehouden in het]*
      Gemeentemuseum Arnhem, 20.9-27.10, 1968. [Voorword door Joh. Mekkrink.
      Inleiding door M. A. Vente.] (Its *Catalogus* 138.) [Arnhem: Gemeentemuseum,
      1968.] [48] pp., 32 pp., photos.
          Copy at DLC(Wc).

ASTEN (Netherlands). BEIAARD-MUSEUM (J93)

Literature

56   Lehr, André. "Het klokkenen beiaardmuseum te Asten," *Mens en melodie* 24
      (1969): 226-28.

57   Maasen, Jacques. "National Beiaard Museum," *Mens en melodie* 30 (1976): 242-
      44. illus.

ATHENS, OHIO (USA). OHIO UNIVERSITY. TRISOLINI GALLERY

58   Thompson, Clyde Henderson. *Representative Ancient and Modern String Instru-*
      ments. October 11-29, 1977, organized by Clyde H. Thompson. Athens: The
      Gallery, [c1977]. [21] pp., illus.

L'AUBERSON (Switzerland). MUSÉE DE MUSIQUES MÉCANIQUES ANCIENNES (J126)

59   Baud, Frédy. *Museum alter mechanischer Musikinstrumente. Gebrüder Baud,*
      L'Auberson. 1972. "Auszug aus den Buche," *Als die Musikdosen Spielten.*
      Lausanne: Mando-Verlag, 1972. unpaged [ca. 100], illus.
          Copy at NL-DHgm.

AUGSBURG (Germany). SCHWÄBISCHE KREISAUSSTELLUNG, 1886

Literature

60   "Die Schwäbische Ausstellung in Augsburg," *ZfI* 6 (1885/86): 483, 485.

61   *Meisterwerke Schwäbischer Kunst aus der. . . .* München: J. Albert, 1886.
          Copy at MH(Cac); not examined.

62   "Musik und Musiker der Fuggerzeit. Ausstellung in Schaetzlerhaus in Augsburg.
      Ausgestellte Instrumente," *Glareana*, vol. 8, no. 3 (1959).

63 Pleijel, Bengt. "Musikvandring i Augsburg [the exhibition, 'Musik und Musiker der Fuggerzeit'] ," *Musikrevy* 15 (1960): 13-15. illus.

> See also under **FUGGER** in Section II; that collection now in Augsburg.

AUSSIG (now Ústí, Czechoslovakia). GEWERBE-, INDUSTRIE- UND LANDWIRTSCHAFT-AUSSTELLUNG, 1893

Literature

64 "Musikinstrumente auf . . . ," *ZfI* 13 (1892/93): 749, 762, 771, 785. "Nachtrag," *ZfI* 14 (1893/94): 29-30.

> List of exhibitors from the official *Katalog* (not located).

AUSSIG (now Ústí, Czechoslovakia). ALLGEMEINE DEUTSCHE AUSSTELLUNG FÜR GEWERBE, INDUSTRIE UND LANDWIRTSCHAFT, 1903

Literature

65 "Die Musikinstrumenten-Industrie auf der . . . ," *ZfI* 23 (1902/3): 367, 502, 825 (exhibitors), 905-7, 937-39, 1002 (prizes). illus.

> Musical instruments, Group X in the exhibition and in the *Amtlicher Katalog* (not located).

BALTIMORE, MARYLAND (USA). MUSEUM OF ART

66 Breeskin, Adelyn D. *Musical Instruments and Their Portrayal in Art.* [*An Exhibition Catalogue That Correlates the Art of Music, Painting and Sculpture.* Foreword by Frederick P. Stieff. Baltimore: 1946.] 48 pp., 12 illus.

> Copies at MiU (AAu), PPULC, NNC (NYcu), MdBP (BApi), DLC (Wc).

BAMBERG (Germany). NEUE RESIDENZ

67 *Führer durch die Ausstellung historischer Musikinstrumente und graphischer Musikdarstellungen in Bamberg, Neue Residenz, 15. Juli-16. August 1953.* Aus Anlass des Internationalen Musikwissen schaftlichen Kongress der Gesellschaft für Musikforschung, 1953. Bamberg: St. Otto-Verlag, 1953. 24 pp.

> Cited from MLAN*, vol. 14 (December 1953).

BARCELONA (Spain). EXPOSICIÓN INTERNACIONAL, 1929

Literature

68 "L'industrie de la musique à l'Exposition Internationale de Barcelone," *M & I* 20 (November 1929): 1465-69, 1473, 1475. Many illus. of exhibits.

69 K., C. M. "Musikinstrumente auf der internationalen Ausstellung Barcelona, 1929," *ZfI* 50 (1929/30): 232-34, 272 (jury report).

General

70 *Offizieller Katalog. Internationale Ausstellung Barcelona 1929.* [Barcelona]: R. Mosse, [1929]. xl, 352, 288 pp., illus.

BARCELONA (Spain). EXPOSICIÓN UNIVERSEL, 1888

Literature

71 "Aussteller-Liste von Barcelona," *ZfI* 9 (1888/89): 21, 50.

72 "Prämiirungen," *ZfI* 9 (1888/89): 112-15, 140-43.

73 *La Exposición, organo oficial. Número 1-75, Agosto 1886 - Septiembre 1889.* 2 vols. Barcelona: 1886-89. illus.
     Copies at NNU-W (NYu), MiD (Dp).

General

74 *Catálogo oficial especial de España de la Exposición Universel de Barcelona de 1888.* Barcelona: Sucesores de N. Ramirez, 1888.
     Cited from Palau*; not located.

BARCELONA (Spain). MUNICIPAL MUSEO DE MUSICA (J112, A361)

Literature

75 Graves, Richard. "The Municipal Museum of Music, Barcelona," *MT* 92 (1956): 209-10. ca. 700 instruments.

BARODA (India). STATE MUSEUM AND PICTURE GALLERY (J70)

76 "A Brief Description of the Musical Instruments in the Museum," *Indian Journal of Sociology,* vol. 2 (?) (1921).
     Jenkins* cites this and a brochure on the "Exhibition of Musical Instruments of India." Neither verified.

BASEL (Switzerland). GEWERBEMUSEUM

Literature

77   Nef, Walter. "Basler Musikinstrumenten Ausstellung," *Deutsche Musik Jahrbuch* (Berlin) 80 (1940): 161-68.

> Cited from *BdZL* *40:1:441; not examined.

BASEL (Switzerland). MUSEUM FÜR VÖLKERKUNDE UND SCHWEIZERISCHES MUSEUM FÜR VOLKSKUNDE   (J120)

78   *Klangzauber. Funktionen aussereuropäischer Musikinstrumente. Sonderausstellung vom 23. Mai bis 17. August 1969. Führer durch das Museum.* [Text] von Urs Ramseyer. Basel: 1969. 339 pp., illus.

> Jenkins*: ca. 2,000 instruments, almost all folk.

Literature

79   Lievense, Willy. "Bazel: Buiten-Europese muziekinstrumenten in Bazel," *Mens en melodie* 24 (1969): 313-14. illus.

BASEL (Switzerland). SCHOLA CANTORUM BASILIENSIS. LOBECK COLLECTION.
See Section II under **LOBECK, OTTO**

BASEL (Switzerland). UNIVERSITÄT. HISTORISCHES MUSEUM   (J120, A399, BB115)
[N.B.: Includes collections of Maurice Bedot-Diodati (1927), Paul Sacher (1956), Albert Riemeyer, and some of Otto Lobeck's.]

80   Nef, Karl. "Katalog der Musikinstrumente im historischen Museum zu Basel." In *Festschrift zum zweiten Kongress der Internationalen Musikgesellschaft.* Basel: 1906. [separately paged], vii, 74 pp., 294 items.

> Duckles* 3:1566.

81   Nef, Karl. *Katalog No. IV, Musikinstrumente.* [Basel: Emil Birkjäuser], 1906. vii, 74 pp., illus., 12 pls.

> Cf. item **80** above. Copies at NN (NYp), CtY (NHu), NjR (PRu).

82   Nef, Walter. *Alte Musikinstrumente in Basel / Instruments de musique anciens á Bâle / Ancient Musical Instruments in Basel.* (The Museum's *Schriften,* n.s., vol. 2.) Bâle: Stiftung für das Historische Museum, 1974. [47] pp., 20 pls., some colored.

> Reviews in *Revue musicale de Suisse Romande* 28 (1975): 52; and by Dale Higbee in *Journal of American Musical Instrument Society* 3 (1977): 132-34.

BASEL (Switzerland). UNITERSITÄT. HISTORISCHES MUSEUM   *continued*

Literature

83   Nef, Karl. "Die Sammlung der Musikinstrumente des historischen Museums in Basel," *Sonntagsblatt der Basler Nachrichten*, Nr. 12 (25 März 1906).

       Cited from *ZiMG*-schau* 7:300.

84   Nef, Walter. "Das neue Musikinstrumenten-Museum," *Jahresbericht der Musik-Akademie der Stadt Basel* 90 (1956/57): 33-39.

85   Nef, Walter. "Das neue Basler Musikmuseum," *Schweizerische Musikforschende Gesellschaft, Mitteilungsblatt*, Nr. 27 (August 1957), pp. 1-4.

86   Nef, Walter. "Das neue Basler Instrumentenmuseum," *Glareana* 6, no. 2 (1957): 1.

87   Nef, Walter. "Die Sammlung alter Musikinstrumente des Historischen Museums in Basel," *PRO,* vol. 18 (1970).

88   Nef, Walter. "Über die Sammlung alter Musikinstrumente des Historischen Museums in Basel. Interview mit Karl Ramstein," *Basler Liedertafel*, vols. 48 & 49 (1971).

89   Nef, Walter. "Die Renaissance-Orgel in der Sammlung alter Musikinstrumentes des Historischen Museums Basel," *Glareana*, vol. 20 (1972).

90   Nef, Walter. *Die Basler Musikinstrumentensammlung.* [Basel?] : Atlantis-Verlag, 1977. 26 pp.; Sonderdruck aus: *Alte und neue Musik II; 50 Jahre Basler Kammerorchester.*

       Citation from *Glareana* 26 (1977): 23; not examined.

BELÉM (Brazil). EXPOSIÇÃO INDUSTRIAL, 1893

Literature

91   Freitas Cavalleiro e Sousa, Augusto Eugenio de. *A Exposição industrial de Belém em 1893.* Lisbon: 1894.

       Cited from Lambertini* (1924); not examined.

BELÉM (Brazil). MUSEO PARANENSE EMILIO GOELDI

General

92   Galvão, Eduardo. *Guia das exposiçoes de antropologia. . . .* (*Sērie Guias*, no. 1.) Belém: 1962. 47 pp., illus.

       Copy at LNHT; not examined. Jenkins* says ca. 400 items.

BELGRADE (Yugoslavia). ETNOGRAFSKI MUZEJ   (J161)

93   *Narodni muzicki instrumenti jugoslavie* [National Musical Instruments of Yugoslavia]. Mitar S. Vlahovič; uvod. Miodrag A. Vasiljevič. [Beograd: 1957.] 60 pp., illus.

> Edited by Z. Markvič-Blagojevic and S. Vasiljevič-Macuoka according to Wilson. Cited from MLAN*.

BENNEBROEK (Netherlands). TENTOONSTELLING "VAN PSALTERIUM TOT PIANO," 1978

94   *Catalogus en wegwijzer voor de Tentoonstelling . . . oorsprong en ontwikkeling van besnaarde clavierinstrumenten, in te Raadhuis . . . 22, 23 en 24 September 1978, georganiseerd door Muziekcentrum 'Het Duintje'. . . .* Bennebroek: 1978. 26 pp., illus., 17 items.

> Copy at NL-DHgm.

BERGEN DAL (Netherlands). AFRIKA MUSEUM   (J94, BB74)

Literature

95   Ligtvoet, A. W. "De Muziekinstrumenten in het Afrika Museum," *Mens en melodie* 23 (1968): 178-80.

BERKELEY, CALIFORNIA (USA). UNIVERSITY OF CALIFORNIA. DEPARTMENT OF MUSIC   (L18)

96   Boyden, David D. *Catalog of the Collection of Musical Instruments in the Department of Music. Part I.* Berkeley: 1972. 104 pp.

> Part II, the Ansley K. Salz collection, in preparation, 1973. Duckles* 3:1567; 88 items.

97   Emerson, John A. *Musical Instruments, East and West. A Catalog of an Exhibit on the Occasion of the 12th Congress of the IMS.* [Berkeley: 1977.]

BERLIN

This section contains literature under the following entries:

Allgemeine deutsche Gewerbe-Ausstellung, 1844
Allgemeine Musik-Ausstellung, 1898

Bach-Ausstellung, 1901
Deutsche Akademie der Künste
Deutsches Museum
Gewerbe-Ausstellung, 1896
Grosse deutsche Funkausstellung und Phonoschau, 1930
Grosse deutsche Funkausstellung und Phonoschau, 1932
Industrie Ausstellung für Gast- und Haus-Wirtschaft, Kochkunst, Erfindungen
     und Neuheiten, 1902
Internationale Handwerkausstellung, 1938
Jubiläums-Ausstellung [der Kgl. Akademie der Künste], 1886
Musik-Fachausstellung, 1906
Musik-Fachausstellung [Third], 1922
Nationale Gewerbe-Ausstellung, 1888
Staatliches Institut für Musikforschung, Stiftung preussischer Kulturbesitz. Musik-
     instrumentenmuseum
Staatliche Museen. Ägyptische Abteilung
Staatliche Museen. Kunstgewerbemuseum
Staatliche Museen. Museum für Völkerkunde

BERLIN (Germany). ALLGEMEINE DEUTSCHE GEWERBE-AUSSTELLUNG, 1844

Literature

98   "Zum fünfzigjährigen Gedenktage der ersten Allgemeinen Deutschen Gewerbe-
ausstellung am 15. August 1844 zu Berlin," *ZfI* 14 (1893/94): 771-73; signed B.

General

99   *Amtlicher Bericht über die. . . .* Berlin: K. Reimarus, 1845-46. 3 vols. in 4.

          Copy, 2 vols. in 3, at MH (CAc), ICU (Cu), CU (BEu),
          MiU (AAu).

BERLIN (Germany). ALLGEMEINE MUSIK-AUSSTELLUNG, 1898

Literature

100   "Die Musikausstellung im Berliner Messpalast," *ZfI* 8 (1897/98): 635-36.

          A list of instrument makers exhibiting.

General

101   *Officieller Katalog . . . Ausstellung . . . im Messpalast, vom 7. Mai bis 12. August
1898.* Berlin: Rudolf Morse, 1989. 56 pp.

          "Königliche Sammlung alter Musik Instrumente in Berlin,"
          pp. 44-56. Other instruments, by firm, pp. 20-26.

BERLIN (Germany). BACH-AUSSTELLUNG, 1901

102 Fleischer, Oskar. *Führer durch die Bach-Ausstellung im Festsaale des Rathauses . . . 21.-31. März 1901.* Berlin: [Bote & Bock], 1901. 46 pp.

> Abthlg. II: Instrumente, pp. 15-36.

BERLIN. BRANDENBURGISCHE HOFKAPELLE. *See Section II under* JOHANN GEORGE II, Prinz von Brandenburg, *and* FRIEDRICH WILHELM DER GROSSE

BERLIN (Germany). DEUTSCHE AKADEMIE DER KÜNSTE [N.B.: For other exhibitions held at the Deutsche Akademie, see under BERLIN (Germany). JUBILÄUMS-AUSSTELLUNG.]

Literature

103 Sachs, Curt. "Die Berliner Instrumentenbau auf den Ausstellungen der Kgl. Preussischen Akademie der Künste, 1794-1844," *ZfI* 32 (1911/12): 1087-89, 1128-30; with a list of the more important items shown, arranged by year.

BERLIN (Germany). DEUTSCHES MUSEUM

Literature

104 Fuchs, Franz. "Führung durch die Abteilung 'Musikinstrumente' des Deutschen Museums," *DIbZ* 27 (1926): 223-24.

BERLIN (Germany). GEWERBE-AUSSTELLUNG, 1896

Literature

105 "Die Musikinstrumente auf der . . . ," *ZfI* 16 (1895/96): 647-49 (Aufsteller), 767-69, 791-94, 817-19, 847-49, 878-82, 909-12; 17 (1896/97): 58 (prizes).

General

106 *Offizieller Haupt-Katalog . . . Illustrirte Prakt.-Ausg.* Berlin: R. Mosse, [1896]. lxiv, 260, 249 pp., illus.

> "Group XII, Musik-Instrumente," pp. 121-26.

107 *Offizieller Special-Katalog I-[X], Gruppe I-[XXII].* Berlin: R. Mosse, [1896]. 10 nos. in 2 vols.

> Group XII, musical instruments, but not found in copy at ICRL.

BERLIN (Germany). GEWERBE-AUSSTELLUNG, 1896 *continued*

General

108 *Allgemeine Führer durch die . . . Gewerbe-Ausstellung.* Berlin: Klinger, 1896. 126 pp., illus.

109 *Illustrirter amtlicher Führer durch die Berliner Gewerbe-Ausstellung. . . .* 2. rev. Aufl. Berlin: "Berliner Börsen-Courier," 1896. 227 pp.

110 *Führer durch die Berliner Gewerbe-Ausstellung. Nebst einem Anhang. . . .* Berlin: A. & J. Hirschberg, 1896. 318 pp., illus.

111 *Amtlicher Bericht der. . . .* Berlin: D. Reimer, 1901. x, 890 pp.

Cited from KaY*; except where indicated items not located.

BERLIN (Germany). GROSSE DEUTSCHE FUNKAUSSTELLUNG UND PHONOSCHAU, 1930

112 *Funkalmanach* [7?] *1930. Offizieller Ausstellungskatalog zur grossen deutschen Funkausstellung und Phonoschau.* Schriftl.: Walter H. Fitze. Berlin: Rothgiesser & Diesing, 1931. 232 pp., illus.

Literature

113 "Deutsche Funkausstellung und Phonoschau Berlin 1930," *ZfI* 50 (1929/30): 678, 742, 772, 780.

BERLIN (Germany). GROSSE DEUTSCHE FUNKAUSSTELLUNG UND PHONOSCHAU, 1932

114 [As above, item no. **112**] , 1933. 184 pp.

BERLIN (Germany). INDUSTRIE AUSSTELLUNG FÜR GAST- UND HAUS-WIRTSCHAFT, KOCHKUNST, ERFINDUNGEN UND NEUHEITEN, 1902

Literature

115 [Notes on the musical instrument industry at . . .] , *ZfI* 22 (1901/2): 389-90, 455, 569 (exhibitors), 633 (prizes).

Article notes an official catalog; not located.

BERLIN (Germany). INTERNATIONALE HANDWERKSAUSSTELLUNG, 1938

Literature

116   "Nach den Ausklang der Internationalen Handwerksausstellung in Berlin," *ZfI* (1937/38), pp. 321-22.

BERLIN (Germany). JUBILÄUMS-AUSSTELLUNG [DER KGL. AKADEMIE DER KÜNSTE], 1886

General

117   *Jubiläums-Ausstellung der kgl. Akademie der Künste im Landes-Ausstellungsgebäude zu Berlin . . . 1886. Illustrirter Katalog.* Berlin: Berliner Verlags-Comptoir, 1886. xxiv, 352 pp. *Nachtrag . . . ibid.* 36 pp.

      Copies at MdBJ (BAu), NN (NYp), DLC (Wc).

118   *Officieller Katalog der Jubiläums-Ausstellung. . . .* Berlin: Berliner Verlags-Comptoir, 1886. xxiv, 210 pp. *Nachtrag . . . ibid.* 36 pp.

119   *Illustrirter praktischer Führer durch die Jubiläums- Kunst-Ausstellung.* Berlin: Berliner Verlags-Comptoir, 1886. 64 pp.

120   *Praktischer Führer durch die grosse akademische Jubiläums- Kunst-Ausstellung in Berlin.* Berlin: Maurer-Greiner, 1886. 71 pp., illus.

      Cited from KaY*; except where indicated items not located.

BERLIN (Germany). MUSIK- FACHAUSSTELLUNG, 1906

Literature

121   "Streiflichter von der Musik-Fachausstellung in Berlin," *ZfI* (1905/6): 740-41, 771-72, 804-6, 836-37.

122   Chop, Max. "Die Berliner Musik-Fachausstellung," *Musikalisches Wochenblatt* 37 (1906): 379-81, 474-76 ("Lehrer und Nutzen").

123   "Die Musik-Fachausstellung in der 'Philharmonie' zu Berlin," *ZfI* 26 (1905/6): 707 (exhibitors), 743-44, 775 (prizes), 809 (prizes), 871 (prizes); 27 (1906/7): 15 ("nachträgliches").

124   Leichtentritt, Hugo. "Die Musik-Fachausstellung in Berlin," *NZfM* 73 (1906): 470-72.

BERLIN (Germany). MUSIK-FACHAUSSTELLUNG [3rd] , 1922

Literature

125   "Die III Musik-Fachausstellung und Messe in Berlin," *ZfI* 42 (1921/22): 807
(announced), 1069, 1133, 1265, 1327 (all exhibitors' lists), 1350, 1502-4 (prizes).

BERLIN (Germany). NATIONALE GEWERBE-AUSSTELLUNG, 1888

Literature

126   [Notes on the musical instrument industry at . . .] , *ZfI* 5 (1884/85): 271;
6 (1885/86): 108, 110, 201, 374, 376, 398.

BERLIN (Germany). PREUSSISCHE AKADEMIE DER KÜNSTE. *See* BERLIN (Germany). DEUTSCHE AKADEMIE DER KÜNSTE

BERLIN (Germany). K. PREUSSISCHE KAPELLE. *See Section II under* JOHANN GEORGE II, Fürst von Brandenburg

BERLIN (Germany). STAATLICHES INSTITUT FÜR MUSIKFORSCHUNG, STIFTUNG PREUSSISCHER KULTURBESITZ. MUSIKINSTRUMENTEN-MUSEUM (J52, A184, BB110)

[N.B.: Formerly the museum of the Kgl. Hochschule für Musik, (i.e., the Staatliche akademische Hochschule für Musik, Schloss Charlottenberg). Part of the Stiftung since 1962. Referred to simply as "Musikinstrumenten-Museum, Berlin."

Collections include two from Paul de Wit—1888, 240 items; 1890, 280 items (covered in Fleischer catalogue of 1892, see below); St. Wenzelskirche, Naumburg; first Snoeck Collection, 1902 (catalogue 1894, q.v.); Spitta (1888); Kaiser Wilhelm I; and from families of Meyerbeer, Weber, Mendelssohn, Joachim, Busoni, etc.

Curators have been: Oskar Fleischer, Curt Sachs (1919-), Georg Schünemann (1933-), Alfred Berner (1948-).]

127   Fleischer, Oskar. *Führer durch die Sammlung alter Musikinstrumente.* Berlin:
A. Haack, 1892. 145 pp.

> This is the official catalogue of the 1,601 instruments from
> the Hochschule exhibited at the International Exhibition for
> Music and the Drama, Vienna, 1892. It includes two groups,
> ca. 500 items, from the WIT collection, q.v., Section II.
> Duckles* 3:1569. Copies generally available.

128   "Raum XII. Königliche Sammlung alterthümlicher Musikinstrumente zu Berlin."
       In Vienna. Internationale Ausstellung für Musik- und Theaterwesen, 1892. *Fach-*
       Katalog . . . Abtheilung Deutschland und Oesterreich-Ungarn, pp. 165-79. Wien:
       Ausstellungs-Commission, 1892.

129   Sachs, Curt. *Sammlung alter Musikinstrumente bei der Staatlichen Hochschule*
       für Musik; beschreibender Katalog von Curt Sachs. Mit 30 Lichtdrucktafeln und
       34 Textabbildungen. Berlin: J. Bard, 1922. viii pp., 384 cols., illus.

              Duckles* 3:1570.

130   Sachs, Curt. *Staatliche Musikinstrumentensammlung: kleiner Führer. Amtliche*
       Ausg. Berlin: J. Bard, [1922]. 15 pp.

              British Museum catalogue puts under Preussische Akademie
              der Künste and dates [1920]. Copy at DLC (Wc).

131   *Führer durch das Musikinstrumenten-Museum. Abteilung III des Instituts für*
       deutsche Musikforschung. Berlin-Charlottenberg: Fänger, 1939. viii, 144 pp.,
       16 pls.

              Compiled by A. Ganse, H.-H. Dräger and K. Reinhard.
              Copies in U.S. not located.

132   Berner, Alfred. "Neuerwerbungen des Staatlichen Instituts für Musikforschung,"
       Stiftung Preussischer Kulturbesitz, Jahrbuch (1964/65), pp. 274-82. illus.

              Copy at NN (NYp).

133   Otto, Irmgard. *Musikinstrumentenmuseum, Berlin. Stiftung Preussischer*
       Kulturbesitz, Staatliches Institut für Musikforschung. Ausstellungsverzeichnis
       mit Personen- und Sachregister, bearb. von Irmgard Otto. Berlin: [the Museum],
       1965. 144 pp., (133-44 illus.).

              Duckles 3:1572. Generally available.

134   Berner, Alfred. "Musikinstrumenten-Museum." In Stiftung Preussischer
       Kulturbesitz, *Preussischer Kulturbesitz; Ausstellungs Katalog Düsseldorf 1967*,
       pp. 158-69 (items 626-89 and pls. 132-35). [Berlin: 1967.]
              Exhibition held in Städtische Kunsthalle, Düsseldorf,
              October 9-December 3, 1967. Copy at MH.

135   Krickeberg, Dieter and Wolfgang Rauch. *Katalog der Blechblasinstrumente.*
       Berlin: Staatliches Institut für Musikforschung, 1976. 199 pp., illus.

              Copy at NBuU-M (BUu).

136   Otto, Irmgard and O. Adelmann. *Katalog der Streichinstrumente.* Berlin:
       Staatliches Institut für Musikforschung, 1975. 336 pp.

              Copies at NRU (Rs), CU (BEu).

BERLIN (Germany). STAATLICHES INSTITUT. . . . *continued*

137   Montagu, Jeremy. "Review of Otto & Adelmann, 'Katalog der Streichinstrumente' and Krickeberg & Rauch, 'Katalog der Blechblasinstrumente, Berlin'," *FoMRHI Bulletin* (October 1977, Communication no. 90).

Literature

138   Fleischer, Oskar. "Die königliche Sammlung alter Musikinstrumente zu Berlin," *ZfI* 10 (1889/90): 137-40. "Abdruck aus der 'Norddeutschen Allgemeinen Zeitung,' Nr. 22, Jan. 14, 1890."

139   Fleischer, Oskar. "Schenkungen für die kgl. Sammlung alter Musikinstrumente [früher de Wit'sche Sammlung]," *ZfI* 11 (1890/91): 315.

140   Seiffert, Max. "Die kgl. Sammlung alter Musik-Instrumente zu Berlin und die Bedeutung für die deutsche Instrumentenindustrie," *Allgemeine Musik-Zeitung* 20, no. 14 (1893): 200-201.

141   Fleischer, Oskar. "Die Snoeck'sche Musikinstrumentensammlung in der k. Hochschule, Berlin," *SiMG* 3 (1902): 565-94. illus.

142   Stempel, Max. "Ein kaiserliches Geschenk an das deutsche Volk," *Der Tag* (May 25, 1902).

        See also the note about this gift in *ZiMG* 3 (1902): 330.

143   Sylvester, H. "Alte Musikinstrumente," *Bühne und Brettl* (Berlin, July 24, 1902).

        About the Snoeck Collection.

144   "Königlichen Sammlung alten Musikinstrumente in neuen Heim [Charlottenberg]," *Beilage zu den Germannia, Blätter zur Unterhaltung,* no. 1 (1903).

        Cited in *BdZL**; not located.

145   Römer, A. "Die kgl. Sammlung alten Musik-Instrumente in Berlin-Charlottenberg," *Ueber Land und Meer* 27 (1902): 601-4. Many illus.

146   Martell, Paul. "Die kgl. Musik-Instrumenten-Sammlung zu Berlin," *Neue musikalische Rundschau* 1, no. 10 (1908): 10-12; "Neuerwerbungen," *ibid.,* no. 13 (1908): 14.

147   Martell, Paul. "Die kgl. Musikinstrumenten-Sammlung zu Berlin," *Musikalisches Wochenblatt* 40, I. Sem. (1909/10): 320-22.

148   Martell, Paul. "Die kgl. Musikinstrumentensammlung zu Berlin," *Musikpflege* (Leipzig), vol. 14, no. 32/33 (1912).

        Cited from *ZiMG*-schau*, vol. 14 (1912/13); no U. S. locations.

149   "Die Königl. Sammlung alter Musikinstrumente in Berlin vor dem drohenden Ruin," *ZfI* 33 (1912/13): 851.

150   Sachs, Curt. "Die staatliche Musikinstrumentensammlung zu Berlin im Jahre 1920," *ZfMW* 3 (1920/21): 382.

151   Sachs, Curt. *Das Klavier.* (Handbücher des Instrumentenmuseums der staatlichen Hochschule für Musik, 1. Bd.) Berlin: Verlag J. Bard, 1923. iv, 54 pp., 16 Taf.
      Examples are from the Museum.

152   Huth, Arno. "Ein javanische Gamelan in das Berliner Instrumenten-Museum," *ZfMW* 12 (1930): 444-45.

153   Sachs, Curt. "A travers un musée d'instruments," *Revue musicale* 13 (1932): 212-14.

154   "Staatliches Musikinstrumentenmuseum in Berlin. Deutschlands grösste Musik-instrumentenschau," *ZfI* 57 (1936/37): 100, 116.

155   *Staatliche Museum, Nationalgalerei und Musikinstrumentenmuseum, Führungen, Arbeitsgemeinschaften, Vorträge* . . . Oktober bis Dezember 1938. . . . [Berlin: 1938.]
      A collection of materials in the British Museum.

156   Berner, Alfred. "Die Berliner Instrumenten-Sammlung," *Stimmen* 15 (1949): 475-79.

157   David, Werner. "Die Berliner Instrumenten-Sammlung," *Musica* (Cassell) 5 (1951): 461-65. illus.

158   Berner, Alfred. *Die Berliner Musikinstrumenten-Sammlung; Einführung mit historischen und technischen Erläuterungen.* Berlin: 1952. 58 pp., 11 pls.
      "Not strictly a catalog, a guide," Duckles 3:1568.

159   Berner, Alfred. "Die Berliner Musikinstrumenten-Sammlung. Eine Fundgrube für den Musikinstrumentenfachmann," *Instrumentenbau-Zeitschrift* 8 (1954): 78.

160   Berner, Alfred. "Sammlung, Restaurierung, Forschung. Aus der Arbeit der Berliner Musikinstrumenten-Sammlung," *Instrumentenbau-Zeitschrift* 10 (1955/56): 236-38.

161   Bauer, Rudolf. "Berliner Musikinstrumentensammlung," *Musica* (Cassell) 17 (1963): 131.

162   Berner, Alfred. "Das Staatliches Institut für Musikforschung," *Stiftung Preussischer Kulturbesitz, Jahrbuch* (1962), pp. 356-68.
      With a bibliography of writings about the Institut.

BERLIN (Germany). STAATLICHES INSTITUT. . . . *continued*

163   Berner, Alfred. *Musikinstrumenten-Sammlung Berlin. Eine Uebersicht.* Berlin: [1963].

164   Fedtke, Traugott. "Wiederöffnung der Berliner Instrumenten-Sammlung," *Instrumenbau-Zeitschrift* 17 (1963): 289-90.

165   Herzog, H. K. "Die 75 Jahre alte Berliner Musikinstrumenten-Sammlung in neuen Räumen," *MIuP* 12 (1963): 299-301.

166   Jones, D. O. "The Berlin Instrument Collection," *Consort* 21 (1964): 311-14.

167   Berner, Alfred. "Die Berliner Musikinstrumenten-Sammlung. Zur Sonderschau 'Historische Musikinstrumente und Klavierlitteratur'," *MIuP* 14 (1965): 527-28.

168   Berner, Alfred. "Die Klavierinstrumenten der Musikinstrumenten-Sammlung Berlin." In *Europiano Kongress, Berlin, 1965. Dokumentation, Kongressbericht . . . ,* pp. 261-71. [Frankfurt a.M.: 1966.]

169   Otto, Irmgard. "Das Musik-instrumenten-Museum Berlin," *Kulturarbeit* 18 (1966): 227-30.

170   *Das Musikinstrumenten Museum Berlin. Eine Einführung in Wort und Bild.* Berlin: 1968. 70 pp., 50 photos.
      Historical essay by Irmgard Otto.

171   *Fortschritte im Instrumentenbau des 19. Jahrhunderts in der Sicht von Hector Berlioz, anlässlich seines 100. Todestages vom 8. März bis 31. Juli 1969.* Berlin: 1969. 8 mimeo pp.

172   Ligtvoet, A. W. "De Muziekinstrumentenverzameling in Berlin," *Mens en melodie* 26 (1971): 277-78.

173   Berner, Alfred. "Der Ruckers-Bestand des Berliner Musikinstrumenten-Museums. Bemerkungen zu der Konstruktionen." In *Colloquium Restauratierproblemen,* pp. 53-62. Antwerp: 1971.

174   Berner, Alfred. "Das 19. Jahrhundert in Musikinstrumenten-Museum." In *Studia musico-museologica* [symposium], pp. 80-89. Nürnberg: 1970.

175   Droysen, Dagmar. "Anforderungen an die audio-visuelle Information in Musik-instrumenten-Museum," *Musik und Bildung* 4 (1972): 372-74.

176   [Brief description], *IAMIC Newsletter* 1 (1973): 14.

177   Berner, Alfred. "Das Berliner Musikinstrumenten-Museum und seine Zupfinstrumente," *Zupfmusik* 27, no. 1 (1974): 5-10.

BERLIN (Germany). STAATLICHE MUSEEN. ÄGYPTISCHE ABTEILUNG

178   Sachs, Curt. *Die Musikinstrumente des algen Ägyptens. Mit 121 Abbildungen im Text und 11 Lichtdrucktafeln.* (Staatliche Museen zu Berlin. Mitteilungen aus der Ägyptischen Sammlung, III. B.) Berlin: K. Curtius, 1921. 92 pp., illus.

> See also his *Altägyptische Musikinstrumenten.* (Alte Orient 21.) Leipzig: Hinrichs'sche Buchhandlung, 1920. 24 pp.
> Copies at IU (Uu), MiU (AAu), ICU (Cu), PU (PHu), DLC (Wc).

BERLIN (Germany). STAATLICHE MUSEEN. KUNSTGEWERBEMUSEUM

General

179   *Führer durch das Kunstgewerbemuseum.* 17. Aufl. (Führer durch . . . staatliches Museen zu Berlin.) Berlin: Vereinigg. wissensch. Verleger, 1915. 154 pp., 30 Taf.

> Not located or examined. Grove's* III and V note a catalogue, including musical instruments, with this date. Museum combined with the Schlossmuseum, 1921; Grove's also mentions a catalogue of that date which has not been found.

BERLIN (Germany). STAATLICHE MUSEEN. MUSEUM FÜR VÖLKERKUNDE (J51, A185, BB110)

180   Ankermann, Bernhard. "Die Afrikanische Musikinstrumente." In Berlin. Museum für Völkerkunde. *Ethnologisches Notizblatt,* vol. 3, pt. 1, pp. 1-134. Berlin: Druck von A. Haack, [1901]; also published separately and reprinted, Leipzig: Zentralantiquariat, 1976.

181   Sachs, Curt. *Die Litauischen Musikinstrumente in der kgl. Sammlung für deutsche Volkskunde zu Berlin.* (Separat-Abdruck aus *Internationales Archiv für Ethnographie* 23.) [Leiden: 1915.] 82 pp.

> Copies at NPV (POvc), NN (NYp).

182   Sachs, Curt. *Die Musikinstrumenten Indiens und Indonesiens, zugleich eine Einführung in die Instrumentenkunde.* (Handbuch der kgl. Museen zu Berlin, [Bd. 15].) Berlin: G. Reimer, 1915. iv, 191 pp., illus.

> Copy at DLC (Wc).

183   Sachs, Curt. *Die Musikinstrumenten Indiens und Indonesiens, zugleich eine Einführung in die Instrumentenkunde.* 2. Aufl. (Handbücher der Staatliche Museen zu Berlin, [Bd. 15].) Berlin und Leipzig: W. de Gruyter & Co., 1923. vi, 192 pp., 117 illus.

> Copies at DLC (Wc), NNMM.

BERLIN (Germany). STAATLICHE MUSEEN. MUSEUM . . . *continued*

184   Nixdorff, Heide. *Tönender Ton. Tongefässflöten und Tonpfeifen aus Europa. Staatliche Museen Preussischer Kulturbesitz. . . .* [Berlin: c1974.] 53 pp., 80 pls. and items.

> Copy at Haags Gemeentemuseum.

Literature

185   Reinhard, Kurt. *Musik exotischer Völker. Bildausstellung: Marie Seidel.* Berlin: Museum für Völkerkunde, 1952. 35, vii pp.

186   Reinhard, Kurt. *Klingende Saiten. Musikinstrumente aus drei Kontinenten. Sonderausstellung.* Berlin: Museum für Völkerkunde, [n.d., 1965?]. [8] pp.

187   Reinhard, Kurt. *Trommeln und Trompeten. Sonderausstellung.* Berlin: Museum für Völkerkunde, [n.d., 1967?]. [6] folded pp.

188   Krieger, Kurt. "Musikinstrumente der Hausa," *Baessler-Archiv; Beiträge zur Völkerkunde* 16 (1968): 373-430.

> Includes catalogue numbers for instruments in the Museum.

189   Hartmann, Günter. "Die Materielle Kultur der Xavante, Zentralbrasilian," *Baessler-Archiv; Beiträge zur Völkerkunde* 18 (1970): 43-70.

> A collection acquired by the Museum in 1966.

General

190   *Führer durch die Museum für Völkerkunde. Die ethnologische Abteilung. . . .* 16. Aufl. Berlin: G. Reimer, 1914. 252 pp.

> Many editions. Lambertini* (*Bibliophilie musicale*) notes that the 1901 edition contains 171 African instruments. Grove's III and V note the catalogs of 1913 and 1898 (7th); neither located.

BERN (Switzerland). HISTORISCHES MUSEUM (J121, A40)

Literature

191   Altenburg, Wilhelm. "Alte Musikinstrumente in dem Bernischen Historischen Museum," *ZfI* 8 (1897/98): 198, 209.

192   Leutenegger, Emil. "Die Musikinstrumenten-Sammlung des Historischen Museum in Bern," *Berner Tagblatt,* no. 69 (1955) and in *Schweizerische Blasmusikzeitung,* vol. 12 (1955).

193　Staehelin, Martin. "Der sogennante Musettenbass: Forschungen zur schweizerischen Instrumenten- und Musikgeschichte des spätern 18. und 19. Jahrhunderts,"
the museum's *Jahrbuch* (1969/70), pp. 93-121. illus.

　　　Jahrbuch at NIC (Iu), CtY (NHu), OClMA (CLm).

194　Geiser, Brigitte. "Die Musikinstrumente des . . . Museums," *Glareana* 19, Nr. 3/4
(1970): 2-7.

195　Centlivres, Pierre. "Les Instruments de musique de Perse et d'Afghanistan au
département d'ethnographie du Musée d'histoire de Berne," the museum's
Jahrbuch 51/52 (1972/72): 305-20. illus.

196　Perret, Denise. "Catalogue des instruments non-européens," the museum's *Jahrbuch*,
vol. 55 (1975); vol. 56 (1976).

　　　Citation from Jenkins*, without pagination; not verified.

BERN (Switzerland). INDUSTRIE-AUSSTELLUNG, 1824

General

197　*Verzeichnis derjenigen Gegenstände des bernischen und schweizerischen Kunstfleisses,*
welche für die Industrie-Ausstellung. Bern: Haller, [1824]. 38 pp.

　　　Musical instruments, pp. 14-17. Information from
　　　Schweizerische Landesbibliothek; no U.S. copies.

BERN (Switzerland). INDUSTRIE-AUSSTELLUNG, 1848

General

198　*Administrativer und technischer Bericht über die 2. allgemeinen Schweizerischen*
Industrie-Ausstellung in Bern . . . in den Monaten Juli, August und September 1848.
Bern & Zürich: Schulthess, 1849. lxviii, 117 pp.

　　　Not located. RINDL-1 notes 33 instruments exhibited by
　　　several makers.

BERN (Switzerland). SCHWEIZERISCHE INDUSTRIEAUSSTELLUNG, 1857

General

199　*Uebersichtliche Darstellung der 1857 in Bern ausgestallten Producte der schweizer-*
ischen Industrie. Bern: Haller'sche Buchdruckerei, 1857. 60 pp.

　　　Musikalische Instrumente, pp. 26-27. Information from
　　　the Schweizerische Landesbibliothek; no U. S. copies.

BERN (Switzerland). SCHWEIZERISCHE LANDESAUSSTELLUNG, 1914

Literature

200   Huber, Hans. "Musikinstrumente. Fachbericht über die 27. Gruppe der Schweizerischen Landesausstellung." In Bern. Schweizerische Landesausstellung, 1914.
Fachberichte, vol. 6, pp. 79- .

> Zürich, Art Institut Orell Füssli, [1916]; citation from
> *DBV*;* not examined.

201   "Die Musikinstrumente auf der . . . ," *ZfI* 34 (1913/14): 971-73, 1283-84, 1299-
1300; 35 (1914/15): 104 (prizes). illus.

General

202   *Offizieller Führer durch die schweizerischen Landesausstellung . . . 15. V. - 15. X.
1914.* Bern: Georgr. Kartenverlag, 1914. 130 pp., illus.

> Citation from *DBV*;* not examined.

BESANÇON (France). MUSÉE HISTORIQUE DE LA FRANCKE-COMTÉ

203   *La vie musicale à Anvers au siècle de Granvelle.* [Exposition] *Musée Granvelle,
Besançon, 1er au septembre 1972. Hôtel de Sully, Paris, 9 octobre au 15 novembre
1972.* [Bruxelles: Laconti, 1974?] [24] pp., illus.

> *RILM** puts under Lambrechts-Douillez, Jeanine and
> G. Thibault de Chambure and says published by
> Ministère de l'Education. Includes a catalogue of
> instruments in the exhibition.

BIRMINGHAM (U. K.). SCHOOL OF MUSIC   (A68, BB52)

204   *Catalogue of Musical Instruments in the Possession of the School.* Birmingham:
1953.

> Not examined. *MGG** says "Autotypie beim Museum."
> Brook and Brody* say "includes part of L.L Key collection."

BLOOMINGTON, INDIANA (USA). INDIANA UNIVERSITY. MUSEUM OF ART

205   Gold, Peter. *Traditional Music of the World; Guide to the Current Exhibit:
December 3, 1968-April 15, 1969, Indiana University Museum.* [Bloomington:
1968.] 44 lvs., illus.

BOCHUM (Germany). MUSEUM (J54)

206 *Musikinstrumente der Völker: Sammlung Hans Grumbt II. 13.12.1975-18.1.1976.*
[Katalog und Layout, Hans Grumbt.] [Bochum] : Museum Bochum, [1976?].
71 pp., [10] lvs.

> The second collection formed by Grumbt, 238 items.
> Copy at DLC (Wc).

Literature

207 "Musikinstrumenten Sammlung Hans Grumbt, Bochum," *Glareana,* vol. 14,
no. 2 (1965).

208 Hiestand-Schnellmann, Josef. "Musikinstrumenten der Völker; Sammlung II von
Hans Grumbt, Bochum," *Glareana* 25 (1976): 20.

BOLOGNA (Italy). CONSERVATORIO DI MUSICA "G. B. MARTINI" (A285)

209 *Raccolta di antichi strumenti armonici conservati nel Liceo musicale del Comune
di Bologna.* Bologna: 1880. ? pp., illus.

> Cited by Lütg* without date, Heyer* without collation.
> NNMM has Ms. copy with English translation, entered
> under Museo Civico and dated 1898. The conservatory's
> collection was transferred to the Museo, 18-?.

BOLOGNA (Italy). MOSTRA INTERNAZIONALE DI MUSICA, 1888

Literature

210 "Die Musikausstellung zu Bologna," *ZfI* 7 (1886/87): 446-48; 8 (1887/88): 2-4,
14-15, 30, 58-60, 110-12, 122-23; (prizes, 76-78).

211 "Ueber die italienische Musikinstrumenten-Industrie auf der Ausstellung," *ZfI*
7 (1886/87): 362-64, 400-2.

General

212 *Catalogo ufficiale. . . .* Parma: Tip. Battei, 1888. 175 pp.

> Grove's* calls this an International Exhibition of Musical
> Instruments. According to Valdrighi (*Nomocheliurgografia,*
> 1884) some of his collection was included in the exhibition.

BOLOGNA (Italy). MUSEO CIVICO (J77). *See above* CONSERVATORIO DI MUSICA "G. B. MARTINI" *and note in Section II under* COSPI, FERDINANDO

BONN (Germany). RHEINISCHES LANDESMUSEUM

Literature

213   Klar, Marlies. "Musikinstrumente der Römerzeit in Bonn," the museum's
       Jahrbuch 121 (1971): 301-33.

BOSTON, MASSACHUSETTS (USA). FOREIGN EXHIBITION, 1883

Literature

214   "Ostindische Instrumente auf der Foreign Exhibition zu Boston [44 items],"
       ZFI 4 (1883/84): 149-50.

General

215   *Official catalogue* . . . , compiled by C. B. Norton. Boston: G. Coolidge, c1883.
       448 (i.e., 256) pp.

             Instruments throughout but note "Indian Musical
             Instruments," pp. 300-306.

BOSTON, MASSACHUSETTS (USA). HORTICULTURAL HALL

216   [Chickering & Sons, Boston.] *Catalogue of the Exhibition, Horticultural Hall,
       Boston, January 11 to 26, 1902.* [Boston: The Barta Press, c1902.] 78 pp., illus.;
       the "Historical Musical Exhibition, under the Auspices of Chickering & Sons. . . ."
             Copies at DLC (Wc), NNMM, MB (Bp), NN (NYp).

Literature

217   J., A. A. "Historical Musical Exhibition [description of some string instruments
       shown]," *The Violinist* 2, no. 7 (March 1902): 7.

218   [Chickering & Sons, Boston]. "The Historical Musical Exhibition under the
       Auspices of . . . ," *Musical Courier* (N.Y.), no. 1141 (1902); reprinted from the
       Boston Herald.

BOSTON, MASSACHUSETTS (USA). MASSACHUSETTS CHARITABLE MECHANIC ASSOCIATION EXHIBITION, 8TH, 1856

Literature

219   Chickering & Sons, Boston. *Pianofortes at the Exhibitions of 1856.* Boston:
       Press of E. L. Balch, 1857. 20 pp., illus.
             Mainly the report of the judges.

BOSTON, MASSACHUSETTS (USA). MUSEUM OF FINE ARTS. LESLIE LINDSEY MASON COLLECTION (L216) [N.B.: Five hundred sixty items from the Francis W. Galpin collection (see Section II) were transferred to the Museum in 1917. Many of those items are shown and described in Galpin's *Old English Instruments of Music* (London: Methuen, 1911). The Mason collection also contains the Edmund Ripon collection.]

220   Bessaraboff, Nicholas. *Ancient European Musical Instruments; An Organological Study of the Musical Instruments in the Leslie Lindsey Mason Collection. . . .* Preface by Edward J. Hipkins and a Foreword by Canon Francis W. Galpin. Cambridge, Mass.: Harvard University Press, 1941. xxxiii, 503 pp., illus.

> See article by Boyden, David, "Nicholas Bessaraboff's *Ancient European Musical Instruments,*" in MLAN* 28 (1971): 21-27.

Literature

221   P., F. V. "The Leslie Lindsey Mason Collections of Musical Instruments, Formerly the Galpin Collection," Boston. Museum of Fine Arts. *Bulletin* 15 (1917): 47-63. With 36 illus.

222   Kinsky, Georg. "Mitteilungen [discusses transfer of Galpin's collection to Boston]," *ZfMW* 3 (1920/21): 639-40.

223   Williamson, N. "The Leslie Lindsey Mason Collection," Boston. Museum of Fine Arts. *Bulletin* 59 (1961): 23-25.

224   Whitehill, W. M. *Museum of Fine Arts, Boston: A Centennial History.* Cambridge, Mass.: 1970; see especially vol. 2, pp. 393, 427, 473, 491, 613-14, 811-12.

BOSTON, MASSACHUSETTS (USA). NEW ENGLAND CONSERVATORY OF MUSIC (L217)

225   *The Sargent Collection of Oriental Instruments, Presented to the Conservatory by Mrs. Horatio A. Lamb in Memory of Mrs. Winthrop Sargent Who Collected Them.* [Boston] : 1920. [4] pp.

> A catalogue; copy at MB (Bp).

226   Burnett, Elizabeth. *A Catalogue of the Collection of Ancient Instruments Owned by the . . . Conservatory.* (Unpublished M. A. thesis, New England Conservatory of Music, 1967.)

BOSTON, MASSACHUSETTS (USA). SYMPHONY ORCHESTRA. CASADESUS COLLECTION OF OLD MUSICAL INSTRUMENTS (L215)

227 *Catalogue of the Collection . . . Presented on October 23, 1926 by Friends, to the Boston Symphony Orchestra.* [Boston: 1926?] [7] pp.

> Copies at CtY (NHu), MB (Bp).

Literature

228 Meyer, Alfred H. "The Casadesus Collection. Ancient Instruments Now Lodged in Boston's Symphony Hall," *Musical Digest* 11 (January 4, 1927): 21, 48.

229 "Boston's Old Instruments," *Musical America* 82 (February 1964): 8-9.

230 "The Casadesus Collection of Ancient Instruments," *Hi Fidelity/Musical America* 15 (December 15, 1965): 152-53. Many illus.

BOURNEMOUTH (U. K.). BROWNSEA CASTLE. *See Section II under* VAN RAALTE, CHARLES

BRANDENBURG HOFKAPELLE. *See* SACHS *Section II under* JOHANN GEORG II, Fürst von Brandenburg

BRATISLAVA (Czechoslovakia). SLOVENSKÉ NÁRODNE MÚZEUM (J29)

231 Mačak, Ivan. *Hudobné nástroje na Slovensku: výstavy Slovenskeho Národného Múzea, Bratislava.* Bratislava: [the Museum], 1975. 64 pp. (20 pp., illus.)

> "Music Instruments in Slovakia"; text by Ivan Mačak.

232 *Hudobné zbierky Slovenskeho narodné muzea = Musiksammlungen des Slowakischen Nationalmuseums.* [Autori] Ľ. Ballová . . . predhovor Jozef Vlachovič. Bratislava: Opus pre Slovenské národné muzeum a Slovenský hudobný fond, 1975. 172 pp., illus.

> The guide includes music. Copy at DLC (Wc).

Literature

233 Mačak, Ivan. "Múzeum hudobných nástrojov," *Slovenská hudba* 9 (1967): 451-52.

> Cited from *RILM** 1:1298.

BREMEN (Germany). FOCKE-MUSEUM (J55)

Literature

234 Hart, Günter. "Die Musikinstrumente im Focke-Museum zu Bremen," *Glareana* 22, no. 3/4 (1973): lvs. 50-57. 36 items.

BREMEN (Germany). NORDWESTDEUTSCHEN GEWERBE- UND INDUSTRIE-AUSSTELLUNG, 1899

Literature

235 Noessel, Louis Carl. "Die Musikinstrumente auf . . . ," *ZfI* 10 (1889/90): 401-4, 418-20.

From *Bremer Nachrichten.*

236 "Aussteller-Liste, nach dem offiziellen Katalog . . . ," *ZfI* 10 (1889/90): 348-50.

Official catalogue not located.

BRENTFORD (U.K.). BRITISH PIANO MUSEUM

237 *The Musical Museum.* Brentford, [1977]. [16] pp., illus.

BRESLAU. *See* WROCŁAW (Poland)

BRIG (Switzerland). STOCKALPERSCHLOSS

238 Geiser, Brigitte. *Das Hackbrett in der Schweiz. Zur Ausstellung im Stockalperschloss Brig, 30. Juni bis 2. September 1973.* [Mitarb.] Karl-Heinz Schickhaus. (Schriften des Stockalper-Archivs in Brig, Heft 25.) Brig: Stockalper-Archiv, 1973. 59 pp., illus.

BROOKLYN, NEW YORK (USA). BROOKLYN MUSEUM

239 Sotheby Parke Bernet, firm. *Musical Instruments, the Property of Various Owners Including the Brooklyn Museum . . . Sold . . . April 5, 1977.* New York: Sotheby Parke Bernet, 1977. [unpaged, 102 items, illus.]

Sale no. 3969.

BROWNSEA CASTLE. *See Section II under* VAN RAALTE, CHARLES

BRÜX. *See* **MOST (Czechoslovakia)**

BRUGES (Belgium). FESTIVAL VAN VLAANDEREN, 1968

240 *Tentoonstelling . . . Het clavicimbel in Europa. Oude en nieuwe instrumenten,*
edities, platen, med de medewerking van de Stad Brugge en 27 clavicimbel-
bouwers en firma's. Stedelijk Concertgebou - Gruuthusmuseum, 17-22 augustus
1968. [n.p.] , 1968. [23] pp., illus.
  Copy at NL-DHgm.

BRUGES (Belgium). STEDELIJK MUSEUM VAN SCHONE KUNSTEN (or GRUUTHUSE-MUSEUM) (A40, BB29)

241 Vermeersch, Valentin. *Stad Brugge. Gids Gruuthemuseum. Stedelijk Museum*
voor Oudheidkunde en Kunstnijverheid. Brugge: 1969. 158 pp., illus.
  Ancient musical instruments (62), pp. 156-58, according to *RILM**.

Literature

242 Hart, Günter. "Die Musikinstrumente im Gruuthuse-Museum zu Brügge," *Glareana*
23, no. 2 (1974): lvs. 25-28. 60 items.

BRUNSWICK (Germany). BRAUNSCHWEIGISCHES LANDESMUSEUM FÜR GESCHICHTE UND VOLKSTUM (J54)

Literature

243 Flechsig, Werner. "Ostfälische Musikinstrumentenmacher des 18. und frühen
Jahrhunderts," *Braunschweigische Heimat; Zeitschrift des Braunschweigischen
Landesvereins für Heimatschutz* 48 (1962): 46, 89, 110; 49 (1963): 9, 42, 83,
109; 50 (1964): 9, 53.
  Cited from Jenkins*; not examined.

244 Hart, Günter. "Musikinstrumente im Landesmuseum Braunschweig," *Glareana*
22, no. 1 (1973): lvs. 12-13. 23 items.

BRUNSWICK (Germany). STÄDTISCHES MUSEUM (J55)

245 Schröder, Hans. *Verzeichnis der Sammlung alter Musikinstrumente im Städtischen
Museum. Instrumente, Instrumentenmacher und Instrumentisten in Braunschweig
(urkundliche Beiträge).* (Werkstücke aus Museum, Archiv und Bibliothek der Stadt
Braunschweig, III.) Braunschweig: E. Appelhans & Comp., 1928. 124 pp., 43 pls.

"Verzeichnis," pp. 5-24. Duckles* 3:1574.
Copies at CU (BEu), NN (NYp), DLC (Wc).

246   "Ausstellung alter Musikinstrumente in Braunschweig," *ZfI* 50 (1930): 550.

Literature

247   Strohbach, Berndt. *Geigenbau in Braunschweig. 125 Jahre Werkstatt Rautmann. Ausstellung Sept.-Oct. 1969.* (Arbeitsberichte aus dem Städt. Museum, 15.) Braunschweig: [the Museum, 1969]. 72 pp., illus.

General

248   [Bilzer, Bert & Rolf Hagen.] *Städtischisches Museum Braunschweig 1861-1961. Ein Ueberblick.* [Braunschweig, 1961.] 152 pp., illus.

Jenkins notes p. 79f; not examined.

249   [Hecht, Dorothea.] *Katalog der afrikanischen Sammlung.* (Braunschweiger Werkstücke, Bd. 37.) Braunschweig: Waisenhaus-Buchdruckerei und Verlag, 1968. 394 pp.

Jenkins* notes musical instruments, pp. 285-373; not examined.

BRUSSELS (Belgium). CONSERVATOIRE ROYAL DE MUSIQUE. MUSÉE INSTRUMENTAL (J18, A43, BB13-14) [N.B.: Begun 1872 with the Fétis Collection. Now includes collections of Coussemaker (1877), S. M. Tagore (1876), Villoteau (1878), Charles, Victor and Joseph Mahillon, A. Tolbecque, Leopold II of Belgium, Correr (1886), and Snoeck second collection (1908). Some catalogues of these private collections are under the collectors' names in Section II, q.v.

A list of the expositions throughout the world where portions of the collection have been shown, 1878-1962, is included in the 1969 exhibition catalogue cited below, no. **262**.]

250   "Musee du conservatoire royal de musique." Under this title, beginning with issue no 25,9me année, Dec. 1877, *L'echo musical* provided information about the Musée, usually a note about new instruments acquired. These notes were doubtless by Victor Mahillon, conservator of the Musée and the founder of the journal.

251   [Mahillon, Victor.] "Catalogue descriptif et analytique . . . Essai de classification methodique de tous les instruments," *BrCA* 2 (1878): 81-159.

252   [Mahillon, Victor.] "Catalogue instruments extra-européens. Instruments offerts au Roi des Belges par le Rajah Sourindo Mohun Tagore . . . et données au Conservatoire par sa Majesté," *BrCA* 2 (1878): 161-256; 3 (1879): 93-183; 4 (1880): 101-91; 5 (1881): 115-64 [642 items]; 10 (1886): 159-228 [792 items]; 14 (1890): 153-211 [878 items]; 16 (1892): 139-236 [1004 items]; 17 (1893): 141-237 [44 items]; 18 (1894): 195-315 [173 items]; 31 (1907): 165-96 [815 items]. illus.

BRUSSELS (Belgium). CONSERVATOIRE ROYAL.... *continued*

253 "Liste des dons faits au Musée du Conservatoire depuis sa fondation." This list, probably prepared by Victor Mahillon, appeared in each of the Conservatoire's *Annuaire* (BrCA*) from volume 2 (1878) through volumes 37 (1913), excepting only volume 34 (1910).

254 [*Album des instruments extra-européens du Musee du Conservatoire royale de musique de Bruxelles.* Bruxelles: n.d., 1879?]

> Consists of twelve mounted photos. Copies at DLC (Wc), CtY (NHu), ICN (Cn), NjP (PRu); at CtY dated [188-?]; at NjP [19--?].

255 Mahillon, Victor. *Catalogue descriptif & analytique du Musée instrumental du Conservatoire royal.* Gand: A. Hoste, 1880-1912. 5 vols., 3,300 items. [Reprint: Les Amis de la musique, 1979. 5 vols. in 2.]

> First edition. Volumes 1-5, dated 1893-1922, called the second edition, but only volumes 1 (1893) and 2 (1909) are literally second edition; 3, 4 and 5 (1900, 1912 and 1922) were each published only once.

256 [Review.] Altenburg, Wilhelm. "Die Instrumentensammlung des Brüsseler Konservatoriums und ihr Katalog," *ZfI* 21 (1900/1901): 55-56.

> Refers to the first three volumes only.

257 [Review.] Altenburg, Wilhelm. "Victor-Charles Mahillon und seine Bedeutung für die Instrumentenkunde," *ZfI* 33 (1912/13): 1000-1004. illus.

258 *Catalogue de la collection iconographique du Musée instrumental du Conservatoire ... 1º Nov. 1901.* Gand: Annot-Braeckman, 1901. 37 pp.

> Copy at NNMM.

259 Mahillon, Ferdinand Victor. *Catalogue abrégé du Musée. Extrait du Catalogue descriptif et analytique de Victor-Charles Mahillon.* Gand: A. Hoste, 1912. vii, 238 pp.

> Copy at MiU (AAu).

260 [Mahillon, Victor.] *Catalogue; resumé des numéros 2962 à 3300.* Bruxelles: Impr. Lombaerts, 1926. 36 pp.

> A résumé of volume 5 of the *Catalogue descriptif et analytique.*
> Copies at MiU (AAu), NN (NYp).

261 Closson, Ernst. "English Musical Instruments in the Museum," *Music & Letters* 7 (1926): 157-64.

262   *Exposition des instruments de musique des XVIème et XVIIème siècles. Organisée par le Musée instrumental de Bruxelles en l'Hôtel de Sully à Paris - Juin 1969.* [Bruxelles: Godenne, 1969?] 89 pp., illus., 97 items.

   "Liste d'expositions [1878-1962]," p. [88].

263   *Europalia 1971. Muziekinstrumenten uit de Nederlanden, 17de-19de eeuw . . . Katalogus.* [Bruxelles] : 197-? 31 pp., 30 items.

264   *Catalogue de l'exposition d'instruments anciens au Château de Boleil 15 juin - 30 septembre 1972.* Bruxelles: Godenne, [1972?].

   Preface signed René de Maeyer; texte par Jacques Tilmans.

265   Varenbergh-Awouters, Mia van. *Catalogus van de tentoonstelling gewijd aan muziekinstrumenten de XVIe en XVIIe eeuw, behorend tot het Instrumenten- museum van Brussel. Kasteel Laarne, septembre-november 1972. Catalogue de l'exposition "Instruments de musique des XVIe et XVIIe siècles". . . Château de Laarne. . . .* Brussel: Drukk. Godenne, 1972. xl, 181 pp., illus., (89 pls.).

266   Lambrechts-Douillez, Jeanine. "Catalogue Ruckers: documenten en instrumenten [catalogue of an exhibition]," *Brussels Museum of Musical Instruments, Bulletin* 4 (1974): 65-70.

   The exhibit in Brussels of instruments and documents from Antwerp Stadtsarchief, Vleeshuis, Museum Plantin-Moretus, and others.

267   Raspé, Paul. *The Brussels Museum of Musical Instruments; A Provisional List of the Pianos. . . .* [Brussels: 1975.] 25 pp.

Literature

268   "La collezione istrumentale del signor A. Tolbecque," *Gazzetta musicale di Milano* 34 (1879): 351-52; observed in the Conservatoire.

269   B[ordes?], Ch[arles]. "Audition d'instruments anciens au Conservatoire," *Echo musical* 12 (1880): 3-5; "La dieuxième audition . . . ," 13 (1881): 301-2.

270   [Mahillon, Victor.] "Musée du Conservatoire Royal," *Echo musical* 12 (1880): 45, 56, 68, 129-30, 142, 311.

271   E. M. [= Echo musical]. "Die alten Instrumente in Museum des königl. Conserva- toriums der Musik in Brüssel," *ZfI* 2 (1881/82): 88-89, 161-62, 315-18. illus.

272   Mahillon, [Victor?]. "Les instruments anciens du Musée . . . ," *Echo musical* 13 (1881): 241-43, 275-78; 14 (1882): 136-38. illus.

273   [A note about the primitive instruments in the Musée], *ZfI* 3 (1882/83): 89-90.

274   "Notice sur les instruments reconstitués par M. V. Mahillon," *BrCA* 14 (1890): 140-43.

BRUSSELS (Belgium). CONSERVATOIRE ROYAL. . . . *continued*

Literature

275 Combaz, Gisbert. "Une visite au Musée du Conservatoire Royal de Musique," *Annales de la Société Royale d'Archéologie* 5 (1891): 285-94.

276 "Die Instrumenten-Sammlung des Brüsseler Conservatoriums," *ZfI* (1893/ 94): 65.

277 "Die Instrumentensammlung des Brüsseler Conservatoriums," *ZfI* 17 (1896/ 97): 469-70.

278 Closson, Ernest. "Le Geigenwerk au Musée du Conservatoire de Bruxelles," *Guide Musical* 50 (1904): 307-9; 15 (1905): 331-34; 16 (1906): 355-57; 17 (1907): 379-82; 18 (1908): 403-6.

279 *Les instruments de musique au Musée . . . Instruments à vent.* Bruxelles: Mahillon, [1906/7]. 3 vols.: I, Le trombone . . . ; II, Le cor . . . ; III, La trompette. . . .
    Copy at NjR.

280 Closson, Ernest. "Un nouvel accroisement du Musée du Conservatoire . . . ," *Guide Musical* 54 (1908): 617-19.

281 Closson, Ernest. "La collection des instruments néerlandais au Musée . . . ," *ZiMG* 11 (1909/10): 71-79.
    About the collection from Snoeck.

282 Closson, Ernest. "Notes sur le Musée . . . ," *BrCA* 51 (1927/28): 113-21.

283 Closson, Ernest. "La collection exotique du Musée . . . ," *BrCA* 53 (1929/30): 124-26.

284 Closson, Ernest. "Hautbois égyptiennes antiques au Musée. . . ." In *Brussels. Fondation égyptologique Reine Elisabeth. Chronique d'Egypte. Bulletin* 13-14 (1932): 50-52. illus.

285 Marinus, Albert. *Le folklore des instruments de musique.* (Extrait du Folklore Brabancon, 13e année, no. 73-74.) Bruxelles: Bull. de Service de recherches historiques et folkloriques du Brabant, 1933. 23 pp., illus.

286 Closson, Ernest. "Gli strumenti italiani al Museo de Conservatorio di Bruxelles," *Musica d'oggi* 16 (1934): 123-25.

287 Closson, Ernest. *La facture des instruments de musique en Belgique. . . .* Bruxelles: [Presses des établissements Degrace à Huy], 1935. 108 pp., pls. [instruments from the Musée].

288   Ernst, Fritz. "Musée d'instruments à Bruxelles," *Schweizerische Musik-zeitung* 98 (1958): 255-56.

289   Moulaert, Pierre. "Das Instrumentenmuseum in Brüssel," *Österreichische Musik-zeitschrift* 17 (1962): 517-21. illus.

290   Bragard, R. "Réaménagement du Musée Instrumental du Conservatoire." In Belgium. Ministère de l'Éducation nationale et de la Culture, *Bulletin* 5 (1964): 84-87. illus.

291   Burnal, Jean. "Das Brüsseler Museum für Musikinstrumente," *Presence de Bruxelles* (October 1964). 6 pp.
           Offprint at NL-DHgm.

292   Wyatt, Lucius R. "The Brussels Museum of Musical Instruments," *Music Educators Journal* 53 (February 1967): 48-51. Well illus.

293   "A Bruxelles. Le Musée instrumental," *Journal musical française* 169 (May 1968): 35-37.

294   Falk, Marguerite. "Het instrumentemuseum te Brussel," *Mens en melodie* 23 (1968): 82-86.

295   "Das Brüsseler Instrumenten-Museum," *Musica* (Cassell) 22 (1968): 190-91.

296   "Instrumentenmuseet i Bryssel," *Musikrevy* 24 (1969): 129-31.

297   Brussels. Museum of Musical Instruments, *Bulletin* [ed. par] René de Maeyer. . . . Bruxelles: 1971- .

298   Boone, Hubert. "De Volksinstrumenten uit de Balkan. 1. Volksinstrumenten uit Bulgarije," Brussels. Museum of Musical Instruments, *Bulletin* 1 (1971): 79-92.
           Includes a catalogue of pertinent music holdings.

299   *Inventaire descriptif des archives du facteur d'orgues Émile Kerkhoff au Musée royal instrumental . . . ,* [par] Jean-Pierre Félix. Bruxelles: [J.-P. Félix] , 1975. 68 pp.

General

300   Bragard, Roger and Ferdinand J. Hen. *Les instruments de musique dans l'art et l'histoire.* Préf. de G. Thibault-Chambure. [Rhode-St-Genèse] : A. de Visscher, [1967] . 261 pp., illus. (119 in color, instruments from the Musée).

301   Bragard, Roger and Ferdinand J. Hen. *Musikinstrumente aus zwei Jahrtausend.* [Translated and edited by Dieter Krickeberg.] Stuttgart: Chr. Belse, 1968. 327 pp., illus.

302   Bragard, Roger and Ferdinand J. Hen. *Musical Instruments in Art and History,* translated by Bill Hopkins. London: Barrie & Rockliff; New York: Viking, 1968. 281 pp., illus.

BRUSSELS (Belgium). EXPOSITION DE L'ART BELGE AU XVIe SIÈCLE, 1910

Literature

303 Closson, Ernest. "L'iconographie instrumentale à l'Exposition de l'art belge au XVIe siècle," *Guide musical* 56 (1910): 669-76.

304 Maass, W. "Ueber d. Klavierbau auf der Brüsseler Weltausstellung," *ZfI* 31 (1910/11): 75-76, 152-55, 191-93, 230-34, 275-79.

BRUSSELS (Belgium). EXPOSITION DES PRODUITS DE L'INDUSTRIE NATIONALE, 1830

305 B[ordes?], Ch[arles?]. "1830 et 1880, Exposition et concours," *Echo musical* 12 (1880): 135-39.

  Extensive quotations and list from the official catalogue.

General

306 *Catalogue des produits de l'Industrie nationale admis à la troisième exposition générale.* . . . Bruxelles: Fond. et Impr. normales, 1830.

  Not located.

BRUSSELS (Belgium). EXPOSITION DES PRODUITS DE L'INDUSTRIE NATIONALE, 1835

307 Faure, ? *La belgique industrielle. Compte rendu de l'exposition.* Bruxelles: Louis Hauman et comp., 1836. xliv, 419 pp.

  Musical instruments, Chapter 27, pp. 166-73; illus.
  Copy at DLC (Wc).

BRUSSELS (Belgium). EXPOSITION DES PRODUITS DE L'INDUSTRIE BELGE, 1841

General

308 *Rapports du Jury et documents.* . . . Bruxelles: Impr. du Musée, 1842.

  Instruments de musique, Chapter 16, pp. 287-99.

309 Perrot, Éduard. *Revue de l'exposition . . . en 1841.* Bruxelles: Chez l'auteur, 1841.

  Instruments de musique, Chapitre XVII, pp. 227-57.
  Copies of both at DLC (Wc).

BRUSSELS (Belgium). **EXPOSITION INTERNATIONALE, 1897**

310   *Catalogue de l'exposition internationale de Bruxelles en 1897. Section francaise, Comité 12: Instruments de musique. Art musical.* Paris: Impr. nationale, 1897. 7 pp.

         Cited from *JbP** 1897; not located.

311   Serpette, Gaston. *Exposition internationale de Bruxelles 1897. Rapport sur les opérations du jury no. 26 (Instruments de musique et art musical).* Bruxelles/ Anvers: Katto, 1897. 47 pp.

         Cited from BrCA* 20:108 and *JbP** 1897; not located.
         Summarized in "Bericht der Jury über die Blasinstrumente auf der Weltausstellung," *ZfI* 3 (1897/98): 164-65.

Literature

312   Jacquot, Albert. Essais de lutherie décorative à l'Exposition de Bruxelles," *Revue des arts décoratives* 17 (1897): 298-301. illus.

313   Liebrecht, Charles. *Musée ethnographique du Congo. Instruments de musique (texte et planches); Guide de la section de l'État Indépendent du Congo à l'Exposition de Bruxelles - Tervueren en 1897.* Bruxelles: V. Monnom, 1897. xiv, 523 pp., illus.

         Copy at NBuU-M (BUu).

314   "Brüsseler Weltausstellung . . . Aussteller, Gruppe XXIV, Klasse 79, Musikinstrumente," *ZfI* 17 (1896/97): 249, 791-92, 818-19, 902 & 911 (prizes); 18 (1897/98): 69-71 ("Offizielle Prämiirungsliste").

BRUSSELS (Belgium). **EXPOSITION INTERNATIONALE, 1910**

Literature

315   A., L. "Les instruments Gelas et les Sociétés d'Estudiantina," *M & I* [1], no. 15 (14 avril 1911): 9. illus.

316   Maas, W. "Über den Klavierbau auf der Brüsseler Weltausstellung," *ZfI* 31 (1910/11): 75-76, 152-55, 191-93, 230-34, 275-79. illus.

317   "Musikinstrumenten-Industrie auf der Weltausstellung in Brüssel," *ZfI* 28 (1907/8): 651; 30 (1909/10): 780, 817-18, 962 (exhibitors), 1132-33 ("Streifzug"), 1137, 1173, 1305, 1330 (prizes); 31 (1910/11): 45-46 (prizes), 81, 507 ("Nachklänge").

318   Daehne, Paul. "Streiflichter von der Brüsseler Weltausstellung," *ZfI* 30 (1909/10): 1060-61.

BRUSSELS (Belgium). EXPOSITION INTERNATIONALE, 1910   *continued*

General

319   Germany. Reichskommissar für die Weltausstellung in Brussels. *Amtlicher Katalog des deutschen Reichs.* . . . Berlin: G. Stilke, 1910. xii, 375 pp.

Cited from KaY* 35:1168; not located.

BRUSSELS (Belgium). EXPOSITION NATIONALE, 1880

Literature

320   B., Ch. "Les instruments de musique à l'Exposition nationale de 1880," *Echo musical* 12 (1880): 206-7, 219-21, 230-31, 242-43, 256-57.

321   S., Ed. V. D. "Les instruments de musique anciens à l'Exposition nationale," *Echo musical* 12 (1880): 267-69; reprinted from *Étoile belge.*

322   Kufferath, Maurice. "Les instruments de musique [Collection de MM. V. et J. Mahillon]." In Roddaz, Camille de. *L'art ancien à l'Exposition nationale,* pp. 291-314. Bruxelles: 1882. illus.

BRUSSELS (Belgium). EXPOSITION RÉTROSPECTIVE D'ART INDUSTRIEL, 1888

323   Mahillon, Charles Victor. "Instruments de musique." In *Exposition rétrospective . . . Catalogue officiel,* pp. 469-74. Bruxelles: [1888].

Copy at NN (NYp).

Literature

324   "Die Musikabtheilung auf der . . . ," *ZfI* 7 (1886/87): 288-90 (exhibitors), 326-28.

325   "Die Prämiirungen auf der . . . ," *ZfI* 9 (1888/89): 74-76, 94, 178, 188.

BRUSSELS (Belgium). FOIRE COMMERCIALE, 1922

Literature

326   "La 3me Foire commerciale de Bruxelles," *M & I* 8 (1922): 169-71.

BRUSSELS (Belgium). FOIRE COMMERCIALE, 1925

Literature

327   [Luthier (Fr.).] *M & I* 11 (1925): 295, 299; 12 (1926): 517 (Belgian).

BRUSSELS (Belgium). INSTRUMENTENMUSEUM. *See* **BRUSSELS (Belgium). CONSERVATOIRE ROYAL DE MUSIQUE**

BRUSSELS (Belgium). MUSÉE DU CONGO BELGE. *See* **TERVUREN (Belgium). MUSÉE ROYALE DE L'AFRIQUE CENTRALE**

BUDAPEST (Hungary). BUDAPESTI ORSZÁGOS ÁLTALÁNOS KIÁLLITAS, 1885

Literature

328 Hofmann, Carl. "Budapester Landesausstellung 1884 [*sic*]," *ZfI* 5 (1884/85): 304, 306.

329 Lauterbach, C. "Ausstellung in Budapest . . . XX. Gruppe sind die Musikinstrumente [with a list of exhibitors]," *ZfI* 5 (1884/85): 319-20.

General

330 *Budapester allgemeine Landes-Ausstellung. Illustrirter Catalog der Abtheilung der bildenden Künste.* [Budapest: 1885.] 161 pp., illus.

   Copy at NN (NyP).

BUDAPEST (Hungary). BUDAPESTI ORSZÁGOS ÁLTALÁNOS KIÁLLITAS, 1937

Literature

331 "Musikinstrumente auf der Landes- Industrie-Ausstellung zu Budapest," *ZfI* 58 (1937/38): 21.

BUDAPEST (Hungary). IPARMÜVÉSZETI MÚZEUM (J68)

Literature

332 "Landes- Musikinstrumenten-Ausstellung in Budapest," *ZfI* 34 (1913/14): 854, 945.

333 Sternegg, Maria Zlinszkyné. "Függőleges húrozáad empire songoráiak." In Budapest. Országos magyar iparmüvészeti muzeum. *Az iparmüvészeti múzeum évkönyvei* 7 (1964): 143-54.

   Copy at NN (NYp).

334 Sternegg, Maria Zlinszkyné. "Függőleges kúrozású empire zongoráink," *Annuaire du Musée des arts decoratifs* 7 (1965): 143-54.

BUDAPEST (Hungary). MAGYAR NEMZETI MÚZEUM   (J69)

Literature

335   Gábry, György. *Régi hangszerek.* [Budapest]: Corvina Kiadó, [1969]. 41 pp., illus., mostly from this museum.

336   Gábry, György. *Old Musical Instruments.* [Translated by Eva Rácz. Budapest]: Corvina Press, [1969]. 42 pp., 55 pls., mostly instruments from the museum.

337   Gábry, György. *Alte Musikinstrumente.* [Translated by Irene Kolbe.] Budapest: Corvina, 1969. 90 pp., illus.

338   Gábry, György. *Anciens instruments de musique,* trad. de János Gergely. Budapest: Corvina, 1969. 42 pp., 24 pls.

339   Gábry, György. *Évszázadok hangszerei. Instrumente der Jahrhunderte.* Tihany: [Veszprém Megyei Múzeumok Igazgatósaga], 1971. 59 pp., illus.

340   Buchner, Alexandr. "Hudební nástroje v maďarském Narodním Museu," *Hudebni Nástroje* 22, no. 4 (August 1975): 99-100. illus.

BUDAPEST (Hungary). MILLENIUMI KIÁLLITÁS, 1896

Literature

341   "Die Musik-Abtheilung der Milleniums-Ausstellung . . . Firmen," *ZfI* 16 (1895/96): 649-51; 17 (1896/97): 142 & 151 (prizes).

BUDAPEST (Hungary). NÉPRAJZI MÚZEUM

342   Bodrogi, Tibor. *Yabim Drums in the [Lajos] Biró Collection.* Budapest: Országos Néprajzi Múzeum, 1950. illus.

> From *Folia Ethnographia,* Budapest, 1949, no. 2-4.
> Copies at MH (CAc), NIC (Iu).

343   *A Néprajzi Múzeum I: Hangszerkiállításának Hanglemezes Katalógusa.* Budapest: 1966.

> Cited from review by Béla Nagy in *Magyar zene* 8 (1967): 84-85; not examined.

General

344   Biró, Lajos. *Német-Uj-Guineai (Astrolabe-Öböl) néprajzi gyüjtéseinek leíró jegyzéke.* (Bud. Magyar Nemzeti Múzeum. Néprajsi gyüjtémenyei, III.) Budapest: Hornyánsky, 1901. 199 pp., illus.

BUENOS AIRES (Argentina). MUSEO DEL TEATRO COLON. FERNANDEZ BLANCO COLLECTION. *See Section II under* **FERNANDEZ BLANCO, ISAAC**

BURGDORF (Switzerland). RITTERSAALVEREIN. HISTORISCHES MUSEUM (J122)

345   Leutenegger, Emil. "Die Musikinstrumenten-Sammlung im Schloss Burgdorf," *Burgdorf-Jahrbuch* 23 (1956): 121-32.

> Woodwind and percussion only in "Instrumentkatalog," pp. 123-30. Copies at CU (BEu), NN (NYp), DLC (Wc).

Literature

346   Leutenegger, Emil. "Alte Musikinstrumente aus den Emmental," *Hochwächter* (Bern) 11 (1955): 14-18.

347   Hiestand-Schnellmann, Josef. "Das Musikzimmer im Schloss Burgdorf," *Glareana,* vol. 9, no. 4 (1960).

BURGSTEINFURT (Germany). FÜRSTLICH BENTHEIMSCHE MUSIKSAMMLUNG. Since 1964 in **MÜNSTER. ERBDROSTENHOF,** q.v.

BURNABY (B. C.). ART GALLERY

348   *Instrument Makers.* [Catalogue. Burnaby, B.C.]: Burnaby Art Gallery, [1974]. [28] pp., illus. (Exhibition, June 5 to July 14, 1974.)

CAIRO (Egypt). AL-MATHAF AL-MISRI (J34)

349   Hickmann, Hans. *Catalogue général des antiquités égyptiennes du Musée du Caire, nos. 69201-69852. Instruments de musique.* Le Caire: Impr. de l Institut francais d'archéologie orientale, 1949. iv, 216 pp., illus., 651 items.

> Duckles* 3:1577.

350   Manniche, Lise. *Ancient Egyptian Musical Instruments.* (Münchner ägyptologische Studien, Heft 34.) München/Berlin: Deutscher Kunstverlag, 1975. xi, 111, xx pp., illus.

> A study of instruments in forty public collections and eight private, but the largest group—nearly ninety—is from the Egyptian Museum, Cairo.

CAIRO (Egypt). AL-MATHAF AL-MISRI   *continued*

General

351   Maspero, G. *Guide to the Cairo Museum,* translated by J. E. and A. A. Quibell. (Fifth ed.) Cairo: Fr. Institute of Oriental Archaeology, 1910. 526 pp.

"Musical Instruments," pp. 318-19.

CALCUTTA (India). INDIAN MUSEUM (J71)

352   *A Guide to the Collection of Musical Instruments Exhibited in the Ethnographical Gallery of the Indian Museum,* by A. M. Meerwarth [Mervart?]. Calcutta: Zoological Survey of India, 1917. 33 pp., illus. (13 pls.)

MGG* says basis was the collection of the Asiatic Society of Bengal, with some additions from the collection of Tagore. Copies at DLC (Wc), ICN (Cn), NN (NYp), NNMM.

CALCUTTA (India). INTERNATIONAL EXHIBITION, 1883-84

Literature

353   "Exhibition internationale de Calcutta [récompenses]," *Echo musical* 16 (1884): 58.

354   [Exhibition announced]," *ZfI* 3 (1882/83): 149, 424.

A note in a later issue terms the exhibition a disaster, the official catalogue, too.

General

355   *Official Report.* Calcutta: Bengal Secretariat Press, 1885. 2 vols., illus.

Instruments in Group 2; copy at ICU (Cu).

CAMBRIDGE (U.K.). GALPIN SOCIETY

356   *Catalogue of the Exhibition of Musical Instruments and Books Held in the Senate House, July 1-3, 1959, on the Occasion of the Joint Congress of the Galpin Society and the International Association of Music Libraries.* [Cambridge: 1959.] 12 pp.

NN (NYp) has fiche copy of typescript.

357   "Catalogue of a Loan Exhibition of Musical Instruments, Manuscripts and Printed Music Held in the Senate House, Cambridge, 30th June - 3rd July, 1959." In *Music, Libraries and Instruments,* pp. 272-79. London: Hinrichsen, 1961.

CASSEL (Germany). HOFKAPELLE. *See Section II under* **MORITZ, Landgraf zu Hessen, 1592-1627**

CÉSKÝ KRUMLOV

358   Záloha, Jiří. "Českokrumlový soupis hudebnin z počátku 18. století [A musical inventory at Cesky Krumlov dating from the beginning of the 18th century]," *Hudební věda* 6 (1969): 365-76.

> Reproducing an inventory of 610 instruments; cited from *RILM**.

CHICAGO, ILLINOIS (USA). NATURAL HISTORY MUSEUM

Literature

359   McAfee, Patricia. "Special Exhibit Shows Exotic Musical Instruments," *Bulletin of the Natural History Museum* 30, no. 7 (1959): 3, 6. illus.

CHICAGO, ILLINOIS (USA). WORLD'S COLUMBIAN EXPOSITION, 1893

360   The Presto, Chicago. *Musical Instruments at the . . . Exposition. A Review of Musical Instruments, Publications and Musical Instrument Supplies of All Kinds, Exhibited at . . . and the Awards Given for These Exhibits (from All Nations). . . .* Chicago: The Presto Co., 1895. [328] pp., illus.

> Prepared by Frank D. Abbott and C. A. Daniell.
> Copies at ICN (Cn), NN (NYp), DLC (Wc).

Literature

361   "Die Weltausstellung zu Chicago," *ZfI* 11 (1890/91): 353-55, 405-7, 449.

362   "Die deutschen Musikinstrumenten-Aussteller auf der Weltausstellung," *ZfI* 13 (1892/93): 520, 585-86, 631-32. With a long list of exhibitors.

363   Hartmann, C. von. "Deutsche Pianos auf der Weltausstellung," *ZfI* 13 (1892/93): 808-9.

364   "Musikinstrumente auf der Welt-Ausstellung," *ZfI* 14 (1893/94): 6, 25, 54 (prizes), 103-4, 154-56 (last two sections by C. von Hartmann).

365   M[athews], W[illiam] S. B. "Music in the Columbian Fair," *Music* (Chicago) 1 (1892): 39-53, 165-73.

366   Maass, W. "Technische Betrachtungen über die amerikaner Piano auf der Chicagoer Weltausstellung," *ZfI* 14 (1893/94): 181-83, 209-12, 236-39, 265-66, 283-84. illus.

CHICAGO, ILLINOIS (USA). WORLD'S COLUMBIAN EXPOSITION, 1893 *continued*

Literature

367   Schiedmayer, Max. "Die Musikinstrumenten-Industrie auf der Weltausstellung," *ZfI* 14 (1893/94): 699-702.

General

368   France. Ministère du Commerce. *Exposition internationale de Chicago en 1893. Rapports publiés sous la direction de M. Camille Krantz . . . Comité 38. Instruments de musique.* [Rapport de M. J. Thibouville-Lamy.] Paris: Impr. nationale, 1894. 25 pp.

> See also "Offizieller Bericht des . . . Thibouville-Lamy über die Musikinstrumente in Chicago," *ZfI* 15 (1894/95): 582-84, 608-9, 638-40.

369   Germany. Reichskommission, Weltausstellung in Chicago, 1893. *Amtlicher Bericht.* 2 vols. München/Berlin: M. Schorz, 1894. (x, 232, 75; iv, v, 1263 pp.), illus.

> See also "Amtlicher Bericht über die Weltausstellung," *ZfI* 15 (1894/95): 377.

370   Germany. Reichskommission, Weltausstellung in Chicago, 1893. *Amtlicher Katalog.* [Berlin: Reichsdruckerei, 1893.]

> "Musik-Instrumente," pp. 182-85, by Paul de Wit; also available in a Spanish translation; instruments, pp. 247-54.

371   Austria. Österr. Central-Commission für die Weltausstellung in Chicago, 1893. *Officieller Bericht, no. 2.* Wien: Gerold, 1894.

> "Musikinstrumente auf der Weltausstellung," pp. 13-32, by Gaston Bodart; see also "Bericht Österreich-Ungarn über Chicago," *ZfI* 15 (1894/95): 409, 430, 439, 465, 467. *Off. Bericht* at ICRL, NjP (PRu), PPF (PHf).

CHRISTIANA (Norway). *See* OSLO (Norway). NORSK FOLKEMUSEUM

CINCINNATI, OHIO (USA). ART MUSEUM (L77)

372   [Winternitz, E.] *Musical Instruments [A Guide to the Permanent Collection].* Cincinnati: [Cincinnati Museum Association], 1949. [23] pp., illus.

> Duckles* 3:1578. Contains the collection of W. H. Doane.

General

373   *Cincinnati Art Museum Handbook.* [Cincinnati: 1975.] 227 pp., illus.

> "Musical Instruments," pp. 72-77, with 13 photos.

CLAREMONT, CALIFORNIA (USA). CLAREMONT GRADUATE SCHOOL. JANSSEN COLLECTION

Literature

374   Boileau, Helen Houston. "Instruments on Display," *Educational Music Magazine* 36 (1956): 12-13. illus.

375   Morgan, Hazel B. "The Janssen Collection of Musical Instruments," *Instrumentalist* 19 (1966): 39-41. illus.

CLUJ (Rumania). MUZEUL DE ISTORIE AL TRANSILVANIEI (J109)

Literature

376   Ardos, A. and S. Lakatos. "Instrumentele muzicale ale muzeului de istorie Cluj," *Acta musei napocensis III, Muzeul de Istorie* (1966), pp. 257-70.
       Cited from Jenkins* not located.

377   Ardacs, A. M. and I. Kakatos. "Musikinstrumente im historischen Museum Klausenberg (Cluj, Koloszvar)," *Studia musicologica* 15 (1973): 235-53. illus.
       Cf. Jenkins* citation, no. **376**.

COEFELD

Literature

378   Brassler, Charles A. "Javanese Musical Instruments [at the Dutch East Indian Art Exhibition]," *Violin Times* 14 (1907): 77-78.
       From Freund's *Musical America;* not located.

COLOGNE (Germany). KÖLNISCHER KUNSTVEREIN

379   Kagel, Mauricio. . . . *Theatrum instrumentorum* . . . [Ausstellung], *Kölnischer Kunstverein, 4. Juni bis 6. Juli 1975.* [Redaktion, Wulf Kerzogenrath et al.] Köln: Der Verein, c1975. [74] pp., illus.

COLOGNE (Germany). MUSIKHISTORISCHES MUSEUM HEYER. *See Section II under* HEYER, WILHELM

COLOGNE (Germany). STADTMUSEUM ((BB141)

Literature

380   Günter. "Das Musikinstrumentensammlung im Kölnischen Stadtmuseum,"
       Glareana 25, no. 1 (1976): lvs. 1-20. 177 items.

   Those from Kaiser collection are marked with K. numbers.

COPENHAGEN (Denmark). MUSIKHISTORISK MUSEUM (J32-33, A57)

381   "Das Kopenhagener Instrumenten Museum [recent acquisitions]," *Deutscher
       Instrumentenbau* (Berlin) (Jg. 1900/1901), pp. 9-10.

   Cited from *ZiMG*-schau* (1900/1901), p. 58; not examined.
   Note that this list appears only three years after the
   museum's founding.

382   [Additions to the Museum], *ZiMG* 6 (1904/5): 261-62.

383   Hammerich, Angul. *Musikhistorisk Museum, beskrivende illustreret katalog.*
       København, Trykt hos Nielsen & Lydiche (A. Simmelkaier): F. Hendriksens
       reproduktions-atelier, 1909. xii, 151 pp., illus.

   Duckles* 3:1580. The Victoria & Albert Museum
   (see LV&A*) and the library of the Gesellschaft der
   Freunde alter Musikinstrumente each have a typescript
   supplement, 8 pp., 1960.

384   Hammerich, Angul. *Das Musikhistorische Museum zu Kopenhagen; beschreibender
       Katalog; deutsch von Erna Bobe.* Kopenhagen: G. E. C. Gad; Leipzig: Kommissions-
       verlag von Breitkopf & Härtel, 1911. 172 pp., illus., 631 items.

   Duckles* 3:1580. Boalch* notes a *Supplement zum
   Katalog,* Kopenhagen, 1960, in typescript which may
   be the same supplement referred to above in no. **383**.

385   Müller, Mette. *Classical Indian Musical Instruments* [an exhibition]. Copenhagen:
       Musikhistorisk Museum, 1969. 20 pp., illus., 24 items.

   Introduction by Erik Kirchheiner.

386   Müller, Mette. *Traek og Tryk, Pust og Sug; fra asiatisk mundorgel til europaeisk
       harmonika* [an exhibition]. Musikhistorisk Museum, 1971-72. [København:
       the Museum, 1971.] 28 pp., illus., 44 items.

387   Müller, Mette. *From Bone Pipe and Cattle Horn to Fiddle and Psaltery. Folk
       Music Instruments from Denmark* [an exhibition]. Copenhagen: Musikhistorisk
       Museum, 1972. 54 pp., illus., 94 items.

Literature

388   Scheurleer, Daniel Francois. "Een navolgenswaardig voorbeeld," *Tijdschrift der Vereeniging voor N.-Nederlands Muziekgeschiedenis* 7 (1901-4): 84-88.

389   Thuren, Hjalmar. "Fra musikhistorisk museum i Köbenhavn," *Nordisk Tidskrift* (1909), pp. 347-64.
         Cited from DaSML* 5194; not located.

390   Thuren, Hjalmar. "Nordische Musikinstrumente im musikhistorischen Museum zu Kopenhagen," *ZiMG* 10 (1908/9): 333-37. illus.

391   Altenberg, Wilhelm. "Das neue musikhistorische Museum in Kopenhagen," *ZfI* 30 (1910): 447-49.

392   Grempe, ?   "Die Schätze des musikhistorischen Museums zu Kopenhagen," *Musik-Industrie* 2, no. 12/13 (192-?): 249-51.
         Cited from *ZiMG*-schau* (1921/22), p. 19; not examined.

393   Boheman, T. "Instrument som tala -ehuru stumma . . . Naagra ord om Musik-historisk Museum i Köpenhavn," *Slöjd och ton* 18 (1948): 68-72.
         Cited from DaSML*.

394   *Ocarina: den lille gås [Exhibition]*. [Copenhagen] : 1971. 4 lvs., typescript.
         Cited in LV&A*.

395   Müller, Mette. "Information om Musikhistroisk Museums virksomhed i København," *Dansk Aarbog for Musikforskning,* 6 (1968-72): 232-36. illus.

396   Müller, Mette. *Musik og mennesker i Thailands bjerge.* København: Musikhistorisk Museum, 1975. 28 pp., illus.

COPENHAGEN (Denmark). NATIONALMUSEET   (J33, A51)

Literature

397   Hammerich, Angul. *Les Lurs de l'âge de bronze au musée national de Copenhague.* Trad. par E. Beauvois. Copenhague: 1894. 32 pp., illus.
         Offprint from *Mémoires de la Société royal des antiquaires du Nord.*

398   Hammerich, Angul and C. Elling. "Studien über die altnordischen Luren im Nationalmuseum zu Kopenhagen," *VfMW* 10 (1894): 1-32.

399   Hammerich, Angul. "Studien über die altnordischen Lüren im National museum zu Kopenhagen," *ZfI* 14 (1893/94): 622-26, 647-49. illus.; [supplemental notes] *ZfI* 23 (1902/3): 62, 69.

COPENHAGEN (Denmark). NATIONALMUSEET   *continued*

Literature

400   Yde, Jens. "Etnografisk samlings Teletrommer," Copenhagen. Nationalmuseet. *Arbejdsmark* (1945), pp. [18]-24. illus.

401   Broholme, Hans Christian. *Bronzelurene i Nationalmuseet.* København: 1958. 122 pp., illus.

> Copies at CtY (NHu), KyU, MH-P, DLC (Wc).

COPENHAGEN (Denmark). NORDISKE INDUSTRI-, LANDBRUGS- OG KUNSTID-STILLING, 1888

Literature

402   Anger, Walter. "Die Musikinstrumente auf der Nordischen Kunst- und Industrie-Ausstellung," *ZfI* 7 (1886/87): 358-62.

General

403   *Officiel katalog.* Kjøbenhavn: H. Hagerup, 1888.

> "Musikinstrumenter" sections under Denmark, Sweden, and Norway; copy at DLC (Wc).

COPENHAGEN (Denmark). UNIVERSITET. CARL CLAUDIUS COLLECTION. *See Section II under* CLAUDIUS, CARL

CORNWALL (U.K.). CORNWALL MUSEUM OF MECHANICAL MUSIC

404   *Souvenir: The Authentic Sounds of an Inventive Age.* [Cornwall: Beric, Tempest & Co., 1977?] 33 pp., illus.

> "First published 1974." The private collections of Douglas R. Berryman and Graham Webb.

COSTA RICA. MUSEO ECLESIASTICO

405   Fournier Facio, Gaston. "Descripcion de algunos instrumentos musicales precolombianos de Costa Rica," *Revista de la Universidad de Costa Rica* 30 (1971): 7-75. Many pls.

> Examples from two museums and two private collections, including that of Oscar Herrera Mata.

CREMONA (Italy). ESPOSIZIONE DI LIUTERIA ANTICA, 1937

406 Cremona. Comitato celebrazioni bicentenario stradivariano. *Catalogo della mostra di liuteria antica cremonese.* [Cremona: Cremona nova, 1937.] 32 pp.

Copy at NN (NYp).

407 Cremona. Comitato celebrazioni bicentenario stradivariano. *L'esposizione di liuteria antica a Cremona nel 1937.* [Cremona: Stab. tip. soc. editoriale "Cremona nova," 1938.] 257, xxvii pp., illus.

Copy at NN (NYp).

Literature

408 Hamma, Fridolin. "Zur 200-Jahr-Feier Antonio Stradivariano' in Cremona," *ZfI* 57 (1936/37): 223-24, 287-88, 330-31. illus.

409 "Zum Beginn der Stradivarius-Feier in Cremona," *ZfI* 57 (1936/37): 257-58, 271-72, 297-99, 316-26.

410 Nicolini, Gualtiero. "The Commemorative Exhibition for the Bicentenary of the Death of Antonio Stradivari." In his *The International School of Cremona,* translated by Helen Palmer, pp. 15-20. [Cremona: 1978.] illus.

Two shows, modern violins (350) in the Palazzo Vidoni, antique violins (136) in the Palazzo Cittanova.

CREMONA (Italy). MUSEO CIVICO (J77, A288) [N.B.: Contains the celebrated collection of Stradivari's tools, molds, and other workshop items gathered by Count Cozio di Salabue.]

411 Sacchi, Federico. *Il Conte Cozio di Salabue. Cenni biografici di questo colletore d'istrumenti ad arco.* Londra: G. Hart (Milano: tip. Cogliati), 1898. 62 pp.

Hirsch no. 1655.

412 Sacchi, Federico. *Count Cozio di Salabue. A Biographical Sketch of This Celebrated Violin Collector, with an Appendix Containing His Unpublished Manuscript and Letters to Vincenzo Lancetti on the Cremonese School . . . ,* edited by A. Towry Piper. London: Dulau & Co., 1898. 47 pp.

Copy at NN (NYp).

413 Bacchetta, Renzo. *Stradivari non e nato nel 1644; vita e opere del celebre liutaro. La Sala Stradivariana del Museo Civico di Cremona. Cozio di Salabue. . . .* [Cremona: Stab. tip. soc. ed. "Cremona nova," 1973.] 174 pp., illus.

Copy at NN (NYp).

CREMONA (Italy). MUSEO CIVICO   *continued*

414   Sacconi, Simone F. *I segreti di Stradivari. Con il catalogo dei cimeli stradivariani del Museo.* . . . Cremona: Libreria del Convegno, 1972. xvi, 261 pp.

> Copy at DLC (Wc).

415   Sacconi, Simone F. *Die Geheimnisse Stradivaris. Mit dem Katalog des Stradivari-Nachlasses* . . . , [translated by] Olga Adelmann. (Fachbuchreihe Das Musikinstrument Bd. 31.) Frankfurt/Main: Verlag Das Musikinstrument, 1976. xx, 238 pp., illus.

Literature

416   Picenardi, Giorgio Sommi. *Notizette biografiche sui liutai cremonesi.* (Atti e communicazione dal Circolo di Studi Cremonesi, 1.) [Cremona?: 1898.]

417   Roberti, Giuseppe. "Un mecenate della liuteria: Il Conte Cozio di Salabue," *Gazzetta musicale di Milano* 54 (1899): 420-23.

418   Hill, W. F., A. F. and A. E. *Antonio Stradivari; His Life and Work.* London: W. E. Hill & Sons, 1902. 2nd ed. London: Macmillan, 1909. Reprint ed. New York: Dover, [1963].

> See the Count's announcement offering his collection of instruments for sale on plate between pp. 276 and 277, and a discussion of his collection, pp. 205-9, 275-77, et passim.

419   Oberberg, Woldemar. "Der Werkstatt-Nachlass des Stradivarius," *ZfI* 58 (1937/38): 250-52, 267-68, 297-99, 325-26.

420   D., E. N. "Count Cozio di Salabue," *Violins and Violinists* 3 (1941): 105-6, 136-39.

421   Möller, Max, Jr. "Voorbereiding tot de Stradivarius-tentoonstelling te Cremona," *Mens en melodie* 2 (1947): 337-40. illus.

422   Cozio di Salabue, Ignazio Alessandro, Count. *Carteggio. Trascrizione di Renzo Bacchetta. Autorizata dal Museo Civico di Cremona.* . . . Milano: S.p.A.A. Cordani, 1950. xxxiv, 515 pp., illus.

423   Disertori, Benvenuto. "Collezionismo settecentesco e il carteggio del Conte di Salabue," *RMI* 53 (1951): 315-22.

424   Frisoli, Patrizia. "The Museo Stradivariano in Cremona," *GSJ* 24 (1971): 33-50.

CREMONA (Italy). INTERNATIONAL EXHIBITION OF VIOLIN MAKING, 1949 (?)

Literature

425   "The Cremona Exhibition," *The Strad* 60 (1949): 140.

CREMONA. ISTITUTO PROFESSIONALE INTERNAZIONALE PER L'ARTIGIANATO LIUTARIO E DEL LEGNO (SCUOLA INTERNAZIONALE DI LIUTERIA)

426   Nicolini, Gualtiero. *The International School of Cremona: Two Score Years of Violin-Making,* translated by Helen Palmer. [Cremona: Edizioni Stradivari, 1978.] 159 pp.

"The Catalogue of the Museum," pp. 106-59 (pp. 107-59, illus.)

CRYSTAL PALACE, LONDON. *See* LONDON (U.K.). INTERNATIONAL LOAN EXHIBITION OF MUSICAL INSTRUMENTS, 1900 *and* LONDON (U.K.). VICTORIAN ERA EXHIBITION, 1897

DARMSTADT (Germany). HESSISCHES LANDESMUSEUM (J57, A196)

General

427   *Führer durch die Kunst- und historischen Sammlungen.* Darmstadt: [Wittisch'sche Hofbuchdruckerei], 1908. v, 132 pp., 48 pls.

Preface signed: Friedrich Bach; "Sammlung der Musik-instrumente (Raum 29)," pp. 64-66.

DEARBORN, MICHIGAN (USA). HENRY FORD MUSEUM (L243)

Literature

428   Eliason, Robert E. *Brass Instrument Key and Valve Mechanisms Made in America Before 1875; With Special Reference to the D. S. Pillsbury Collection.* (Unpublished D.M.A. thesis, University of Missouri, Kansas City, 1969.) 225 pp., illus.

429   Angelescu, Victor. "The Henry Ford Collection of Instruments," *Violins* 21 (1960): 3-9, 46, 48-53, 97-102, 138-44, 173. Heavily illus.

Contents: Part I, Nicolo Amati; Part II, The Ford Strads; Part III, Carlo Bergonzi and Guarneri del Gesu; Part IV, Italian violin making after Cremona.

430   Eliason, Robert E. *Graves & Company; Musical Instrument Makers.* Dearborn, Mich.: [1975?]. 24 pp., illus.

DELHI (India). SANGEET NATAK AKADEMI (J73)

431   Kothari, Komal S. *Indian Folk Musical Instruments* [an exhibition catalogue]. [New Delhi]: Sangeet Natak Akademi, [1968]. 90 pp., illus.

Copy at NN (NyP).

DELHI (India). SANGEET NATAK AKADEMI *continued*

432 *Folk Musical Instruments of Rajasthan. An Exhibition. Triveni Kala Sangam. From 1st April to 5th April 1963.* Jodhpur: Rajasthan Law Weekly Press, 1963. 38 pp., 73 items.

Copy at NL-DHgm.

DETMOLD (Germany). LIPPISCHE GEWERBE-AUSSTELLUNG, 1881

Literature

433 "Original-Bericht, Gruppe VI. Musikalische Instrumente," *ZfI* 1 (1880/81): 294, 296.

No "official" *Berichte* or *Katalog* located.

DETMOLD (Germany). MUSIKALIEN-KAMMER. *See Section II under* SIMON AUGUST, Graf . . . *and* SAYN-WITTGENSTEIN, CASIMIR

DETROIT, MICHIGAN (USA). INSTITUTE OF ARTS. EDITH J. FREEMAN COLLECTION. *See under* MINNEAPOLIS, MINNESOTA (USA). UNIVERSITY OF MINNESOTA. UNIVERSITY GALLERY

DONDO (Angola). MUSEUM (J1)

Literature

434 De Vilhena, Julio. "A Note on the Dundo Museum of the Companhia de Diamantes de Angola," *Journal of the International Folk Music Council* 7 (1955): 41-43.

435 Companhia de Diamantes de Angola. *Folclore musical de Angola; coleccao de fitas magneticas e discos. I. Povo Quioco . . . Lunda. . . .* Lisboa: Servicos Culturais, 1961. 296 pp., illus.

"Musical Instruments," Chapter 3; review in *Ethnomusicology* 9 (1965): 176-77.

DRESDEN (Germany). DEUTSCHE KUNSTGEWERBE-AUSSTELLUNG, 1906

Literature

436 "Die Musikinstrumenten-Industrie auf der . . . ," *ZfI* 26 (1905/6): 775-76, 783 (exhibitors), 930-31 (prizes), 1128, 1135.

General

437   *Officieller Katalog der sächsischen Kunst-Ausstellung . . . von dem Sächs. Kunst-verein.* Dresden: C. Heinrich, 1906. 40 pp., illus.; 2. Aufl., *ibid.*, 40 pp., 31 pp., illus.

Cited from KaY* 33:1089; not located.

438   *Offizieller Katalog der 3. deutschen Kunstgewerbe-Ausstellung Dresden 1906.* Dresden: W. Baensch, [1906]. xviii, 146 pp.; 2. Aufl., Illustrierte Ausg., *ibid.*, xxi, 210, 63 pp., illus.

Cited from KaY* 33:1089; not located.

DRESDEN (Germany). EXPORT-VEREIN IM KÖNIGREICH SACHSEN

Literature

439   R., D. "Ausstellung des Exportmusterlagers des Exportvereins für das Königreich Sachsen 1886," *ZfI* 6 (1885/86): 429-30, 432.

DRESDEN (Germany). INTERNATIONALE HYGIENE-AUSSTELLUNG, 1911

Literature

440   "Musikinstrumenten-Aussteller . . . ," *ZfI* 31 (1910/11): 943; 32 (1911/12): 21 (Bericht), 59, 122 (prizes).

General

441   *Offizieller Katalog der international Hygiene-Ausstellung Dresden Mai—Oktober 1911.* Berlin: R. Mosse, [1911]. 440 pp.

Cited from *DBV* * 1:1395; not located.

DRESDEN (Germany). KÖRNER-MUSEUM

Literature

442   Roeder, Ernst. "Zwei historische Instrumente," *ZfI* 6 (1885/86): 432, 434, 436.

DRESDEN (Germany). K. SÄCHSISCHE MUSIK-KAPELLE

443   "Inventarium uber die Instrumenta, welche vor dieser Zeit dem Hoforganisten Christoff Walthern in Vorwarhrunge gegeben, nunmehr aber nach desselben Absterben Augustus Nöringern, welcher an seine Stelle verordnet. . . . Auffgerichtet

DRESDEN (Germany). K. SÄCHSISCHE MUSIK-KAPELLE *continued*

durch Michael Kronbergern . . . Rogier Michael . . . und Augustus Nöringer. . . . Dresden den 2. Aprilis 1593." Reprinted in Fürstenau, Moritz. *Ein Instrumenten-inventarium vom Jahre 1593.* [1872] 11 pp.

> Copy at NBuU-M (BUu).

444 ———, *Mittheilungen des Kgl. sächsis. Altertums-vereins,* Heft 22 (1872): 1-11.

445 Kittel, Christian. "Verzeichnis derer in das Churfürstl. Sächs. Jüngste Gerichte- und Instrument-Kammer gehörigen Musicalischen Sachen und Instrumenten. . . ." From Ms. loc. 7027, dated 1681 in the Sächsischen Hauptstaatsarchiv. Reprinted in Drechsel, F. A. "Alte Dresdner Instrumenteninventare," *ZfMW* 10 (1927/28): 495-99.

Literature

446 "Instrumenten-Kammer mit Streich und Blasinstrumente." In Fürstenau, Moritz. *Beiträge zur Geschichte des Königlich Sächsischen musikalischen Kapelle.* Dresden: 1849. x, 206 pp.

> Copies at DLC (Wc), MB (Bp).

447 "Des Augsburger Patriziers Philipp Hainhofer's Angaben über die Musik-Instrumenten-sammlung des kurfürstlichen Schlosses zu Dresden vom Jahre 1629," *ZfI* 21 (1900/1901): 622-23.

DRESDEN (Germany). SÄCHSISCHEN HANDWERK- UND KUNST-GEWERBE AUSSTELLUNG, 1896

Literature

448 "Ein Rundgang durch die Ausstellung. 'Tasten-Instrumente' auf der . . . ," *ZfI* 17 (1896/97): 1-2.

DRESDEN (Germany). SAMMLUNGEN FÜR KUNST UND WISSENSCHAFT

Literature

449 Drechsel, F. A. "Alte Musikinstrumente in Dresdner Kunstsammlungen," *ZfI* 48 (1927/28): 454-56.

DUBLIN (Ireland). FEIS CEOIL, 1899

450   O'Donoghue, David J. *Catalogue of the Musical Loan Exhibition Held in Connection with the Above Festival in the National Library and National Museum* . . . May 15th-20th, 1899. Dublin: Office of the Feis Ceoil, 1899. 32 pp.

  Copy at NN (NYp).

DUBLIN (Ireland). NATIONAL MUSEUM   (A278, BB206)

Literature

451   Grattan-Flood, W. H. "Dublin Harpsichord and Pianoforte Makers," *Journal of the Royal Society of Antiquaries of Ireland* 39 (1909): 137-45.

  Many of the museum's instruments are mentioned according to Boalch*; not examined.

452   Doyle, Paul. "18th Century Musical Instruments in the . . . with Notes on an English Guitar 1764 by Gibson of Dublin," *FoMRHI,* no. 13 (October 1978), pp. 21-24.

DUBLIN (Ireland). ROYAL IRISH ACADEMY   (A279, BB206)

453   Taylor, Meadows. "Catalogue of Indian Musical Instruments, Presented by Colonel P. T. French," *Proceedings of the Royal Irish Academy* 9, part 1: 106-25. 50 items described.

  Reprinted in following.

454   Tagore, S. M. "Catalogue of Indian Musical Instruments." In his *Hindu Music from Various Authors,* pp. [243]-73. Calcutta: 1875.

  "Collection presented by P. T. French to the Academy."

General

455   Wilde, W. R. *A Descriptive Catalogue of the Antiquities in the Royal Irish Academy.* Vol. 1: Articles of stone, earth, vegetable, and animal materials, and of copper and brozne. Dublin: 1863.

  Not examined.

DÜSSELDORF (Germany). DEUTSCHE MUSIKMESSE, 3rd, 1951

456   *Fachmesse für Musikinstrumenten und Musikalien. Offizieller Messekatalog.* Düsseldorf: Nowea, Nordwestd. Ausstellungs-Gesellschaft, 1951. 82 pp.

  Numbers 1 and 2 under **MITTENWALD**, q.v.

DÜSSELDORF (Germany). DEUTSCHE MUSIKMESSE, 4th, 1952

457   *Fachmesse für Musikinstrumenten und Musikalien. Offizieller Messekatalog.*
Düsseldorf: Nowea, Nordwestd. Ausstellungs-Gesellschaft, 1952. 80 pp.

DÜSSELDORF (Germany). DEUTSCHE MUSIKMESSE, 5th, 1953

458   *Fachmesse für Musikinstrumenten und Musikalien. Offizieller Messekatalog.*
Düsseldorf: Nowea, Nordwestd. Ausstellungs-Gesellschaft, 1953. 52 pp.

DÜSSELDORF (Germany). INDUSTRIE- UND GEWERBE-AUSSTELLUNG, 1902

Literature

459   Maass, W. "Die Musikinstrumente auf der Düsseldorfer Industrie-, Kunst-
und Gewerbe-Ausstellung," *ZfI* 22 (1901/2): 813-17, 847-49, 873-79, 906-7,
937-38. Many illus.; 23 (1902/3): 33 (Nachtrag), 88 (prizes).

460   D., J. "Rückblicke auf die Düsseldorfer Ausstellung," *Gregorius-Blatt*
(Düsseldorf), vol. 27, no. 10 (1902).

461   Eccarius-Sieber, A. "Die Musikinstrumente auf der . . . ," *Die Musik* (Berlin)
2 (1902): 60-61.

462   "Illustrationen zur Düsseldorfer Ausstellung," *DIbZ,* vol. 3, no. 26 (1901/2).

463   Pudor, Heinrich. "Die Düsseldorfer Industrie- und Gewerbe-Ausstellung 1902,"
DIbZ, vol. 3, no. 22 (1901/2).
Not examined.

General

464   *Amtlicher Führer durch die Industrie- und Gewerbe-Ausstellung.* Düsseldorf:
[Schmitz & Olbertz], 1902. 78, xxiii, 332 pp., illus.
Copies at ICU, CU (BEu); not examined.

465   *Amtlicher Katalog der . . . Ausstellung.* Düsseldorf: [Schmitz & Olbertz], 1902.
306, cxxviii pp., illus.
Copy at ICJ; not examined.

DÜSSELDORF (Germany). KUNST- UND GEWERBE-AUSSTELLUNG, 1880

Literature

466   Z., V. "Die Musikinstrumente auf der . . . ," *ZfI* 1 (1880/81): 34-35.

DUNDEE (Scotland). CENTRAL MUSEUM (J141, A346, BB173)

467   *The Simpson Collection of Musical Instruments.* [List of. . . .] [Dundee, 1972.] 3 lvs.

>   Typescript in Victoria & Albert Museum.

Literature

468   Millar, A. H. "The Simpson Collection of Musical Instruments in the Dundee Central Museum," *Museum Journal* (Great Britain and Ireland Museums Association) 19 (October 1919): 60-62.

DUNDO (Angola). *See* **DONDO (Angola)**

EDGWARE (U. K.). BOOSEY & HAWKES GROUP. MUSEUM

469   Baines, Anthony. *Antique Musical Instruments of Historical Interest.* Edgware: [1972]. 30 pp., 743 items.

>   Copy at NbuU-M (BUu).

Literature

470   Harwood, W. "Boosey & Hawke's Antique Instrument Collection," *Crescendo International* 12 (November 1973): 27.

EDINBURGH (Scotland). EDINBURGH FESTIVAL SOCIETY

471   *An Exhibition of Music and Dance in Indian Art. Sponsored by the . . . Society at the Royal Scottish Museum.* Edinburgh: [1963?]. 32 pp., pls.

>   Instruments—described, pp. [8-12] and pls. [2-5] —
>   are from the Victoria & Albert and the Ashmolean
>   museums, and elsewhere. Copies at OU (COu), MH.

EDINBURGH (Scotland). INTERNATIONAL EXHIBITION [OF INDUSTRY, SCIENCE AND ART], 1886

472   "Catalogue of the Historical Musical Collections, Consisting of Instruments and Appliances, Mss and Books [etc.] Formed by Robert A. Marr, Assisted by William Cowan." In Bapty, Lee. *Official Catalogue. International Exhibition of Electrical Engineering, General Inventions and Industries,* pp. 157-80. Edinburgh: 1890. 192 pp.

>   "Printed in gold throughout," according to BM*.

EDINBURGH (Scotland). INTERNATIONAL EXHIBITION . . . *continued*

473   "Catalogue of the Historical Musical Collections, Consisting of Instruments and Appliances, Mss and Books [etc.] Formed by Robert A. Marr, Assisted by William Cowan." In Bapty, Lee. *Official Catalogue. International Exhibition of Electrical Engineering, General Inventions and Industries,* pp. 157-80. 2nd ed. Edinburgh: T. & A. Constable, 1890. 296 pp.

         Cited from Marr*.

Literature

474   Marr, Robert A. *Music and Musicians at the Edinburgh Exhibition.* Edinburgh: T. & A. Constable, 1887. 217 pp.

         Copy at NN (NYp).

475   "Internationaler Ausstellung zu Edinburgh [with a list of exhibitors]," *ZfI* 6 (1885/86): 411; 7 (1886/87): 86-88 (prizes).

EDINBURGH (Scotland). INTERNATIONAL FESTIVAL OF MUSIC AND DRAMA, 1968

476   Galpin Society. *An Exhibition of European Musical Instruments. Edinburgh International Festival, Aug. 18th-Sept. 7th, 1968, Reid School of Music, Edinburgh University.* [Edinburgh: 1968.] 99 pp., 40 pls., 716 items.

         Duckles* 3:1582; catalogue edited by Graham Melville-Mason.

EDINBURGH (Scotland). NATIONAL MUSEUM OF ANTIQUITIES   (A350, BB167)

General

477   *Catalogue of the National Museum.* New and enlarged ed., with illus. Edinburgh: Society of Antiquaries of Scotland, 1892. iv, 380 pp., illus.

         Instruments on pp. 152, 311, 314, 317, according to Heyer*; copies at CU (BEu), CtY (NHu), OCl (CLp).

EDINBURGH (Scotland). ROYAL SCOTTISH MUSEUM

478   Thomson, Alistair G. *Phonographs & Gramophones* [exhibition]. Edinburgh: 1977. 24, viii, 32 pp., (illus.).

         158 items displayed; descriptions of 44 others not in show.

EDINBURGH (Scotland). UNIVERSITY [N.B.: Collections include: Russell collection of keyboards, Rendall collection of wind instruments, and the Langwill collection.]

479   Department of Early Keyboard Instruments. *The Russell Collection and Other Early Keyboard Instruments in Saint Cecilia's Hall.* [Compiled by Sidney Newman and Peter Williams.] Edinburgh: Edinburgh U.P., 1968. xi, 79 pp., 36 pls., 28 items.

        Duckles* 3:1581.

Literature

480   Barnes, John. "The Flemish Instruments of the Russell Collection." In *Colloquium Restauratieproblemen . . .* , pp. 35-39. Antwerp: 1971.

EINDHOVEN (Netherlands). PHILIPS ONTSPANNINGS CENTRUM

481   *Een wereld vol muziekinstrumenten. Catalogus tentoonstelling in de Galerie 'de Zonnewijzer' van 4 Oktober tot en met 15 november 1968. . . .* [Eindhoven?] : 1968. 30 pp., illus.

482   *Van onwillige kanaries fluitende klokken en een pierement. Beknopt historisch overzicht van de mechanische muziekinstrumenten. Uitgave . . . ter gelegenheid van de tentoonstelling "Van Speeldoos tot Cassettofoon," in Galerie De Zonnewijzer, 11 februari - 29 maart 1970.* [Eindhoven?] : 1970. 66 pp., mostly illus.

EISENACH (Germany). BACHMUSEUM

483   Bornemann, G. and E. Buhle. "Verzeichnis der Sammlung alter Musikinstrumenten im Bachhaus zu Eisenach." In *Bach-Jahrbuch,* pp. 109-28. Leipzig: 1911.

        Basis of the collection was that of Dr. Aloys Obrist.
        See below, no. **484**.

484   "Die Instrumenten-Sammlung des verstorbenen Dr. Aloys Obrist," *ZfI* 31 (1910/11): 89.

485   Buhle, Eward and Georg Vormann. *Verzeichnis der Sammlung alter Musikinstrumente im Bachhause zu Eisenach.* Leipzig: Breitkopf & Härtel, 1913. 43 pp.

        Copies at CtY (NHu), MB (Bp), MiU (AAu), PP (PHf), NN (NYp), DLC (Wc).

486   Sachs, Curt. *Verzeichnis der Sammlung alter Musikinstrumente im Bachhause zu Eisenach.* [Neue Ausg.] Leipzig: Breitkopf & Härtel, [1919]. iv, 51 pp., illus. 184 items.

        Copies at NcU (CHHu), IaU (IOu), CU (BEu), CtY (NHu), DLC (Wc).

EISENACH (Germany). BACHMUSEUM *continued*

487 Breidert, Friedrich and Conrad Freyse. *Verzeichnis der Sammlung alter Musik-instrumente im Bachhause zu Eisenach.* 3., verm. Ausg. Leipzig: Breitkopf & Härtel, [1939]. 64 pp., illus., 233 items.

>   Copies at NcU (CHHu), IaU (IOu), CU (BEu), CtY (NHu), DLC (Wc).

488 Breidert, Friedrich and Conrad Freyse. *Verzeichnis der Sammlung alter Musik-instrumente im Bachhause zu Eisenach, hrsg. von der Neuen Bachgesellschaft.* 4., erweiterte Aufl. Leipzig: Breitkopf & Härtel, 1964. 97 pp., illus., 15 pls., 320 items.

>   Duckles* 3:1583.

489 Heyde, Herbert. *Historische Musikinstrumente im Bachhaus Eisenach.* Eisenach: Bachhaus, 1976. 297 pp., illus., 196 items.

>   Supersedes lists in the *Bach-Jahrbuch* (above).

ERFURT (Germany). THÜRINGER GEWERBE- UND INDUSTRIE-AUSSTELLUNG, 1893

Literature

490 "Gesammt-Ausstellung der Erzeugnisse Thüringer Gewerbefleisses," *ZfI* 13 (1892/93): 771 (exhibitors).

491 "Thüringer Gewerbe- und Industrie-Ausstellung," *ZfI* 14 (1893/94): 587-89 (exhibitors), 823-25, 856 (jury).

>   Each article notes an official *Katalog* and a *Bericht* which include musical instruments in Gruppe XVI. Neither work located.

ERLANGEN (Germany). UNIVERSITÄT. KOLLEGIENHAUS. MUSIKINSTRUMEN-TENSAMMLUNG (J58)

Literature

492 Steglich, Rudolf. "Vom Klang der Zeiten; historische Musikinstrumente in Erlangen," *Musica* (Kassel) 2 (1948): 19-24. illus.

>   Includes some of the Ulrich Rück collection; the remainder is now in the **NUREMBERG, GERMANISCHES NATIONALMUSEUM**, q.v.

493 Steglich, Rudolf. "Kostbare Sammlung. Frankische Musikinstrumente," *Bayerische Handwerkzeitung* 4, no. 24 (1952): 8.

FENTON HOUSE, HAMPSTEAD. *See* **LONDON (U.K.). FENTON HOUSE, HAMPSTEAD**

FLORENCE (Italy). CONSERVATORIO DI MUSICA LUIGI CHERUBINI. MUSEO
(J78, A291)   [N.B.: Includes collections from the Palazzo Pitti in Florence; L. F. Casamorata; the Contessa Editta Rucellai; Ferdinand I de Medici, duke of Tuscany (see catalogues in Section II); and Grand Duke Cosimo III, his father.]

494   Mariotti, Olimpo. "Inventario stimativo degli strumenti musicale esistenti nella guardaroba del R. Palazzo Pitti che si consegnano al Sig. Segret.º Olimpo Mariotti in ordine all'officio del di' 10 marzo 1863." Reprinted in Gai, Vinicio. *Gli strumenti musicali della corte medicea e il Museo del Conservatorio . . . ,* pp. 33-38. Firenze: LICOSA, 1969.
>   See no. **497** below.

495   Bargagna, Leto. *Gli strumenti musicali raccolti nel Museo del R. Istituto L. Cherubini a Firenze.* Firenze: G. Ceccherini & c., [1911]. 70 pp.
>   Duckles* 3:1584. Copies at CU(BEu), FMU(CGu), IU(Uu), DLC(Wc).

496   Fedeli, Vito. [A notice of the instruments in the collection and of the catalogue], *ZiMG* 13 (1911/12): 201-2.

497   Gai, Vinicio. *Gli strumenti musicali della corte medicea e il Museo del Conservatorio Luigi Cherubini. Cenni storici e catalogo descrittivo.* Presentazione di Antonio Veretti. Firenze: LICOSA, 1969. xvi, 286 pp., illus.
>   Duckles* 3:1585. Copies at NBuU-M (BUu), NN (NYp), DLC(Wc). Pp. 2-5: "Elenco di alcuni documenti che si trovano nell' Archivio di Stato di Firenze (Guardaroba Mediceo)," which cites inventories of 1640, 1652, 1654, 1669, 1670, 1691, 1700, 1716, 1732, 1732-65. These are set out in full here, nos. **1960-72**, Section II.
>   See review in *GSJ* 23 (1970): 154-56.

498   Hammond, Frederick. "Musical Instruments at the Medici Court in the Mid-Seventeenth Century," *Analecta musicologica* 15 (1975): 202-19. illus.

Literature

499   Casamorata, Luigi Ferdinando. "Relazione di antichi e speciosi strumenti donati al R. Istituto dal Cav. Vittorio Mahillon . . . ," *Atti dell' Accademia del R. Istituto musicale di Firenze* 18 (1880): 116-18.

500   Piccolellis, Giovanni de. *Della autenticità e pregio di taluni strumenti ad arco appartenenti al R. Istituto musicale di Firenze.* (Atti dell' Accademia del R. Istituto musicale di Firenze, Anno XXVII.) Firenze: Tip. Galletti e Cocci, 1889. 34 pp.

FLORENCE (Italy). CONSERVATORIO DI MUSICA. . . . *continued*

Literature

501   Sacchi, Federico. "Gli strumenti di Stradivari alla Corte Medicea," *Gazzetta musicale di Milano* 23 (June 5, 1892): 367-69.

502   Bonaventura, Arnaldo. "Cimeli bibliografici e strumenti musicali all' Esposizione del R. Istituto musicale di Firenze," *La Bibliofilia* 14 (1912/13): 46-60. illus.

503   Damerini, Adelmo. *Esposizione nazionale dei conservatori musicale e delle biblioteche Palazzo Davanzati- 27 ottobre 1949 - 8 gennaio 1950.* Firenze: Barbèra, 1950. xx, 121 pp., illus.

>   Hirsch* no. 340.

504   Parigi, Luigi. "L'esposizione musicale a Palazzo Davanzati," *Arte mediterranea* (nov.-dic. 1949), pp. 23-25. illus.

505   Gai, Vinicio. "Gli strumenti di Antonio Stradivari conservati nel museo del Conservatorio. . . ." In his *Gli strumenti musicali della Corte Medicea,* pp. 48-62. Firenze: LICOSA, 1969. illus. (Cf. no. **501** above.)

FLORENCE (Italy). ESPOSIZIONE ITALIANA, 1861

506   Casamorata, Luigi Ferdinando. *Gli strumenti musicali all'esposizione italiana del anno 1861. Descrizione sommaria e motivi del giudizii pronunziati della terza sezione della Classe IX . . . Relatore della suddetta Sezione.* Firenze: coi tipi di Felice Le Monnier, 1862. 51 pp.

>   Cited from Gaspari*; not located.

FLORENCE (Italy). ESPOSIZIONE STORICA NELLE ONORANZE A BARTOLOMEO CRISTOFORI, 1876

507   "Nota degl' istrumenti storici che figurano nell'esposizione dello stabilimento Brizzi e Niccolai." In Ponsicchi, Cesare. *Il pianoforte, sua origine e sviluppo e rassegna dell'esposizione,* pp. 75-77. Firenze: G.-C. Guidi, 1876. (33 items)

>   Copy at DLC(Wc).

Literature

508   "Exposition retrospective de pianos a Florenze. A l'occasion des fêtes en l'honneur de Cristofori," *Echo musical* 8, no. 11 (1876): 3-4. Notes 53 items with owners' names

FLORENCE (Italy). GALLERIA DEGLI UFFIZI

509 Bernardi, Marziano and Andrea Della Corte. *Gli strumenti musicale nei dipinti della Galleria degli Uffizi.* [Torino: Edizioni radio italiana, 1952.] 177 pp., illus., pls.

Copies at IU (Uu), ICU (Cu), OrU (EUu), NN (NYp), DLC (Wc).

510 Marcucci, Luisa. *Mostra di strumenti musicali in disegni degli Uffizi. Catalogo,* a cura di Luisa Marcucci, con pref. di Luigi Parigi. Firenze: L. S. Olschki, [1952]. 47 pp., illus., 14 pls.

Copies at NPv (POvc), NBuU-M (BUu).

FLORENCE (Italy). MUSEO DI STORIA DELLA SCIENZA

511 *Catalogo degli strumenti del Museo di Storia dell Scienza.* Firenze: L. S. Olschki, 1954. vii, 394 pp., illus., pls.

Copies at IaU (ICu), NN (NYp), NIC (Iu), WaU (Su), DLC (Wc).

FLORENCE (Italy). MUSEO NAZIONALE DI ANTROPOLOGIA

512 Puccioni, Nello. "Gli oggetti musicali del Museo Nazionale di Antropologia," *Archivio per la Antropologia e la Etnologia* 36 (1906): fasc. 1, 59-84. 152 items.

Copies at MnU (MSu), CtY (NHu), CU (BEu), MBM (Bfa).

Literature

513 Kraus, Alessandro. "Illustrazione degli strumenti musicali portati dal prof. Mante. gazza dal suo ultimo viaggio nell'India," *Archivio per l'Antropologia e la Etnologia* 13 (1883): 532-42.

514 Kraus, [Alessandro]. "Du alcuni strumenti della Micronesia e della Melanesia, regulati al Museo nazionale d'antropologia e di etnologia dal Dott. Otto Finsch," *Archivio per l'Antropologia e la Etnologia* 17 (1887): fasc. 1, 35-41. illus.

FRANKFURT a.M. (Germany). ALLGEMEINE DEUTSCHE PATENT- UND MUSTERSCHÜTZ-AUSSTELLUNG, 1881

Literature

515 "Die Musikinstrumente auf . . . ," *ZfI* 1 (1880/81): 301-2, 304.

FRANKFURT a.M. (Germany). ALLGEMEINE DEUTSCHE . . . *continued*

General

516   *Officieller Catalog der allgemeinen deutschen Patent- und Musterschutz- und der Local- Gewerbe-Ausstellung zu . . . Eröffnet am 10. Mai 1881.* Frankfurt a/M: [Keller] ,-1881. 426 pp., illus.

Cited from KaY* 21:254; not located.

FRANKFURT a.M. (Germany). BIBLIOTHEK FÜR NEUERE SPRACHEN UND MUSIK. MANSKOPFISCHES MUSEUM. *See under* **FRANKFURT a.M. (Germany). STADT- UND UNIVERSITÄTSBIBLIOTHEK**

FRANKFURT a.M. (Germany). HISTORISCHES MUSEUM (J58, BB155)

517   Epstein, Peter. *Katalog der Musikinstrumente im Historischen Museum der Stadt Frankfurt am Main.* Frankfurt am Main: 1927. 32 pp., 8 pls., 149 items.

Copies at DSI, NN (NYp), DLC (Wc).

Literature

518   Quilling, Fritz. "Die Sammlungen des städtischen historischen Museums. Die Musik-Instrumente," *Frankfurter Nachrichten* (April 1900).

519   Schweizer, G. "Kostbarkeiten und Kuriosotäten in der Instrumentenabteilung des Frankfurter historischen Museums," *MIuP* 13 (1964): 748-49.

520   Ernst, Friedrich. "Historische Tasteninstrumente im Frankfurter Besitz," *MIuP* 13 (1964): 126-28.

Discusses keyboard instruments in four collections:
the Historisches Museum, the Goethehaus,
the Museum für Handwerk, and the Stadt- und
Universitäts-Bibliothek, with references to entries
in Epstein's 1927 *Katalog* (no. **517** above).

General

521   "[Abthlg. 2.] Die Musikinstrumente, bearb. von Dr. F. L. Limbert," [4 pp.]. In Quilling, Fritz. *Die Sammlungen des historischen Museums zu Frankfurt am Main.* 2 vols. Frankfurt a/M: Kern & Birner, 1899-1904.

Identical to no. **518**, also published separately.

FRANKFURT a.M. (Germany). INTERNATIONALE AUSSTELLUNG, MUSIK IM LEBEN DER VÖLKER, 1927

522   Meyer, Kathi. *Katalog der Internationalen Ausstellung.* Frankfurt a/M: Hauserpresse, 1927. viii, 340 pp., 49 pls.

>Includes instruments from the Neupert Museum in Nuremberg (see **NEUPERT** in Section II) and from the **BRUSSELS, CONSERVATOIRE ROYALE.** . . .

523   Bottenheim, S. *De Nederlandsche afdeeling op de Internationale muziektentoonstelling.* . . . *Catalogus samengesteld door.* . . . [Amsterdam: 1927.] 22 pp., illus.

>Copy at NN (NYp).

524   Cesari, G. *Catalogo della sezione italiana.* Roma: 1927. 161 pp., illus., pls.

>Copy at NN (NYp).

525   Herriot, Eduard. *Catalogue de la section francaise.* Paris: Palais-royal, 1927. 172 pp.

>Copy at NN (NYp).

Literature

526   Daehne, Paul. "Musik im Leben der Völker; Ein Rückblick auf die . . . ," *ZfI* 47 (1926/27): 1100-1103.

527   Holde, Arthur. "Internationale Ausstellung 'Musik im Leben der Völker'," *Allgemeine Musik Zeitung* 54 (June 17, 1927): 721-23.

528   Closson, Ernest. "L'Exposition musicale de Francfort," *Revue musicale belge* 3 (September 20, 1927): 4-6.

>About the instruments from the Brussels Conservatoire.

FRANKFURT a.M. (Germany). STADT- UND UNIVERSITÄTSBIBLIOTHEK. MUSIK- UND THEATERABTEILUNG. MANSKOPFISCHES MUSEUM (A205, BB154)

[N. B.: Consists of the former Stadtbibliothek, Manskopfisches Museum für Musik- und Theatergeschichte; Gymnasialbibliothek; Bibliothek für neuere Sprachen und Kunst (formerly Carl von Rothschild Bibliothek); and libraries of Peters- und Barfüsskirche.]

Literature

529   P., H. "Das Frankfurter musikhistorische Museum von Fr. Nicolas Manskopf," *Frankfurter Nachrichten,* no. 296 (1900).

>Cited from *ZiMG*-schau* 2 (1900/1901): 148; not examined.

FRANKFURT a.M. (Germany). STADT- UND UNIVERSITÄTSBIBLIOTHEK....
continued

Literature

530   Münster, Emil. "Das Fr. Nikolas Manskopf'sche musikhistorische Museum zu
Frankfurt a.M.," *Neue Musik-Zeitung* (Stuttgart) 21, no. 17 (1900?): 209.

> Cited from *ZiMG*-schau* 2 (1900/1901): 33; not examined.

531   *Das Musikhistorische Museum von Nicolas Manskopf.* Frankfurt a.M.: R. Th.
Hauser & Co. [n.d., 1920?] . 64 pp., illus.

> Copies at DLC (Wc), NNMM.

532   *Das musikhistorische Museum von Nicolas Manskopf, Frankfurt a.M.*
[A collection of extracts from newspapers, illustrations, and a portrait.
Frankfurt a.M., ca. 1902.]

> Copy at GB-Lbl (Hirsch no. 459).

533   "The English Coronation Exhibition . . . at Frankfort-on-the-Main," *MT* 43
(1902): 464.

> Exhibition contained 100 items, part of Manskopf collection.

534   Meister, ? "Das musikhistorische Museum von Nic. Manskopf zu Frankfurt
a.M. und seine Bedeutung," *Mitteilungen aus dem Frankfurter Schulmuseum*,
vol. 4, no. 4/5 (1920).

> Cited from *ZiMG*-schau* 3 (1920/21): 18; not examined.

FREDERICKSBURG, VIRGINIA (USA). MARY WASHINGTON COLLEGE

535   *An Exhibition of Early Musical Instruments [Chiefly from the Collection of
Frederick Selch, New York] with Original Prints Showing the Instruments
As a Prominent Feature.* Dupont Galleries March 19-April 5. Fredericksburg:
[1959] . [16] pp., illus.

> Copy at NN (NYp).

FREIBURG, i. B. (Germany). DOMKAPELLE

536   Müller, F. E. "Die Musikinstrumente in der Freiberger Domkapelle," *AfMW* 14
(1957): 193-200. With a brief inventory.

FREIBURG i. B. (Germany). OBERRHEINISCHE GEWERBEAUSSTELLUNG, 1887

Literature

537   "Oberrheinische Gewerbeausstellung zu . . . ," *ZfI* 7 (1886/87): 405-7 (exhibitors), 459 (notes).

General

538   *Offizieller Katalog d. oberrheinischen Gewerbeausstellung.* Freiburg i/B: [Stoll & Bader], 1887. lxxvii, 231 pp.

>   Cited from KaY* 25:697; not examined.

FREIBURG i. B. (Germany). UNIVERSITÄT

Literature

539   Graevenits, Dr. von. "Sammlung alter Klavierinstrumente der Freiburger Universität," *Neue Musik-Zeitung* (Stuttgart) 42, no. 9 (1921): 138-39.

>   Cited from NN (NYp) catalogue.

GENEVA (Switzerland). EXPOSITION INTERNATIONALE DE LA MUSIQUE, 1927

540   *L'exposition . . . Genève, 1927.* Genève: [1927]. 143 pp., illus.

>   Preface: Karl Nef. "Instruments à clavier," A. Mathu; "Les instruments à cordes," A. Vidoudez; "La collection des instruments anciens allemands," Curt Sachs; "Les instruments à clavier," A. Mathu; "Les instruments à vent," Frank Martin; "Les luthiers," A. Vidoudez; "La machines parlantes," E. Combe.
>   Copy at NN (NYp).

Literature

541   "Die internationale Musikausstellung in Genf," *ZfI* 47 (1926/27): 297, 428, 595, 664 (German exhibitors), 859-60 (prizes), 915-16, et passim.

542   Neisser, Artur. "Von der internationalen Musikausstellung zu Genf," *Neue Musik-Zeitung* (Stuttgart) 48 (1927): 405-7, 425-26. illus.

543   Tobler, Ernst and S.-W., K. "Internationale Musikausstellung in Genf," *Schweizerische Musikzeitung* 67 (1927): 212-14, 234, 251-52.

GENEVA (Switzerland). EXPOSITION NATIONALE SUISSE, 1896

Literature

544   "Musikinstrumente auf der . . . Gruppe XVI . . . Firmen," *ZfI* 16 (1895/96): 744, 753.

        Notes an official catalogue; not located.

General

545   *Deutscher Führer durch Genf und d. Landes-Ausstellung.* Genf: P. G. Drehmann, 1896. 61 pp., illus.

        Cited from KaY* 29:545; not located.

GENEVA (Switzerland). MUSÉE D'ART ET D'HISTOIRE (BB104)

546   Chavannes, R. "Catalogue descriptif des instruments de musique à cordes frottées ou pincées du Musée," *Geneva* 9 (1931): 234-54.

Literature

547   Kling, Henry. "La collection des anciens instruments de musique au Musée d'Art et d'Histoire," *Schweizerische Zeitschrift für Instrumentalmusik*, vol. 2 (September 1, 1913).

        About the collection of Camille Galopin; cited from Altenburg*; not examined.

548   Nef, Karl. "Instruments de musique anciens: A propos d'une visité au Musée d'art et d'histoire," *M & I* 12 (1926): 1047, 1049.

GENEVA (Switzerland). MUSÉE DES INSTRUMENTS ANCIENS DE MUSIQUE (J124, A411, BB103-4)

Literature

549   Haldenwang, Jacques. "Le Musée des instruments anciens de musique," *Musées de Genève* 4, no. 33 (1963): 17-19. illus., 240 items.

        Formerly the private collection of Dr. Fritz Ernst (see private catalogue, Section II).

550   Boresel, Alfred. "Das klingende Museum aus Genf," *Instrumentenbau-Zeitschrift* 20 (1966): 134-36.

551   Muggler, F. and K. Hofer. "Den Genfer Musée d'instruments anciens de musique," *Neue Zürcher Zeitung,* vol. 357 (June 15, 1969).

552 Junge, Sylvia. "Old Instruments Seen and Heard," *Music in Education* 36 (1972): 131-32.

553 Clerc, E. I. *Musée d'instruments anciens de musique.* Genf: 1973.
   Cited from Jenkins*; not located.

GENEVA (Switzerland). MUSÉE ET INSTITUT D'ETHNOGRAPHIE (J123)

554 Montandon, George. *La généalogie des instruments de musique et les cycles de civilisation; étude suivie du Catalogue raisonné des instruments de musique du Musée ethnographique de Genève.* Genève: Impr. A. Kundig, 1919. 120 pp., illus.
   From *Archives suisses d'anthropologie générale* 3 (1919): 1-120.
   Copies at CtY (NHu), DLC (Wc).

GHENT (Netherlands). EXPOSITION UNIVERSELLE ET INTERNATIONALE, 1913

Literature

555 "Weltausstellung in Gent," *ZfI* 33 (1912/13): 1015, 1219, 1247-48 (exhibitors).

GHENT (Netherlands). FESTIVAL VAN VLAANDEREN (A45)

Literature

556 Lievense, Willy. "Klavicimbels van de familie Ruckers [at the exhibition at St. Peters Abbey]," *Mens en melodie* 22 (1967): 296-99. illus.
   Instruments from various collections, including the Brussels Conservatoire.

GHENT (Netherlands). MUSEUM VAN OUDHEDEN DER BYLOKE

557 Hollebosch-van Reck, Y. and Ignace de Keyser. *Catalogus van de muziekinstrumenten.* . . . Gent: Oudheidkundige Musea, Bijlokemuseum, [1978?]. 47 pp., [5] lvs., illus.

GIJON (Spain). MUSEU INTERNACIONAL DE LA GAITA

558 Mere, Rafael. *Catalogo.* [1. ed.] Gijon: Ayuntamiento, [1970]. 152 pp., illus., mostly col.
   Duckles* 3:1586: a museum devoted to the bagpipe.

GLASGOW (Scotland). KELVINGROVE ART GALLERY AND MUSEUM (J144, A352, BB157) [N.B.: Includes the Glen and Euing collections, the Dyer group of Japanese instruments, and the Farmer purchase, 1945.]

559   *Instruments of Music; History and Development.* [Glasgow] : Corporation of Glasgow Art Gallery and Museum, 1941. 17 pp., illus.

    Introduction by Henry George Farmer; collaborator, S. M. K. Henderson.

560   Farmer, Henry George. *The Glen Collection of Musical Instruments.* Glasgow: 1945. 7 pp., illus.

    From *Art Review,* vol. 1 (1946).

Literature

561   Farmer, Henry George. "Some Oriental Musical Instruments at Kelvingrove," *The Scottish Art Review* 8 (1961): 1-4. illus.

General

562   *Dept. of Ethnography Catalogue.* [Introduction by H. G. Farmer.] [Glasgow: 1944?] 15 pp., illus.

    Copy at DLC (Wc); not examined.

GLASGOW (Scotland). INTERNATIONAL EXHIBITION, 1901

Literature

563   "Musical Exhibits at Glasgow Exhibition," *Musical Opinion* 24 (1900/1901): 715-18. illus.

564   Lancastrian. "String Instruments at the Glasgow Exhibition," *The Strad* 12, no. 141 (1902): 274-76.

GNIEZNO (Poland). ARCHIVUM ARCHIDIECEZIAJNE

Literature

565   Zientarski, Wladyslaw. "Przycznyki z archowaliow Gnieznienskich I. O Instrumentach muzycznych kapeli gnieznienskiej na przestrzeni XVIII wieku," *Z dziejow muzyki polskiej* 13 (1969): 1-21.

GÖRLITZ (Germany). NIEDERSCHLESISCHE GEWERBE- UND INDUSTRIE-AUSSTELLUNG, 1885

Literature

566   Schlemüller, Gustav. "Gewerbe- und Industrie-Ausstellung in Görlitz," *ZfI* 5 (1884/85): 337-38.

567   [Notices, list of exhibitors and prizes for Group XVII, musical instruments], *ZfI* 5 (1884/85): 295; 6 (1885/86): 5-6, 63-64.

General

568   *Führer durch die Gewerbe- und Industrie-Ausstellung . . . 1885.* Görlitz / Leipzig: Stauffer, 1885. 35 pp.

   Cited from KaY* 23:346; not located.

GÖRLITZ (Germany). NIEDERSCHLESISCHE GEWERBE- UND INDUSTRIE-AUSSTELLUNG, 1905

Literature

569   ["Die Musikinstrumenten-Industrie auf der . . . "], *ZfI* 25 (1904/5): 455, 791 (exhibitors), 951.

GÖTEBORG (Sweden). ETNOGRAFISKA MUSEUM (J115). *See also Section II under* KAUDERN, WALTER

570   Izikowitz, Karl Gustav. *Musical and Other Sound Instruments of the South American Indians.* (Göteborgs kungl. vetenskaps- och vitterhets-samhälles handlingar, 5. fjölden, ser. A, Bd. 5, no. 1.) Göteborg: Elanders boktr., 1935. Reprint ed. East Ardsley: S. R. Publ., 1970. xii, 433 pp., illus.

   " . . . founded on studies of . . . collections in numerous museums . . . pre-eminently those of the Gothenburg Museum."

GÖTEBORG. MUSEUM. HISTORISKA AVDELNINGEN (A383)

571   Lagerberg, Carl. *Göteborgs museum. Vägledning för besökare inom historiska afdelningen samlingar.* Göteborg: Wettergran & Kerber, 1912. 228 pp.

   "Musikinstrument," pp. 197-212. illus., 104 items.

572   Anrep Nordin, Birger. *Musikhistoriska avdelningen.* Göteborg: Göteborgs litografiska aktiebolag, 1923. 24 pp., illus., 112 items.

   Copy at DLC (Wc).

GÖTEBORG. MUSEUM. HISTORISKA AVDELNINGEN   *continued*

573   Thulin, Otto. *Historiska avdelningen . . . Musik-instrument.* [Göteborg, Elanders Boktryckeri, 1931.] 37 pp., 16 pls.

        Cited from BM*.

GÖTTINGEN (Germany). STÄDTISCHES MUSEUM

Literature

574   Hart, Günter. "Die Musikinstrumente im Städtischen Museum," *Glareana* 24, no. 2 (1975): lvs. 32-39. 46 items.

GÖTTINGEN. UNIVERSITÄT. MUSIKWISSENSCHAFTLICHEN INSTITUT, MUSIK-INSTRUMENTSAMMLUNG (J59)   [N. B.: Now contains Hermann MOECK collection (see catalogue in Section II).]

GÖTTWEIG (Austria). BENEDICTINE ABBEY. MUSIKARCHIV

575   Fitzpatrick, Horace. "Jacob Denner's Woodwinds for Göttweig Abbey," *GSJ* 21 (1968): 81-87.

        Facsimile plate after page 88 is Denner's "Specificatione," his Ms. bill, ca. 1720, from the Arch. Gött. RAR 1700-1709.

576   Wondratsch, Heinrich. *Catalogus operum musicalium,* 1830.

        A Ms. according to Jenkins* which includes: "Inventarium über die vorhandenen Instrumente auf dem Musikchor des löbl. Stiftes." Not located.

GRAND RAPIDS, MICHIGAN (USA). ART GALLERY.   [Exhibit, Music and Art] *See under* MINNEAPOLIS, MINNESOTA (USA). UNIVERSITY OF MINNESOTA. UNIVERSITY GALLERY

GRAZ (Austria). JOANNEUM   (J7, A17)

577   Sowinski, Hans. "Steirische Volksmusikinstrumente," *Das Joanneum* 3 (1940): 188-202. illus.

        Most of the illustrations are from Sowinski's collection on loan to the Joanneum since 1940.

GRAZ (Austria). MUSEUM FÜR KULTURGESCHICHTE UND KUNSTGEWERBE
(BB59)   [N.B.: Its collection of instruments now with the **JOANNEUM,** above.]

GRAZ (Austria). STEIERMÄRKISCHES LANDESZEUGHAUS

578   Stradner, Gerhard. *Die Musikinstrumente im Steiermärkischen Landeszeughaus in Graz.* [Graz]: 1976. 30 pp., illus.

> Sonderdruck aus: Veröffentlichungen des Landeszeughaus Graz, Nr. 6.
>
>   Includes texts "of inventories of instruments from 1590 to 1769" [review by Jeremy Montagu in *FoMRHI Comm.* 109 (January 1978): 69-70].

"GRAZER INSTRUMENTENKAMMER" [N.B.: The collections of KARL von Steiermark, Erzherzog von Innerösterreich, 1540-1590 and FERDINAND II, Erzherzog von Innerösterreich, 1596-1619. (See inventories under their names in Section II.) The Archduke Ferdinand became King of Bohemia in 1617, King of Hungary in 1618, and Holy Roman Emperor in 1619, when he transferred his household and the Kapelle to Vienna. By 1765, according to Schlosser* (p. 17) "wurde aufgelöst und nach Wien übertragen; von ihren Instrumenten ist jedoch hier nichts mehr vorhanden."]

GRINDELWALD (Switzerland). HEIMATMUSEUM

579   Geiser, Brigitte and Markus Römer. *Das Alphorn in der Schweiz. Katalog der Ausstellung im Heimatmuseum Grindelwald Sommer 1972.* Grindelwald: 1972. 48 pp., illus.

> *RILM*,* vol. 6, no. 2795.

GUELPH, ONTARIO (Canada). UNIVERSITY

Literature

580   Coleman, Barbara. "Musical Heirlooms of Canadian Pioneers," *Dolmetsch Foundation Bulletin,* no. 20 (September 1973). [3] pp.

HAARLEM (Netherlands). GROTE KERK

581   "Catalogus der Tentoonstelling Nederlandse Orgelpracht, 3-30 Juli 1961 te
Haarlem. Samengesteld en ingericht door H. P. Baard, Klaas Bolt, Piet Kee
[etc.] ." In *Nederlandse Orgelpracht*, pp. 151-88 [and illus.] . Haarlem: H. D.
Tjeenk Willink & Zoon, 1961.

   Copies at CU (BEu), WU (MAu), MH.

HÄLSINGBORG (Sweden). MUSEUM   (J115). *See also Section II under* FRYKLUND, LARS AXEL DANIEL for many works relating to his collection while private

582   *Utställning av musikinstrument ur Daniel Fryklunds samling i Hälsingborg;
katalog.* Med förord av Tobias Norlind. [Hälsingborg: Schmidts boktr., 1945.]
80 pp., 14 pls., 304 items.

   Copies at DLC (Wc), NjR (PRu).

HAGUE (Netherlands). GEMEENTEMUSEUM   (J94, A262, BB75)   [N.B.: Includes the collections of Boers, Alsbach, and the Amsterdam Rijksmuseum. Its nucleus was the Scheurleer collection, its latest important addition that of van Leeuwen Boomkamp (see entries for each in Section II).]

583   Scheurleer, Daniel Francois. *Die muziek-historische afdeeling (Verz. D. F.
Scheurleer) door Dirk J. Balfoort.* [s'Gravenhage] : 1935. 50 pp., illus.

   Copies at ViU (CHu), CtY (NHu).

584   *Tentoonstelling van toegelaten strijkinstrumenten, violen, altviolen, violoncellen,
contrebassen, strijkkwartetten. Internationale manifestatie van hedendaagse
vioolbouw, concours Hendrik Jacoby beroepsklasse. s'Gravenhage, 19 Juni-
17 Juli 1949.* s'Gravenhage: 1949. [60] pp., illus.

   Copy at ICN. See also no. 585.

585   "The Hague Exhibition [with a list of prizewinners] ," *The Strad* 60 (1949):
114, 128.

586   *Tentoonstelling van manuscripten, oude drukken, gravures, portretten en
muziek-instrumenten . . . uit de muziekhistorische afdeling van het Gemeentemuseum.* s'Gravenhage: 1950. 16 pp.

   Typescript in the Victoria and Albert Museum.
   Exhibition: Bach en zijn Tijdgenoten, 1685-1750.

587 Ligtvoet, A. W. _Exotische en oude europese muziekinstrumente in de muziek-afdeling van het haagse gemeentemuseum. Exotic and Ancient European Music Instruments._ . . . s'Gravenhage: Nijgh & Van Ditmar, [1955]. 51 pp.

> Duckles* 3:1589. Copies at MH (Cac), PP (PHf).

588 _Het muzikale hart van Nieuw-Guinea. Muziekinstrumenten van de Papoea's. 7 juli tim 16 augustus 1959._ [Den Haag]: 1959. unpaged, 66 items.

589 Ligtvoet, A. W. and W. Lievense. _Europese muziekinstrumenten in het Haagse Gemeentemuseum._ s'Gravenhage: the Museum, 1965. 160 pp., 64 illus.

> Duckles* 3:1588.

590 _Catalogus van de muziekinstrumenten van het Haags Gemeentemuseum._ (Catalogi van de Muziekbibliotheek en de collectie muziekinstrumenten, onder red. van C. C. von Gleich.) [Amsterdam: Knuf, 1970- .]

> Six volumes are planned. Vol. 1: _Hoorn- en trompetachtige blaasinstrumenten,_ door Leo J. Plenckers. (88 pp., illus., 135 items.)

591 Ligtvoet, A. W. "Neuerwerbung des Haager Gemeindemuseums," _Sonorum Speculum,_ no. 43 (1970), pp. 37-39.

592 Lievense, Willi. _Oude Europese muziekinstrumenten_ [exhibition catalogue]. [s.p., s.d., 197-?] 50 pp., illus.

593 _Historische Blaasinstrumenten, de ontwikkeling van de blaasinstrumenten vanaf 1600. Kasteel Ehrenstein te Wereldmuziekconcours Kerkrade, 6-28 juli 1974._ [s'Gravenhage]: Haags Gemeentemuseum-Gemeente Kerkrade, 1974. 80 pp., illus., 224 items.

> Red.: R. J. M. van Acht, C. C. J. von Gleich, D. M. Klerk.

594 Gleich, Clemens Christoph von. _Toetsinstrumenten uit de Lage Landen / Keyboard Instruments from the Low Countries._ ([The Museum's] Kijk-boekjes, 4.) The Hague: Knuf, 1977. 60 pp., 25 pls. [announced]

595 _Traditionele muziekinstrumenten van Japan; Traditional Musical Instruments of Japan._ [Text and translation by Onno Mensink.] ([The Museum's] Kijkboekjes, [3].) [Buren: Frits Knuf, 1979.] 64 pp., illus. plus recording.

Literature

596 Monnikendam, Marius. "Exotische muziekinstrumenten: Die Collectie 'Scheurleer' in het nieuwe museum te's-Gravenhage," _Het R. K. Bouwblad_ 8, no. 10 (December 1936): 152-56. illus.

597 _Internationale Tentoonstelling van moderne Blaasinstrumenten_ . . . _27. Juli - 4. September 1951._ [Den Haag]: 1951. unpaged, 289 items.

HAGUE (Netherlands). GEMEENTEMUSEUM   *continued*

598 Ligtvoet, A. W. "Het Haagse Gemeentemuseum verrijkt," *Mens en melodie* 7 (1952): 37-38. illus.

599 Lievense, Willi. "Die Instrumentensammlung des Gemeinde-Museums den Haag," *Das Orchester* 5 (1957): 2-4.

600 Lievense, Willi. "Die Instrumentensammlung des Gemeinde-Museums den Haag," *NZfM* 118, Heft 1 (1957): 16-18. illus.

601 Piroen-Roodvoets, D. R. "Oude muziekinstrumenten in het Gemeentemuseum te s'-Gravenhage," *Mens en melodie* 18 (1963): 364-66.

602 Kullberg, Barbara L. "Klingende Vergangenheit 'Haags Gemeentemuseum'," *NZfM* 129 (1968): 14-16. illus.

   About the Scheurleer collection.

603 Ligtvoet, A. W. "Aanwisten voor het Haags Gemeentemuseum," *Mens en melodie* 23 (1968): 282-83; 24 (1969): 313-14.

604 Ligtvoet, A. W. *Gids buiten-europese muziekinstrumenten.* Den Haag: Gemeente- museum, 1962. 32 pp., 8 pls.

605 Acht, Rob van. "Waarom bezit het Haags Gemeentemuseum een kollektie oude muziekinstrument?" *Huismuziek,* 22, no. 4 (juli 1973): 47-48.

606 Verveen, Arie and Magda Klerk. "The Gemeentemuseum at the Hague," *Fontes artis musicae* 21 (1974): 106-9.

   Mostly about the Scheurleer collection.

607 Klerk, Magda and Onno Mensink. *Japanese prenten met muziek / Japanese Woodcuts with Music.* ([The Museum's] Kijkboekjes, 1.) Den Haag: Gemeente- museum, [1976?]. 60 pp., 25 illus.

608 Scheurwater, Wouter and Rob van Acht. *Oude klavecimbels, hun bouw en restauratie / The Making and Restoring of Old Harpsichords.* ([The Museum's] Kijkboekjes, 2.) The Hague: Knuf, [1976?]. 60 pp., 32 pls.

HAIFA (Israel). HA MUZE'ON VE-SIFRIYAT AMLI LE'MUSIKAH HEFAH (THE AMLI MUSEUM AND LIBRARY FOR MUSIC)   (J76)

609 Ben-Zvi, Yaakov. *ha-Musikah ba-'olam ha-'atik. . . . Music in the Ancient World* [exhibition]. Haifa: The AMLI Museum, [1971]. 1 vol., unpaged, illus.

610 Ben-Zvi, Yaakov. *Music in the Ancient World.* 2nd enl. ed. [Haifa: Haifa Music Museum], 1979. unpaged.

611   Gorali, Moshe. *Music in Ancient Israel.* [Haifa: The Haifa Museum & AMLI Library], 1972-73. [49] pp., illus., 87 items, some reconstructed. 2nd enl. ed., 1974. [64] pp., illus; 3rd enl. ed., [1977]. [66] pp.

Literature

612   Sachs, Julius. "In Haifa klingen antike Musikinstrumente," *Instrumentenbau-Zeitschrift* 25 (1971): 552.

About the exhibition, May 1971.

HALLE (Germany). GEWERBE- UND INDUSTRIE-AUSSTELLUNG, 1881

Literature

613   W[it, Paul de]. "Die Musikinstrumente auf der . . . ," *ZfI* 1 (1880/81): 293-94.

614   [Notes on exhibitors, exhibits and prizes], *ZfI* 1 (1880/81): 25, 78, 234-35, 261-62, 283.

615   Laffert, Oscar. [Further notes], *ZfI* 1 (1880/81): 333-34, 338.

HALLE (Germany). HÄNDEL-HAUS

616   Sasse, Konrad. *Musikinstrumentensammlung. Besaitete Tasteninstrumente.* (Katalog zu den Sammlungen, 5. Teil.) Halle: Händel-Haus, 1966. 292 pp., illus.

Duckles* 3:1590: One of the largest collections of keyboard instruments; based on the Neupert collection.
Review: Theurich, Jutta in *Musik und Gesellschaft* 17 (1968): 343-44.

617   Sasse, Konrad. *Musikinstrumentensammlung. Streich- und Zupf-Instrumente.* (Katalog zu den Sammlungen, 6. Teil.) Halle: [Union-Druck (VOB)], 1972. 337 pp., illus.

HAMBURG (Germany). AUSSTELLUNG MUSIKGESCHICHTEICHER DRUCKE . . . [etc.] 1925. *See under* HAMBURG (Germany). MUSEUM FÜR HAMBURGISCHE GESCHICHTE

HAMBURG (Germany). GEWERBE- UND INDUSTRIE-AUSSTELLUNG, 1889

618   Sittard, Joseph. *Die Musik-Instrumente auf der Hamburger Gewerbe- und Industrie-Ausstellung, 1889.* Altona: Reher, 1890. 49 pp.

Cited from Lütg* (dates 1889) and KaY*; not located.

HAMBURG (Germany). GEWERBE- UND . . . *continued*

Literature

619 "Aussteller-Liste," *ZfI* 9 (1888/89): 348-49.

Notes an official catalogue, not located; Gruppe XVI, instruments.

620 "Ueber die Musikinstrumente auf der . . . ," *ZfI* 9 (1888/89): 397-99.

General

621 *Offizieller Katalog der Hamburgischen Gewerbe- und Industrie-Ausstellung in Jahre 1889.* Hamburg: Persiehl, 1889. xxvii, 161 pp.

Cited from KaY* 25:697; not located.

HAMBURG (Germany). MUSEUM FÜR HAMBURGISCHE GESCHICHTE (J60, BB165)

622 Gesellschaft der Freunde des vaterländischen Schul- und Erziehungswesens. *Musikalisches Schaffen und Wirken aus drei Jahrhunderten. Ausstellung musikgeschichtlicher Drucke, Handschriften und alter Musikinstrumente. Staats - und Universitätsbibliothek. Museum für hamburgische Geschichte.* Hamburg: 1925. vi, 89 pp., illus.

"2. Alte Musikinstrumente in Museum für hamburgische Geschichte, von Dr. Hans Schröder," pp. 11-16. Copies at NN (NYp) and DLC (Wc).

623 Schröder, Hans. *Verzeichnis der Sammlung alter Musikinstrumente im Auftrage der Museumsverwaltung.* Hamburg: Alster-Verlag, 1930. 95 pp., 20 pls.

Copies at ViU (CHu), DLC Wc).

Literature

624 Mayer-Reinach, Albert. "Die Sammlung alter Musikinstrumente," *Die Musikwelt* (Hamburg) 11 (1930/31): 69.

HAMBURG (Germany). MUSEUM FÜR KUNST UND GEWERBE (J60, BB165)
[N.B.: Basis of the instrument collection, that of Hans von Bülow, with additions from Friedrich Chrysander's.]

Literature

625 Nirnnheim, Hans. *Die hamburgischen Musikinstrumente - Das Hamburgische Museum für Kunst und Gewerbe, dargestellt zur Feier des 25 jährigen Bestehens.* Hamburg: J. F. Richter, 1902.

Cited from Heyer*; not located.

626   Conradt, Arnim. "Hamburger Musikinstrumente des 18. Jahrhunderts mit Lackmalerei," *Jahrbuch der Hamburger Kunstsammlungen* 9 (1964): 29-48.

>   Most of the instruments considered are in the Museum für Kunst und Gewerbe.

HAMPSTEAD (U.K.). FENTON HOUSE. *See* **LONDON (U.K.). FENTON HOUSE, HAMPSTEAD**

HARBURG (Germany). OETTINGEN-WALLERSTEIN'SCHE HOFKAPELLE

627   Hart, Günter. "Musikinstrumente auf Schloss Harburg," *Glareana* 23, no. 3 (1974): lvs. 38-39. 19 items.

   Literature

628   Schiedermaier, Ludwig. "Die Blütezeit der Oettingen-Wallerstein'schen Hofkapelle. Ein Beitrag zur Geschichte der deutschen Adelskapellen," *SiMG* 10 (1907): 83-130.

629   Piersol, Jon Ross. *The Oettingen-Wallerstein Hofkapelle and Its Wind Music.* 2 vols. (Thesis, University of Iowa, 1972.)

HASLEMER (U. K.). DOLMETSCH COLLECTION. *See Section II under* **DOLMETSCH, ARNOLD**

HAVANA (Cuba). BIBLIOTECA NACIONAL "JOSÉ MARTÍ"

   Literature

630   *Instrumentos y atributos folklóricos cubanos [Exhibicion, Habana].* [Habana?] : 1961. 1 folded sheet.

>   Cited from University of Texas, *Catalogue of Latin American Collection;* not examined.

HESSE-CASSEL (Germany). HOFKAPELLE. *See Section II under* **MORITZ, Landgraf zu Hessen, 1592-1627**

HOLBORN (U.K.). MUSIC TRADES EXHIBITION, 1898

Literature

631   "Exhibition of Instruments at the Holborn Town Hall [by the Music Trades
Association]," *Musical Opinion* 21 (1897/98): 702-3.

HOLYOKE, MASSACHUSETTS (USA). BELLE SKINNER COLLECTION. *See under* NEW HAVEN, CONNECTICUT (USA). YALE UNIVERSITY

HONOLULU (Hawaii). BERNICE PAUAHI BISHOP MUSEUM (L118)

General

632   *A Preliminary Catalogue . . . of Polynesian Ethnology and Natural History.*
5 vols. Honolulu: 1892-93.
          "Hula [instruments]," vol. 2, pp. 61-64, et passim.

IASI (Rumania). MUZEUL POLITECHNIC. SECTIA INREGISTRAREA SI REDAREA SUNETULUI

633   *Complexul muzeistic Iasi* [prezentare, text si documentare Eugenia Urescu,
Antoaneta Garabedeanu, Maria Nica]. Iasi: 1974. 29 pp., illus.
          Mechanical instruments. Summaries in French and English.

INGOLSTADT (Germany). SCHLOSSMUSEUM

634   Hart, Günter. "Die Musikinstrumentensammlung im Schlossmuseum zu
Ingolstadt/Donau," *Glareana* 17, no. 1 (1968): lvs. 2-7.
          Nucleus of the collection from Frauenkirche in Ingolstadt.
          Hart's inventory based on that of Otto Schmelz.

INNSBRUCK (Austria). MUSEUM FERDINANDEUM (J8, A19) [N.B.: Formerly TIROLER LANDESMUSEUM FERDINANDEUM.]

635   "Verzeichnis der Musikinstrumente in der Sammlung des Museums Ferdinandeum,"
Zeitschrift der Ferdinandeums für Tirol und Vorarlberg, vol. 59 (1915). Anhang.
(2 pls., 22 pp.)
                    Also issued separately; copy at CtY (NHu).
                    See also *Vienne à Versailles* under **VERSAILLES**
          (France). MUSÉE NATIONAL.

Literature

636　Pass, Walter. "Die Instrumentensammlung des Tiroler Landesmuseums Ferdinandeum," *Österreichische Musikzeitschrift* 25 (1970): 693-98. illus.

General

637　*Führer durch das Tiroler Landesmuseum Ferdinandeum.* . . . Innsbruck: 1933.

> Note on page 29: "Ein gedrucktes Verzeichnis der ausgestellten Instrumente ist beim Saalausfeher zu haben."

INNSBRUCK (Austria). SCHLOSS AMBRAS. *See under* VIENNA (Austria). KUNSTHISTORISCHES MUSEUM

INNSBRUCK (Austria). TIROLER LANDESAUSSTELLUNG, 1893

Literature

638　Eichhorn, Hermann. "Die Musikinstrumentenbranche auf der . . . Landesausstellung," *ZfI* 13 (1892/93): 715-16.

IOWA CITY, IOWA (USA). UNIVERSITY OF IOWA

639　Ross, David. *Musical Instruments at the University of Iowa: A Catalogue.* Iowa City: 1979. 23 pp., 39 items.

ISOLA BELLA (Italy). ESPOSIZIONE VIOLINI STRADIVARI, 1963

640　*Mostra di Antonio Stradivari, Palazzo Borromeo, Isola Bella, 26 agosto - 10 settembre 1963.* Novara: Ent provinciale del turismo, 1963. 77 pp.

> "Presentazione di G[uido] Piamonte."

JENA (Germany). STAATSMUSEUM

Literature

641　"Eine Sammlung alter Musikinstrumente in Jena," *Weltkunst* (Berlin) 7 (April 2, 1933): 2-3.

> Includes items from the W. Danckert collection.

JERSEY (Channel Islands). SOCIÉTÉ JERSIAISE. MUSEUM (J156)

642   Falle, Raymond. "A List of the Musical Wind Instruments in the Museum of the
Société Jersiaise," *Société Jersiaise Bulletin* 16 (1954): 202-6.

> " . . . the greater part . . . presented . . . by M. W. Brunt."

JERUSALEM (Israel). BEZALEL MUSEUM

643   *Musical Instruments Bequeathed by the Late Conductor Dr. Serge Koussevitzky
to the State of Israel, and Loans from Other Collections, [Exhibited] 14
February - March 1953.* Jerusalem: National Museum Bezalel, 1953. 15 pp.
(English); 17 pp. (Hebrew), 151 items, 59 of them from Koussevitzky bequest.

> Since 1963 at the Rubin Academy of Music. Copy at
> NBuU-M (BUu).

JERUSALEM (Israel). RUBIN ACADEMY OF MUSIC (J77)

644   Gerson-Kiwi, Edith. *Permanent Exhibition of Musical Instruments. Catalogue
and Classified Check-list Compiled . . . for the International Conference, "East
and West in Music," August 5-12, 1963.* Jerusalem: the Academy, 1963. iv, 34 pp.

> The exhibition contains items from many collections,
> public and private; the Foreword by Prof. Gerson-Kiwi
> notes that its basis was the Koussevitzky Collection,
> ca. 60 items. See no. **643**, above. Copy at NBuU (BUu).

Literature

645   "Exhibitions of Musical Instruments in Israel (prefaces of the catalogues)," *Tatzlil*,
no. 12 (1972), pp. 31-35.

> In Hebrew with brief English abstracts. The exhibit was
> originally organized by Prof. Gerson-Kiwi in 1943 and first
> shown in the Conservatory of Music, in 1953 in the Bezalel
> Museum (see no. **643** above), and finally in the Rubin
> Academy in 1963. The 1943 exhibition did not include the
> Koussevitzky instruments which were not given until 1951,
> and Prof. Gerson-Kiwi says there was no catalogue issued.
> (Information and copies of catalogues kindly furnished by
> Mr. Claude Abravanel of the Rubin Academy.)

JOHANNESBURG (South Africa). AFRICANA MUSEUM (J110)

646   Kirby, Percival Robson. *Catalogue of the Musical Instruments in Collection of . . . Compiled by Margaret M. de Lange.* Johannesburg: Africana Museum, 1967. 155 lvs.

> Kirby Collection in the Museum since 1952.
> Duckles* 3:1594. Copy at NBuU-M (BUu).
> See additional catalogues of the Kirby Collection, while it was still private, in Section II.

KÄRNTEN (Austria). BENEDICTINERKLOSTER ST. PAUL

647   Federhofer, Helmut. "Alte Musikalien-Inventare der Kloster St. Paul und Göss (Steiermark)," *KmJ* 35 (1951): 97-112.

> Music and musical instruments.

KAMPALA (Uganda). UGANDA MUSEUM (J131)

648   Trowell, Kathleen Margaret and K. P. Wachsmann. *Tribal Crafts of Uganda.* London: Oxford U. P., 1953. xxi, 442 pp., illus.

> African musical instruments in the museum, pp. 309-417, according to *MGG*; not examined.

KANSAS CITY, MISSOURI (USA). HOMER CONSERVATORY OF MUSIC

Literature

649   "Carl Busch Collection of Old Instruments of the Homer Conservatory of Music," *The Violinist* 47 (1931): 16-17. illus.

KASSEL (Germany). HOFKAPELLE (catalogues of 1573, 1613 and 1638). *See Section II under* MORITZ, Landgraf zu Hessen, 1592-1627

KÖTHEN (Sachsen-Anhalt, Germany). HOFKAPELLE

650   Bunge, Rudolf. "Johann Sebastian Bachs Kapelle zu Cöthen und deren nachgelassene Instrumente," *Bach-Jahrbuch* 2 (1905): 14- .

KÖTHEN (Sachsen-Anhalt, Germany). HOFKAPELLE *continued*

> Reprints an inventory of 1773 by C. F. von Horn:
> "Inventarien der fürstlichen Musikalienkammer vom
> 9. Oktober 1773" (Ms. in Herzögl. Haus- und Staats-
> Archiv, Abteilung Cöthen, St. 12, Nr. 68), pp. 37-43;
> and another, undated, pp. 38-41.

651 "Die nachgelassenen Instrumente der Kapelle Johann Sebastian Bachs zu
Cöthen," *ZfI* 27 (1906/7): 33-35.

> Reprints Bunge's list of 1773, see no. **650**.

KOLBERG (Germany). ALLGEMEINE GEWERBE- UND INDUSTRIE-AUSSTELLUNG, 1881

Literature

652 [Reference to Sekt. XI, Musikalische Instruments (2 classes) and to the
commissioner for music, Moritz Reiter]," *ZfI* 1 (1880/81): 163.

> No general catalogue identified.

KOLDING (Denmark). MUSEET

653 Skov, Sigvard. *Militaere Musikinstrumenter paa Koldinghus.* [Kolding]:
Koldinghusmuseet, 1947. 15 pp., illus.

> Copy at DLC (Wc).

654 Skov, Sigvard. *Musikinstrumenten paa Koldinghus.* [Kolding: Museet for
Koldinghus len og Kolding musikforening af 1880, 1944.] 10 pp., illus.

> Copies at NN (NYp), DLC (Wc).

KOSMONOSY (Czechoslovakia). PIARISTICÉ KOLEJE

655 Culka, Zdeněk. "Inventáře hudebních nástrojů a hudebnín Piaristické Koleje
v Kosmonosích. . . ." In *Prispevky k dějinam české hudby, II. Sborník studii
a Mertialovych Státi hudebne,* pp. 5-43. Praha: Acadamia, 1972.

KRASLICE (Czechoslovakia). FACHSCHULE FÜR MUSIKINSTRUMENTENERZEUGUNG

Literature

656 Keller, Jindřich. "Kraslická sbiřka hudebnich nástrojů [music instrument collection in Kraslice (Groslitz)]," *Hudebni nástroje* 5 (1968): 155-56. illus.

Collection made by F. Maresko.

KREMSMÜNSTER (Germany). BENEDIKTINERABTEI [N.B.: Schlosser* says the instruments of the Abbey's Musikkammer went to the Francisco-Carolinum in Linz in 1839. *See under* LINZ (Austria). OBERÖSTERREICHISCHES LANDESMUSEUM.]

Jenkins* also notes that forty instruments belonging to the Abbey are now in what she calls the "Kunstsammlungen des Stiftes." See no. **657**.

KREMSMÜNSTER (Germany). STIFTES

657 "Ein Instrumenteninventar des Stiftes Kremsmünster aufgenommen im Jahre 1747 durch Josef Kinniger und Ignatius Dansky." A summary in *MfM* 20 (1888): 109-10.

KUALA LUMPUR (Malaysia). SELANGOR MUSEUM. *See* catalogue *under* TAIPING (Malaysia). PERAK STATE MUSEUM

KUCHING (Malaysia). SARAWAK MUSEUM (J89)

658 Shelford, Robert Walter Campbell. "An Illustrated Catalogue of the Ethnographical Collection of the Sarawak Museum. Part I, Musical Instruments," *Journal of the Straits Branch of the Royal Asiatic Society*, no. 40 (June 1904). 59 pp., 8 pls. Reprint ed. New York: Kraus, 1965.

LANCASHIRE (U.K.). CHORLEY PUBLIC LIBRARY

Literature

659 Rhodes, Ernest. "Old Musical Instruments at Chorley," *Musical Opinion* 64 (February 1940): 202-3.

Part of Dr. ? Parker's collection at Bolton; not identified.

LAUCHA (Sachsen-Anhalt, Germany). GLOCKENMUSEUM (J48)

Literature

660   Ohk, Vera. *Das Glockenmuseum in Laucha a.U.* Nebra [Unstrut]: Rat d. Kreises,
1962. 14 pp., illus.
Cited from *JdMM**.

LEEDS (U.K.). CITY MUSEUM (J148)

661   "Exhibition of Musical Instruments at Leeds," *The Strad* 61 (1950): 244-46.
illus., ca. 50 items.
In conjunction with the Leeds Musical Festival,
an exhibition by L. P. Balmforth and Son.

662   *An Exhibition of Master Violins and Antique Stringed Instruments, 11-18 October,
1958.* [Leeds?] : 1958. unpaged, 119 items.
Foreword: Earl of Harewood.

Literature

663   Woodhouse, John C. "Exhibition of Musical Instruments at Leeds," *The Strad*
69 (1958): 258-60. over 150 items.
By Balmforth and Son.

LEIPZIG (Germany). ALLGEMEINE DEUTSCHE MUSIKVEREIN

Literature

664   "Der Allgemeine deutsche Musikverein und dessen historische und ethnographische
Ausstellung in Leipzig," *Die Gartenlaube* 22 (1883): 356-60. illus.

LEIPZIG (Germany). GRASSI MUSEUM. *See* LEIPZIG (Germany). UNIVERSITÄT. MUSIKINSTRUMENTENMUSEUM

LEIPZIG (Germany). INTERNATIONALE BAU-FACH-AUSSTELLUNG, 1913

665   Daehne, Paul. "Die Musikinstrumente auf der . . . ," *ZfI* 33 (1912/13): 926
(exhibitors), 1080-82, 1303; 34 (1913/14): 140, 179, 229 (prizes).

General

666   *Offizieller Katalog der internationalen Baufach-Ausstellung mit Sonderausstellungen.* [Schriftl.: Fel. Schloemp.] Leipzig: C. F. Müller, [1913]. 264 pp., illus.

Cited from *DBV** 1:1393; not located.

667   *Offizieller Führer durch die internationalen Baufach-Ausstellung mit Sonderausstellungen.* Leipzig: C. F. Müller, 1913. 128 pp., illus.

Cited from *DBV** 1:832; not located.

LEIPZIG (Germany). MUSEUM FÜR VÖLKERKUNDE

668   Richter, Arno. " . . . historische und ethnologische Ausstellung musikalischer Instrumente . . . ," *ZfI* 3 (1882/83): 244, 255-56, 267-68.

669   *. . . Führer durch das Museum für Völkerkunde. . . .* Leipzig: Spamerschen Buchdruckerei, 1913. Listed on the cover of the Museum's *Jahrbuch,* vol. 6 (1913/14, publ. 1915).

Not located.

670   Wagner, Eduard. Verzeichnis chinesischer Musikinstrumente," *Jahrbuch für Völkerkunde* 11 (1952): 23-33.

Wagner's private collection given to the museum.

Literature

671   Drost, Dietrich. "Tönerne Trommeln in Afrika," *Jahrbuch für Völkerkunde* 14 (1955): 31-61. illus.

Many descriptions of instruments in this museum—and others.

LEIPZIG (Germany). MUSIKFACHAUSSTELLUNG, 1909

672   "Musikfachausstellung Leipzig Juni 1909," *ZfI* 29 (1908/9): 185, 189, 224, 409-10, 899-900 (exhibitors), 947, 977-79 (by Paul Daehne), 980, 981-82 (prizes), 1014-16 ("Streichinstrumente auf . . . ," by Gustav Seifert), 1018-20 (prizes), 1052-53 ("Ergebnis").

LEIPZIG (Germany). [HERBST-] MUSTERMESSE, 1922

Literature

673   "Die Musikinstrumenten-Industrie auf der . . . ," *ZfI* 42 (1921/22): lvs. 1459-71.

LEIPZIG (Germany). [FRÜJAHRS-] MUSTERMESSE, 1923

Literature

674   "Musikinstrumenten-Industrie auf der . . . ," *ZfI* 43 (1922/23): 534, 579-87
(recto only), 608, 661-71 (recto only); the same type of reports for subsequent
fairs were carried in vol. 44 (1923/24) and vol. 45 (1924/25), q.v.

LEIPZIG (Germany). MUSIKINSTRUMENTEN-MESSE, 1929

Literature

675   "Les instruments de musique à la Foire de Leipzig," *M & I* 20 (1929): 447, 1223.

LEIPZIG (Germany). MUSIKINSTRUMENTEN-MESSE, 1936

Literature

676   "[Musikinstrumenten auf der . . .]," *ZfI* 56 (1935/36): 362-63, 382-83, 402-3.

LEIPZIG (Germany). MUSIKINSTRUMENTEN-MESSE, 1937

Literature

677   "Musikinstrumente und Leipziger Herbstmess 1937," *ZfI* 57 (1936/37): 187-88,
341-42, 355-56, 370, 372-73, 377-78; "Die gut verlaufene Sitzung wurde mit einem
'Sieg-Heil' auf den Führer beendet."

LEIPZIG (Germany). MUSIKINSTRUMENTEN-MESSE, 1938

Literature

678   "Der Leipziger Musikinstrumenten-Messe im Messhaus Petershof," *ZfI* 58 (1937/
38): 148-49, 163-64, 180-82 (exhibitors), 187-89 and 203-5 ("Rückblick"), 265-
66 ("Ergebnis").

LEIPZIG (Germany). MUSIKINSTRUMENTEN-MESSE, [Herbst] 1938

Literature

679   "Der Leipziger Musikinstrumenten-Messe im Messhaus Petershof," *ZfI* 58 (1937/38):
335-36, 347-48 (exhibitors), 355-56 (view), 371-74.

LEIPZIG (Germany). SÄCHSISCH- THÜRINGISCHE INDUSTRIE- UND GEWERBE-AUSSTELLUNG, 1897

680   "Die Musikinstrumente auf der . . . ," *ZfI* 17 (1896/97): 624-26, 652-55, 684-87, 713, 737-40, 764-65, 790-91, 819-20, 846-48, 876-78, 901-2, 923-26. illus.

   Literature

681   "Die Musikinstrumenten-Industrie auf der . . . ," *ZfI* 17 (1896/97): 549-50, 559, 602, 611; 18 (1897/98): 51-53 (prizes).

   General

682   *Offizieller Katalog . . . ,* bearb. von Johannes Kleinpaul. Leipzig: G. L. Daube, [1897?] . xl, 297 pp., illus.

   "Musikalische Instrumente und Bestandsteile, Gruppe XIX," pp. [220]-28, items 2696-2795. Copy at NIC (US).

683   *Offizieller Führer durch d. sächsischethüringische Industrie- und Gewerbe-Ausstellung . . . ,* bearb. von Leon Fraenkel. Leipzig: F. E. Fischer, 1897. iv, 107 pp., illus.

   Cited from KaY* 29:546; not located.

LEIPZIG (Germany). KARL-MARX-UNIVERSITÄT. MUSIKINSTRUMENTENMUSEUM
(J49)   [N.B.: Basis for the museum was the Wilhelm Heyer Collection purchased in 1926. For information about the collections which made up the Heyer museum, see Section II under **HEYER, WILHELM.**]

684   Schultz, Helmut. *Führer durch das musikwissenschaftliche Instrumentenmuseum der Universität Leipzig.* Mit einem Vorwort von Theodor Kroyer und einem Bilderanhang. Leipzig: Breitkopf & Härtel, 1929. 85 pp., illus.

   Duckles* 3:1497. Copy at NBuU-M (BUu).

685   Rubardt, Paul. *Führer durch das Musikinstrumenten-Museum der Karl-Marx-Universität, Leipzig.* Mit einem Vorwort von W. Serauky und einem Bilderanhang. Leipzig: Breitkopf & Härtel, 1955. 83 pp., xvi pls.

   Duckles* 3:1596. Copy at DLC (Wc).

686   Rubardt, Paul. *Führer durch das Musikinstrumenten-Museum.* 2. ver. Aufl. Leipzig: 1964.

   Not examined. Verified by the Museum.

LEIPZIG (Germany). KARL-MARX-UNIVERSITÄT. . . . *continued*

687 Schrammek, Winfried. *Musikinstrumenten. Aus dem Musikinstrumenten-Museum der Karl-Marx-Universität. Einführung und Erläuterungen.* 32 Tafeln von Rolf Langematz. [Leipzig]: Prisma-Verlag, [1970]. xii, 41 pp. (pp. 1-32, illus.).

> Some of the collection in photos; not a complete catalogue.
> Copy at DLC (Wc).

688 Heyde, Herbert. *Flöteninstrumente Karl-Marx-Universität zu Leipzig.* (Musik-instrumenten-Museum, Gesamtkatalog, Band 1.) Leipzig: VEB Deutscher Verlag für Musik, 1978. 160 pp., [8] lvs., pls.

689 Henkel, Hubert. *Kielinstrumente.* . . . (Musikinstrumenten-Museum, Gesamt-katalog, Band 2.) Frankfurt a.M.: Das Musikinstrument, [1979]. 250 pp.

Literature

690 Heuss, Alfred. "Einweihung des Instrumente-Museums der Universität Leipzig," *Zeitschrift für Musik* 96 (1929): 391-92.

691 Zenck, Hermann and Helmt Schulz. "Museums Eröffnung und Orgelweihe in Leipzig," *ZfMW* 11 (1929): 584-87.

692 "Besinnlicher Spaziergang durch das Leipziger Instrumenten-Museum," *ZfI* 61 (1941): 81-83.

693 "Ausgewählte instrumentenkundliche Probleme in einem Musikinstrumenten-museum." In *Bericht über den Internationalen Musikwissenschaftlichen Kongress, Bamberg 1953,* pp. 82-85. Kassel und Basel: Bärenreiter-Verlag, [1954].

694 "Klingende Jahrhunderte: Bericht aus dem Musikinstrumenten-Museum in Leipzig," *Deutscher Export* (Berlin) 10 (1962): 13-15.

695 Schrammek, Winfried. "Der Bachsaal im Musikinstrumenten-Museum der Karl-Marx-Universität." In *II. Internationales Bachfest Leipzig 1970* . . . , pp. 67-69. Leipzig: 1970.

696 "3000 Musikinstrumenten im Musikinstrumentenmuseum Leipzig," *Musikhandel* 21 (1970): 110.

697 Zeraschi, Helmut. *Geschichte des Museums.* (Schriftenreihe des Musikinstrumenten Museums, 2.) Leipzig, Musikinstrumenten-Museum . . . 1977. 43 pp., pls., illus.

698 "Zum 50. Todestag von Paul de Wit. . . ." In Leipzig. Universität. Musik-instrumentenmuseum. *Schriftenreihe,* vol. 1, pp. 7-12. [Leipzig]: 1975.

LENINGRAD (USSR). ERMITAZH

699   Ginzburg, S[emen L'vovich?]. *Muzika v muzeĭ*. Leningrad: 1934. 65 pp., 12 pls.
Copy at NNMM.

LENINGRAD (USSR). GOSUDARSTVENNAĬA AKADEMICHESKAĬA FILARMONIĬA. MUZEĬ

700   Akimova-Malova, N. P. *Kratkiĭ katalog muzykal'nykh instrumentov. i ikh izobrazheniĭ*. Predisl. N. Findeĭzena. Leningrad: Gos. akad. filarmoniĭa, 1927. 55 pp.

Cited from *JbP** (1927); not located.

LENINGRAD (USSR). GOSUDARSTVENNYI INSTITUT TEATRA, MUZYKI I KINEMATOGRAFII   (J133)

701   Petukhov, Nikhail O. *Narodnye muzykal'nye instrumenty muzeĭa S-Peterburgskoĭ konservatorii. (Balalaika, kobza, panskaĭa bandura. . . .)* S. Petersburg: Tip. Akademii nauk, 1884. 56, 2 pp.

Citation from Waterman*; Emsheimer* says with 29 plates.
Not located.

702   Petukhov, Mikhail O. *Opyt sistematicheskogo kataloga instrumental'nogo muzeĭa S.-Peterburgskoĭ konservatorii. (S portretem A. I. Rubtsa, osnovatelĭa muzeia i s risunkami v tekste.)* S.-Peterburg: Tip. V. Demakova, 1893. 35 pp., illus., 54 items.

Copy at DLC (Wc).

703   Blagodatov, Georgii Ivanovich and K. A. Vertkov. *Postoĭannaĭa vystavka muzykal'nykh instrumentov; putevoditel'*. Leningrad: 1962. 105 pp., illus.

Copy at DLC (Wc). *BdMS** dates 1964; collates, 128 pp.

704   Blagodatov, Georgii. *Katalog sobraniĭa muzykal'nykh instrumentov*. Leningrad: Edition "Muzyka," 1972. 127 pp., pls.

Review: *GSJ* 28:135-36.

Literature

705   *Putevoditel' po vystavke muzykal'nykh instrumentov*. Leningrad: 1902.

Cited from Jenkins*; not verified.

706   M. "Die Musikabteilung in der Haus- Industrie-Ausstellung," *St. Petersburger Zeitung*, no. 80 (April 3, 1902).

Cited from *ZiMG*-schau* 3:343.

LENINGRAD (USSR). GOSUDAESTVENNYI INSTITUT TEATRA, ... *continued*

707   Johnson, John Henry. "The Exhibition in St. Petersburg, Department for Musical Instruments," *Musical Opinion* 25 (1901/2): 471.

708   Vertkov, K. A. "Sobranie muzykal'nykh instrumentov." In the Institute's *Uchennye Zapiski, T. 2. Sektor Muzyki,* pp. 477-92. Leningrad: 1958.

   Cited from Koltypina*.

709   Seaman, Gerald. "An Unknown Leningrad Museum," *Tempo,* no. 60 (1961-62), pp. 17-18.

710   Buchner, Alexander. "Leningradské hudebnich nástrojů," *Hudnástroje* 8 (1971): 102-4. illus.

   Cited from *RILM**.

LENINGRAD (USSR). [INDUSTRIAL EXPOSITION], 1889

Literature

711   Bormann, Emil. "Klavierinstrumente auf der St. Petersburger Gewerbe-Ausstellung 1899," *NZfM* Bd. 96, Tl. 1 (1900): 89-90, 101-2.

LENINGRAD (USSR). PERVAIĀ VSEROSSIĪSKAIĀ VYSTAVKA MUZYKAL'NYKH INSTRUMENTOV, 1907

712   *Pervaiā vserossiĭskaiā vystavka muzykal'nykh instrumentov, ikh prinodlezhnostei i proizvodstva "Muzykal'nyĭ Mir." Katalog.* S. Peterburg: Tip. Glavn. upr. Udelov, [1907]. [22], 33 pp.

   Cited from Koltypina*; 80 exhibitors.

LEWISBURG, PENNSYLVANIA (USA). BUCKNELL UNIVERSITY. DEPARTMENT OF MUSIC (L85)

713   Hill, Jackson. *A Checklist of Musical Instruments in the Harold E. Cook Collection.* [Lewisburg, Pa.: Bucknell University Press, 1971?]   4 lvs.

   Copy at NBuU-M (BUu).

714   Hill, Jackson. *The Harold E. Cook Collection of Musical Instruments. An Illustrated Catalogue.* Lewisburg, Pa.: Bucknell University Press, [1975]. 67 pp., 32 pls.

LEYDEN (Netherlands). RIJKSMUSEEN VOOR VOLKENKUNDE (J95, BB76)
[N.B.: Formerly **RIJKS ETHNOGRAPHISCH MUSEUM.**]

715   Markwart, Josef and J. D. E. Schmeltz. *Ethnographisch album van het stroomgebied van den Congo.* (Publicatien van's Rijks ethnographisch museum, Ser. II, no. 2.) 's-Gravenhage: Nijhoff, 1904-16. 2 pp., 242 pls.

> Musical instruments (ca. 90 items), pls. 183-98.
> Copies at CU (BEu), IU (Uu), ICN (Cn), DLC (Wc).

716   Farmer, Henry George. *Meccan Musical Instruments* [presented to the Museum by Dr. C. Snouck Hurgronje]. [London: 1929.]

> From the *Journal of the Royal Asiatic Society,* July,
> 1929, pp. [489]-505, pls. VII-VIII.

LIÈGE (France). CONCOURS INTERNATIONAL DE QUATUOR À CORDES, 1954

717   Koenig, Adolf Heinrich. *Le violon et ses ancêstres. Catalogue de l'exposition presentée à l'occasion de Concours.* Liège: 1954. 16 pp.

> Copy at NN (NyP).

718   *Lutherie* [oblong album with photos of instruments exhibited, names of exhibitors, and lists of prizewinners]. [Liège: Impr. DUP, 1954.] [22] pp., mostly photos.

> Copy at NBuU-M (BUu).

LIÈGE (France). EXPOSITION UNIVERSELLE ET INTERNATIONALE, 1905

Literature

719   "Die internationale Weltausstellung in Lüttich 1905," *ZfI* 25 (1904/5): 135, 273, 691, 761, 1065.

General

720   *Catalogue géneral officiel.* . . . Liège: C. Desoer; Bruxelles: A. Mertens et fils, [1905]. 3 vols.

> Instruments in Classe 17 in section for each country
> (e.g. Belgium, vol. 2, pp. 39-40). Copy at ICRL.

LIÈGE (France). MUSÉE DE LA VIE WALLONE

721   Gason, Pierre Marie, Marie Claude Gaspar, Jerome Lejeune and Bernard Tholomier. *Univers du pianoforte. Exposition (organisée par le Festival de Liège dans le cadre des XIVes Nuits de septembre). Musée de la vie wallonne, Liège, septembre 1970.* [Liège: Festival de Liège], 1970. 71 pp., illus., 9 pls., 24 items.

LIEGNITZ (Germany). KUNST- UND KUNSTGEWERBE-AUSSTELLUNG, 1902

Literature

722   "Von der schlessischen Kunst- und Kunstgewerbe-Ausstellung in Liegnitz
        [behandelt die ausgestellten Musikinstrumente] ," *DIbZ*, vol. 3 (1902).
        Cited from *ZiMG*-schau* 4:92.

LIMA (Peru). MUSEO DE LA CULTURA PERUANA. COLLECCION ARTURO JIMÉNEZ BORJA

723   *Instrumentos musicales del Perú.* Lima: 1951. 48 pp., [107] pp. of illus.
        "Sobretiro de la Revista del Museo Nacional, tomos
        XIX y XX," 1951, pp. [37]-190.

Literature

724   "Exposición de instrumentos musicales peruanos," *Cultura peruana* (Lima)
        11 (sept./oct. 1951): [18-19]. illus.

LIMA (Peru). MUSEO NACIONAL DE ANTROPOLOGIA Y ARQUEOLOGIA   (J103)

725   Sas, André. "Ensayo sobre la música nazca," *Boletin Latino-america de musica*
        4 (1938): 221-33. illus.

726   Sas, André. "Ensayo sobre la música nazca," *Revista del museo nacional* (Lima)
        1 (1939): 123-28.

LINZ (Austria). INDUSTRIE- UND GEWERBS-PRODUKTION AUSSTELLUNG, 1847

Literature

727   Mayer, Emil. "Die vierte Industrie- und Gewerbs-Produktion-Ausstellung zu
        Linz im September 1847 in musikalischer Beziehung," *Wiener allgemeine Musik-
        Zeitung* 7 (1847): 533-34, 537, 541-42.

LINZ (Austria). OBERÖSTERREICHISCHES LANDESMUSEUM   (J8, BB60)
[N.B.: Formerly the Museum Francisco-Carolinum. Instrument collection begun in
1835 with 46 instruments from the Benedictine Abbey in Kremsmünster, contributed
by P. Robert Mittermayr.]

728   Wessely, Othmar. *Die Musikinstrumentensammlung des Oberösterreichischer
        Landesmuseum Linz.* (Katalog des Oberösterreichisches Landesmuseums, 9.)

Linz: Druck- und Verlags-Gesellschaft, [1952]. 47 pp.

Copies at NIC (Iu), NjP (PRu), NN (NYp), NNMM.

Literature

729   Wesseley, Othmar. "Die Musikinstrumentensammlung des Oberösterreichischen
Landesmuseums zu Linz," *Instrumentenbau-Zeitschrift* 16 (1962): 396, 398,
400, 402.

General

730   *Führer durch das Museum Francisco-Carolinum.* [Many eds.] 3. Aufl. Linz:
1910.

Contains: "Saal IV, Musikinstrumente," pp. 41-43.

LISBON (Portugal). ASSOCIAÇÃO DOS ARQUEOLOGOS PORTUGUESES. MUSEU

General

731   *Catalogo do Museu da Real Associação dos Architectos Civica e Archeologos
portuguezes.* Lisbon: Typ. universal, 1891. 121 pp.

Lambertini (1924)*: "pièces intéressantes pour l'histoire
des instruments." Copy at DLC (Wc); not examined.

LISBON (Portugal). CONSERVATORIO NACIONAL. MUSEU (J108) [N.B.: The
somewhat difficult history of the collection is set out in the article by Cruz (below). It now
includes the collections of Michel'angelo Lambertini; Antonio Lamas; King D. Louis I; and
the collection which serves as its nucleus, that owned by Alfredo Keil. For catalogs and
articles about the Keil Collection before 1915 when it came to the Museum, see Section II.]

Literature

732   Lambertini, Michel'angelo. *Bibliophilie musicale....* [Lisboa: Typ. do Annuario
commercial], 1918. 302 pp., illus.

733   Lambertini, Michel'angelo. *Bibliophilie musicale....* Éd. abregée. Viseu: Tip.
Andrade & cie, 1924. 247 pp.

A 2,339-item bibliography of works about musical
instruments to complement Lambertini's collection
of instruments which went to the Museu.

734   Cruz, Maria Antonieta de Lima. "O Museu instrumental," *Boletim do Conservatorio
Nacional* 1 (1947): 70-81.

"Aquisicoes [etc., 1942-47]," pp. 78-81.

LISBON (Portugal). CONSERVATORIO NACIONAL. . . . *continued*

Literature

735 [Article, unverified, cited by Jenkins*.] *Boletim do Conservatorio nacional e revista panorama,* no. 13 - IV serie (March 1965), pp. 19-26.

736 Doderer, Gerhard. *Clavicordios portugueses do século XVIII - Portugiesische Klavichorde des 18. Jahrhunderts.* Lisboa: Fundação Calouste Gulbenkian, 1971. 102, 105 pp., illus.

    Discusses 13 from the Conservatorio collection.

LISBON (Portugal). FESTIVAL GULBENKIAN DE MÚSICA, 1961

737 . . . *Exposicão Internacional de Instrumentos Antigos. V. Festival Gulbenkian de Música, Junho 1961, Palacio Foz.* [Catálogo.] Lisboa: 1961. 34 pp., illus.

    Cited from BM*; LV&A says 82 pages.

Literature

738 Ribeiro, Mario de Sampaio. "A exposicão internacional de instrumentos antigos," *Coloquio,* no. 15 (1961), pp. 36-40.

LISBON (Portugal). FUNDAÇÃO CALOUSTE GULBENKIAN

739 Oliveira, Ernesto Veiga de. *Instrumentos musicais populares Portugueses.* Lisboa: Fundação Calouste Gulbenkina, 1966. 239, xxii pp., 439 pls.

    Describes the instruments he collected for the Fundação.
    Copy at NcU (CHHu).

LIVERPOOL (U.K.). INTERNATIONAL EXPOSITION, 1886

Literature

740 "Die Ausstellung zu Liverpool," *ZfI* 6 (1885/86): 400 (exhibitors); 7 (1886/87): 86 (prizes).

LIVERPOOL (U.K.). MERSEYSIDE COUNTY MUSEUMS. DEPARTMENT OF DECORATIVE ARTS. RUSHWORTH & DREAPER COLLECTION [N.B.: Purchased the Rushworth & Dreaper Collection in 1967. All catalogues were issued before then; see Section II.]

LONDON

This section includes literature under the following entries:

American Exhibition, Crystal Palace, Sydenham, 1902
Austrian Exhibition, 1906
British Crafts Centre
British Museum. Department of Egyptian Antiquities
British Museum. Department of Western Asiatic Antiquities
British Music Exhibition, 1913
College of Furniture
Colonial and Indian Exhibition, 1886
Cremona Society
Crystal Palace
Devonshire House
Exhibition of Early Musical Instruments, 1977
Fenton House
Festival of Britain Exhibition, 1951
First Annual Piano Exhibition, 1936
Furniture Trades Exhibition, 1883
German Exhibition, 1891
Great Exhibition of the Works of Industry of All Nations, 1851
Horniman Museum
Imperial Victorian Exhibition, 1897. *See* Victorian Era Exhibition
International Exhibition, 1862
International Exhibition, 1872
International Exhibition, 1884
International Inventions Exhibition, 1885
International Loan Exhibition of Musical Instruments, Crystal Palace, 1900
International Pianoforte and Music Trades Exhibition, 1903
International Pianoforte and Music Trades Exhibition, 1904
International Pianoforte and Music Trades Exhibition, 1905
International Pianoforte and Music Trades Exhibition, 1911
Music Trades Exhibition, 2nd, 1895
Music Trades Exhibition, 3rd, 1897
Music Trades Exhibition, 4th, 1898
Music Trades Exhibition, 5th, 1903. *See* International Pianoforte . . .
Musicians' Company. Loan Exhibition, 1904
Olympia Exhibition, 1913. *See* British Music Exhibition
The Retford Centenary Exhibition
Royal Aquarium
Royal College of Music
Royal Military Exhibition, 1890

Victoria & Albert Museum
Victorian Era Exhibition, 1897
World Exhibition, 1851. *See* Great Exhibition of the Works . . .

LONDON (U.K.). AMERICAN EXHIBITION, CRYSTAL PALACE, SYDENHAM, 1902

Literature

741 "An American Exhibition at the Crystal Palace," *Musical Opinion* 25 (1901/2): 315.

742 "American Musical Instruments at the Crystal Palace," *Musical Opinion* 25 (1901/2): 387.

LONDON (U.K.). AUSTRIAN EXHIBITION, 1906

Literature

743 "The Austrian Exhibition at Earl's Court," *London and Provincial Music Trades Review* 29, no. 346 (1906): 31-32; no. 347 (1906): 31-33. illus.

LONDON (U.K.). BRITISH CRAFTS CENTRE

744 [*Catalogue for the Exhibition of Musical Instruments, May 1974.* London?: n.d.] 10 pp., 92 items.
    Copy at NBuU-M (BUu).

745 Review by H. M. Brown. "Exhibition by Contemporary Craftsmen," *Early Music* 2 (1974): 215-16. illus.

LONDON (U.K.). BRITISH MUSEUM. DEPARTMENT OF EGYPTIAN ANTIQUITIES
(J150, A94)

746 Anderson, Robert D. *Catalogue of Egyptian Antiquities in the British Museum. III. Musical Instruments.* London: the Museum, c1976. viii, 86 pp., illus.
    See Anderson's notes on the catalogue, no. **747**.

747 "Ancient Egyptian Musical Instruments; A Catalogue and Its Problems," *MT* 117 (October 1976): 824.

LONDON (U.K.). BRITISH MUSEUM. DEPARTMENT OF WESTERN ASIATIC ANTIQUITIES

748 Rimmer, Joan. *Ancient Musical Instruments of Western Asia.* London: British Museum, 1969. 51 pp., 26 pls., ca. 178 items.

Duckles* 3:1599. Appendices by Terence Mitchell.

LONDON (U.K.). BRITISH MUSIC EXHIBITION, 1913

749 . . . *Official Catalogue of the British Music Exhibition, Olympia.* London: 1913. ? pp., illus.

Cited from LV&A*; copies in the U.S. not located.

Literature

750 "The British Music Exhibition at Olympia, September 6th-20th. List of Prize Winners," *Organist and Choirmaster* 21 (1913): 240-41.

On page 64 in the same issue, the show is called, "the greatest exhibition of Art and Manufacture ever held."

751 "The British Music Exhibition, Olympia, September 6-20," *MT* 54 (1913): 663, 758. Notes 63 firms exhibiting.

752 "Die allbritische Musik-Ausstellung in der Olympia-Halle zu London," *ZfI* 34 (1913/ 14): 13-14.

LONDON (U.K.). COLLEGE OF FURNITURE

Literature

753 Thomson, J. M. "High Standards at the London College of Furniture [exhibits of students' work]," *Early Music* 3 (1975): 191.

LONDON (U.K.). COLONIAL AND INDIAN EXHIBITION, 1886

Literature

754 "Die Colonial- und Indische-Ausstellung in London," *ZfI* 6 (1885/86): 386, 388.

General

755 *Official Catalogue.* London: Wm. Clowes & Sons, 1886. 580 pp.

Copies at PPF (PHf), PPL (PHlc).

LONDON (U.K.). CREMONA SOCIETY

756   . . . *Exhibition of violes d'amour, Books and Sundries Relating to That Instrument on the Occasion of Reading a Paper on the viole d'amour by G. Carnaby Harrower, Esq., Written and Musically Illustrated by Prof. Carli Zoelker.* London: 1889.

> Cited by Fryklund in *Svensk Tidskrift for Musikforskning* 3 (1921): 36; not located.

LONDON (U.K.). CRYSTAL PALACE   [N.B.: Various exhibitions held at this location. *See* LONDON, INTERNATIONAL LOAN EXHIBITION OF MUSICAL INSTRUMENTS, 1900 *and* VICTORIAN ERA EXHIBITION, 1897.]

LONDON (U.K.). DEVONSHIRE HOUSE

757   Fletcher, Benton. "Early Music at Devonshire House," *The Listener* (October 6, 1938), pp. 713-14.

> Collection now reassembled at Hampstead, Trinity College of Music, Fenton House; later catalogues under LONDON, FENTON HOUSE, q.v.

LONDON (U.K.). EXHIBITION OF EARLY MUSICAL INSTRUMENTS, 1977

758   Sotheby & Co. *Good Musical Instruments, Comprising Violins and Violas . . . Woodwind Instruments . . . Stringed Instruments . . . Keyboard, Brasswind and Free Reed Instruments Which Will Be Sold by Auction by. . . . At the London Exhibition of Early Musical Instruments, The New Horticultural Hall . . . Saturday, the 17th September, 1977.* [London: 1977.]   28 pp., illus., 115 lots.

> Copy at NBuU-M (BUu).

Literature

759   Schott, Howard. "Third London Exhibition of Early Musical Instruments," *Early Music* 6, no. 1 (1978): 133.

LONDON (U.K.). FENTON HOUSE, HAMPSTEAD   (J150, BB23)

760   Russell, Raymond. *The Musical Instruments in Fenton House, Hampstead, a Property of the National Trust.* London: 1953.

> Cited from *MGG;* copies in the U.S. not located.

761   Russell, Raymond. *The Benton Fletcher Collection of Early English Musical Instruments at Fenton House.* London: 1955.

>   *MGG* says, "Autotypie beim Museum." Copies in the U.S. not located.

762   Russell, Raymond. *Catalogue of the Benton Fletcher Collection of Early Keyboard Instruments at Fenton House, Hampstead.* London: Country Life Ltd., for the National Trust, 1957. 26 pp., illus.

>   Duckles 3:1600. Copy at NN (NYp).

763   Russell, Raymond. *A Catalogue of Early Keyboard Instruments: The Benton Fletcher Collection.* Photographs by John Bethell. [London]: The National Trust, 1976. 21 pp., [4] pp., pls.

LONDON (U.K.). FESTIVAL OF BRITAIN EXHIBITION, 1951

764   Galpin Society. *British Musical Instruments; An Exhibition, August 7-30, 1951. The Galpin Society, by Arrangement with the Arts Council of Great Britain.* [London]: The Society, [1951?]. 35 pp., illus., 616 items.

>   Duckles* 3:1601.

Literature

765   "Music Lover's Diary [interesting exhibits in the Festival of Britain]," *Music Parade* 2 (1951): 1-4. illus.

766   "Antique Instruments at the Festival of Britain: the Galpin Society," *Violins* 12 (1951): 196-97.

767   Winternitz, Emanuel. "British Musical Instruments; An Exhibit in London," *MLAN* 9 (1952): 395-98.

LONDON (U.K.). FIRST ANNUAL PIANO EXHIBITION, 1936

768   *The First Annual Piano Exhibition Held at Dorland Hall, September 12th to 26th, 1936, under the Direction of J. Skinner.* London: 1936. 56 pp., illus.

>   Cited from LV&A*; copies in the U.S. not located.

LONDON (U.K.). FURNITURE TRADES EXHIBITION, 1883

Literature

769   "Musikalische Instrumente auf der 'Furniture Exhibition' in der Agricultural Hall," *ZfI* 3 (1882/83): 268-270.

LONDON (U.K.). FURNITURE TRADES EXHIBITION, 1883 *continued*

Literature

770　"Die Musikinstrumente in der Ausstellung von Hausgeräthen und der landwirt-schaftlichen Halle zu London," *ZfI* 2 (1881/82): 259, 261.

General

771　*Ye Catalogue of ye Furniture Trades' Exhibition, Held in . . . 1883.* [London]: C. Messent & Son, 1883. 229 pp.

　　　　　Cited from BM*.

LONDON (U.K.). GALPIN SOCIETY. *See under* LONDON (U.K.). FESTIVAL OF BRITAIN EXHIBITION, 1951

LONDON (U.K.). GERMAN EXHIBITION, 1891

Literature

772　"Deutsch-nationale Ausstellung zu London," *ZfI* 11 (1890/91): 345, 389-91, 477 (prizes).

773　"Musikinstrumente auf der deutschen Ausstellung in London," *ZfI* 11 (1890/91): 429-31.

774　"The German Exhibition [enumeration of instruments on view]," *Musical Opinion & Music Trades Review,* vol. 15 (July 1, 1891).

LONDON (U.K.). GREAT EXHIBITION OF THE WORKS OF INDUSTRY OF ALL NATIONS, 1851　[N.B.: General comprehensive works which are normally placed in a section labelled *"General"*: are here placed in a primary position because they offer the best catalogues of materials shown in this exhibition.]

775　. . . *Official Descriptive and Illustrated Catalogue.* London: Spicer Bros., 1851. 3 vols.

　　　　　[Musical Instruments, Class 10], vol. 1, Section II, pp. 464-74, item nos. 468-562, with illus.

776　. . . *Reports by the Juries on the Subjects in the Thirty Classes.* London: Spicer Bros., 1852. 4 vols.

　　　　　"Class Xa. Report on Musical Instruments &c. H. R. Bishop, Reporter," vol. 3, pp. 324-35, " . . . a faithful and impartial register of the state of musical instruments and their manu-

facture in the year 1851." Carse (no. **789**, below) notes
that a London newspaper said of [this] report, "a more
miserably weak and worthless document never appeared
on a great public occasion."

777 Pole, William. *Musical Instruments in the Great Industrial Exhibition of 1851.*
London: Privately printed, 1851. 99 pp.

> Reprinted, with additions, from *Newton's London Journal
> of Arts.* Copy at NN (NYp).

778 France. Commission française sur l'industrie des nations, London, 1851.
Instruments de musique. (Rapport: X^e jury, 1re subdivision.) Par Hector
Berlioz. (Exposition universelle de 1851. Travaux de la Commission française
sur l'industrie des nations, Tome III, 2^e partie.) Paris: Impr. Imper., 1855.

> Cited from BN*; not located.

779 Zollverein. *Amtlicher Bericht über die Industrie . . . und Kunst-Ausstellung
zu London im Jahre 1851.* 3 vols. Berlin: Verlag der Deckerschen ober-
Hofbuchdr., 1852-53.

> "Musikalische Instrumente," vol. 1, pp. 845-99;
> "Mitglieder der Unterjury X.a," and "Preisvertheilung,"
> pp. 934-39. Copy at DLC (Wc).

780 Streicher, J. B. "Klavierbau." In *Mittheilungen über die Industrie-Ausstellung
aller Völker (London, 1851). Aus den Berichten der von der österreichischen
Regierung delegierten Sachverständigen,* pp. 312-56. Wien: 1853.

> Citation furnished by Österr. Nationalbibliothek;
> no U.S. locations.

781 [Cronham, J. P. and J. E. Bäckstrom.] *Berättelser om musik och musikalska
instrumenter vid verldsexpositionen i London aar 1851.* Stockholm: 1851. 15 pp.

> Cited from DaSML*, no. 5142; not located.

Literature

782 Érard, firm. *London Exhibition 1851. Erard's Piano-forte.* [Whitefriars:
Bradbury and Evans, 1851?] 8 pp., pls.

> Copy at IaU (IOu).

783 Cazalet, W[illiam Wahab]. *On the Musical Department of the Late Exhibition.
Read before the Society of Arts, May, 1852.* [n.p.: 1852?] 16 pp.

> Copies at MB (Bp), NN (NYp).

LONDON (U.K.). GREAT EXHIBITION OF THE WORKS ... *continued*

Literature

784 Fischhof, Joseph. *Versuch einer Geschichte des Klavierbaues. Mit besonderem Hinblicke auf die Londoner grösser Industrie-Ausstellung.* Wien: Wallishausser, 1853. 142 pp.

> Cited from DBV; not examined.

785 Fétis, F. J. "Ueber die Instrumente auf der Londonder Ausstellung," *Niederrheinische Musik-Zeitung* 1 (1853): 226f; 3 (1855): ?; unable to verify.

786 "The Exhibition of 1851 [exhibitors]," *London and Provincial Music Trades Review* 28, no. 329 (December 1904): 25-29.

787 Mathew, A. G. "Under Glass," *Musical Opinion* 70 (1947): 401; 71 (1947): 7-8.

788 King, George J. S. "Music and the Great Exhibition," *Tempo*, no. 18 (1950/51), pp. 6-11. illus.

789 Carse, Adam. "Music in the 1851 Exhibition," *Monthly Musical Record* 81 (1951): 171-75.

790 Shillitoe, E. J. "Violin Making at the Great Exhibitions [VI, London, 1851]," *The Strad* 90 (1979): 125-28.

LONDON (U.K.). HORNIMAN MUSEUM (J150, A95, BB24) [N.B.: Frederick J. Horniman collection given to London in 1901. Other collections added: ethnic instruments from the Victoria and Albert Museum (1870); Adam Carse collection (1947); Percy A. Bull collection (1948).]

791 ... *A List of the Instruments Included in the Adam Carse Collection of Musical Wind Instruments, with an Introduction Prepared by Mr. Carse.* London: London County Council, 1947. 16 pp., brief list of 320 items.

> Copy at DLC (Wc).

792 Carse, Adam. "The Adam Carse Collection of Wind Instruments," *GSJ*, no. 2 (March 1949), pp. 3-9.

793 *The Adam Carse Collection of Old Musical Wind Instruments.* London: London County Council, [1951]. 88 pp., drawings.

> Introduction by Adam Carse; illus. by Henry Trivick.
> Duckles* 3:1602. Copy at DLC (Wc).

794   Jenkins, Jean. *Musical Instruments; [A Handbook to the Collection]*. London: London County Council, 1958. 109 pp., illus.

>   Copy at DLC (Wc).

795   Jenkins, Jean. *Musical Instruments; [A Handbook to the Collection]*. 2nd ed. London: Inner London Education Authority, 1970. 104 pp., 32 pls., 160 instruments illus.

>   Duckles* 3:1603. Jenkins* notes a 3rd ed., 1977; not examined.

796   Ridley, Edward Alexander Keane. *Wind Instruments of European Art Music.* London: Inner London Education Authority, c1974. 107 pp., 10 lvs., pls., 92 illus.

>   "The Adam Carse Collection," pp. 65-70 (334 items); "Catalogue," pp. 71-101. Copy at NBuU-M (BUu).

797   Montagu, Jeremy. "Notes on the Horniman Museum's Handbook: Wind Instruments of European Art Music, 1974," *FoMRHI Bulletin* (October 1976), Communication no. 43.

798   Jenkins, Jean and Poul Rovsing Olsen. *Music and Musical Instruments in the World of Islam* [catalogue of an exhibition, April-October, 1976]. London: World of Islam Festival Publishing Co., Ltd., 1976. iv, 100 pp., [8] pp., pls.

Literature

799   "African Music in London (Horniman's Museum)," *African Music* 2 (1961): 81-82.

800   E., L. "Horniman Museum," *Music and Musicians* 20, no. 11 (July 1972): 14-15.

801   [Description of current projects], *IAMIC Newsletter* 1 (1973): 18-19.

LONDON (U.K.). IMPERIAL VICTORIAN EXHIBITION, 1897. *See* **LONDON (U. K.). VICTORIAN ERA EXHIBITION, 1897**

LONDON (U.K.). INTERNATIONAL EXHIBITION, 1862

802   . . . *The Illustrated Catalogue of the Industrial Departments. British Division - Vol. II.* [London: For his Majesty's Commission, 1862.]

>   "Class XVI, Musical Instruments [items 3360-3454]," pp. 87-116, illus. Copy at DLC (Wc).

LONDON (U.K.). INTERNATIONAL EXHIBITION, 1862 *continued*

803 Zollverein. *Amtlicher Bericht über die Industrie- und Kunst-Ausstellung zu London im Jahre 1862.* Berlin: Verlag der kgl. Geheimen Ober-Hofbuchdruckerei, 1865.

> "16. Klasse. Musikalische Instrumente [von] Ernst Pauer," pp. 55-125. Copy at DLC (Wc).

Literature

804 "The Exhibition of 1862 [list of makers from the catalogue]," *London and Provincial Music Trades Review* 28, no. 328 (November 1904): 13-15.

805 Pohl, Carl Ferdinand. *Londoner Industrie-Ausstellung. Zur Geschichte der Glas-Harmonika.* Wien: 1862.

> Cited from BM*; not located.

806 Pohl, Carl Ferdinand. *International Exhibition of 1862. Cursory Notices on the Origin and History of the Glass Harmonica.* London: Potter and Galpin, 1862. 16 pp.

> Copy at NN (NYp).

807 Pontécoulant, Louis Adolph le Doulcet, marquis de. *Douze jours à Londres. Voyage d'un mélomane à travers l'exposition universelle.* Paris: F. Henry, 1862. vi, 328 pp.

> Cited from BN*.

808 Romero y Andia, Antonio. *Memoria sobre los instramentas de música, presentados en la esposicion internacional do Londres.* Madrid: Imprenta nacional, 1864. 29 pp., illus.

> Copy at DLC (Wc).

809 Shillitoe, E. J. "Violin Making at the Great Exhibitions [VIII, 1862]," *The Strad* 90 (1979): 197-200.

General

810 France. Commission ouvrière, Exposition universelle de Londres, 1862. *Rapports des Délégués de la Commission . . . [pour les instruments de musique à vent, cuivre et bois].* Paris: M. Chabaud, 1862-64. 888 pp.

> Cited from Lambertini* (1924); not located.

811 Broadwood and Sons, firm. *List of Pianofortes, and of Various Samples and Models . . . Exhibited . . . With an Historical Introduction.* London: Printed by W. S. Johnson and Co., 1862. 56 pp., 7 pls.

> Cited from BM* and Fétis*, no. 4071.

812   Chappell and Co., firm. *Chappell and Co.'s Illustrated Catalogue of Music and Musical Instruments for 1862.* London: Chappell and Co., [1862]. 32 pp.

> Cited from BM*; not located.

813   Collard and Collard, firm. *A List of Pianofortes and Models of Actions . . . Exhibited by Them at the International Exhibition, South Kensington.* London: 1862. 8 pp., 11 pls.

> Cited from Fétis*, no. 4072.

814   Rudall, Rose, Carte, and Co., firm. *A Description of the Musical Instruments Manufactured by . . . and Exhibited by Them at the International Exhibition, 1862.* London: 1862.

> Cited from Fétis*, no. 4030; not in BM*.

815   *Illustrirter Katalog der Londoner Industrie-Ausstellung von 1862.* Leipzig: Brockhaus, 1862-64. 2 vols.

> Cited from Kay* 15/16; not located.

LONDON (U.K.). INTERNATIONAL EXHIBITION, 1872

816   "Musical Instruments at the International Exhibition," *Journal of Society of Arts* 20 (1872): 889-94.

> Article says no official catalogue was issued for the 1872 "annual display."

LONDON (U.K.). INTERNATIONAL EXHIBITION, 1884

Literature

817   "Eine internationale Ausstellung im Crystallpalast zu London," *ZfI* 4 (1883/84): 43, 121, 130, 184, 269 (exhibitors, from *London and Provincial Music Trades Review*), 405 (reprinted from *Musical Opinion*).

818   "Aussteller-Liste [and notes on exhibits]," *ZfI* (1883/84): 294-95 (translated from May 1884 *Musical Opinion*).

819   "Die deutschen Prämiirungen auf der internationalen Ausstellung im Krystallpalast," *ZfI* 4 (1883/84): 403-4; 5 (1884/85): 226.

LONDON (U.K.). INTERNATIONAL INVENTIONS EXHIBITION, 1885 [N.B.: Some instruments from the Brussels, Conservatoire Royal and some from the Royal College of Music (Tagore collection) were shown.]

820 *Guide to the Loan Collection and List of Musical Instruments, Manuscripts, Books, Paintings, and Engravings, Exhibited in the Gallery and Lower Rooms of the Albert Hall.* [London] : William Clowes and Sons, Ltd., 1885. vi, 136 pp.

> Preface signed: A. J. Hipkins. The collection was formed and catalogue edited by Hipkins, according to Marr*.
> Second and third editions identical dates and collations.
> Copy at CtY (NHu).

821 Dale, William. *Brief Description of Spinets, Virginals, Harpsichords, Clavichords, and Pianos Shown in the Loan Collection of the . . . Exhibition, 1885.* [London: Fargues & Co., 188-.] 37 pp.

> Copy at MH (CAc).

Literature

822 B., Ch. "L'incendie de South Kensington," *Echo musical* 17 (1885): 145-46.

> Regarding instruments from the Brussels Conservatoire at the exhibition.

823 C[houquet?] , G[ustave?]. "Exposition de Londres," *Le Ménestrel* 51 (1884/85): 364-65.

824 Hueffer, Francis. "La musique en Angleterre: La musique à l'exposition de South-Kensington," *Le Ménestrel* 51 (1884/85): 348-50.

825 "Die South Kensington Ausstelling," *ZfI* 5 (1884/85): 156, 158, 166-72 and 209-10 (exhibitors), 370 (jury).

826 "Die internationale Erfindung- und Musik-Ausstelling in London 1885," *ZfI* 5 (1884/85): 328, 330, 349-50, 352, 402, 404; 6 (1885/86): 53-54 and 56 (prizes).

827 [Long note about contents and organizations] , *MT* 25 (1884): 529.

828 *Historical Notes on Queen Elizabeth's Virginal, on Exhibition at the Historic Musical Loan Collection.* London: [1885] . 20 pp., illus.

> Cited from LV&A*.

829 "Music at the Inventions Exhibition, 1885," *Art Journal* (1885), pp. 152-56, 220-32, 305-8, 349-52. illus.

830 Broadwood, John, & Sons, firm. [List of . . . exhibits.] London: 1885. 26 lvs.

> Cited from LV&A*.

LONDON (U.K.). INTERNATIONAL LOAN EXHIBITION OF MUSICAL INSTRUMENTS, CRYSTAL PALACE, 1900
[N.B.: Included in the show were items from the private collections of F. W. Galpin, F. Erckmann, Henry Watson, William Cummings, and Colonel Shaw-Hellier. See catalogues of some in Section II.]

831   *Musical Instruments and Memorials of Musicians. Being the Catalogue of the International Loan Exhibition, Crystal Palace, from July Till Nov. 1900. Also Abstracts of Lectures Delivered by S. F. Jacques, W. H. Cummings, and the Rev. F. W. Galpin.* London: Published at the Office of the "Musical News," 1900. 94 pp.

> Cited from Lütg*, *JbP** (1900) and elsewhere; not located.

832   *. . . Official Catalogue. . . .* Sydenham: The Crystal Palace, 1900. 55 pp.

> Cited from BM*. NNMM has copy of 64, 2 pp. (with an introduction by F. W. Galpin) called "second ed."

Literature

833   "The Crystal Palace International Loan Exhibition of Musical Instruments," *Organist and Choirmaster* 8, no. 88 (1900): 81-83.

834   Smith, Herman. "Musical Legacies: The Loan Exhibition at the Crystal Palace," *Musical Opinion* 24 (1900/1901): 58-59, 131-32.

835   Maclean, Charles. [Comments about some of the items in the exhibition], *ZiMG* 2 (1900/1901): 249.

836   ["Notice"], *MT* 41 (1900): 527.

837   "John Broadwood and Son's Exhibition," *Piano, Organ and Music Trades Journal,* vol. 17, no. 203 (1901).

> Cited from *ZiMG*-schau* 2 (1900/1901): 253.

838   "Historical Musical Instruments; A Grand Show at the Crystal Palace," *Piano, Organ and Music Trades Journal,* no. 217 (1901).

> Cited from *ZiMG*-schau* 2 (1900/1901): 31.

LONDON (U.K.). INTERNATIONAL PIANOFORTE AND MUSIC TRADES EXHIBITION, 1903

Literature

839   "Crystal Palace Exhibition. Some of the Exhibits; A Preliminary Description," *London and Provincial Music Trades Review* 26, no. 311 (June 1903): 19-25; 312 (July 1903): 17-31. illus.

840   "Musical Instrument Exhibition at the Crystal Palace," *London and Provincial Music Trades Review,* vol. 26, no. 306 (January 1903).

LONDON (U.K.). INTERNATIONAL PIANOFORTE AND MUSIC TRADES EXHIBITION, 1904

Literature

841   "Agricultural Hall Exhibition. Description of Exhibits," *London and Provincial Music Trades Review* 28, no. 325 (August 1904): 29-33. illus.

LONDON (U.K.). INTERNATIONAL PIANOFORTE AND MUSIC TRADES EXHIBITION, 1905

Literature

842   "Agricultural Hall Exhibition; Description of Exhibits," *London and Provincial Music Trades Review* 29, no. 337 (August 1905): 23-31; no. 338 (September 1905): 31-36.

LONDON (U.K.). INTERNATIONAL PIANOFORTE AND MUSIC TRADES EXHIBITION, 1911

Literature

843   [Brief report], *ZfI* 31 (1910/11): 559, 1323, 1325.

LONDON (U.K.). MUSIC TRADES EXHIBITION, 2nd, 1895

Literature

844   "The Chiel." "The Music Trades Exhibition," *Musical Opinion and Music Trades Review* 18 (1895): 665-69. illus.

845   "Eine musikindustrielle Ausstellung in London 1895," *ZfI* 15 (1894/95): 270-71, 425-26, 454, 465, 480-81.

846   "In eigener Sache," *ZfI* 16 (1895/96): 853-54, 863-65.

847   "Nochmals Mr. Benjamin," *ZfI* 17 (1896/97): 368-69.

848   "De aanstaande internationale tentoonstelling van muziekinstrumenten te London," *Weekhlad voor Muziek* 2 (1895): 97-98.

LONDON (U.K.). MUSIC TRADES EXHIBITION, 3rd, 1897

Literature

849   "Music Trades Exhibition," *Musical Opinion* 20 (1896/97): 636-37, 704, 775-76.

850   "International Music Trades Exhibition," *MT* 38 (1897): 546.

LONDON (U.K.). MUSIC TRADES EXHIBITION, 4th, 1898

Literature

851   "Trade Exhibition at Agricultural Hall," *Musical Opinion* 21 (1897/98): 557.

LONDON (U.K.). MUSIC TRADES EXHIBITION, 5th, 1903. *See* INTERNATIONAL PIANOFORTE AND MUSIC TRADES EXHIBITION, 1903

LONDON (U.K.). MUSICIANS' COMPANY. LOAN EXHIBITION, 1904

852   *. . . A Special Loan Exhibition of Musical Instruments, Manuscripts, Books, Portraits, and Other Mementoes of Music and Musicians, Formed to Commemorate the Tercentenary of the Granting of a Charter to the Worshipful Company of Musicians in 1604.* [London: J. Truscott and Son, Ltd., 1904.] xxv, 159 pp.
Copy at DLC (Wc).

853   *An Illustrated Catalogue of the Music Loan Exhibition Held . . . by the Worshipful Company of Musicians of Fishmongers' Hall, June and July 1904.* London: Novello and Company, Ltd., 1909. 5 pp., xxiii, 353 pp., illus.
"Musical Instruments," pp. 165-73. Copy at NBuU-M (BUu).

854   *English Music (1604 to 1904) Being the Lectures Given at the Music Loan Exhibition. . . .* London: Scott Publ. Co., Ltd.; New York: C. Scribner's Sons, 1906. 539 pp., illus. drawn from the exhibition.
Copy at NBuU-M (BUu).

Literature

855   Dotted Crochet. "The Tercentenary Exhibition of the Musicians' Company," *MT* 45 (1904): 380, 429-35, 501-12, 730. illus.

856   "Two Important Books on Music: Catalogue of the Musicians' Company Exhibition," *MT* 50 (1909): 574-75.

857   Krummel, Donald W. "An Edwardian Gentlemen's Music Exhibition," *Music Library Association Notes,* 2nd ser., 32 (1976): 711-18.

LONDON (U.K.). OLYMPIA EXHIBITION. *See* **BRITISH MUSIC EXHIBITION**

LONDON (U.K.). THE RETFORD CENTENARY EXHIBITION

858   *The Retford Centenary Exhibition.* Foreword by M[alcolm] R. S[adler].
London: Ealing Strings, 1975. 63 pp., 100 pls.

> Bows made by Retford and others from 1780 to 1966.
> Collection went to Oxford, Faculty of Music; see *Consort*,
> no. 29 (1973), p. 4.

LONDON (U.K.). ROYAL AQUARIUM

859   *. . . First Musical Art Exhibition, September 13th to October 8th. The Catalogue
Compiled and Arranged by Mr. E. A. Du Plat.* London: R. E. King, [1892?]. 64 pp.

> Copy at MiU (AAu). See note in *MT* 33 (1892): 602.

LONDON (U.K.). ROYAL COLLEGE OF MUSIC (J151, A95, BB26) [N.B.: Includes
the collections of Tagore (1884); King Edward VII (1886); A. J. Hipkins (1903); Charles
R. Day; Sir George Donaldson (1894); E. A. K. Ridley (1968). Catalogues of some of these
in Section II.]

860   *Catalogue of the Musical Instruments and Objects Forming the Donaldson
Collection Presented to . . . the Royal College . . . 1894.* London: Waterlow
for the author, [1898-99]. 53 (3 col.) pls.

> Cited from LV&A*. Boalch* says "not reliable".

861   *. . . Catalog of Historical Musical Instruments, Paintings, Sculpture and Drawings.*
[London: Royal College, 1952.] 16 pp.

> Duckles* 3:1604; foreword by George Dyson.
> "Based on Karl Geiringer's notes," according to
> Wells article, below.

Literature

862   "The Royal College of Music a Londra," *Ars et Labor* 61 (1906): 792-94. illus.

863   Colson, Percy. "Early Musical Instruments in the Donaldson Collection,"
Connoisseur 96 (1935): 341-44; 97 (1936): 262-66. Many illus.

864   Wells, E. "The RCM Collection of Instruments," *Royal College of Music
Magazine* 63 (1967): 83-87.

865   Wells, Elizabeth. "The Opening of the Museum of Historical Instruments," *Royal College of Music Magazine* 66 (1970): 46-48. illus.

866   "The Museum of Instruments," *Royal College of Music Magazine* 68 (1972): 51.

867   Monk, Christopher. "Where the Wind Blows [exhibition of early musical instruments, Royal College of Music]," *Early Music* 2 (1974): 31. illus.

868   Baines, Francis. "Exhibition of Early Music [i.e., musical instruments]," *Music Teacher and Piano Student* 54 (November 1975): 13.

>   An exhibition organized by R. Wood of the Early Music Shop in London.

869   Wells, Elizabeth. "The R. C. M. Collection of Instruments," *Royal College of Music Magazine* 72 (1976): 39-43.

LONDON (U.K.). ROYAL FESTIVAL HALL EXHIBITION, 1957

870   *"Private Musicke" Arranged by the Galpin Society, 17 Sept. - 3 Nov. 1957.* London: 1957. 10 pp.

LONDON (U.K.). ROYAL MILITARY EXHIBITION, 1890

871   Day, Charles Russell. *A Descriptive Catalogue of the Musical Instruments Recently Exhibited at the Royal Military Exhibition, London, 1890. Issued under the Orders of Colonel Shaw-Hellier, and Compiled by Captain C. R. Day.* London: Eyre & Spottiswoode, 1891. ix, 262 pp., illus., 457 items.

>   Duckles* 3:1605. Copies at MiU (AAu), ViU (CHu), DLC (Wc).

General

872   . . . *Official Catalogue and Guide.* [Preface signed F. C.] London: W. Clowes & Sons, [1890]. xxii, 196 pp.; pp. 95-114, the 458 instruments on exhibit.

>   According to Marr*; not examined.

LONDON (U.K.). VICTORIA & ALBERT MUSEUM   (J152, A94, BB27)   [N.B.:
Nucleus of musical instrument collections purchased from the **GREAT EXHIBITION OF 1851**, q.v. Collections were at Marlborough House 1852-57, as the Museum of

LONDON (U.K.). VICTORIA & ALBERT MUSEUM *continued*

Manufactures, later the Museum of Ornamental Art. Moved in 1857 to the South
Kensington Museum. Since 1900 as Victoria & Albert Museum.]

873   Arundel Society, London. *Musical Instruments in the South Kensington
      Society,* [by Carl Engel] . (Arundel Society. Examples of Art Workmanship
      of Various Ages and Countries.) London: 1869. 8 pp., 20 pls.

> Cited from Russell*, LV&A*, and BM*; not examined.

874   Engel, Carl. *A Descriptive Catalogue of the Musical Instruments in the South
      Kensington Museum.* London: Printed by G. E. Eyre and W. Spottiswoode,
      1870. 2, 82 pp., 18 illus., 60 items.

> Copy at DLC (Wc).

875   Rühlmann, Julius. "Die Gründung eines Instrumenten-Museum; Worte zur
      Anregung," *MfM* 5 (1873): 4-10.

> Notes on instruments in the Museum, including those
> displayed at the Great Exhibition of 1851 and in
> Engel's 1870 catalogue (above), as well as comments
> on the Contarini-Correr collection.

876   Engel, Carl. *A Descriptive Catalogue of the Musical Instruments in the South
      Kensington Museum, Preceded by an Essay on the History of Musical Instruments.*
      2nd ed. London: G. E. Eyre and W. Spottiswoode, 1874. Reprint ed. [N.Y.] :
      B. Blom, [1971] . viii, 402 pp., 6 photos.

> Includes 107 instruments from Engel's private collection
> and 30 from the Donaldson collection now in the Royal
> College of Music. Copies at ICN (Cn), IU (Uu), MiU (AAu),
> NN (NYp), OCl (CLp).

877   [Engel, Carl.] *Catalogue of the Special Exhibition of Ancient Musical Instru-
      ments. . . .* London: Printed by J. Strangeways, 1872. xi, 48 pp., 16 mounted
      photos, 518 items.

> Preface signed: Carl Engel. Forty-four instruments "from
> Windsor Castle" are listed under no. 543. Valdrighi, in the list
> of his instrument collection in his *Nomocheliurgografia* of
> 1884 ("Corollarii IV. Collezione Valdrighi") marks with an
> asterisk those shown at this exhibition. It was a loan exhibition,
> however, with many participants.

878   [Engel, Carl.] *Catalogue of the Special Exhibition of Ancient Musical Instru-
      ments, 1872.* Edited with an introduction by C. E. London: South Kensington
      Museum, [1873] . ? pp., 9 pls., 204 items.

Cited from BM*, Lütg*, none of whom supply
collation; not located. Pages [v-vi], 6-18 were
reprinted as Section I of Dissmore's *Violin Gallery,*
1895 (see no. **881** below).

879 [Engel, Carl?] *Some Account of the Special Exhibition, Being Appendix 2 to
the Catalogue.* . . . London: 1874.

Found only in Heyer*; unable to verify.

880 Engel, Carl. *Musical Instruments.* (South Kensington Museum, Art Handbook,
no. 5.) London: Chapman and Hall, [1875]; New York: Scribner, Welford &
Armstrong, 1876. vii, 128 pp., illus.

Copies at MB (Bp), NN (NYp).

881 Dissmore, George A. *The Violin Gallery. Comprising: Sect. I. South Kensington
Special Exhibition, 1872* . . . [etc.]. Des Moines, Ia.: 1895.

Section I is a reprint of pages [v-vi], 6-18, with the
original plates of Engel's 1872 *Catalogue of the Special
Exhibition* (see no. **878** above). Copy at DLC (Wc).

882 [Engel, Carl?] *Music Instruments.* (South Kensington Museum, Art Handbooks,
edited by W. Maskell.) London: Chapman and Hall, 1880.

Cited from EngCat*; not located.

883 Engel, Carl. *Musical Instruments. With Seventy-eight Illustrations.* Rev. ed.
(Victoria and Albert Museum, South Kensington, Board of Education.) London:
H.M.S.O., 1908. x, 146 pp., 52 pls.

Copies at MB (Bp), NN (NYp). Mummery antiquariat
catalogue N.S.2, no. 2576 says 78 plates.

884 . . . *Photographs of Objects in the Museum: List. Part 8* . . . *Sect. G. Musical
Instruments.* London: H.M.S.O., [1930].

Cited from *JbP* * (1930); not located. Compare
with the following.

885 *A Picture Book of Keyboard Musical Instruments.* (Victoria & Albert Museum,
South Kensington, Picture books, [no. 37].) London: South Kensington Museum,
[1929]. [4] pp., 20 pls.

Copy at NNMM.

886 Russell, Raymond. *Early Keyboard Instruments.* (Victoria & Albert Museum,
Small picture book, no. 48.) London: H.M.S.O., 1959. [32] pp.

Copy at NPV (POvc).

LONDON (U.K.). VICTORIA & ALBERT MUSEUM   *continued*

887   . . . *Musical Instruments As Works of Art.* (Victoria & Albert Museum, Large special miscellaneous publications, no. 10.) London: H.M.S.O., 1968. [101] pp. of illus.

> Duckles* 3:1608. Copy at DLC (Wc).

888   Russell, Raymond and Anthony Baines. *Catalogue of Musical Instruments [in the] Victoria and Albert Museum.* London: H.M.S.O., 1968. 3 vols., pls., illus.

> Vol. 1: Keyboard instruments, by R. Russell.
> Vol. 2: Non-keyboard instruments, by A. Baines
> [N.B.: strings and winds only]. Vol. 3: Additional
> and detailed photographs of the collection [N.B.:
> vol. 3 not examined; cited from antiquarian's
> catalogue]. Duckles 3:1607 (vols. 1, 2 only).
> See also no. **889**.

889   Dawes, Frank. "Musical Instruments at the V & A," *MT* 109 (October 1968): 915-18. illus.

> Comments on the exhibition and a review of the
> catalogue (vols. 1, 2 only).

[N.B.: The following entries all refer to the traveling exhibition organized by the Circulation Department of the V & A Museum, catalogued by Genevieve Thibault (and others). It was subsequently shown at the Horniman Museum, in Edinburgh, and elsewhere.]

890   Thibault, Genevieve. *Eighteenth Century Musical Instruments, France and Britain. Les instruments de musique au XVIIIe Siècle, France et Grande-Bretagne [catalogue of an exhibition].* [Exhibition designed and catalogue written by] G. Thibault (Mme de Chambure), Jean Jenkins, Josiane Bran-Ricci. [Exhibition organized by the Circulation Department.] London: Victoria and Albert Museum, 1973. xxx, 229 pp., illus., over 150 pls., 126 items.

Literature (about the 1973 exhibition)

891   "Victoria and Albert Museum," *The Strad* 84 (1974): 677.

892   Thomson, J. M. "Music in the 18th Century [at the Horniman Museum]," *Recorder & Music Magazine* 4 (1973): 241-42.

893   Brown, Howard Mayer. "Exceptional Exhibition: 18th Century Musical Instruments in France and Britain," *Early Music* 2 (1974): 75-76. illus.

894   Lewin, R. "South Kensington saga (special exhibition of 18th century French and English instruments)," *The Strad* 84 (1974): 717.

895   Remnant, M. "18th-Century Musical Instruments: A French and British Exhibition," *MT* 115 (January 1974): 31.

896   Godwin, Sheila M. "A Note on the Exhibition of Eighteenth Century Musical Instruments of France and Germany [*sic*]," *Consort*, no. 30 (1974), p. 82.

897   Montagu, Jeremy. "Comments on the Catalogue of the Victoria and Albert Museum Travelling Exhibition of 1973," *FoMRHI Bulletin, Communication* no. 9, January 1976.

Literature (about the Victoria & Albert Museum collections in general)

898   "Musical Instruments at Kensington," *Musical World* 50 (1872): 359, 691.

899   Altenburg, W. "Die Instrumentensammlung der South Kensington Museum und ihr Katalog [von Carl Engel]," *ZfI* 21 (1900/1901): 518.

900   "The Musical Instruments of South Kensington," *Musical News* 37 (1909): 35-37.

901   Ligtvoet, A. W. "Muziekinstrumenten collectie in Londen," *Mens en melodie* 23 (1968): 374-76. illus.

902   Wilson, Michael I. "The Case of the Victorian Piano," *Victoria & Albert Museum Yearbook,* no. 3 (1972), pp. 133-53. illus.
        Mostly instruments from the Museum.

LONDON (U.K.). VICTORIAN ERA EXHIBITION, 1897

Literature

903   "Victorian Era Exhibition," *MT* 38 (1897): 335, 383-84.

LONDON (U.K.). WORLD EXHIBITION, 1851. *See* LONDON (U.K.). GREAT EXHIBITION OF THE WORKS OF INDUSTRY OF ALL NATIONS, 1851

LOS ANGELES, CALIFORNIA (USA). THE CRAFT AND FOLK ART MUSEUM

Literature

904   Ashin, Deborah. "Stringed Musical Instruments Exhibition," *Early Music* 4 (1976): 294-95. illus.

LOS ANGELES, CALIFORNIA (USA). UNIVERSITY OF SOUTHERN CALIFORNIA. ALLAN HANCOCK MUSEUM

905 Norvell, Philip J. *A History and a Catalogue of the Albert Gale Collection of Musical Instruments.* (Master's thesis, University of Southern California, 1952.)

LOS ANGELES, CALIFORNIA (USA). UNIVERSITY OF SOUTHERN CALIFORNIA. ERICH LACKMANN COLLECTION. *See Section II under* LACHMANN, ERICH

LUANDA (ANGOLA). MUSEU DE ANGOLA

906 *Exposição etnográfica de instrumentos musicais e máscaras dos Povos de Angola. Organização da Divisão de Etnologia e Etnografia do I.I.C. A. e do Museu de Angola.* [Luanda: 1964.] 34 pp., illus., 219 items.

     Copy at DLC(Wc).

LUCERNE (Switzerland). INDUSTRIE-AUSSTELLUNG, 1855. *See* WILLISAU (Switzerland). INDUSTRIE-AUSSTELLUNG, 1855

LUCERNE (Switzerland). RICHARD-WAGNER MUSEUM (J124, A418) [N.B.: Of three hundred rare instruments gathered by the Lucerne collector, Heinrich Schumacher, the municipality bought one hundred fifty in 1943 to begin the collection in this Museum.]

907 Vannes, René. *Katalog der städtischen Sammlung alter Musikinstrumente im Richard-Wagner-Museum, Tribschen/Luzern.* Erstellt im Auftrag der Museums-Kommission von Rene Vannes. Vorwort von Otto Dreyer. [Tribschen/Luzern]: Richard-Wagner-Museum, 1956. 40 pp., illus., 95 items.

     Duckles* 3:1609. Copy at NN(NYp).

Literature

908 Dreyer, Otto. "Sammlung alter Musikinstrumente im Wagner-Museum, Luzern," *Pro Arte* (Genève) (juil-août, 1944), pp. 299-304.

909 Roelli, Eva. "Beim Betrachten alter Instrumente Besuch in der neugeordneten städtischen Sammlung alter Musikinstrumente im Richard-Wagner-Museum," *Luzerner Tagblatt*, Nr. 197 (1967).

LÜBECK (Germany). DEUTSCH-NORDISCHE HANDELS- UND INDUSTRIE-AUSSTELLUNG, 1895

Literature

910 "Deutsch-Nordische Handels- und Industrie-Ausstellung," *ZfI* 15 (1894/95): 194, 765-66, 816-18; 16 (1895/96): 15-17.

General

911 *Officieller Katalog der . . . Ausstellung zu Lübeck vom 21. Juni bis 30. September 1895.* Berlin: R. Mosse, 1895. 196 pp.

> Musical instruments, Gruppe XX. Cited from KaY* 29:920-21; not located.

LÜBECK (Germany). ST. ANNEN MUSEUM. SAMMLUNG ALTER MUSIK-INSTRUMENTE (J62, A224)

912 Karstädt, Georg. *Die Sammlung alter Musikinstrumente im St. Annen-Museum.* (Lübecker Museums-Heft, 2.) Lübeck: the Museum, 1959. 10 pp., 6 pls., ca. 110 items.

> Copy at DLC (Wc).

913 Hart, Günter. "Glossen zu einem Verzeichnis [see preceding] einer Instrumentensammlung. Alte Musikinstrumente im St. Annen-Museum in Lübeck," *Instrumentenbau-Zeitschrift* 14 (1960): 88-89.

Literature

914 Karstädt, Georg. "Blasinstrumenten des Barock," *Musica* 4 (1950): 460-62. illus.

915 "Alte Musikinstrumente in Lübeck," *Musica* 12 (1958): 563-64.

> About its new "Saal".

916 Hart, Günter. "Literaturhinweise an Hand eines Museumsführers," *Musikforschung* 14 (1961): 65-68.

917 Karstädt, Georg. "Bildzeugnisse mittelalterlicher Musikinstrumente im St. Annen-Museum," *Der Wagen; ein lübeckisches Jahrbuch* (1964), pp. 51-57.

LÜTTICH. *See* LIEGE

LUND (Sweden). KULTURHISTORISKA MUSEET

General

918 *En handbok för besök och självstudium av G. J:son Karlin.* Lund: Ohlssons Boktryckeri, 1918. illus.

"Musikhistoria [and instruments]," pp. 57-60.

LUSAKA (Zambia). UNIVERSITY OF ZAMBIA. INSTITUTE FOR AFRICAN STUDIES [formerly RHODES-LIVINGSTONE INSTITUTE]

919 Brelsford, W. Vernon. "Rhodes-Livingstone Museum Collection of Musical Instruments." In Jones, A. M. *African Music in Northern Rhodesia,* pp. [32]-36. [Lusaka] : 1949.

Copy at MH-P.

LUTON (U.K.). PUBLIC MUSEUM

920 *The Ridley Collection of Musical Wind Instruments in Luton Museum.* [Luton] : Museum & Art Gallery, 1957. 32 pp., illus., 75 items.

"Historical Note [by E. A. K. Ridley]," pp. 3-21; "Catalogue," pp. 22-[32]. See also same title in *Monthly Musical Record* 88 (1958): 11. Copies at NN (NYp), DLC (Wc).

L'VOV (USSR). GALIZISCHEN LANDESAUSSTELLUNG, 1894

Literature

921 "Musik und Musikinstrumente auf der Galizischen Landesausstellung [zu Lemberg]," *ZfI* 15 (1894/95): 5-6.

LYONS (France). EXPOSITION UNIVERSELLE ET COLONIAL, 1894

Literature

922 "Die Prämiirungen auf der Ausstellung . . . Klasse XII (Musik-instrumente)," *ZfI* 15 (1894/95): 71.

General

923 . . . *Catalogue général officiel.* Lyon: 1894. 10 pts.

Cited in BM*.

LYONS (France). FOIRE, 4th, 1919

Literature

924   "La foire de Lyon," *M & I* 5 (1919): 3.

LYONS (France). FOIRE, 6th, 1920

Literature

925   "La 6me Foire de Lyon," *M & I* 6 (1920): 71-73.

LYONS (France). FOIRE, 7th, 1921

Literature

926   "La Foire de Lyon," *M & I* 7 (1921): 81-83, 133.

LYONS (France). FOIRE, 11th, 1925

Literature

927   [List of French exhibitors] , *M & I* 11 (1925): 203.

MADISON, WISCONSIN (USA). UNIVERSITY. SCHOOL OF MUSIC. PRESTIA FLUTE COLLECTION

Literature

928   Cole, Robert M. "Historical Flute Exhibit," *Woodwind World-Brass & Percussion,* 16, no. 6 (1977): 8-10. illus., (19 items).

MADRAS (India). GOVERNMENT MUSEUM

929   Sambamoorthy, P. *Catalogue of the Musical Instruments Exhibited in the Madras Government Museum.* (Bulletin of the Madras Government Museum, N.S., Gen'l. Sect. 2, pt. 3.) Madras: Government Printing Office, 1932. [4], 25 pp., 9 pls., ca. 125 items.
        NNMM and PU (PHu) date 1931.

930   Sambamoorthy, P. *Catalogue of the Musical Instruments Exhibited in the Madras Government Museum.* (Bulletin of the Madras Government Museum, N.S., Gen'l Sect. 2, pt. 3.) Rev. ed. Madras: Printed by the Superintendent, Government Press, 1955. 32 pp., 11 pls.
            Copy at Miu (AAu). *IAMIC Newsletter* for Spring 1973
            notes a 4th rev. ed. in preparation.

155

MADRAS (India). SANGITA VADYALAYA [MUSICAL INSTRUMENT DEVELOP-MENT CENTER] (J73)

931   Sambamoorthy, P. *Sruti Vadyas, drones.* (Sangita Vadyalaya series, 1.) New Delhi: All India Handicrafts Board, [1957]. 48 pp., illus.

"Appendix III. List of Musical Instruments in the Gallery of the Sagita Vadyalaya," pp. 47-48, pls. I-XXIII. Copies at CtY (NHu), DLC (Wc).

932   Sambamoorthy, P. *Laya Vadyas (Time-Keeping Instruments).* (Sangita Vadyalaya series, 2.) New Delhi: All India Handicrafts Board, 1959. 90 pp. illus.

Copies at CtW (MIu), CU (BEu).

MADRID (Spain). BIBLIOTECA MUSICAL CIRCULANTE (J113, A369)

933   *Catalogo. Edición ilustrada.* Madrid: Ayuntamiento de Madrid, Sección de cultura e información, Artes gráficas municipales, 1946. xv, 610 pp., illus.

Copy at NN (NYp).

MADRID (Spain). MUSEO ARQUEOLÓGICO NACIONAL

934   Janer, Florencio. "De los antiguos instrumentos músicos de los Americanos, conservados en el Museo nacional de arqueología," *Museo español de antigüedades* 2 (1873): 265-71. illus.

MADRID (Spain). MUSEO DEL ARTE

Literature

935   *Recital y Esposición de instrumentos musicales del Antiguo Perú del 15 al 29 setiembre de 1961.* [Madrid, 1961.] [19] pp., illus.

"Presentación" by Federico Kauffmann Doicy.

MADRID (Spain). MUSEO ETNOLÓGICO

936   Garciá, Matos M. "Catalogo de los instrumentos musicales 'igorrotes' conservados en el Museo," *Antropología y etnología* 4 (1951): [9]-19. illus.

MADRID (Spain). PALACIO NACIONAL

937 "Instrumentos de música tasados por Joan de Rojas Carrion, violero en Madrid à 13 de Mayo de 1602. Las cosas de su oficio y pipharos y otras cosas se tasaron por Alonso de Morales." Ms. in Madrid, Biblioteca nacional, Dept. of Mss. 14017/6, translated into English by McLeish, Martin, "An Inventory of Musical Instruments at the Royal Palace, Madrid, in 1602," *GSJ* 21 (1968): 108-28. 77 items.

> Dispersed by Francisco Hidalgo, auctioneer, 1608 and 1609. The inventory includes dates and names of purchasers, and prices fetched.

MAINZ (Germany). RÖMISCH-GERMANISCHE ZENTRAL-MUSEUM

Literature

938 "Antike Musikinstrumente im . . . ," *ZfI* 32 (1911/12): 365.

MALBORK [MARIENBURG] (Poland). SCHLOSS BLANKENBURG

Literature

939 Hart, Günter. "Musikinstrumente auf der Marienburg," *Glareana* 24 (1975): lvs. 11-13.

MALMÖ (Sweden). BALTISKA UTSTÄLLNING, 1914

Literature

940 "Die Musikinstrumenten-Industrie auf der baltischen Ausstellung," *ZfI* 34 (1913/14): 987 (exhibitors); 35 (1914/15): 184 (prizes).

941 Göbel, Josef. "Die baltische Ausstellung in Malmö," *ZfI* 34 (1913/14): 1170-71, 1208-10. illus.

General

942 *Amtlicher Katalog für die deutsch Abteilung der baltischen Ausstellung Malmö 1914.* Schriftl.: Rud. Hauptner. Berlin: [Klasing & Co., 1914]. xxvii, 224 pp.

> Cited from *DBV** 1:1393; not located.

943 *Officiell berättelse öfver. . . .* Utg. af H. Fr. Ahlström. [Malmö: Förlagsaktiebolagets i Malmö boktryckeri, 1915-21.] 2 vols.

> Copy at MnU (MSu); not examined.

MANCHESTER (U.K.). MUSIC TRADES EXHIBITION, 1901

Literature

944   "Manchester Music Trades Exhibition," *Musical Opinion* 25 (1901/2): 58-61, 940-42.

945   "The Manchester Music Trades Exhibition," *Piano, Organ and Music Trades Journal,* vol. 17, no. 230 (1901).

MANCHESTER (U.K.). MUSIC TRADES EXHIBITION, 1903

Literature

946   "An Imposing Show at Manchester," *London and Provincial Music Trades Review* 27, no. 314 (September 1903): 11, 17-31.

947   "First List of Exhibitors," *London and Provincial Music Trades Review* 27, no. 313 (August 1903): 31.

MANCHESTER (U.K.). MUSIC TRADES EXHIBITION, 1904

Literature

948   "The Manchester Music Trades Exhibition," *London and Provincial Music Trades Review* 28, no. 326 (September 1904): 25-35. illus.

MANCHESTER (U.K.). MUSIC TRADES EXHIBITION, 1905

Literature

949   "Manchester Trades Exhibition," *London and Provincial Music Trades Review* 29, no. 337 (August 1905): 31; no. 338 (September 1905): 23.

MANCHESTER (U.K.). ROYAL MANCHESTER COLLEGE OF MUSIC. HENRY WATSON COLLECTION OF MUSICAL INSTRUMENTS (J153)

950   *Descriptive and Illustrated Catalogue of the Henry Watson Collection of Musical Instruments.* With an Introduction by Stanley Withers. Manchester: Sherratt & Hughes, [1906]. 32 pp., illus., 155 items.

   MGG* says catalogue by Henry Watson.

Literature

951   "The Henry Watson Collection of Old Musical Instruments," *Musical Opinion* 30 (1907): 265.

952   "Henry Watson. The Man. The Books. The Instruments," *MT* 50 (1909): 365-72. illus. include instruments.

953   Duck, L. W. "The Henry Watson Music Library [and Instruments]," *Library World* 63 (December 1961): 132-36.

MARIENBURG BEI NORDSTEMMEN

954   Hart, Günter. "Musikinstrumente auf der Marienburg," *Glareana* 24, no. 1 (1976): lvs. 11-13. 32 items in the Schloss of Princess Ortrud of Hannover.

MARKNEUKIRCHEN (Germany). GEWERBE- UND INDUSTRIE-AUSSTELLUNG, 1897

Literature

955   "Die Musikinstrumente auf der Markneukircher Gewerbe- und Industrie-Ausstellung, von 8. bis 15. August 1897," *ZfI* 17 (1896/97): 844-46, 873-76, 897-99.

MARKNEUKIRCHEN (Germany). GEWERBEMUSEUM

956   "Die Sammlung mittelasiatische Musikinstrumente im Gewerbemuseum," *ZfI* 10 (1889/90): 300-302.

   Describes 15 instruments given to the Museum by A. Reichel.

957   . . . *Katalog des Gewerbemuseums zu Markneukirchen.* Markneukirchen: 1908. 97 pp.

   Copies at ICU.

MARKNEUKIRCHEN (Germany). FACHSCHULE FÜR MUSIKINSTRUMENTENBAUER

958   Drechsel, F. A. "Die Ausstellung alter Musikinstrumente in Markneukirchen vom 25.9. bis 2.10. 1927," *ZfI* 48 (1927/28): 60-62.

MARKNEUKIRCHEN (Germany). MUSIKINSTRUMENTEN-MUSEUM (J49)

959   Wild, Erich. *Führer durch das Musikinstrumenten-Museum.* Markneukirchen: 1967.

> Cited from Jenkins*; not located.

960   Wild, Erich. *Führer durch das Musikinstrumenten-Museum.* [3. Aufl.] Markneukirchen: Rat d. Stadt, 1971. 72 pp., 22 pls.

> Copy at DLC (Wc).

Literature

961   Buchner, Alexander. "Muzeum hudebních nástrojů v Markneukirchenu," *Hudební nástroje* 7 (1970): 106-7, 137-38, 170-71.

MEININGEN (Germany). STAATLICHE MUSEEN. MUSIKGESCHICHTLICHE ABTEILUNG (J50)

Literature

962   Weinitz, Franz. "Die lappische Zaubertrommel in Meiningen," *Zeitschrift für Ethnologie* 42 (1910): Heft 1, pp. 1-14.

MELBOURNE (Australia). INTERNATIONAL EXHIBITION, 1880-81

Literature

963   "Die Pianos auf der Welt-Ausstellung zu Melbourne 1880. Bericht des Melbourner 'The Argus'," *ZfI* 1 (1880/81): 105-7.

964   [Exhibitors and prizes], *ZfI* 1 (1880/81): 77, 210, 240.

General

965   *Official Record; Containing Introduction, Description of Exhibition and Exhibits . . . Catalogue of Exhibits.* Melbourne: Mason, Firth & McCutcheon, 1882.

> "Musical Instruments and Printed Music, [by L. Moonen]," pp. 46-57. Copy at DLC (Wc).

966   *Official Catalogue of the Exhibits. 2d Ed. of First Issue.* Melbourne: Mason, Firth of McCutcheon, 1880. 2 vols., illus.

> Class 13 under each country includes some musical instruments. Copies at NN (NYp), CSt (STm), MWA.

MELBOURNE (Australia). CENTENNIAL INTERNATIONAL EXHIBITION, 1888-89

Literature

967   "Die Melbourner Ausstellung in französischer Beleuchtung," *ZfI* 9 (1888/89): 96.

968   "Die Musikinstrumenten-Prämiirungen," *ZfI* 9 (1888/89): 258-60, 457-59.

969   "Die deutsche Musik-Industrie auf der . . . ," *ZfI* 8 (1887/88): 271-75.

General

970   *Official Catalogue of the Exhibits. . . .* 2 vols. Melbourne: M. L. Hutchinson, 1888.

> Musical instruments under most countries in class 13; worthwhile. Copy at DLC (Wc).

MELBOURNE (Australia). UNIVERSITY. GRAINGER MUSEUM (J4)

Literature

971   Prescott, Anthony. "The Grainger Museum [summary of contents]," *Australian Journal of Music Education*, no. 18 (April 1976), pp. 3-5.

MELBOURNE (Australia). VICTORIA PUBLIC LIBRARY, MUSEUMS AND NATIONAL GALLERY, MELBOURNE MUSEUM

Literature

972   Massola, Aldo. "Drum Types of Eastern New Guinea [. . . reported in the relevant literature and existing in the Collections of the National Museum] ." In the Museum's *Memoirs,* no. 22 (1957), pp. [1]-12. 2 pls.

MERAN (Germany). LANDFÜRSTLICHE BURG

Literature

973   Roos, Wilhelm. "The Musical Instrument Collection at Meran," *GSJ* 32 (1979): 1-23. 4 pls.

MERAN (Germany). PFARRKIRCHE ST. NIKOLAUS

974   Senn, Walter. "Ein Musikalienverzeichnis der Pfarrkirche . . . aus dem Jahre 1682." In *Symbolae historiae musicae; Helmut Federhofer zum 60. Geburtstag,* pp. 103-16. Mainz: 1971.

> Reprints the inventory; the appendix lists instruments.

MEXICO CITY (Mexico). INSTITUTO NACIONAL DE BELLAS ARTES (J90)

975   Sordo Sodi, Carmen. *Catalogo de la primera esposición internacional de instrumentos musicales.* Mexico, D. F.: Instituto Nacional de Bellas Artes, 1969. 30 pp., illus.

From various sources.

MEXICO CITY (Mexico). MUSEO NACIONAL DE ARQUEOLOGIA, HISTORIA Y ETNOGRAFIA (J90)

Literature

976   Campos, R. M. "Los instrumentos musicales de los antiguos Mexicanos," [the Museum's] *Anales,* ep. 4, t. 3 (1925), pp. 333-37.

977   Campos, R. M. "The Musical Instruments of the Ancient Mexicans," *Pan American Union, Bulletin* 60 (1926): 380-89. illus.

A translation of the preceding.

MILAN (Italy). CONSERVATORIO DI MUSICA GIUSEPPE VERDI. MUSEO (J79, A299)

978   Guarinoni, Eugenio de'. *Gli strumenti musicali nel Museo . . . cenni illustrativi e descrittivi . . . con 32 tavole.* Milano: U. Hoepli, [1908]. vi, 109 pp., illus., 278 items.

Basis of the collection was the group exhibited at the Esposizione musicale in 1881, q.v. Copies at CtY (NHu), NN (NYp), DLC (Wc).

Literature

979   "R. Conservatorio musicale Giuseppe Verdi in Milano. II. Biblioteca e Museo," *Musica e musicisti* 59, no. 1 (1904): 1-11. illus. (including instruments).

MILAN (Italy). ESPOSIZIONE INDUSTRIALE NAZIONALE, 1881   [N.B.: The Esposizione musicale of 1881 was a part of the over-all industrial exposition.]

980   *Esposizione musicale sotto il patrocinio di S. M. la Regina. Milano 1881. Catalogo. Gruppi I [-VI].* Milano: Tip. Luigi di Giacomo Pirola, 1881. x, 54, [2], 68 pp.

According to Lambertini* materials shown constitute the basis of the Milan Conservatorio's collections. Copies at NcU (CHu), NN (NYp).

981   . . . *Catalogo degli oggetti artistici musicali spediti dalla Giunta Italo-Portughese ala Esposizione il Milano.* Lisbon: 1881.

        Cited from Lambertini*; not verified.

Literature

982   "Die Claviere italienische Fabrikanten auf der Ausstellung zu Mailand 1881," *ZfI* 1 (1880/81): 292-93; 2 (1881/82): 34-35.

983   [Reports, descriptions, invitations, regulations, etc.] , *Gazzetta musicale di Milano* 36 (1881): 50, 158, 178-79, 213-14, 234, 237 (juries), 369 and 386-87 (prizes), 427-28 and 436 and 444-45 ("Echi" by "Edwort").

984   Ricordi, Giulio. "L'Esposizione nazionale e la musica," *Gazzetta musicale di Milano* 36 (1881): 33-34, 177-78, 193-94, 250.

985   *Esposizione musicale, sotto il patrocinio di S. M. la Regina.* (Atti del congresso dei Musicisti italiani riunito in Milano dal 16 al 22 giugno 1881.) Milano: Ricordi, 1881. 187 pp.

        Cited from PaG* and Lambertini*; not examined.

986   Montuoro, A[chille?]. *Instrumenti musicale e loro parti.* (Relazione dei giurati, Sez. XXVI, Classe 54ª.) Milano: Hoepli, 1883.

        Cited from Torri* and BM*; not located.

General

987   Roggero, Candido. *Riccordo dell' Esposizione industriale nazionale in Milano, 1881. Telegrafo acustico-musicale.* Milano: [s. d.] .

        Cited from Lambertini*; unable to verify.

MILAN (Italy). ESPOSIZIONE INTERNAZIONALE, 1906

Literature

988   "Musikinstrumente auf der . . . ," *ZfI* 27 (1906/7): 105, 107 (exhibitors), 199, 838-39 (prizes).

General

989   Marius. "L'esposizione del 1906," *Musica e musicisti* 60 (1905): 151-62, 716-24; *Ars et labor* 61 (1906): 13-16, 509-14, 713-15, 909-14, 1016. illus.

        Little about instrument collections.

990   Germany. Zentralkommission, Internationale Ausstellung in Mailand, 1906. *Amtlicher Katalog.* Berlin: G. Stilke, [1911] . 192 pp., illus.

        Copy at ICRL.

MILAN (Italy). ESPOSIZIONE INTERNAZIONALE, 1906 *continued*

991   *Catalogo descrittivo della mostra storico-artistica all'esposizione internationale di Milano.* Milano: Tip. La Prealpina, 1907. 118 pp.

>   Cited from PaG*; not located.

992   *Catalogo ufficiale della esposizione dell'impero tedesco.* . . . Berlino: Stilke, 1908. 2 vols.

>   Cited from PaG*; not located.

MILAN (Italy). MUSEO DI ANTICHI STRUMENTI MUSICALI (J79)   [N.B.: The private collection of Natale Gallini formed the basis of the collection. For clarity, the catalogue of the "Mostra" (below), held before the collection became the Museo's property, is included here instead of in Section II.]

993   Gallini, Natale. *Mostra di antichi strumenti musicali della collezione N. Gallini. Maggio 1953, Villa comunale (ex reale) Milano.* [Milano: Tip. di Rizzoli, 1953.] 42 pp., 32 pls., 200 items.

>   Duckles* 3:1613. Copies at NN (NYp), DLC (Wc).

994   . . . *Catalogo descrittivo a cura di Natale Gallini.* [Milano] : Comune di Milano, [1958]. 128 pp., 77 pls., [9] pp., indexes, 358 items.

>   After the Gallini collection became property of the Museo.
>   Copies at NN (NYp), OrU (EUu), DLC (Wc).

995   Milan. Museo degli strumenti musicali. *Catalogo, a cura di Natale e Franco Gallini.* [Milano] : Castello Sforzesco, [1963]. 448 pp., 151 pls., 641 items.

>   Duckles* 3:1612. Copies at NPV (POvc), DLC (Wc).

Literature

996   "La collection d'instruments anciens de Natale Gallini au 'Museo di Milano'," *Schweizerische Musikzeitung* 99 (1959): 215.

997   Morelli-Gallet, Wina. "Das Museum alter Musikinstrumente in Mailand," *Oesterreichische Musikzeitschrift* 16 (1961): 175-76. illus.

MILAN (Italy). MUSEO NAZIONALE DELLA SCIENZA E DELLA TECNICA

998   Curti, Orazio. *Museoscienza.* Milano: [Stab. Grafico Matarelli, 1971.] 479 pp. illus

>   "Riproduzione del Suono," pp. 85-89, illus. "Strumenti musicali, Sala Emma Vecla," pp. 90-93, illus. Copy at DLC (Wc).

MILAN (Italy). MUSEO TEATRALE ALLA SCALA (J80)

999   . . . *Catalogo del Museo teatrale alla Scala, Milano.* (Il piccolo cicerone moderno, nr. 12.) Milano: Alfieri & Lacroix, 1914. 116 pp., illus.

> Preface signed: G[iuseppe] M[orazzoni]. Copies
> at CU (BEu), NcU (CHHu), MiU (AAu), NN (NYp),
> DLC (Wc).

1000   Vittadini, Stefano. *Catalogo . . . Edita a cura del Consiglio direttivo; pref. di Renato Simoni.* Milano: E. Bestetti, 1948. xviii, 401 pp., illus.

> Copies at CoU (BOu), CtY (NHu), IaU (IOu),
> NcU (CHHu), DLC (Wc).

Literature

1001   Neisser, Artur. "Aus dem Theatermuseum des Scala-theaters in Mailand," *Neue Musik-Zeitung* 48 (1927): 102-5. illus.

MILAN (Italy). PINACOTECA DI BRERA

Literature

1002   Antolini, Francesco. *Osservazioni su due violini esposti nelle sale dell'I. R. Palazzo di Brera, uno dei quali di forma non comune.* Milano: Luigi di Giacomo Pirola, 1832.

> Cited from Fétis* (4051) and Torri*; not located.

MINNEAPOLIS, MINNESOTA (USA). UNIVERSITY OF MINNESOTA. UNIVERSITY GALLERY

1003   *Music and Art.* [*Exhibition.*] *University Gallery, April 4-May 18, 1958. Grand Rapids Arts Gallery, Michigan, June 15-July 29, 1958.* [n.p., 1958.] [16] pp., illus.

> Includes some of the Edith J. Freeman collection
> from the Detroit Institute of Arts, according to L246.

MITTENWALD (Germany). DEUTSCHE MUSIKINSTRUMENTENMESSE, 1949.

1004   *Amtlicher Messekatalog. Mittenwald im Karwendelgebirge [1] 1949.* Mittenwald: Verlag Duo-Graphik, 1949. 63 pp., illus.

> Cited from *DBH*; not located.

MITTENWALD (Germany). DEUTSCHE MUSIKINSTRUMENTENMESSE UND MUSIKWOCHE, 1950

1005   *Amtlicher Messekatalog. Mittenwald im Karwendelgebirge. 2. 1950, vom 3 - 10. Sept. 1950. Nebst Messebedingungen, Anmeldung. . . .* Mittenwald: Verlag Duo-Graphik, [1950]. 36 pp., illus.

> Cited from *DBH*;* not located. The "Musikinstru-
> mentenmesse" nos. 3-5 were held in Düsseldorf, q.v.

MITTENWALD (Germany). GEIGENBAU- UND HEIMAT-MUSEUM   (J62)

Literature

1006   "Das Geigenbau- und Heimat-Museum in Mittenwald," *ZfI* 50 (1929/30): 735-36. illus.

1007   Seidel, Max. *Geigenbaumuseum Mittenwald-Bayern.* [n.p., n.d.] [20] pp.
> Copy at NL-DHgm.

MITTENWALD (Germany). GEIGENBAUSCHULE

1008   *Ausstellung des 100 jährigen Bestehens und der Einweihung ihres erweiterten Neubaues, veranstaltet vom Verein "Die Freunde der Geigenbauschule" . . . 15. August - 13 September 1959.* [n.p., 1959?] 19 pp., illus., 311 items.

MODENA (Italy). MOSTRA DI ANTICHI STRUMENTI MUSICALI, TEATRO COMUNALE, 1963-64

1009   Cervelli, Luisa. *Mostra di antichi strumenti musicali 1963-1964. Catalogo . . . premessa di G. Guandalini.* Modena: Coop. Tip., 1963. 38 pp., 16 pls.
> Mostly the collection of Count Valdrighi; see earlier
> catalogues under **VALDRIGHI** in Section II.

MODENA (Italy). MUSEO CIVICO   (J90)

1010   Crescellani, Arsenio. *Catalogue of Old Musical Instruments (Valdrighi Collection).* [n.p., n.d.] 3 lvs.
> Typewritten copy at NNMM. See also **VALDRIGHI** in Section II.

1011   Vienna. Internationale Ausstellung für Musik- und Theaterwesen, 1892. *Fachkatalog der musik-historischen Abtheilung des königreiches Italien*. Wien: 1892.

> Instruments from the Modena, Museo Civico, including some of the Valdrighi collection, pp. 293-94, according to Boalch*.

MOSCOW (USSR). [Several Institutions]

Literature

1012   Keller, Jindřich. "Organologická procházka Moskvou," *Hudebni nástroje* 10 (1973): 143-44.

> An organologist describes the Glinka Central State Museum of Musical Culture and the State Musical College; cited from *RILM*.

MOSCOW (USSR). DASHKOVSKOM EITNOGRAFICHESKOM. MUZEE

1013   Maslov, A. L. *Illiùstrirovannoe opisanie muzykal'nykh instrumentov, khraniùatsikhsiùa v Dashkovskom etnograficheskom muzee v Moskve*. Moskva: 1909. 64 pp., illus., 237 items.

> Copy at DLC (Wc).

MOSCOW (USSR). GOSUDARSTVENNAIÄ KONSERVATORIIÄ. MUZEE

1014   Arakishvili, Dmitrii I. "Kavkazskie muzyal'nyi instrumenty v muzee . . . ," *Russkaiä muzykal'naiä gazeta* 20 (1905): 338-43.

> Cited from Emsheimer*.

MOSCOW (USSR). GOSUDARSTVENNYĬ ŤSENTRAL'NYĬ MUZEĬ MUZYKAL'NOĬ KUL'TURY (J133)

1015   *Muzykal'nye instrumenty narodov Sovetskogo Soiùza v fondakh Gosudarstvennogo ťsentral'nogo muzeiä muzykal'noi kul'tury imeni M. I. Glinki. Katalog*. Moskva: 1977. 63 pp., [8] lvs., illus.

MOSCOW (USSR). VSEROSSIISSKAIÄ VYSTAVKA, 188 (2?)

Literature

1016   "Auf der Allgemeinen Russischen Kunst- und Industrie-Ausstellung," *ZfI* 2 (1881/82): 294 (exhibitors); 3 (1882/83): 26 and 28-29 ("Bericht").

MOST (Czechoslovakia). NORDWESTBÖHMISCHE AUSSTELLUNG FÜR DEUTSCHE INDUSTRIE, GEWERBE UND LANDWIRTSCHAFT, 1898

1017   "Katalog . . . Firmen der Musikinstrumenten-Industrie . . . nach dem officiellen Kataloge," *ZfI* 18 (1897/98): 854; 19 (1898/99): 125 (prizes).

        Official catalogue not located.

MÜNSTER (Germany). ERBDROSTENHOF

1018   Reuter, Rudolf. "Das Instrumentarium des Fürstlich-Bentheim-Tecklenbur-gischen Hofmusik im Erbdrostenhof zu Münster," *Verein für Geschichte und Altertumskunde Westfalens, Mitteilungen* 56 (1968): 129-45. illus., 20 items.

MUNICH (Germany). ALLGEMEINE DEUTSCHE INDUSTRIE-AUSSTELLUNG, 1854

1019   Schafhäutl, Karl Emil von. *Bericht der Beurtheilungs-Commission bei der allgemeinen deutschen Industrie-Ausstellung zu München. 6. Heft. IV. über musikalische Instrumente.* München: Franz, [1854]. 234 pp.

        Cited from Fétis* (4022) and Torri*; not located.

1020   Schafhäutl, Karl Emil von. *Die Pianofortebaukunst der deutschen, repräsentiert auf der . . . Ausstellung.* Aus dem Bericht der Beurtheilungs Commission über die musikalischen-Instrumente. München: Franz, 1855. Pp. 69-110.

        Copy at NN (NYp).

MUNICH (Germany). AUSSTELLUNG ALTE MUSIK, 1951

1021   Ott, Alfons. *Ausstellung alte Musik. Instrumente, Noten und Dokumente aus drei Jahrhunderten. Katalog* [Veranstaltet durch die Stadt München im Bayerischen Nationalmuseum, November-Dezember 1951]. München: M. Hieber, 1951. 71 pp., 23 pls., 636 items.

        Vorw.: H. L. Held. Duckles 3:1614. Copy at NN (NYp).

MUNICH (Germany). AUSSTELLUNG "DAS BAYERISCHE HANDWERK," 1927

Literature

1022   "Ausstellung 'Das bayerische Handwerk' in München," *ZfI* 47 (1926/27): 716, 911 and 913 (exhibitors).

General

1023   *Amtlicher Katalog. Ausstellung München 1927, "Das bayerische Handwerk."*
        2. Aufl. München: M. Müller & Sohn, [1927]. 284, xii, 112 pp., illus.

> Cited from *DBV** 13:549; not located.

MUNICH (Germany). AUSSTELLUNG VON MEISTERWERKEN MUHAMMED-ANISCHER KUNST, 1910

1024   . . . *Muster-Ausstellung von Musik-Instrumenten Amtlicher Katalog.* [2. Aufl.]
        München: R. Mosse, 1910. 151 pp., 4 plans, illus.

> The first edition of the *Amtlicher Katalog* appears
> to have excluded instruments. Copy at DLC (Wc).

1025   . . . *Muster-Ausstellung von Musik-Instrumenten Amtlicher Katalog.* [3. Aufl.]
        München: R. Mosse, [1911]. 287, 1 plan, illus.

> Copy at NN (NYp). NNMM has the same collation
> but calls it 4. Aufl., and dates it [1910].

MUNICH (Germany). BAYERISCHE NATIONALMUSEUM (J62). *See also* MUNICH (Germany). AUSSTELLUNG ALTE MUSIK, 1951

1026   Bierdimpfl, K. A. *Die Sammlung der Musikinstrumenten des baierischen
        Nationalmuseums. Offizielle Ausg.* München: Akademische Buchdruckerei
        von F. Straub, 1883. 73 pp.

> Copy at DLC (Wc).

Literature

1027   Pottgiesser, Karl. "Die Sammlung der Musikinstrumente im neuen bayrischen
        National-Museum," *Allgemeine Musik-Zeitung* 1 (1901): 5-6. illus.

1028   Smith, Douglas Alton. "The Lutes in the Bavarian National Museum," *Journal
        of the Lute Society of America,* 11 (1978): 36-44, 50-55 (pls.).

> "Will also appear in German in the periodical *Musik
> in Bayern, 1979.*"

MUNICH (Germany). DEUTSCH-NATIONALE KUNSTGEWERBE-AUSSTELLUNG, 1888

Literature

1029   "Musikinstrumente auf der . . . Ausstellung," *ZfI* (1886/87): 313 (exhibitors);
        8 (1887/88): 62-63, 90 (prizes).

MUNICH (Germany). DEUTSCH-NATIONALE ... *continued*

General

1030 *Officieller Katalog der deutschnationalen Kunstgewerbe-Ausstellung zu München.*
München: [Verlag d. Academ. Monatshefte], 1888. 160 pp.

1031 *Officieller Katalog der deutschnationalen Kunstgewerbe-Ausstellung zu München.*
2. [verb.] Aufl. München: [Verlag d. Academ. Monatshefte], 1888. 203 pp., illus.

Both cited from KaY* 25:698; not located.

**MUNICH (Germany). DEUTSCHES MUSEUM VON MEISTERWERKEN DER NATUR-
WISSENSCHAFT UND TECHNIK** (J63, BB183)

1032 *Amtlicher Führer durch die Sammlungen.* München: Knorr und Hirth, [1925].
359 pp., illus.

Musical instruments, pp. 258-67.

1033 Wallner, Bertha Antonia. "Die Musikinstrumentensammlung des Deutschen
Museums in München," *ZfMW* 8 (1926): 239-47.

1034 Seifers, Heinrich. *Die Blasinstrumenten im Deutschen Museum; beschreibender
Katalog.* (Deutsches Museum, Abhandlungen und Berichte; Jahrg. 44, 1976,
Heft 1.) München: R. Oldenburg, 1976. 108 pp., illus.

Literature

1035 "Liste wünchenswerter Sammlungs-gegenstände aus dem Bebiete des Musik-
instrumentenbaues für das Deutsch Museum," *ZfI* 26 (1905/6): 448, 457, 459.

1036 Williams, C. F. Abdy. "Ancient Pianos and Organs at the German Museum,
Munich," *Musician* (Philadelphia/Boston) 14 (1909): 531-32, 566. illus.

1037 Koch, Markus. "Die Instrumentensammlung des deutschen Museums in München,"
Deutsche Musikerzeitung 44 (1913): 367-68, 435.

1038 Fuchs, Franz. "Führung durch des Abteilung 'Musikinstrumente' des Deutschen
Museums," *Deutsche Instrumentenbau-Zeitung* 27 (1926): 223-24.

1039 Fuchs, Franz. *Der Aufbau der technischen Akustik (Musikinstrumente) im Deutschen
Museum.* (Deutsches Museum, Abhandlungen und Berichte, 31. Jg., 1963, 2. Heft.)
München: R. Oldenburg; Düsseldorf: VDI-Verlag, 1963. 59 pp., 40 pls.

1040 Ligtvoet, A. W. "Muziekinstrumenten in het Deutsches Museum te Muenchen,"
Mens en melodie 24 (1969): 113-14. illus.

1041   Voelckers, Jürgen. "Streichzither-Klavierharfe und der älteste Kielflügel; Die Instrumentensammlung des Deutschen Museums in München," *Instrumentenbau-Zeitschrift* 25, no. 6 (1971): 279-81. illus.

General

1042   *Führer durch die Sammlungen.* Leipzig: B. G. Teubner, [1907]. 158 pp., illus.
"Saal Nr. 23, Technische Akustik" [von] Oskar Fleischer, pp. 78-82. Copy at CU (BEu).

1043   Conzelmann, Theodor. *Rundgang durch die Sammlungen.* 4. erw. Aufl. [München: 1939.] 198 pp., illus.
"Raum 194 [-203], Musikinstrumenten," pp. 124-28.

1044   *Objekt- und Demonstrationsverzeichnis: Stand Oktober 1976.* München: R. Oldenburg, 1976.
Not examined; noted by H. M. Brown in *Early Music* (1977), p. 403.

MUNICH (Germany). GLASPALAST. *See* MUNICH (Germany). MÜNCHENER JAHRES-AUSSTELLUNG, 1908

MUNICH (Germany). INTERNATIONALE GITARRISTENTAG, 1904. *See Section II* WIT, PAUL de

MUNICH (Germany). MÜNCHENER JAHRES-AUSSTELLUNG, 1908

Literature

1045   "Ausstellung München 1908 [nach dem amtlichen Katalog]," *ZfI* 28 (1907/8): 945-46 (exhibitors), 982.

General

1046   *Amtlicher Katalog der Ausstellung.* . . . Hrsg. von der Ausstellungsleitung, [Vorw. von Walter Riezler]. München/Berlin: R. Mosse, 1908. 184 pp.
Though this is the only catalogue cited here, the show was an annual event for many years, and many general catalogues and guides for those years exist but were not examined.

MUNICH (Germany). MUSIKFACHAUSSTELLUNG, 1910

Literature

1047   "Musikinstrumente auf der . . . Ausstellung," *ZfI* 30 (1909/10): 1031-32.

MUNICH (Germany). STAATLICHES MUSEUM FÜR VÖLKERKUNDE   (J63)

1048   Sachs, Curt. *Die Musikinstrumenten Birmas und Assams in K. Ethnographisches Museum zu München.* (K. Bayerische Akad. der Wissenschaften. Sitzungsberichte. Philos.-philol. und hist. Klasse. Jg. 1917, Abh. 2.) München: G. Franzscher Verlag in Komm, 1917. 47 pp., pls.

Copies at NN (NYp).

MUNICH (Germany). STÄDTISCHE MUSIKINSTRUMENTENSAMMLUNG   (J63, A233, NN184)

Literature

1049   Dreimüller, Karl. "Schicksal und Zukunst der Sammlung Georg Neuner in München," *Musikforschung* 2 (1949): 54-56.

1050   Schmidt-Garre, Helmut. "Magie afrikanischer Musikinstrumente; zu einer Ausstellung in München," *Musikleben* 8 (1955): 177-78. illus.

NANCY (France). EXPOSITION INTERNATIONALE DE L'EST DE LA FRANCE, 1909

1051   Laffitte, Louis. *Rapport général. . . .* Paris/Nancy: 1912.

"Les instruments de musique: Les exposants, par M. Acoulon; La Rétrospective de la Musique, par Albert Jacquot; L'industrie de la lutherie à Mirécourt," pp. 172-78. illus.

NAPLES (Italy). R. CONSERVATORIO DI MUSICA. MUSEO STORICO MUSICALE (J80, A302)

1052   Santagata, Ettore. *Il museo storico-musicale di "S. Pietro a Majella."* Napoli: Giannini, 1930. 153 pp., illus.

Copy at NN (NYp). See also Cervelli (1970) under **ROME (Italy). MUSEO NAZIONALE. . . .**

NARA (Japan). SHÔSÔIN JIMUSHO (J86)

1053   *Musical Instruments in the Shôsôin.* Edited by the Shôsôin Office [for the Imperial Household Agency]. English summary by Kenzo Hayashi et al, translated by Shigetaka Kaneko. Tokyo: Nihon Keizai Shimbum Sha, 1967. xxii, 234 pp., illus.

> Copy at NBuU-M (BUu).

NAUMBURG AN DER SAALE (Germany). ST. WENZELSKIRCHE

1054   Werner, Arno. "Die alte Musikbibliothek und der Instrumentensammlung an St. Wenzel in Naumburg a.d.S.," *AfMW* 8 (1927): 390-415.

> Instruments, pp. 397-415. Some of the instruments eventually went to the Berlin Instrumentenmuseum (see Droysen under that entry).

NEUCHÂTEL (Switzerland). MUSÉE D'ETHNOGRAPHIE (J124)

1055   Estreicher, Z. "Collection Gaston Bardout [acquise par le Musée par l'intermédiaire de André Schaeffner en 1954]," *Rapport annuel des Bibliothèques et Musées de la ville de Neuchâtel* (1954), pp. 43-71. 409 items.

> See also *Glareana*, vol. 7, no. 2 (1958).

NEW DELHI. *See* DELHI (India). SANGEET NATAK AKADEMI

NEW HAVEN, CONNECTICUT (USA). YALE UNIVERSITY (L87) [N.B.: Includes collections of Morris and son, Albert, Steinert (on loan from the School of Art, Providence, R.I.); the Belle Skinner collection (formerly at Mt. Holyoke, Mass.); and the collection of Emil Herrmann. See catalogues of these private collections in Section II.]

1056   Marcuse, Sibyl. *Musical Instruments at Yale; A Selection of Western Instruments from the 15th to 20th Centuries.* Exhibition directed by Stanton L. Catlin; February 19-March 27, 1960. [New Haven: 1960.] [47] pp., illus.

> Duckles* 3:1615. Copies at NN (NYp), DLC (Wc).

1057   Willson, Theodore Booth. *Historical Catalogue of the M. Steinert Collection of Musical Instruments.* New Haven: Yale University, 1913. 18 pp., 83 items.

> Copy at DLC (Wc). See earlier Steinert catalogues, Section II.

NEW HAVEN, CONNECTICUT (USA). YALE UNIVERSITY *continued*

1058 Marcuse, Sibyl. *Checklist of Western Instruments in the Collection of Musical Instruments* [in the School of Music]. New Haven: Yale University, 1958.

>   Vol. 1 only, Keyboard instruments. Copy at NPV (POvc).

1059 Rephann, Richard. *Checklist: Yale Collection of Musical Instruments.* New Haven: Yale University, 1968. 43 pp., 310 items.

>   Duckles* 3:1616. Copy at DLC (Wc).

Literature

1060 Conant, Robert. "The Yale Collection of Musical Instruments," *The Consort* 20 (1963): 174-81.

1061 Bolster, Caitriona. "The Yale Collection of Musical Instruments," *Current Musicology* 7 (1968): 41-43. 350 items.

NEW YORK, NEW YORK (USA). AMERICAN MUSEUM OF NATURAL HISTORY
(L67)

1062 Mead, Charles Williams. *The Musical Instruments of the Incas. A Guide Leaflet to the Collection on Exhibition.* (Guide leaflet no. 11.) [New York]: the Museum, 1903. 31 pp., illus.

>   Supplement to the *American Museum Journal,* vol. 3, no. 4, July 1903.

1063 Mead, Charles Williams. "The Musical Instruments of the Incas," *Anthropological Papers of the American Museum of Natural History,* 15, pt. 3 (1924): 313-47.

>   "Most of the text . . . appeared . . . in 1903 as a Guide leaflet."

NEW YORK, NEW YORK (USA). COOPER UNION [N.B.: Collection on loan to Yale University, 1957; given to the Smithsonian in 1960. See respective catalogues.]

NEW YORK, NEW YORK (USA). CULTURAL CENTER

1064 *Musical Instruments of World Cultures, from the Laura Boulton Collection* [exhibition]. [New York: Intercultural Arts Press, 1972.] vii, 89 pp.

>   Copy at DLC (Wc).

1065 "Musical Instruments and Art of World Cultures, New York Cultural Center [an exhibit assembled by Laura Bolton]," *Connoisseur* 180 (1972): 135. illus.

NEW YORK, NEW YORK (USA). EXHIBITION OF THE INDUSTRY OF ALL NATIONS, 1853-54

1066 Fry, William Henry. *Jury on Musical Instruments. Report.* New York: Baker, Goodwin & Co., 1853. 16 pp.

> Copy at MB (Bp).

NEW YORK, NEW YORK (USA). LIBRARY AND MUSEUM OF THE PERFORMING ARTS

1067 Francois, Jacques. *Violins of France; A Retrospective Exhibition.* January 29 - March 31, 1971. Amsterdam Gallery. [New York: 1971?] 17 pp., 95 items.

> Includes numerous items on loan from the private collections of Jacques Francois, Janos Scholz and (anonymously) Henryck Kaston.

1068 *Jacques Francois Presents Collectors Choice; Musical Instruments of Five Centuries from American Private Collections* . . . April 4 to June 21, 1975. [New York: 1975.] 18 lvs.

> Copy at NN (NYp).

Literature

1069 Rosenbaum, R. M. "Collectors' Choice [exhibit sponsored by the American Musical Instrument Society]," *Early Music* 3 (1975): 440.

1070 American Musical Instrument Society. [Photos and notes about the exhibit in Lincoln Center in Connection with the Society's annual meeting], *American Musical Instrument Society Newsletter* 4, no. 2 (June 1975): 1-6.

NEW YORK, NEW YORK (USA). METROPOLITAN MUSEUM OF ART (L69)
[N.B.: Includes collections of Mrs. J. Crosby Brown, Mary Flagler Cary, Andre Mertens, and Joseph Drexel. Catalogues and literature devoted to these specific gifts and collections follow the general selection below.]

1071 Winternitz, Emanuel. "The Evolution of the Baroque Orchestra. [Exhibition]," *New York (City) Metropolitan Museum of Art Bulletin*, N.S. 12 (1954): 258-76. illus.

NEW YORK, NEW YORK (USA). METROPOLITAN MUSEUM OF ART   *continued*

1072   Winternitz, Emanuel. *Keyboard Instruments in the Metropolitan Museum of Art; A Picture Book.* New York: 1961. 48 pp.

1073   [Libin, Laurence.] *Musical Instruments in the Metropolitan Museum.* [New York: The Metropolitan Museum of Art, c1978.] 48 pp. + 7" LP disc. Lavishly illus.

Literature

1074   Marling, F. H. "Musical Instruments in the Metropolitan Museum," *Music* (Chicago) 10, no. 11 (1905): 451-53; 11, no. 1 (1906): 11-13.

1075   "The Remarkable Collection of Antique Instruments in the Metropolitan Museum," *Music Trades* 42 (1911): 3-4.

1076   R[ansom], C. L. "Egyptian Furniture and Musical Instruments," *New York City. Metropolitan Museum of Art, Bulletin* 7 (1913): 72-79.

1077   "Metropolitan Museum of Art," *Violins* 15 (1954): 222-23.

1078   Holde, Arthur. "Die Sammlung in New-Yorker Metropolitan Museum," *Musikleben* 7 (1954): 305-8. illus.

1079   "Instruments of the Ages [about the exhibition, 'Musical instruments of five continents'] ," *Musical Courier* 163, no. 7 (1961): 14-16.

1080   Winternitz, Emanuel. "Pleasing Eye and Ear Alike," *New York City. Metropolitan Museum of Art, Bulletin* 3 (1971): 66-73.

1081   Libin, Laurence. "The 'Restored' Stradivari and Amati Violins of the Metropolitan Museum," *Violin Society of America Journal* 4, no. 1 (1977/78): 34-39. 8 pls.

General

1082   Hayes, William C. *The Scepter of Egypt; A Background for the Study of Egyptian Antiquities in the [Museum].* 2 vols. New York: Harper, 1953, 1959.
>   Musical Instruments, vol. 1, pp. 247-48; vol. 2, pp. 23-25, et passim.

1083   Lerman, Leo. *The Museum.* New York: Viking Press, [1969]. 400 pp.
>   See index under "Musical Instruments," etc.

1084   Metropolitan Museum of Art. *Guide to the . . .* [First edition]. New York: the Museum, [1972]. 320 pp., illus.
>   "Musical Instruments," pp. 225-40.

1085   "Acquisitions in 1977 at the Metropolitan," *American Musical Instrument Society, Newsletter* 7, no. 1 (March 1978): 2-4. illus.

NEW YORK, NEW YORK (USA). METROPOLITAN MUSEUM OF ART. CROSBY BROWN COLLECTION

1086   Brown, Mrs. Mary Elizabeth. *Musical Instruments and Their Homes, by Mary E. Brown and Wm. Adams Brown; With Two Hundred and Seventy Illustrations. . . . The Whole Forming a Complete Catalogue of the Collection of Musical Instruments Now in the Possession of Mrs. J. Crosby Brown.* New York: Dodd, Mead and Co., 1888. xvii, 380 pp., pls.

> Copies at NN (NYp), NNUT (NYts), PU (PHu), DLC (Wc).

1087   *. . . Preliminary Catalogue of the Crosby-Brown Collection of Musical Instruments of All Nations. Prepared under the Direction, and Issued with the Authorization of the Donor. I. Gallery 27.* (Metropolitan Museum of Art, Handbook no. 13.) New York: Metropolitan Museum of Art, 1901. 94 pp.

> Copy at NN (NYp).

1088   *. . . Catalogue of the Crosby Brown Collection of Musical Instruments of All Nations, Prepared under the Direction, and Issued with the Authorization of the Donor.* (Metropolitan Museum of Art, Handbook no. 13.) 4 vols. in 5. New York: The Metropolitan Museum of Art, 1902-7. illus.

> Duckles* 3:1619. Copies at ICJ, MiU (AAu), NN (NYp), DLC (Wc).

1089   *. . . The Crosby Brown Collection of Musical Instruments of All Nations; Catalogue of Keyboard Instruments, Prepared under the Direction and Issued with the Authorization of the Donor. Galleries 25, 26, 27, 28, 29, Central Cases.* New York: The Metropolitan Museum of Art, 1903.

> This is in part a reprint, in part a supplement, to Handbook no. 13, 1901, no. **1087** above, according to Preface.

1090   *Guide to the Crosby Brown Collection of Musical Instruments, 1905, [by] Mrs. Crosby Brown.* [New York: the Museum, 1905.] 4 lvs.

> Copy at NN (NYp).

1091   Morris, Frances. *Catalogue of the Musical Instruments of Oceanica and America.* (Metropolitan Museum of Art. Catalogue of the Crosby Brown Collection . . . , vol. 2.) New York: 1914. xxi, 333 pp., illus.

> Copies at ICJ, ICN (Cn), MWElC (WElc), NN (NYp), DLC (Wc).

1092   B[rown], M[ary] E[lizabeth]. *The Crosby Brown Collection of Musical Instruments in the Metropolitan Museum of Art. . . .* [n.p., n.d.] 2 vols. of mounted pls.

> Vol. 1: Galleries 35-39, Keyboard instruments. Vol. 2: Galleries 35-39, Wall cases. Copy at DLC (Wc) only.

NEW YORK, NEW YORK (USA). METROPOLITAN MUSEUM. . . . *continued*

1093   . . . *Catalogue of the Crosby Brown Collection of Musical Instruments of All Nations*. . . . [A reissue of no. **1092** above.] 5 vols. New York: [W. L. Davids, printer], 1914.
> Copies at ICU (Cu), MiU (AAu), NN (NYp), NBuG (BUp).

[N. B.: Portions of the collections covered in nos. **1086**-**93** have been re-examined, and the following checklists issued.]

1094   *A Checklist of Western European Flageolets, Recorders, and Tabor Pipes.* [New York] : The Metropolitan Museum of Art, [c1976]. 15 pp., illus.
> Introduction by Laurence Libin.

1095   *A Checklist of Western European Fifes, Piccolos, and Transverse Flutes.* [New York] : The Metropolitan Museum of Art, [c1977]. 16 pp., illus.
> Introduction by Laurence Libin.

1096   *A Checklist of Bagpipes.* [New York] : The Metropolitan Museum of Art, [c1977]. 22 pp., illus.
> Introduction by Laurence Libin.

1097   *A Checklist of Viole da Gamba (Viols).* [New York] : The Metropolitan Museum of Art, [c1979]. 20 pp., illus.
> Preface by Laurence Libin; Introduction by William L. Monical.

1098   *A Checklist of European Harps.* [New York] : The Metropolitan Museum of Art, [1979]. 16 pp., illus.
> Introduction by Laurence Libin.

Literature

1099   Brown, William A. "Rare Musical Instruments," *Outlook* 70 (1902): 564-70.
> A description of the start of the Crosby Brown collection.

1100   Winternitz, Emanuel. "The Crosby Brown Collection of Musical Instruments: Its Origin and Development," *Metropolitan Museum Journal* 3 (1970): 337-56.
> Reviewed in *Galpin Society Journal* 25 (1972): 135-36.

1101   "Mrs. Brown's Magnificent Obsession," *Time* 98 (December 27, 1971): 50-51.

1102   I., B. "A nagyvilág zenéje," *Muzsika* 15 (July 1972): 13-14. illus.

NEW YORK, NEW YORK (USA). METROPOLITAN MUSEUM OF ART. MARY FLAGLER CARY COLLECTION

Literature

1103 Heinsheimer, Hans. "Neue Instrumentsammlung in Metropolitan Museum (New York)," *NZfM* 133, no. 2 (1972): 89-92. illus.

NEW YORK, NEW YORK (USA). METROPOLITAN MUSEUM OF ART. JOSEPH DREXEL COLLECTION

General

1104 *A Guide to the Collections in the.* . . . 7th ed. New York: 1931. 127 pp., illus.

"Musical Instruments," pp. 60-62, notes 45 instruments from the Drexel collection.

NEW YORK, NEW YORK (USA). METROPOLITAN MUSEUM OF ART. ANDRE MERTENS GALLERIES OF MUSICAL INSTRUMENTS

Literature

1105 "Mertens Galleries [opened November 18, 1972]," *American Musical Instrument Society Newsletter* 1, no. 2 (1972): 3-4.

NEW YORK, NEW YORK (USA). PUBLIC LIBRARY. MUSIC DIVISION

1106 Širola, Božidar. *Native Musical Instruments of Kingdom of Yougoslavia;* collected and described by Dr. Božidar Širola. Translated by Lav Medanić. 1 vol. [n.p., 1938.] Mounted illus., 35 items.

Typewritten copy at NN (NYp). Collection, presented to Metropolitan Museum of Art but not accepted, "now in the possession of the New York Public Library." (from printed catalogue card)

NEWARK, NEW JERSEY (USA). NEWARK MUSEUM (L61)

1107 Kerr, Robert Riggs. *Musical Instruments in the Museum's Collections.* Newark, N. J.: Newark Museum Association, 1962. 24 pp., illus.

Constitutes the complete issue of the *Museum,* vol. 14, no. 1 (Winter 1962). Copy at NBuU-M (BUu).

NIZHNI-NOVGOROD (USSR). VSEROSSIISKAIA VYSTAVKA, 1896

1108   Lipaev, I. *Muzyka na XVI Vserossiĭskoĭ vystavke 1896 g. v Nizhnem-Novgorode.* S.-Peterburg: Izd. "Russkoi muzykal'noi gazeti," 1896. 86 pp.

> Cited from Koltypina* (542); instruments, pp. 40-82.

Literature

1109   Findeĭsen, N. F. "So vserossiĭskoĭ vystavki v Nizhnem-Novgorode. Russkie i inorodnicheskie muzykal'nyi instrumenty," *Russkaia muzykal'naia gazeta* (1896), pp. 1008-19.

> Cited from Emsheimer*; not examined.

1110   "Musik-Instrumente und Prämiirungen auf der Russischen National-Ausstellung," *ZfI* 17 (1896/97): 5-6, 191-92.

NONESUCH CASTLE (U.K.)

1111   Warren, C. W. "Music at Nonesuch," *MQ* 54 (1968): 47-57.

> Reprints an inventory of instruments from a 1606 copy of the catalogue of the Nonesuch Library, dated 1596.

Literature

1112   Cust, Lionel Henry. "The Lumley Inventories," *The Walpole Society* (London) 6 (1918): [15]-35.

NUREMBURG (Germany). BAYERISCHE LANDES- INDUSTRIE- GEWERBE- UND KUNST-AUSSTELLUNG, 1882

Literature

1113   Laffert, Oscar. "Die Bayerische Landes- Industrie- Gewerbe- und Kunstausstellung in Nürnberg," *ZfI* 2 (1881/82): 266, 268, 285-86, 298, 300, 314-15, 332-33, 346-48.

1114   "Prämiirungen," *ZfI* 2 (1881/82): 306-7, 309, 357; 3 (1882/83): 17-18.

General

1115   ... *Berichte über die bayerische ... Kunst-Ausstellung zu ... 1882.* Red. von E. Hoyer. München: Literarisch-artist. Anstalt: 1884.

> Cited from KaY* 25:93; not located.

NUREMBURG (Germany). BAYERISCHE LANDES- INDUSTRIE- GEWERBE- UND KUNST-AUSSTELLUNG, 1896

Literature

1116 "Musikinstrumente auf der . . .," *ZfI* 16 (1895/96): 651-53, 941-43, 971-73; 17 (1896/97): 2-3, 916 (prizes).

1117 "Musikinstrumente auf der [II.] Bayerischen Landesausstellung," *Neue Musik-Zeitung* 17 (1896): 235.

General

1118 . . . *Offizieller Katalog*. . . . Nürnberg: J. L. Schrag, 1896. 444 pp., illus.
Cited from KaY* 29:922; not located.

NUREMBURG (Germany). BAYERISCHE JUBILÄUMS- LANDES- INDUSTRIE- GEWERBE-KUNSTAUSSTELLUNG, 1906

Literature

1119 "Die Musikinstrumenten-Industrie in der Bayerischen Landesausstellung zu Nürnberg," *ZfI* 26 (1905/6): 898-900, 1123-25 (prizes).

1120 Flatau. "Musik-Instrumente in der Nürnberger Jubiläums-Ausstellung," *Musikalische Rundschau* (Munich), vol. 2 (October 15, 1906).

General

1121 . . . *Offizieller Bericht . . . verfasst von Paul Johannes Ree*. Nürnberg: Bayerisches Gewerbemuseum, 1907. vi, 502 pp.
Copies at ICJ, ICRL; not examined.

1122 *Offizieller Katalog*. . . . Nürnberg: Vertriebstelle der offiziellen Drucksachen der Bayer. Jubiläums- Landes-Ausstellung, 1906. 120 pp.
Cited from KaY* 33:1089; not located.

1123 *Offizieller Katalog*. . . . 2. Aufl. Nürnberg: 1906. 376 pp.
Cited from KaY* 33:1089; not located.

NUREMBURG (Germany). GERMANISCHES NATIONALMUSEUM (J64, A237, BB192) [N.B.: Includes the Neupert collection, acquired 1968 (see 1938 and 1964 catalogues in Section II), and the Rück collection, acquired 1962. See also Marvin article (1972), no. 1625 under VIENNA (Austria). KUNSTHISTORISCHES MUSEUM.]

1124 *Instrumental Catalogue*. . . . [n.p., n.d.] [61] pp.
A Ms. at NNMM; not examined.

NUREMBURG (Germany). GERMANISCHES NATIONALMUSEUM *continued*

1125   "Die Sammlung musikalischer Instrumente im germanischen Museum," *Anzeiger für Kunde der deutschen Vorzeit* (1860), cols. 6-8, 44-46.

> A list of 65 of the most interesting instruments, sixteenth-eighteenth centuries.

1126   Meer, John Henry van der. "Die Klavierhistorische Sammlung Neupert," *Anzeiger des germanischen Nationalmuseums* (1969), pp. 255-66. illus.

> An inventory of the 298 items in the Neupert collection is included.

1127   Meer, John Henry van der. *Wegweiser durch die Sammlung historischer Musikinstrumente.* Nürnberg: the Museum, [1971?]. 88 pp., illus.

1128   Meer, John Henry van der. Die europäischen Musikinstrumente im Germanischen Nationalmuseum Nürnberg. (Quellenkataloge zur Musikgeschichte, 16: Instrumentenkataloge des Germanischen Nationalmuseums Nürnberg, 1- .) Wilhelmshaven [etc.]: Heinrichshofen, 1979-

> Bd. 1: Hörner und Trompeten, Membranophone, Idio-phone.
> 1979. 137 pp. 195 Abbildungen.

Literature

1129   Hampe, T. "Das Germanische Museum und seine musikhistorische Sammlung," *Nordbayerischen Zeitung,* no. 75 (27. Juli 1912).

1130   Jahn, Fritz. "Das Germanische Nationalmuseum zu Nürnberg und seine Musikinstrumenten-Sammlung," *ZfMW* 10 (1927/28): 109-11.

1131   Jahn, Fritz. "Eine Musik-instrumentensammlung vor dem Verfall," *Signale für die musikalische Welt* 87, no. 41 (1929): 1210-13.

1132   Wittkowski, Josef. "Kommt ohne Instrumente nit! Von Instrumentensammlungen in Franken," *Unser Bayern* (Munich) 3 (1954): 92-93.

1133   Berner, Alfred. "Gutachten über die Musikinstrumenten-Sammlung von Dr. h. c. Ulrich Rück," *Instrumentenbau-Zeitschrift* 17 (1963): 290-93.

1134   Jahnel, Franz. "Die Sammlung historische Musikinstrumenten Dr. Ulrich Rück dem Germanischen Nationalmuseum in Nürnberg einverleibt," *Das Musikinstrument* 12 (1963): 389-91.

1135   Meer, John Henry van der. "Typologie der Sackpfeife," *Anzeiger der germanischen Nationalmuseums* (1954), pp. 123-46.

1136   Talsma, Willem R. "Die Muziekinstrumentenverzameling te Neurenberg," *Mens en melodie* 24 (1969): 264-67. illus.

1137   Meer, John Henry van der. "Die klavierhistorische Sammlung Neupert," *Anzeiger des Germanischen Nationalmuseum* (1969), pp. 255-66. illus.

1138   Meer, John Henry van der. "Curt Sachs and Nuernberg [illustrations of instruments from the museum in Sachs' *Handbuch der Instrumentenkunde,* Leipzig, 1920]," *GSJ* 23 (1970): 120-25.

1139   Meer, John Henry van der. "Die Musikinstrumentensammlung des germanischen Nationalmuseums und ihre Darbeitung." In *Studia musico-museologica* [symposium], pp. 32-47. Nürnberg: 1970.

About an exhibition of ca. 400 items from the Museum.

1140   Meer, John Henry van der. "Flämische Kielklaviere im germanischen National- museum." In *Colloquium Restauratieproblemen* . . . , pp. 63-67. Antwerp: 1971.

Information about the Colloquium in "Neueste Verfahren für alte Instrumente," *Instrumentenbau-Zeitschrift* 25 (1971): 28.

1141   Hellwig, Friedemann. "Die Sammlung historischer Musikinstrumente im . . . ," *Musica* 26 (1972): 123-24, 125-26. 1 pl., illus.

1142   Meer, John Henry van der. "Musikinstrumentenbau in Bayern bis 1800." In *Musik in Bayern, Bd. II: Katalog der Augsburger Musikausstellung, hrsg. von Folker Göthel.* Tutzing: Hans Schneider, 1972.

1143   Meer, John Henry van der. *Der "alte" Musikinstrumentenbestand des . . . Museums.* [Nürnberg: 1972.] 26 pp., mimeo.

1144   [Current projects and productions] , *IAMIC Newsletter* 1 (1973): 21-22.

General

1145   *Die Kunst- und kulturgeschichtlichen Sammlungen des germanischen Museums. Wegweiser für die Besucher.* Nürnberg: Verlag des germanischen Museum, 1912.

"Musikinstrumente (Saal 92)," pp. 199-203, according to *MGG**; many earlier editions, 1877-1910, not examined.

NYON (Switzerland). EXPOSITION. TRÉSORS MUSICAUX DES COLLECTIONS SUISSES, 1949. *See Section II under* **ERNST, FRITZ**

OPORTO (Portugal). MUSEU INDUSTRIAL E COMMERCIAL

1146   [Delerue, Joseph.] *Os piànos portuguezes . . . Edição para o Museu Industrial e Commercial do Porto.* Porto: 1886.

Cited from Lambertini*; not located or examined.

OSEK (Czechoslovakia)

1147 "Inventarium sive Catalogus Musicalium cum annexa Specificatione Instrumentorum Musicorum Ecclesiae B. V. Mariae de Ossecco Combinatum et hoc ordine digestum, Anno 1706." Transcribed by Paul Nettl in "Weltliche Musik des Stiftes Ossegg (Böhmen)," *ZfMW* 4 (1921/22): 351-57.

> "Specificatione," p. 357.

Literature

1148 "Inventarium sive Catalogus Musicalium cum annexa Specificatione Instrumentorum Musicorum Ecclesiae B. V. Mariae de Ossecco Combinatum et hoc ordine digestum, Anno 1706." In Nettl, Paul. *Beiträge zur böhmischen und mährischen Musikgeschichte,* pp. 33-40. Brünn: R. M. Rohrer, 1927.

OSLO (Norway). MUSIKKHØYSKOLEN (J101)

1149 Kjeldsberg, P. A. [Checklist of Olav Gurvin's Instrument Collection.] Oslo: 1975.

> Cited from Jenkins*; not verified.

OSLO (Norway). NORSK FOLKEMUSEUM (J101)

1150 Fett, Harry Per. *Musik-instrumenter. Katalog.* (Norsk folkemuseums Saerudstilling, 2.) Kristiana: Trykt i centraltrykkeriet (C. Thorvaldsen), 1904. 72 pp., [6] pp., illus.

> Copy at NN (NYp), DLC (Wc).

OSLO (Norway). UNIVERSITET. ETNOGRAFSKE MUSEUM (J101)

Literature

1151 Aarflot, Olav. *Kinesisk musikk.* (Handbøker utg. av Etnografske museum, 2.) Oslo: A. W. Brøgger, 1948. 127 pp., illus.

> Copy at DLC (Wc).

General

1152 Klausen, Arne Martin. *Totem, tam-tam, duk-duk. Glimt fra Universitets Etnografiske Museums samlingar.* Oslo: 1961. 39 pp., illus.

> Cited from BM-S*; not located.

OSTEND (Belgium). MUSEUM VOOR SCHONE KUNSTEN

1153   [A list of fourteen ancient instruments in the collection.]
                In Bergmans*, p. 7.

OXFORD (U.K.). UNIVERSITY. ASHMOLEAN MUSEUM   (J155, A110, BB91)

1154   Boyden, David D. *Catalogue of the Hill Collection of Musical Instruments in the Ashmolean Museum.* London, N.Y.: Oxford U. P., 1969.

> Reviews: Albi Rosenthal in *Music & Letters* 110 (1969): 506-8, and Kurt Wegerer in *Österreichische Musikzeitschrift* 24 (1969): 663-64.

Literature

1155   Dart, Thurston. "The Instruments in the Ashmolean Museum," *GSJ* 7 (1954): 7-10.

> "A fuller catalogue is in preparation."

OXFORD (U. K.). UNIVERSITY. FACULTY OF MUSIC. BATE COLLECTION (J155, A111, BB92)

1156   *Handlist to the Collection. . . .* Oxford: 1970. 24 pp.
                Copy of typescript, according to Baines, below.

1157   Baines, Anthony. *The Bate Collection of Historical Wind Instruments. Catalogue.* Oxford: 1976. iv, 64 pp.

Literature

1158   Baines, Anthony. "The Bate Collection at Oxford," *MT* 112 (1971): 25-26. illus.
                About Philip Bate's gift in 1968.

OXFORD (U. K.). UNIVERSITY. FACULTY OF MUSIC. RETFORD GIFT COLLECTION. *See* LONDON (U.K.). RETFORD CENTENARY EXHIBITION

OXFORD (U. K.). UNIVERSITY. MUSICK SCHOOL   (BB93)

1159   Goodson, Richard, snr., d. 1718. *Transcript of the Papers Cattalougs of the Instruments and Books Belonging to the Musick School.*
                Ms. BM* Add. 30493 (ff. 9).

OXFORD (U.K.). UNIVERSITY. PITT RIVERS MUSEUM (J155, A111, BB93)
[N.B.: The gift of General Pitt Rivers in 1883.]

1160   Balfour, Henry. "Report on a Collection of Musical Instruments from the
        Siamese Malay States and Perak." In Annandale, Nelson. *Fasciculi Malayensis,
        Part IIa, Anthropology,* pp. [1]-18. Liverpool: 1904. Pls. XX-XXi.
>   Copy at DLC (Wc).

1161   Baines, Anthony. *Bagpipes* [A survey based upon the collection in the Museum].
        (Pitt Rivers Museum Occasional Papers on Technology, 9.) Oxford: [1960].
        140 pp., illus., including 17 pls.
>   Many of the items illustrated are from the
>   Henry Balfour collection.

Literature

1162   Penniman, T. K. "The Waterloo and Other Musical Boxes in the Pitt Rivers
        Museum at Oxford," *Museums Journal* 55 (1946): 192-93.

PALERMO (Sicily). MUSEO ETNOGRAFICO PITRÈ (J81)

1163   Cocchiara, Giuseppe. *La vita e l'arte del popolo siciliano nel Museo Pitrè.*
        Palermo: Ciuni, 1938. 228 pp., illus.
>   "Balocchi, Giocatolli e strumenti musicali," pp. 121-31.
>   Copies at NIC (Iu), IU (Uu), MH (CAc), DLC (Wc).

PAPEETE (Tahiti). MUSÉE (J128)

1164   Lavandes, Anne. *Catalogue des collections éthnographiques et archéologiques.* . . .
        Papeete: 1966. vii, 409 pp., illus.
>   Musical instruments, pp. 273-80, according to Jenkins*.
>   Copies at CtY (NHu), MU, PPiU, DLC (Wc).

PARIS

This section includes literature under the following entries:

Conservatoire national superieur de musique. Musée
Conservatoire national des arts et métiers. Musée
Exposition de la musique francaise, 1934

Exposition de physique et de T. S. F., 1923

Exposition des produits de l'industrie francaise, 1818

Exposition des produits de l'industrie francaise, 1823

Exposition des produits de l'industrie francaise, 1827

Exposition des produits de l'industrie francaise, 1834

Exposition des produits de l'industrie francaise, 1839

Exposition des produits de l'industrie francaise, 1844

Exposition des produits de l'industrie francaise, 1849

Exposition du travail, 1925

Exposition internationale, 1937

Exposition internationale d'électricité, 1881

Exposition internationale des arts décoratifs et industriels modernes, 1925.
     Section artistique et technique

Exposition internationale du théâtre et de la musique, 1896

Exposition universelle, 1855

Exposition universelle, 1867

Exposition universelle, 1878

Exposition universelle, 1889

Exposition universelle, 1900

Foire, 11th, 1919

Foire, 13th, 1923

Foire, 14th, 1924

Galerie la Boëtie

Hôtel de Cluny. *See* Musée des thermes et de l'Hôtel de Cluny

Musée de la Monnaie

Musée de l'homme

Musée des arts et traditions populaires

Musée des thermes et de l'Hôtel de Cluny

Musée du Louvre

Musée national des arts et traditions populaires. *See* Musée des arts . . .

Saint-Germaine-en-Laye. Musée

Salon, 1912

Salon de la musique, 1st, 1923

Salon de la musique, 2nd, 1924

Salon de la musique, 3rd, 1925

Salon de la musique, 4th, 1926

Salon de la musique, 5th, 1927

Salon de la musique, 6th, 1928

Salon de la musique, 7th, 1929

PARIS (France). CONSERVATOIRE NATIONAL SUPERIEUR DE MUSIQUE. MUSÉE
(J40-41, A155) [N.B.: Began with the Louis Clapisson collection, 1861 (see catalogue
in Section II). Opened with Clapisson its first conservator; Berlioz was second, to 1869.]

1165 Pontécoulant, Louis Adolphe Le Doulcet, marquis de. *Musée instrumental du
      Conservatoire de musique. Histoire et anecdotes. Première partie.* Paris:
      Michel-Lévy freres, 1864. v, 197 pp.

> Cited from BN*; not located.

1166 Chouquet, Gustave. *Le musée du Conservatoire national de musique. Catalogue
      raisonné des instruments de cette collection,* par . . . Chouquet, conservateur du
      musée. Paris: Firmin-Didot frèrers, fils, et cie., 1875. ix, 145 pp., 630 items.

> Copies at NcU (CHhu), CtY (NHu), MH (CAc),
> ViU (CHu), DLC (Wc).

1167 Bannelier, Charles. "Le Musée du Conservatoire National de Musique.
      Publication du Catalogue par M. Gustave Chouquet," *Revue et gazette
      musical de Paris* 42 (1875): 211-12.

1168 Chouquet, Gustave. *Le musée du Conservatoire national de musique. Catalogue
      descriptif et raisonné.* Nouv ed., ornée de figures. Paris: Firmin-Didot et cie,
      1884. xvi, 276 pp., illus.

1169 *1er Supplément au catalogue de 1884* . . . par Léon Pillaut. Paris: Fischbacher,
      1894. xiv, 89 pp. (Nos. 1007-1313).

1170 *2e Supplément au catalogue de 1884* . . . par Léon Pillaut. Paris: Fischbacher,
      1899. 47 pp.

1171 *3e Supplément au catalogue de 1884* . . . par Léon Pillaut. Paris: Fischbacher,
      1903. 35 pp.

> Duckles* 3:1622. Copies at MdBP (BApi), ViU (CHu),
> DLC (Wc).

Literature

1172 Lacome, Paul. "Le Musée instrumental du Conservatoire de Musique. Collection
      de Mr. Clapisson," *Musée des familles* 34 (April 1867): 199.

1173 Liquier, Gabriel. "Le Musée du Conservatoire," *L'art* 11 (1877): 121-27. illus.

1174 Pillaut, Léon. "Dans fait au Musée instrumental," *Le Ménestrel* 53 (1886/87):
      100-101, 244-45.

1175 Pillaut, Léon. Le Musée instrumental du Conservatoire," *Revue politique et
      litteraire* 2 (1886): 756.

1176   Lenotre, G. "The Museum of the Paris Conservatoire," *Violin Times* 5, no. 59, Supplement (1898): 217-18.

1177   Brancour, René. "Le Musée du Conservatoire de musique de Paris," *RMI* 26 (1919): 66-93, 265-90.

1178   Gauther, Maximilien. "Le Musée instrumental: épinettes et virginales, luths, mandores, tympanons," *Renaissance de l'art francaise* 7 (1924): 524-34. illus.

1179   Chambure, Geneviève Thibault de. "Recherches effectuées au Musée Instrumental du Conservatoire de Paris (1962-1965)," *Fontes artis musicae* 12 (1965): 209-12.

1180   Chambure, Geneviève Thibault de. "Les clavecins et épinettes des Ruckers au Musée instrumental du Conservatoire national superieur de musique." In *Colloquium restauratieproblemen . . . Museum Vleeshuis,* pp. 77-85. Antwerp: Ruckers Genootschap, 1971.

1181   Garden, Greer. "Models of Perfection. Woodwind Instruments from the Museum of the Paris Conservatoire," *Recorder & Music Magazine* 4 (1972): 116-17.

1182   Chambure, Geneviève Thibault de. [Descriptions of holdings and projects], *IAMIC Newsletter* 1 (1973): 24-25.

PARIS (France). CONSERVATOIRE NATIONAL DES ARTS ET MÉTIERS. MUSÉE (J41, A155)

1183   . . . *Catalogue du Musée. Section Z: Automates et méchanismes à musique.* Paris: 1960. 65 pp., illus.

>   Copy at NhD (DMu).

General

1184   *Catalogue officiel des collections du Conservatoire des arts et métiers. . . .* Huitième éd. 2e fasc.: Physique. Paris: E. Bernard, 1905.

>   Musical instruments, pp. 71-78; acoustique, pp. 62-69; cited from Heyer* 2:673.

PARIS (France). EXPOSITION DE LA MUSIQUE FRANCAISE, 1934

1185   Gastoué, Amédée, V. Leroquais, [et al]. *La musique francaise du moyen âge à la Révolution. Catalogue. . . .* [Paris]: Éditions des Bibliothèques nationales de France, 1934. 196 pp., illus.

>   "Instruments anciens," pp. 185-87, item nos. 631-48.
>   Copy at NBuU-M (BUu).

PARIS (France). EXPOSITION DE PHYSIQUE ET DE T. S. F., 1923

1186   "La facture instrumental francaise à l'Exposition de Physique et de T. S. F.,"
M & I 9 (1923): 893-97.

PARIS (France). EXPOSITION DES PRODUITS DE L'INDUSTRIE FRANCAISE, 1818

1187   *Rapport du jury central* . . . [par] le Comte Decazes . . . rédigé par M. L. Costaz.
Paris: Impr. royale, 1819.
  "Chap. XXVII, Instruments de musique," pp. 266-69.

PARIS (France). EXPOSITION DES PRODUITS DE L'INDUSTRIE FRANCAISE, 1823

General

1188   *Rapport du jury central* . . . 1823. Paris, 1824.
  "Instruments," pp. 350-58.

PARIS (France). EXPOSITION DES PRODUITS DE L'INDUSTRIE FRANCAISE, 1827

Literature

1189   Fétis, F. J. "Exposition des produits de l'industrie . . . ," *Revue musicale* 2 (1827):
25-36, 82-88, 128-35.

1190   Shillitoe, E. J. "Violin Making at the Great Exhibitions [I, 1827] ," *The Strad*
89 (1979): 911-15.

General

1191   *Rapport du jury central* . . . 1827. Paris, 1828.
  "Instruments," pp. 391-402.

PARIS (France). EXPOSITION DES PRODUITS DE L'INDUSTRIE FRANCAISE, 1834

Literature

1192   Érard, firm. *Perfectionnements appartés dans le mécanisme du piano par les Érard,
depuis l'origine de cet instrument jusqu'à l'Exposition de 1834.* [Paris: P. Érard,
1834.] 16 pp., 8 pls.
  Copy at ICN (Cn).

1193   Shillitoe, E. J. "Violin Making at the Great Exhibitions [III, 1834]," *The Strad*
89 (1979): 915-17.

General

1194   Dupin, Charles, baron. *Rapport du Jury Central sur les produits.* 3 vols. Paris:
Impr. royale, 1836.

> "III. Chap. XXXI, Instruments de musique," vol. 3,
> pp. 281-99. Copy at NBuU-M (BUu).

1195   Flachat-Mony, Christophe Stéphane. *L'Industrie. Exposition de 1834,* par
Stéphane Flachet. Paris: L. Tenré, [s.d.]. 160 pp., illus.

> "Chapitre VI. Lutherie-Pianos," pp. 97-101.
> Copies at CU (BEu), MiU (AAu).

PARIS (France). EXPOSITION DES PRODUITS DE L'INDUSTRIE FRANCAISE, 1839

1196   Jobard, J. B. A. M. *Rapport sur l'Exposition de 1839. . . .* 3 vols. Bruxelles:
Chez l'auteur, 1842.

> "Instruments de musique," vol. 2, pp. 89-187.
> Copy at DLC (Wc).

Literature

1197   Pontécoulant, Adolphe Le Doulcet, marquis de. *Pianos. Analyse des produits de
la manufacture de M. Henri Herz.* Paris: Impr. C. Bajat, 1839.

> Cited from Fétis* (4066); not located.

1198   [Reports], *Allgemeine musikalische Zeitung* 41 (1839): cols. 490, 506, 545-46,
616-18; 46 (1844): col. 726.

1199   Shillitoe, E. J. "Violin Making at the Great Exhibitions [III, 1839]," *The Strad*
89 (1979): 1011-15.

General

1200   *Rapport du Jury Central. . . .* Paris: Impr. Royale, 1839.

> "Instruments de musique [par M. Savart]," vol. 2,
> Sect. IV, pp. 327-76. Copy at DLC (Wc).

PARIS (France). EXPOSITION DES PRODUITS DE L'INDUSTRIE FRANCAISE, 1844

Literature

1201   Érard, firm. *Le piano d'Érard à l'Exposition le 1844. Le piano orné.* Paris:
F. Didot frères; Londres: 1844. 27 pp., 10 pls.

> Copy at ICN (Cn).

PARIS (France). EXPOSITION DES PRODUITS . . . *continued*

Literature

1202   Pontécoulant, Louis Adolphe le Doulcet. "Exposition de l'industrie. Facture instrumentale," *La France musicale* 7 (1844): 139-40, 146-48, 165-67, 170-72, 180-82, 188-90, 196-97, 213-14, 219-20, 239-40 (Récompenses).

1203   Édouard [engineer]. *E. Guérin, ingénieur mécanicien . . . inventeur et fabricant breveté du pianographe, de la clef de piano à engrenages. . . . Description sommaire avec planches de ces instruments; mémoire explicatif sur leur emploi.* St. Germain: Impr. Fleur-Petitjean, 1845.

       Cited from Fétis* (4080); not located.

1204   Shillitoe, E. J. Violin Making at the Great Exhibitions [IV, 1844]," *The Strad* 89 (1979): 1125-33.

General

1205   *Catalogue officiel.* . . . [Paris: Typ. de Cosson, 1844?]   3, 274 pp.

       Copy at MH-BA only; not examined.

1206   Burat, Jules. *Description méthodique, t. 2, 4. ptie.: Application des beaux-arts* [instruments de musique, pp. 50-54, with plates]. Paris: Challamel, [1844?].

1207   *Rapport du jury central* . . . 1844. Paris: Impr. de Fain et Thunot, 1844.

       "Instruments de musique," par M. Savart, vol. 2, pp. 529-88.

PARIS (France). EXPOSITION DES PRODUITS DE L'INDUSTRIE FRANCAISE, 1849

Literature

1208   Érard, firm. *Exportation. Pianos d'Érard en Espagne, Italie et le Levant, Suisse, Russie, Prusse, Belgique, Hollande, Angleterre et le Indes, Amerique.* Paris: F. Didot frères, [1849?].

       Cited from Fétis* (4065).

1209   Shillitoe, E. J. "Violin Making at the Great Exhibition [V, 1849]," *The Strad* 89 (1979): 1133-39.

PARIS (France). EXPOSITION DU TRAVAIL, 1925

Literature

1210   [A report on French instrument manufacturers], *M & I* 11 (1925): 103, 205.

PARIS (France). EXPOSITION INTERNATIONALE, 1937

Literature

1211 Schünemann, Georg. "Die Musikinstrumente auf der Pariser Weltausstellung," *Allgemeine Musikzeitung* 65 (1938): 21-22.

1212 "Die deutschen Musikinstrumente auf der Pariser Weltausstellung," *ZfI* 58 (1937/38): 5-6, 55-56.

PARIS (France). EXPOSITION INTERNATIONALE D'ÉLECTRICITÉ, 1881

Literature

1213 "La musique a l'exposition de l'électricité de Paris," *Echo musicale* 13 (1881): 244-45.

PARIS (France). EXPOSITION INTERNATIONALE DES ARTS DÉCORATIFS ET INDUSTRIELS MODERNES, 1925. SECTION ARTISTIQUE ET TECHNIQUE

1214 "Jouets, appareils scientifiques, instruments de musique, moyens de transport." In *Rapport général de l'Exposition,* T. VIII, pp. 1-105. Paris: Larousse, 1928.
> "Instruments de musique," pp. [51]-62, pls. 52-57.
> Copy at NNMM.

Literature

1215 "L'Industrie de la musique à l'Exposition," *M & I* 11 (1925): 671-73, 755, 759, 831, 833, 837; 12 (1926): 107 (prizes and juries).

1216 Fréchet, André. "Les pianos modernes à l'Exposition," *M & I* 11 (1925): 917, 919, 1019.

PARIS (France). EXPOSITION INTERNATIONALE DU THÉÂTRE ET DE LA MUSIQUE, 1896

General

1217 *Catalogue officiel. 25 juillet - 25 nov. Palais de l'industrie.* [Paris: Impr. Wattier, 1896.] 296 pp.
> Cited from *JbP** 1896; not located.

PARIS (France). EXPOSITION UNIVERSELLE, 1855

1218 Fétis, Francois Joseph. "XXVIIe classe. Fabrication des instruments de musique. Exposé historique de la formation et des variations de systems dans la fabrication des instruments de musique." In *Rapports du Jury Mixte International* . . . , part 2, pp. 1321-72. Paris: Impr. Imperiale, 1856.

   Copies at IaU (IOu), ICN (Cn), DLC (Wc).

1219 Comments on the *Rapports* by Th. Nisard, "VII. Exposition universelle de 1855. Rapports du Jury mixte . . . ," *Revue de musique ancienne et modern* 1 (1856): 713-14.

1220 Helmesberger, Joseph and Edmund Schebek. "XXVII Classe, Musik-Instrumente." In Jonak, Eberhard A. *Bericht über die allgemeine Agricultur- und Industrie-Ausstellung zu Paris,* pp. 1-130 [in the middle of vol. 3] . Wien: k.-k. Hof- und Staatsdruckerei, 1856-57.

   Copies at CLU (LAu), DLC (Wc).

1221 Robin, Charles Joseph Nicolas. *Histoire illustre de l'Exposition universelle, par catégories d'industries.* . . . Paris: Furne, 1855.

   "Instruments de musique," pp. 78-133, illus.
   Copy at DLC (Wc).

Literature

1222 Alexandre, Édouard. *Les orgues-mélodium d'Alexandre père et fils. Exposition Universelle de 1855. Orgues expressive. Pianos-mélodium, pianos à prolongement. Piano Liszt.* Paris: Alexandre père et fils, [n.d.] .

   Cited from Fétis* (4143), "Premiere partie par M. Ad.
   Adam; deuxième partie par M. Frélon"; not located.

1223 Érard, firm. *Paris. Exposition universelle, 1855. Notice sur les travaux de mm. Érard, facteurs de pianos et harpes de Leurs Majestés impériales.* [Paris] : Firmin-Didot frères, [1855?] . 39 pp., illus.

   Copy at DLC (Wc).

1224 LaFage, Juste Adrien Lenoir de. *Quinze visites musicales à l'Exposition universelle* . . . *suivies d'une Post-exposition, de la liste des exposants et de celle des récompenses, et d'un Rapport sur l'orgue de Saint-Eugène.* Paris: Tardif, 1856. viii, 232 pp.

   Article previously published in *Revue et gazette musicale* (Paris). Copies at NN (NYp), DLC (Wc).

1225   *Orgue à piston pour église et pour salon inventé par mm. Claude, frères, de
        Mirécourt (Vosges); brevet d'invention et de perfectionnement.* Paris: typ.
        Soupe, 1855.

>   Cited from Fetis* (4195); not located.

1226   Pontécoulant, Adolphe Le Doulcet, marquis de. *Organographie, ou analyse des
        travaux de la facture instrumentale admise aux expositions des produits de l'industrie
        de la France et de la Belgique . . .* 3e livre. . . . Paris: impr. de C. Bajat, [n.d.] .

>   Volume 2 of his *Essai sur la facture instrumentale . . .*
>   1857-61. Copy at OU (COu).

1227   Shillitoe, E. J. "Violin Making at the Great Exhibitions [VII, 1855] ," *The Strad*
        90 (1979): 197-200.

>   *General*

1228   France. Commission Impériale, Exposition universelle, 1855. *Catalogue
        officiel.* . . . 2e ed. Paris: E. Panis, [1855] .

>   Class XXVII in each section, "Fabrication d'instruments
>   de musique." Copy at DLC (Wc).

PARIS (France). EXPOSITION UNIVERSELLE, 1867

1229   Comettant, Jean Pierre Oscar. *La musique, les musiciens et les instruments de
        musique chez les differents peuples du monde; ouvrage enrichi de textes musicaux,
        orné de 150 dessins d'instruments rares et curieux.* . . . Paris: Michel Lévy frères,
        1869. v, 737 pp.

>   Parts appeared first in *Le Ménestrel.* Copy at DLC (Wc).

1230   Fétis, Francois Joseph. *Exposition universelle de Paris, 1867. Rapport du Jury
        internationale (Vol. IIe, Groupe II^2, Classe 10: Instruments de musique).* Paris:
        Paul Dupont, 1867. 86 pp.

>   Copies at CtY (NHu), NjR (NBu).

1231   Fétis, Francois Joseph. *Exposition universelle de Paris, 1867. Rapport du Jury
        internationale (Vol. IIe, Groupe II^2, Classe 10: Instruments de musique).* In
        Belgium. Commission belge de l'Exposition universelle. Paris: 1867. *Documents
        et rapports,* vol. 1, pp. 471-560. Bruxelles: E. Guyot, 1868.

>   Copy at DLC (Wc).

1232   Fétis, Francois Joseph. *Exposition universelle de 1867 à Paris. Extrait des rapports
        du Jury International . . . Instruments de musique.* Paris: impr. de P. Dupont,
        [1868] . 7 pp.

>   Cited in BN* separately from no. **1230** above; not located.

PARIS (France). EXPOSITION UNIVERSELLE, 1867   *continued*

1233   Gallay, Jules. *Les instruments à archet à l'Exposition universelle de 1867.*
Paris: Imprimerie Jouaust, 1867. 3, 57 pp.

> Copies at MB (Bp), MH (CAc), DLC (Wc).

1234   Pontécoulant, Adolphe LeDoulcet, marquis de. *La musique à l'Exposition
universelle de 1867.* Paris: Au Bureau du journal de l'Art musical, 1868.
3, lxxi, 237 pp., illus.

> Copy at DLC (Wc).

Literature

1235   [Herce, A.] *Exposition universelle de 1867, section francaise, groupe II, classe
X. A Herce inventeur d'un nouveau piano. (Paris 1e 1er mai 1867. . . .)*

> Ms. in Fétis* (4076).

1236   [Steinway & Sons, firm.] *Apercu général sur l'origine et le developpement de la
fabrication de pianos aux États-Unis et description spéciale des pianos fabriques
par MM. Steinway. . . .* [n.p., n.d.]

> Fetis* (4075) says New York: 1861; not located.

1237   Paul, Oscar. *Geschichte des Klaviers . . . nebst einer Uebersicht über der
musikalische Abtheilung der Pariser Weltausstellung, 1867.* Leipzig: A. H. Payne,
1868. 256 pp.

> Copy at NN (NYp).

General

1238   "Instrumente für Kunst und Wissenschaft." In Austria. Central Comite für die
Weltausstellung, Paris. *Berichte . . . ,* 3. Heft, 1. Lfg. Wien: W. Braunmüller,
1869. 199 pp.

> Copy at DLC (Wc).

1239   "Class 10, Instruments de musique." In Belgium. Commission belge de
l'exposition universelle. *Catalogue des produits industrials et des oeuvres d'art,*
pp. 115-20. Bruxelles: 1867.

1240   "Class X, Musical Instruments." In *Complete official catalogue . . . September
edition,* pp. 167-75. London and Paris: J. M. Johnson and Sons, [1867].

> Copy at DLC (Wc).

1241   Fecit, Pietro. *L'industria cremonese manufatturiera e agricola e l'Esposizione
universale di Parigi. Relazione.* Cremona: Ronzi e Signori, 1873. 90 pp.

> "Violini," pp. 58-67.

1242   Boudoin, Felix. "Les instruments de musique [Classe XIX]." In *Études sur l'Exposition de 1867, ou Les Archives de l'Industrie au XIXe siècle.* 2e ed., 1er Sér., Fasc. 1 à 5, pp. 321-26. Paris: Lacroix, 1868.

>   Copy at DLC(Wc).

1243   France. Commission Impériale . . . *Catalogue général.* . . . 2e ed. Paris: E. Dentu, [1867].

>   Groupe 2 [Classe] 10 under each country, "Instruments de musique." Copy at DLC(Wc).

1244   LeRoux, Jules. *L'industrie moderne au champ de Mars.* Paris: Impr. Générale de Ch. Lehure, [1867].

>   "III. Musique," pp. 221-27. Copy at DLC(Wc).

1245   Spain. Commissario regio de España en la exposicion universal de Paris. *Catalogue général* . . . trad. de l'espagnol. Paris: Impr. Générale, 1867.

>   "Classe 10, Instruments de musique (Palais)," pp. 119-21.

1246   Switzerland. Commission d'exposition. *Rapports sur la participation de la suisse.* . . . Berne: Impr. C.-J. Wyer, 1868.

>   "Classe 10. Instruments de musique," pp. 32-37.

1247   Stevens, Paran. *Report upon Musical Instruments.* Washington, D.C.: Government Printing Office, 1869. 18 pp.

>   From *Reports* of the U. S. Commissioners, vol. 5.

PARIS (France). EXPOSITION UNIVERSELLE, 1878 [N.B.: See report on the Kraus collection at the Exposition, nos. 1841-42.]

1248   Boudoin, Felix, Florimond Hervé, ——— Du Moncel, and Nicolas Boquillon. *La musique historique, méthodes et instruments, historique . . . Application de l'électricité aux instruments musicaux. Etudes recueillies dans les derniers Expositions.* 2 vols. Paris: Lacroix, 1886.

>   Cited from BM*; not located.

1249   Chouquet, Gustave. *Rapport sur les instruments de musique et les éditions musicales.* (Paris. Exposition universelles, 1878. Jury international. Rapports, Groupe II, Classe 13.) Paris: Impr. nationale, 1880. 68 pp.

>   Copies at NN (NYp), DLC (Wc).

1250   Chouquet, Gustave. "La musica all'esposizione di Parigi," *Gazzetta musicale di Milano* 36 (1881): 13-15, 43-45, 59-61, 67-68, 77-78, 86.

>   Comments on official reports.

PARIS (France). EXPOSITION UNIVERSELLE, 1878 *continued*

1251   Wit, Paul de. "Gustave Chouquet's Bericht über die musikalischen Instrumente auf der Pariser Weltausstellung, 1878 . . . aus der 'Gazette musical' von Paul de Wit," *ZfI* 1 (1880/81): 167-68, 181-82, 197-98, 213-14, 229.

1252   Hervé, F. "Rapports . . . III. La musique, les méthodes et les instruments par M. [F.] Hervé." In *Études sur l'Exposition de 1878,* pp. 30-67. Paris: Lacroix, [1878]. [illus.]

        Cited from BM* and BN*; not located.

1253   LeComte, Eugène. *Exposition historique de l'art ancien. Catalogue des instruments anciens de musique, documents, curiosités, suivi du catalogue de l'Exposition faite par la Belgique dans l'aile droite du Trocadéro.* Paris: Gand et Bernardel frères, [1878]. 48 pp., pls.

        Copy at MB.

1254   Samuel, Adolphe. "Les instruments de musique." In Belgium. Comité des collaborateurs, Exposition universelle. *La belgique à l'exposition,* vol. 1, pp. 109-26. Bruxelles: A.-N. Lebègue, 1878.

        Copy at DLC.

1255   Samuel, Adolphe. "La belgique à l'exposition universelle de 1878. Les instruments de musique," *Echo musical* 10, no. 20 (1878): 3-4; no. 21 (1878): 3-4; no. 22 (1878): 2-3; no. 23 (1878): 2-3; no. 24 (1878): 2-3.

Literature

1256   [Chanot, George, firm.] *Paris Universal Exhibition. Descriptive Catalogue of Violins, Violas, Violoncellos, and a Double Bass, Exhibited by George Chanot. . . .* London: Mitchell & Hughes, 1878. 1 pl., 7 pp.

        Copy at NN (NYp).

1257   Sievers, G. L. B. "Über die neu verbesserten Geigeninstrumente des Herrn Chanot in Paris," *Gazzetta musicale di Lipsia* 22 (18--): 85.

        Cited from Torri*.

1258   "Les récompenses à l'exposition de Paris. Art musical (Belgique)," *Echo musical* 10, no. 22 (1978): 1.

1259   "Una collezione [A. Kraus] di strumenti musicali all'esposizione di Parigi," *Gazzetta musicale di Milano* 33 (1878): 198.

General

1260 *Catalogue special de la section portugaise à l'exposition universelle de Paris de 1878.* [Paris?] : 1878.

Cited from Lambertini*; not located.

1261 *Illustrirter Katalog der Pariser Weltausstellung . . .* hrsg. von W. H. Uhland. 2 vols. Leipzig: Brockhaus, 1880.

Cited from KaY* 21:787; not located.

PARIS (France). EXPOSITION UNIVERSELLE, 1889

1262 Arnold, G. *Bericht über Classe 13: Musikinstrumente schweizerisches Ursprungs an der Weltausstellung in Paris, 1889.* Zürich: 1890. 15 pp.

Cited from Nef*; not located.

1263 Pierre, Constant Victor Désiré. *La facture instrumentale à l'Exposition universelle de 1889; notes d'un musicien sur les instruments à souffle humain nouveaux & perfectionnés.* Paris: Librarie de l'Art indépendant, 1890. xii, 316 pp., illus.

Copy at NN (NYp).

1264 Thibouville-Lamy, M. J. *Rapports du Jury international . . . sous la direction de M. Alfred Picard . . . Classe 13. Instruments de musique.* Paris: Impr. nationale, 1891. 83 pp.

Cited from BM*; not located. See comments on the reports
by Pierre (above) and Thibouville-Lamy in Eichhorn, no. **1265**.

1265 Eichhorn, M. "Noch einmal der französische Ausstellungsbericht von 1889 über Blasinstrumente," *ZfI* 12 (1891/92): 542-43.

Literature

1266 "Exposition Universelle de Paris 1889 . . . classe 13 (Instruments de musique)," *Echo musical* 19 (1889): 5 (jury), 88-90 (prizes), 102-3 ("nouveautés," by A. Tolbecque).

1267 "Liste der Musikinstrumenten-Aussteller auf der Weltausstellung," *ZfI* 9 (1888/89): 346-48, 364.

1268 Pillaut, Leon. *L'expositions de l'État au Champ-de-Mars et à l'esplanade des Invalides en 1889.* Paris: Impr. du "Journal Officiel," [1889?] .

Cited from Pillaut supplement to Chouquet's *Catalogue*
(nos. **1169-71**, above).

PARIS (France). EXPOSITION UNIVERSELLE, 1889 *continued*

Literature

1269   [Pleyel, Wolff et cie, Paris.] *Exposition universelle de 1889. Classe XIII, Pleyel, Wolff et Cie. Paris, 1807-1889.* Paris: 1889.

   Cited from Lambertini*; not located.

1270   Pougin, Arthur. "Distribution des récompenses à l'exposition universelle," *Le Ménestrel* 55 (1889): 316-17.

1271   Saint-Saëns, Camille. "Les instruments de musique à l'exposition . . . ," *Echo musical* 19 (1889): 137-39, 148-52.

1272   "Betrachtungen von C. Saint-Saëns über Musik und Musikinstrumente gelegentlich der Pariser Weltausstellung," *ZfI* 10 (1889/90): 44-46, 68-70.

1273   Tiersot, Julien. "Promenades musicales à l'exposition," *Le Ménestrel* 55 (1889): 165-66, 179-80, 188-89, 195-96, 203-5, 210-12 [published as a book with title *Musique pittoresques.* Paris: Fischbacher, 1889. 120 pp.] .

General

1274   *Rapport général, par M. Alfred Picard. Tome quatrième: Les beaux arts.* Paris: Impr. nationale, 1891.

   "Instruments de musique," vol. 4, pp. 493-521.
   Copy at DLC (Wc).

PARIS (France). EXPOSITION UNIVERSELLE INTERNATIONALE, 1900

1275   Bricqueville, Eugène de. *Rapports du Jury international . . . Classe XVII, Instruments de musique, par M. de Bricqueville.* (France. Ministère du Commerce, de l'industrie des postes et de télégraphes. Rapports du Jury international. Group III.) Paris: Impr. nationale, 1902. Pp. [491]-573.

   Copy of the *Rapports* at DLC (Wc).

1276   Jacquot, Albert. *Musée rétrospectif de la classe 17. Instruments de musique: matérial, procédés et produits. Rapport du comité d'installation, suivie du catalogue des instruments et accessories ayant figure à l'Exposition Centennial et Rétrospective de 1900 . . .* par MM. Albert Jacquot, E. de Bricqueville et Decescaud. Paris: Impr. de A. Eyméaud, [1900]. 119 pp., illus.

   Copies at ICU (Cu), CU (BEu), IaU (IOu), MH (CAc), DLC (Wc).

1277   Pierre, Constant. *La facture instrumentale à l'Exposition de 1883 et de 1900.* Paris: Librairie de l'Art, 1901. xii, 316 pp.

   Copies at IaU (IOu), CtY (NHu), NIC (Iu), DLC (Wc).

1278   Krehbiel, Henry Edward. *Official Report . . . Class XVII, Group III. Musical Instruments.* [Washington, D. C.] : Government Printing Office, 1901. 16 pp.

>   "Reprinted from the Report of the Commissioner-General for the U. S., 1901."

Literature

1279   Bailly, Éd[ouard?]. *Le pittoresque musical à l'Exposition.* Paris: L'Humanité nouvelle, 1900. 32 pp.

>   Cited from antiquariat's catalogue; not located.

1280   Imbert, Hugues. "Les instruments anciens à l'Exposition universelle de 1900," *Guide musical* 44 (1900): 790-95.

1281   "Intimes van der Pariser Weltausstellung," *ZfI* 20 (1899/1900): 846, 855.

1282   Jacquot, Albert. "La décoration des instruments de musique de 1800 à 1899. [La décoration des instruments . . . à l'Exposition de 1900]," *Revue des arts décoratifs* 22 (1902): 202-13. illus.

1283   Kratochwill, Carl. "Weltausstellung Paris 1900 [about the Austrian instrument-makers at the exhibition]," *Neue musikalische Presse* (Vienna), vol. 9, no. 17 (1900).

1284   "Musical Exhibits at Paris," *Musical Opinion* 23 (1899/1900): 855-56.

1285   "The Musical Instruments Section at the Paris Exhibition," special number of the *Piano, Organ and Music Trades Journal,* October 1900.

>   According to Schles*; not located.

1286   Presto music times. *European Export Supplement of the Special Exposition Issue.* Paris & Chicago: 1900. 40 pp., illus.

>   Copy at NBuU-M (BUu).

1287   Le Monde musical. *[Numero special de l'Exposition de 1900.]* Paris: 1900. illus.

>   Cited from LV&A*; not located in U.S.

1288   Solenière, Eugène de. *La musique à l'Exposition de 1900. Projet présenté à la Commission.* [Paris] : E. Sagot, 1895[?]. 15 pp.

>   Cited from BN*; not located.

1289   Vogt, Felix. "Musik auf der Weltausstellung," *Frankfurter Zeitung,* nos. 200, 232, 288 (1900?).

>   Cited from IBZ* 7:228; not examined.

1290   Westhoven, H. von. "Die Musik auf der Pariser Weltausstellung," *Neue Musik Zeitung* 21 (1900): 185-86, 202-3, 216, 218.

PARIS (France). EXPOSITION UNIVERSELLE ... *continued*

Literature

1291   [Wit, Paul de.] "Die Betheiligung der deutschen Musikinstrumenten-Industrie an der Weltausstellung," *ZfI* 20 (1899/90): 347-48.

1292   "Aussteller ... ," *ZfI* 20 (1899/90): 730, 760, 769, 771-73.

1293   "Prämiirungen," *ZfI* 20 (1899/90): 961-62, 990-94, 997.

1294   Wit, Paul de. "Die Musikinstrumente auf der Pariser Weltausstellung," *ZfI* 20 (1899/90): 811-14, 842-45, 873-75, 901-3, 929-30, 957-61, 1020-23, 1051; 21 (1900/1901): 5, 55-56, 82-83.

1295   Bruneau, Alfred. *La musique francaise: ... La musique à Paris en 1900, au theatre, au concert, à l'Exposition.* Paris: E. Fasquelle, 1901. viii, 255 pp.
        Copy at NN (NYp).

General

1296   Austria. General-Commissariat für die Weltausstellung, Paris. *Katalog der österreichischen Abtheilung.* 11 vols. Heft 1-11. Wien: k. k. Hof- und Staatsdruckerei, [1900].
        "Classe 17: Musikinstrumente," by Friedrich Ehrbar, vol. 1-2, pp. 112-20. Copies at ICRL, NN (NYp), DLC (Wc).

1297   Austria. General-Commissariat für die Weltausstellung, Paris. *Berichte. ...* 12 vols. Wien: C. Gerold's Sohn, 1901-2.
        "Die Musikinstrumente," by Friedrich Ehrbar, vol. 12, pp. 41-53 [483 exhibitors, over 5,000 instruments]. Copies at ICRL and DLC (Wc).

1298   Ehrbar, Friedrich. "Amtlicher Bericht des österreichischen-ungarischen General-Kommissariates über die Musikinstrumente auf der Pariser Weltausstellung 1900," *ZfI* 21 (1900/1901): 779, 802-4, 830-31.

1299   Germany. Reichscommissar für die Weltausstellung, Paris. *Official catalogue of the Exhibition of the German Empire of the International Exposition.* Berlin: [J. A. Stargardt, 1900.] vi, 424 pp., illus.
        "Musik-Instrumente (Champ de Mars)," by Paul de Wit, pp. 150-57; also issued in French and German editions containing de Wit's section. Copies at DLC (Wc).

1300   ... *Catalogue général officiel.* 20 vols. Paris: Lemercier, [1900].
        "Groupe III., Classe 17, Instruments de musique," 51 pp., 424 items. Copy at DLC (Wc).

PARIS (France). FOIRE, 11th, 1919

Literature

1301　"Marché des produits francais," *M & I* 5 (1919): 53.

PARIS (France). FOIRE, 13th, 1923. *See also* PARIS (France). SALON DE MUSIQUE, 1st, 1923

Literature

1302　"La 13me Foire," *M & I* 7 (1923): 165, 203, 207-9.

PARIS (France). FOIRE, 14th, 1924

Literature

1303　"La 14e Foire de Paris," *M & I* 8 (1924): 221-24, 317.

PARIS (France). GALERIE LA BOËTIE

Literature

1304　T., P. de. "L'exposition Pleyel. Pianos modernes de style ancien. Série Albert de Montry," *M & I* 4, no. 105 (1914): 97.

PARIS (France). HÔTEL DE CLUNY. *See* MUSÉE DES THERMES ET DE L'HÔTEL DE CLUNY

PARIS (France). HÔTEL DE SULLY [Exhibit, October 9-November 15, 1972] . *See* BESANCON. MUSÉE HISTORIQUE

PARIS (France). MUSÉE DE LA MONNAIE

1305　*Louis XV. Un moment de perfection de l'art français.* Paris: Hôtel de la Monnaie, 1974. lxvi, 682 pp., illus.

　　　　Catalogue of an exhibition, which included musical
　　　　instruments, at the Hotel. "Les instruments de musique,"
　　　　prepared by Mme. Bran-Ricci, according to *RILM* * 8:1500.

PARIS (France). MUSÉE DE L'HOMME [until 1937 the MUSÉE D'ETHNOGRAPHIE] (J40)

1306   Sachs, Curt. *Les instruments de musique de Madagascar.* (Université de Paris. Travaux et mémoires de l'Institut d'Ethnologie, 28.) Paris: Institut d'Ethnologie, 1938. ix, 96 pp., illus., 15 pls.

> Includes a catalogue of instruments in the Musée.
> Copy at NN (NYp).

1307   Dournon-Taurelle, Geneviève and John Wright. *Les guimbardes du Musée. . . .* Préface de Gilbert Rouget. Paris: Institut d'Ethnologie . . . , 1978. 150 pp., illus.

> Catalogue: pp. 56-129 (155 items).

PARIS (France). MUSÉE DES ARTS ET TRADITIONS POPULAIRES (J39, A156)

Literature

1308   Marcel-Dubois, Claude. "The Objectives of Music and Musical Instrument Collections in a National Ethnological Museum." In *Studia musico-museologica* [symposium], pp. 98-102. Nürnberg: Germanisches Nationalmuseum, 1970.

1309   [Description of activities and projects], *IAMIC Newsletter* 1 (1973): 26-27.

PARIS (France). MUSÉE DES THERMES ET DE L'HÔTEL DE CLUNY

1310   Grillet de Givry, Émile Angelo. *Notice sur les instruments de musique exposés au Musée de Cluny.* Paris: A. Bourlon, 1914. 19 pp.

> Cited from LoR*; not examined.

General

1311   Du Sommerard, Eduard. *Catalogue et description des objets d'art, de l'antiquité, du moyen âge et de la renaissance exposés. . . .* Paris: Hôtel de Cluny, 1883. 693 pp.

> "[Classe] XVI. Instruments de musique," pp. 560-61;
> at least 25 editions listed in LC-NUC*.

PARIS (France). MUSÉE DU LOUVRE. DEPARTEMENT DES ANTIQUITÉS ÉGYPTIENNES (J41)

1312   Ziegler, Christianne. *Les instruments à musique égyptiens au Musée de Cluny. . . .* Paris: Édition de la Réunion des Musées Nationaux, 1979. 135 pp., illus.

PARIS (France). MUSÉE NATIONAL DES ARTS ET TRADITIONS POPULAIRES.
See PARIS (France). MUSÉE DES ARTS ET TRADITIONS POPULAIRES

PARIS (France). OPÉRA. BIBLIOTHÈQUE, ARCHIVES ET MUSÈE

1313   *Musique d'Asie. Instruments de la collection Kwok On* [exposition] . *Bibliothèque de l'Opéra, 1977. Département des arts du spectacle de la Bibliothèque nationale.* Paris: Bibliothèque nationale, c1977. [27] pp., illus.

PARIS (France). SAINT-GERMAINE-EN-LAYE. MUSÉE

1314   Daubresse, Mathilde. *La musique au Musée de Saint-Germain-en-Laye.* Paris: Fischbacher, 1912. 22 pp., illus.

　　　　Copy at NN(NYp).

PARIS (France). SALON, 1912

　　　　Literature

1315   *La musique, la danse. Catalogue. Exposition rétrospective, organisée par la Société nationale des beaux-arts dans les Palais du Domaine de Bagatelle.* [Paris] : Évreux, 1912. 100 pp.

　　　　BM* says 60 pp. Copies at INU(BLu), NN(NYp).

PARIS (France). SALON DE LA MUSIQUE, 1st, 1923

1316   "Premier Salon de la Musique. Organizé à la Foire à Paris (10-25 mai 1923)," *M & I* 8 (1922): 659; 9 (1923): 5, 73; and whole Special issue no. 165 (10 mai 1923), lxvii pp.; 9 (1923): 421, 439-99, 533.

PARIS (France). SALON DE LA MUSIQUE, 2nd, 1924

1317   "Le 2e Salon de la Musique," *M & I* 9 (1923): 889, 951-52; 10 (1924): 11, 89, 171, 249-53; whole issue no. 177 (10 mai, 1924), lxxxiv pp.; 10 (1924): 491-538.

PARIS (France). SALON DE LA MUSIQUE, 3rd, 1925

1318   "Le 3^e Salon de la Musique," *M & I* 11 (1925): 5-7, 97-101, 197, 279, 283, 285; whole issue no. 189 (mai, 1925), lxxxvi pp.; 11 (1925): 544-81 (illus.).

PARIS (France). SALON DE LA MUSIQUE, 4th, 1926

1319   "Le 4^e Salon de la Musique," *M & I* 12 (1926): 11, 113, 211, 213, 309, 311-13, 317; whole issue no. 201 (mai 1926), civ pp.; 12 (1926): 599-646 (illus.).

PARIS (France). SALON DE LA MUSIQUE, 5th, 1927

1320   "Le 5e Salon de la Musique," *M & I* 12 (1926): 1265.

PARIS (France). SALON DE LA MUSIQUE, 6th, 1928   [N.B.: Held? No literature found.]

PARIS (France). SALON DE LA MUSIQUE, 7th, 1929

1321   "7e Salon de la Musique et du phonographe organisé à la Foire de Paris . . . 26 mai 1929," *M & I* 20 (1929): 413-17, 421; whole issue no. 237 (10 mai 1929), cxx pp.; 20 (1929): 675.

PESSARO (Italy). LICEO MUSICALE ROSSINI

1322   Fara, Giulio. "Il Liceo musicale Rossini di Pessaro e i suoi strumenti musicali etnici," *Musica d'oggi* 14 (1932): 421-28.

PHILADELPHIA, PENNSYLVANIA (USA). CENTENNIAL EXHIBITION, 1876

Literature

1323   "Ouverture dell'Exposition de Philadelphia," *Echo musical* 8, no. 11 (mai, 1876): 4-5.

General

1324   U. S. Centennial Commission. *International Exhibition 1876. Reports and Awards. Group XXV.* Philadelphia: Lippincott, 1878.

> "Musical Instruments," by Henry K. Oliver, pp. 27-56;
> [Exhibitors of musical instruments and prizes], pp. 140-51.
> Copy at DLC.

1325   Germany. Reichskommission, Weltausstellung in Philadelphia, 1876. *Amtlicher Katalog / Official Catalogue.* Berlin: R. v. Decker, 1876.

>   "Class 327, Musical Instruments," pp. 87-90; (English and German in parallel columns). Copy at DLC (Wc).

PHILADELPHIA, PENNSYLVANIA (USA). COMMERCIAL MUSEUM

1326   Barone, Joseph. *A Handbook of the Musical Instrument Collection of the Commercial Museum.* [Philadelphia: 1961.] 63 pp., illus.

>   Copy at NBuU-M (BUu).

PHILADELPHIA, PENNSYLVANIA (USA). MUSEUM OF ART (L88). *See Section II under* FRISHMUTH, Mrs. WILLIAM D.

PHILADELPHIA, PENNSYLVANIA (USA). PENNSYLVANIA UNIVERSITY. UNIVERSITY MUSEUM (L87)

Literature

1327   Fernald, Helen Elizabeth. "Ancient Chinese Musical Instruments As Depicted on Some of the Early Monuments in the Museum," *Pennsylvania University. University Museums Journal* 17 (1926): 325-71. illus.

PHILADELPHIA, PENNSYLVANIA (USA). PENNSYLVANIA UNIVERSITY. FREE MUSEUM OF SCIENCE AND ART. FRISHMUTH COLLECTION. *See Section II under* FRISHMUTH, Mrs. WILLIAM D.

PHILADELPHIA, PENNSYLVANIA (USA). SESQUICENTENNIAL INTERNATIONAL EXPOSITION, 1926

1328   Friedrich, John & Bro., firm, N.Y. *Souvenir Brochure of John Friedrich Instruments Exhibited at the Sesquicentennial International Exposition . . . June 1 to December 1 . . . Palace of Liberal Arts & Manufactures.* New York: J. Friedrich & Bro., Inc., [1927?]. 22 pp., illus.

>   Copy at NN (NYp).

POZNÁN (Poland). MUZEUM NARODOWE W POZNANIU (J105)

1329 Szulc, Zdislaw. *Katalog instrumentów muzycznych ze zbiorow Zdislawa Szulca Wystawionych na Wystawie Muzycznej w Muzeum Miejskin w Poznaniu* 2-9 X 1938. Poznań: Zarzad Miejski, 1939. 15 pp.

   Cited from Michalowski* (211).

1330 Kamiński, Włodzimierz. "Muzeum instrumentów muzycznych," *Kronika miasta Poznania* 27 (1959): 22-32.

   Cited from *BdMS*.

1331 Kamiński, Włodzimierz. *Skrzypce polskie.* Krákow: PWM, 1969. 96 pp., illus.

   "The instruments studied are mostly from the collection of the Museum" (Michalowski in *RILM*).

POZNAŃ (Poland). MUZEUM WIELKOPOLSKIE

1332 Szulc, Zdzislaw. *Katalog instrumentów muzycznych.* [Przedm. Adolf Chybinski.] Poznań: druk. Zaklad Doskonalenia Rzemiosla, 1949. 11 pp., illus.

   Cited from Michalowski*; not examined.

PRAGUE (Czechoslovakia). ALLGEMEINE LANDESAUSSTELLUNG, 1891

Literature

1333 "Musikinstrumente auf der Landesausstellung," *ZfI* 11 (1890/91): 375-77, 389.

General

1334 *Katalog der collectiv-Ausstellung.* . . . Prag: Im Verlag der fürstl. Schwarzenberg'schen Centralkanzlei, 1891. 103 pp.

   Musical instruments, group 22. Copy at DGS (Wgs).

PRAGUE (Czechoslovakia). NÁRODNÍ MUZEUM (J30-31)

1335 Buchner, Alexander, ed. *Průvodce výstavou Česke hudebni nástroje minulosti v břevnovském klášteře sv. Markety.* [V Praze: 1950.] 87 pp., illus., 495 items.

   "Les instruments de musique tcheque du passe," from summary in French. Includes Lobkowitz collection according to Grove's*. Copy at DLC (Wc).

1336   *Katalog der Dauerausstellung der Musikinstrumente der Musikabteilung des Nationalmuseums Prag.* Deutschsprachige Aufl. Prag: 1974. 48 pp., 13 pls.

> Reviewed in *Glareana* 26, no. 2 (June 20, 1977):
> lvs. 32-33; not examined.

Literature

1337   Jetel, Rudolf O. "Státní sbirky hudebních nástrojů otevřeny," *Hudebni rozhledy* 7 (1954): 529.

1338   Buchner, Alexandr. *Hudebni nástroje od pravěku k dnešku.* [1. vyd.] Praha: Orbis, 1956. 279 pp., illus.

> Nearly half of illustrations depict instruments in this collection.

1339   Buchner, Alexandr. *Musical Instruments Through the Ages.* [Translated by Iris Unwin.] London: Spring Books, [1956?]. xv, 38 pp., pls.

1340   Buchner, Alexandr. *Musikinstrumente im Wandel der Zeiten.* Prag: Artia, [1956]. 50, vi pp., illus.

1341   Buchner, Alexandr. *Gli strumenti musicali attraverso i secoli.* Pref. di Massimo Mila. [Milano]: Edizioni la Pietra, [1964]. 52 pp., 331 pls.

> Copy at DLC (Wc).

1342   Buchner, Alexandr. *Musical Instruments; An Illustrated History.* [Translated by Borek Vancura.] [New York]: Crown, [1973]. 274 pp., chiefly illus.

1343   Buchner, Alexandr. *Musical Instruments; An Illustrated History.* [Translated from the Czech MS by Borek Vancura.] London: Octopus Books, 1973. 275 pp., chiefly illus.

1344   Buchner, Alexandr. *České automatofony . . . Czech automatophones.* (Sbornik Národního musea v Praze, sv. 11 - A. Historický. čis 2/3.) Praha: 1957. 69 pp., 16 pls.

> Inventory of the museum's collection, pp. 46-47.
> Copy at DLC (Wc).

1345   Montagu, Jeremy. "The [Galpin] Society's First Foreign Tour," *GSJ* 21 (1968): 4-23.

> Most of the article about the Prague museum.

1346   Hradecký, Emil. "Die Musikabteilung des Prager Nationalmuseums mit besonderer Berücksichtigung der Musikinstrumenten-sammlung," *Glareana* 18, no. 3/4 (1969): 2-16.

1347   Keller, Jindřich. "Alte Trompetendämpfer," *Glareana* 18, no. 1 (1969): lvs. 2-9.

> Eighteen mutes from the Prague museum described.

PRAGUE (Czechoslovakia). NÁRODNÍ MUZEUM   *continued*

Literature

1348   Hradecký, Emil. "Die Darbeitungs-probleme einer Musikinstrumentensammlung in historischen Ausstellungsraumen." In *Studia musico-museologica* [symposium], pp. 55-63. Nürnberg: Germanisches Nationalmuseum, 1970.

1349   Keller, Jindřich. "Pozvanka do muzea [Invitation to the musical instruments in Prague]," *Hudební nástroje* 7 (1970): 22-23, 54-55, 87, 118, 149-50, 185.

   Cited from *BdMS**.

1350   Oromszegi, Otto. "Bassoons at the Narodní Museum," *GSJ* 24 (1971): 96-101. illus., 36 items.

General

1351   *Führer durch die Sammlungen des Museums des Königreiches Böhmen, in Prag.* Prag: Verlag des Museums, 1897. 108 pp.

   Boalch* mentions; not examined.

PRAGUE (Czechoslovakia). NÁPRSTKOVO MUZEUM ASIJSKÝCH, AFRICKÝCH A AMERICKÝCH KULTUR

1352   *Hudební nástroje severní Afriky a arabského Orientu. Katalóg výstavy Náprstkoveho musea v Praze.* Praha: the museum, 1970. 23, [3] pp., illus., 25 photos, 20 items.

   Copy at DLC (Wc).

PROVIDENCE, RHODE ISLAND (USA). RHODE ISLAND SCHOOL OF DESIGN, MUSEUM OF ART   (L90)

1353   Chapman, W. L. "The Albert Steinert Collection of Harpsichords," *Rhode Island School of Design, Bulletin* 16, no. 1 (1928): 4-8.

1354   Neilson, Katherin B. "Keyboard and Strings; Early Instruments and Performers. [Exhibition . . . of the Albert M. Steinert collection]," *Rhode Island School of Design Museum, Museum Notes* 8, no. 3 (1951): unpaged. 6 pp., illus.

QUITO (Ecuador). CASA DE LA CULTURA ECUATORIANA. MUSEO DE INSTRUMENTOS MUSICALES "PEDRO TRAVERSARI" (J33)

1355   *Catalogo general del Museo de Instrumentos Musicales de la Casa de Cultura Ecuatoriana.* Quito: 1961. 71 pp., 22 photos.

> Copies at TxU (AUSu), NN (NYp), DLC (Wc).

1356   *Museo de Instrumentos Musicales "Pedro Pablo Traversari."* [Quito] : Casa de la Cultura Ecuatoriana, 1971. 62 pp., illus.

> Copy at DLC (Wc).

REICHENBERG i. B. (Germany). DEUTSCH-BÖHMISCHE AUSSTELLUNG, 1906

Literature

1357   Ströbe, P. "Die Musikinstrumente auf der deutsch-böhmischen Ausstellung," *ZfI* 26 (1905/6): 1059-61, 1091-92, 1125-26; see also pp. 776, 783 (exhibitors) and 1097 (prizes).

General

1358   *Katalog der . . . Ausstellung.* Reichenberg: [P. Sollons Nachf.] , 1906. 247 pp.

> Cited from KaY* 33:1088; not located.

1359   [Moissl, F.] *Deutsch-Böhmische Musikausstellung.* Reichenberg: 1906. 221 pp.

> Bayreuther Musikantiquariat catalogue, 1957; not located.

RHEDA (Germany). FÜRSTEN ZU BENTHEIM-TECHLENBURG MUSIKBIBLIOTHEK since 1967 at MÜNSTER. ERBDROSTENHOF, q. v.

RIO DE JANEIRO (Brazil). BIBLIOTECA NACIONAL

1360   Camêu, Helza. *Instrumentos musicais dos indígenas brasileiros: catálogo da exposição.* Rio de Janeiro: Biblioteca Nacional, 1979. 69 pp., illus.

RIO DE JANEIRO (Brazil). EXPOSIÇÃO DO CENTENARIO DO BRASIL, 1922-23

Literature

1361   "L'Industrie musicale française à l'Exposition de Rio-de-Janeiro," *M & I* 8 (1922): 533-37, 539.

RIO DE JANEIRO (Brazil). EXPOSIÇÃO DO CENTENARIO ... *continued*

Literature

1362   Goebel, Josef. "Deutsche Klavier-Industrie auf der Weltausstellung," *ZfI* 42 (1921/22): 1026-27, 1093, 1545, 1547.

RIO DE JANEIRO (Brazil). INSTITUTO NACIONAL DE MUSICA. MUSEU INSTRUMENTAL

1363   *O museum instrumental do Instituto nacional de musica do Rio de Janeiro.* Rio de Janeiro: 1905. 52 pp.

        Cited from antiquariat's catalogue; unable to verify or locate.

ROME (Italy). R. ACCADEMIA NAZIONALE DI SANTA CECILIA. MUSEO STRUMENTALE (A310) [N.B.: Some of the private collections included are those of Margaret of Savoy, Prospero Colonna, Evan Gorga, Gioacchino Pasqualini.]

1364   Re, Lucie Del. *Mostra di strumenti musicali, per gentile concessione del Museo strumentale del l'Accademia Nazionale di S. Cecilia, Roma 9-19 ottobre 1963. Catalogo.* Roma: Associazione via del Babuino e Alitalia, 1963. 60 pp., illus.

        Preliminary notes by A. Bustini and F. Lampronti.

Literature

1365   "Museo (L'incipiente) di strumenti musicali nella R. Accademia," *Bollettino musicale Romano,* vol. 2, no. 6-9 (1900).

        Cited from Torri* and *ZiMG*-schau*; not located.

1366   "Raccolta d'istrumenti ... da Alberto Cametti," *R. Accademia di Santa Cecilia, Annuario* 5 (1900): 22-54. illus.

1367   "Il Museo di strumenti musicali dell'Accademia Nazionale di Santa Cecilia," *St. Cecilia* 9 (1960): 45-46.

1368   Pasqualini, Gioacchino. "Donazione di strumenti antichi fatta dal prof. Gioacchino Pasqualini all'Accademia Nazionale di S. Cecilia," *St. Cecilia* 11 (1962): 21-27. illus.

ROME (Italy). MOSTRA CORELLIANA, 1953-54

1369   *Catalogo della Mostra corelliana; a cura del Comitato nazionale per la celebrazione del III Centenario della nascita di Arcangelo Corelli . . . Manoscritti documenti, edizioni antiche e rare, iconografia, strumenti musicali . . .* [etc.] *Roma, Palazzo Braschi, dicembre 1953-gennaio 1954.* Roma: Tip. Filli Palombi, 1953. 48 pp., illus.

> Section on musical instruments by Luisa Cervelli, pp. 41-48, includes some items from Evan Gorga collection. See Winternitz in *MQ* 40 (1954): 614.

Literature

1370   DeLitala, N. "Exhibition at Rome [of old Italian instruments]," *Violins and Violinists* 15 (1954): 160-61.

ROME (Italy). MUSEO DELL'AFRICA ITALIANA

Literature

1371   Caravaglios, Cesare. *Saggi di folklore.* Napoli: Ed. Rispoli anonima, [1938]. 205 pp., illus.

> "Notizie sommario sugli strumenti musicali del Museo," p. 159. Copies at CU (BEu), NjP (PRu), DLC (Wc).

ROME (Italy). MUSEO NAZIONALE DELLE ARTI E DELLE TRADIZIONI POPOLARI (J81)

1372   Scotti, Pietro. *Etnologia.* Seconda ed., completamente rinnovata. Milano: Hoepli, 1955.

> "Strumenti musicali," pp. 304-15; Figs. 141-57 (mostly from this museum).

1373   Grottanelli, Vinigi L. [About the instruments in this museum], *Etnologia,* Vol. III, pp. 637-57.

> Cited from Jenkins*; unable to verify or locate.

ROME (Italy). MUSEO PREISTORICO-ETNOGRAFICO "LUIGI PIGORINI" (J82)

1374   Scotti, Pietro. *Gli strumenti musicali africani del R. Museo Pigorini, Rome.* Firenze: Palazzo Nonfinito, 1940. 60 pp., 16 pls.

> Issued separately from: *Archivio per antropologia e la etnologia* 70 (1940): fasc. 1/4, pp. [5]-60.

ROME (Italy). RACCOLTA STATALE DI STRUMENTI MUSICALI — FONDO EVAN GORGA   (Entry from J/Jenkins*, p. 81)

1375   Cervelli, Luisa. *Mostra di strumenti musicali dell'Estremo Oriente della collezione Gorga. Catalogo. Roma, Palazzo Venezia, Salo Barbo, 27 marzo - 6 aprile 1965.* Roma: Ministero P. I. . . . , 1965. 24 pp., illus.

> Cited from Gai* and *BNI*; not located in U. S.
> Cf. nos. **1364-67** and **1369**, above.

1376   Cervelli, Luisa. *Mostra di strumenti musicali del '600 e '700. Catalogo . . . Roma, S. Marta al Collegio Romano, dicembre 1965 - gennaio 1966.* Roma: Ministero P. I. . . . , 1966. 30 pp., 3 tables.

> Cited from Gai* (who dates 1965) and *BdMS*;
> not located in U. S.

1377   Cervelli, Luisa. "Museographische Kriterien und Arbeitsplanung, dargestellt anhand der Instrumentenmuseen von Rom und Neapel." In *Studia musico-museologica* [symposium], pp. 64-67. Nürnberg: Germanisches Nationalmuseum, 1970.

> The Naples collection is that in the Conservatorio
> "S. Pietro a Majella."

ROME (Italy). SOCIETA NAZIONALE "DANTE ALIGHIERI." COMITATO DI TUNISI

1378   Nataletti, Giorgio. "Gli strumenti musicali etnici della Sez. musicale 'Giuseppe Verdi' di Tunisi," *Musica d'oggi* 16 (1934): 414-21.

> A "catalogo sommario" of Tunisian, Tripolitanian,
> Madagascan and Chinese instruments.

1379   Nataletti, Giorgio. *Catalogo descrittivo degli strumenti musicali raccolti nel Museo strumentale.* Rome: [Tip. "La Speranza"] anno XIV, [1936]. 61 pp., illus., 17 pls.

> Includes items from the collection of Antonin Laffage.
> Copies at NN(NYp), DLC(Wc).

ROME (Italy). TEATRO DELL'OPERA

Literature

1380   Angelis, Alberto de. "L'erigendo Museo del Teatro reale dell'Opera in Roma," *Musica d'oggi* 14 (1931): 158-62.

> Notes the gift of Emma Carelli.

ROME (Italy). VATICAN. MUSEO MISSIONARIO ETNOLOGICO (J83)

1381   Palazzo, Elena. *Musica e strumenti di terre lontane (con la riproduzione degli strumenti musicali conservati nel Pontificio Museo Missionario Etnologico Lateranense)*. Roma: A. Signorelli, 1933. 95 pp., illus.

>   Copy at DLC(Wc).

1382   Forno, Mario. "La raccolta di strumenti musicali Ghivaro (Ecuador e Peru) del Museo missionario salesiano di Colle Don Bosco (Asti)," *Pontificio museo missionario etnologico, già Lateranensi, Annali* 33 (1969 [publ. 1971]): 9-30.

>   Cited from *BdMS**; not examined.

ROTTERDAM (Netherlands). TENTOONSTELLING VAN MUZIEKINSTRUMENTEN, 1909

Literature

1383   "Musikausstellung in Rotterdam," *ZfI* 29 (1908/9): 154, 271, 336, 901 (exhibitors), 937-38, 974-76 (reports), 991 (Dutch exhibitors), 1053 (Epilogue), 1094-96 ("Schlussbericht").

1384   "De tentoonstelling van muziekinstrumenten te Rotterdam," *Weekblad voor muziek* 16 (1909): 271-72 (awards and juries).

1385   *International Tentoonstelling van Muziekinstrumenten, met daaraan Verbonden National Concours voor Harmonie- en Fanfarekorpsen te houden van 19 Mei tot 1 Juni 1909*. Rotterdam: 1909. [8] pp.

RUDOLSTADT (Germany). HOF-KAPELLE

1386   Anemüller, B. "Instrumenteninventarium einer kleinen Hofkapelle [compiled originally by Ph. H. Erlebach, d. 1741]," *Anzeiger für Kunde der deutschen Vorzeit* (1833), pp. 326-27.

>   From a Ms. in the Staatsarchiv.

1387   "Musikalisches Instrumenten-Inventarium der fürstlichen Hof-kapelle zu Rudolstadt vor 180 Jahren," *ZfI* 17 (1896/97): 307. 27 items.

>   Reprints Erlebach's inventory.

1388   Erlebach, Ph. H. "Inventarium Ueber die, zur Hochgräffl. Rudolstädtischen Hoff Capell gehörigen musicalischen Sachen und Instrumenta. An Instrumenten." In Erlebach, Philip Heinrich. *Harmonische freude . . .* , hrsg. von Otto Kinkeldey, p. xxviii. Leipzig: Breitkopf & Härtel, 1914. (*DDT*, Band XLVI)

RZESZOW (Poland). MUZEUM OKREGOWE   (J106)

1389   Lew, Stefan. *Instrumenty muzyczne Pogorza Karpachiego; katalog wystaw.* . . .
Dynow: 1969.

> Cited from Jenkins*; not located.

ST. ALBANS (U. K.). ENGLISH CHURCH HISTORY EXHIBITION, 1905

1390   *Exhibition . . . at the Town Hall St. Albans from 27th June to 15th July 1905.*
[Catalogue. London: 1905.] vii, 191 pp.

ST. GALLEN (Switzerland). [HISTORISCHES MUSEUM?]   (J125)

Literature

1391   "Musikinstrumente aus aller Welt," *Glareana*, vol. 7, no. 3 (1958).

> Not examined.

ST. LOUIS, MISSOURI (USA). LOUISIANA PURCHASE EXPOSITION, 1904

Literature

1392   "St. Louis Exhibition: the British [etc.] Exhibits," *London and Provincial Music
Trades Review* 27, no. 322 (1904): 15-16, 23.

1393   "Die Weltausstellung in St. Louis," *ZfI* 24 (1903/4): 356, 384, 389, 395, 632
(German exhibitors), 662 (French exhibitors), 759, 1059; 25 (1904/5): 67, 103,
134-35, 165, 262, 273, 389 (all, lists of prizes), 610, 621.

General

1394   Germany. Reichskommission, Weltausstellung in St. Louis, 1904. *Amtlicher
Katalog.* . . . Berlin: G. Stilke, [1904]. 548 pp., illus.

> "Musikinstrumente," pp. 189-95, by Paul de Wit;
> "Group 21 - Musikinstrumente," pp. 426-27.
> Copies at NIC (Iu), NNC (NYcu).

1395   Germany. Reichskommission. . . . *Official Catalogue of the Exhibitions of the
German Empire.* Berlin: G. Stilke, [1904].

> "Musical Instruments," pp. 186-92, by Paul de Wit.
> Copy at DLC (Wc).

SALEM, NORTH CAROLINA (USA). MORAVIAN MUSICAL ARCHIVES

1396 Pressley, Ernest Wayne. *Musical Wind Instruments in the Moravian Musical Archives*. D. M. A. dissertation, University of Kentucky, 1975.

SALZBURG (Austria). MOZART-MUSEUM (J9, A25, BB17)

Literature

1397 Kinsky, Georg. "Die Klaviere im Mozart-Museum," *ZfI* 54 (1933/34): 322-25. illus.

1398 Schurich, Hans. *W. A. Mozarts Original-Instrumente im Mozart-Museum*. Salzburg: Internationale Stiftung Mozarteum, 1960.

      Cited from Jenkins*; not located.

1399 "Diebstahl in Mozarts Wohnhaus in Salzburg," *Musica* 26 (1972): 380.

SALZBURG (Austria). MUSEUM CAROLINO-AUGUSTEUM (J9-10)

1400 Süss, Maria V. "Die Instrumenten-Stube . . . ," *Museum Carolino-Augusteum, Jahresbericht* (1865), pp. 55-64.

1401 *Verzeichnis über die seit dem Jahre 1865 neuerworbenen Musikinstrumente zwechs Vermehrung der Instrumenten-Sammlung des Museums . . . als Nachtrag des Süss'schen Aufsatzes im Kataloge von 1865*. Ms.

      Heyer* indicates that the Ms. is in the Museum.

1402 Geiringer, Karl. *Alte Musik-instrumente im Museum Carolino Augusteum, Salzburg. Führer und beschreibendes Verzeichnis*. Leipzig: Breitkopf & Härtel, 1932. 45 pp., 4 pls.

      Copy at NPV (POvc).

1403 Birsak, Kurt. *Die Holzblasinstrumente im Salzburger Museum Carolino Augusteum; Verzeichnis und entwicklungsgeschichtliche Untersuchungen*. (Publikationen des Instituts für Musikwissenschaft der Universität Salzburg, 9; Museum Carolino Augusteum, Jahresschrift, 18, 1972.) Salzburg: 1973. 211 pp. [8] lvs. of pls., 128 items.

Literature

1404 Altenberg, Wilhelm. "Die Blasinstrumente im städtischen Museum in Salzburg," *ZfI* 24 (1903/4): 4-5.

SALZBURG (Austria). MUSEUM CAROLINO-AUGUSTEUM *continued*

Literature

1405   Gassner, Josef. "Die Musikaliensammlung im Salzburger Museum," *Museum Carolino Augusteum, Jahresschrift* 7 (1961): 119-365.

> Also published separately; included here in order
> to point out that it does *not* contain instruments.

1406   Meer, John Henry van der. "Die Kielklaviere im Salzburger Museum," *Museum Carolino Augusteum, Jahresschrift* 12/13 (1966-67): 83-96.

1407   Birsak, Kurt. "Die Sammlung alter Musikinstrumente im Salzburger Museum Carolino Augusteum," *Österreichische Musikzeitschrift* 7 (1970): 399-402. illus.

SALZBURG (Austria). ÖSTERREICHISCHE MUSEUM FÜR VOLKSKUNDE

Literature

1408   Schmidt, Leopold. *Volksmusik: Zeugnisse ländlichen Musizierens.* Salzburg: Residenz Verlag, 1974. 175 pp., lavish illus.

SALZBURG (Austria). STÄDTISCHES MUSEUM. *See* MUSEUM CAROLINO-AUGUSTEUM

SAN FRANCISCO, CALIFORNIA (USA). GOLDEN GATE PARK. MEMORIAL MUSEUM

Literature

1409   Coxhead, Edith. "Curious Musical Instruments in the Park Museum," *Overland* 39 (1902): 533-43.

SANTIAGO DE CHILE. EXPOSICIÓN INTERNACIONAL, 1875

General

1410   *Catalogo official . . . Seccion Primera.* Santiago: Mercurio, 1875.

> Musical instruments, pp. 195-213, et passim.
> Copy at DLC (Wc).

SAO PAULO (Brazil). DISCOTECA PUBLICA MUNICIPAL   (J24)

1411   Alvarenga, Oneyda, ed. *Catalogo illustrado do museu folklorico.* (Sao Paulo,
        Discoteca publica municipal, Arquivo folklorico, 2.) [Sao Paulo] : 1950.
        xviii, 235 pp. of illus.

>   Copy at DLC (Wc).

SARAWAK (Malaysia). MUSEUM.   *See* KUCHING (Malaysia)

SCHAFFHAUSEN (Switzerland). MUSEUM ZU ALLERHEILIGEN

1412   "Musikinstrumente aus der Bach'schen Zeit," *Glareana,* vol. 6, no. 2 (1957).

>   Not examined.

SCHIEDAM (Netherlands). GEMEENTE-MUSEUM

Literature

1413   Möller, Max. "Tentoonstelling van oud-Hollandse meesters der vioolbouw te
        Schiedam," *Mens en melodie* 5 (1950): 48-51.

>   In connection with the Concours Hendrik Jacobz.

1414   Smits, C. H. L. *Oud Hollandse strykinstrumenten en hun bouw . . . 10 tot en met
        26 Februari 1950.* [n. p.] , 1950. 13 pp. (70 items)

SCHÖNBACH (Austria). MUSIKINSTRUMENTENBAU-AUSSTELLUNG

Literature

1415   "Die Musikinstrumentenbau-Ausstellung in Schönbach," *ZfI* 41 (1920/21): 1200.

SCHWETZINGEN (Germany). SCHLOSS

1416   Feil, Arnold and Rudolf Schnellbach. *Alte Musikinstrumente. Ausstellung in
        Verbindungen mit dem Festspielen im Schwetzinger Schloss vom 8. Mai bis 30
        Juni 1954.* Stuttgart: Süddeutscher Rundfunk, 1954. 16 pp., 36 items.

>   Copy at Oru (EUu).

SEGOVIA (Spain). ALCAZÁR.   *See Section II under* ISABEL I, la Catolica

SEOUL (Korea). NATIONAL TRADITIONAL MUSIC INSTITUTE (J88)

1417   Lee, Hye-ku. *Photographs of the Musical Instruments in the Royal Conservatory.*
Seoul: 1939.

> Cited by Jenkins*; unable to verify.

1418   *Korean Classical Music Instruments.* Seoul: 1959.

> Cited by Jenkins*; unable to verify.

1419   Lee, Hveku. *Musical Instruments of Korea Illustrated.* [Seoul: 1966.] 257 pp.
59 pls. In Korean and English.

> "Majority of instruments in this book belong
> to the . . . Institute." Copy at NBuU-M (BUu).

1420   Suh, Injuna. *Traditional Korean Stringed Instruments.* M. M. thesis, Indiana
University, 1972. 63 pp., illus.

> " . . . 15 stringed instruments preserved in the
> Institute. . . ." Cited from *RILM*.*

SHEFFIELD (U. K.). SHEFFIELD FESTIVAL EXHIBITION, 1967 (J157). *See Section II under* MONTAGU, JEREMY

SINGAPORE (Malaysia). RAFFLES MUSEUM AND LIBRARY. *See* Blacking citation *under* TAIPING (Malaysia)

SKARA (Sweden). VÄSTERGÖTLANDS FORNMUSEUM (J116)

1421   Welin, S. *Musikhistoriska avdelningen vid Västergötlands Fornmuseum i Skara.*
Skara: 1924.

> Cited from *MGG*;* not located.

SMOLENSK (USSR). ISTORIKO-ETNOGRAFICHESKIĬ MUZEE

1422   Bartsevskiĭ, I. *Katalog muzykal'nykh instrumentov, nakhodiãtsikhsiã v Smolenskom
istoriko-etnograficheskogo instituta, sobrannom kn. M. K. Tenishevoĭ. Sostavil
khranitel' muzeĩa I. Bartsevskiĭ.* Moskva: 1915. 36 pp.

> Cited from Koltypina*.

SNOWSHILL MANOR, GLOUCESTERSHIRE (U. K.)

General

1423   M., H. W. *Snowshill Manor . . . A Property of the National Trust.* London:
        Country Life, 1954. 23 pp.

> Cited from BM*; not located in U. S. Jenkins* says the
> Manor contains an unusual collection of instruments,
> mainly the collection of Charles Wade.

SPAIN — General

1424   Reuter, Rudolf. *Organos españoles.* [*Exposición de fotografías de organos
        españoles, septiembre 1963.* Fotografías: Heinrich Vossing.] (Spain. Dirección
        General de Bellas Artes. [Publicaciones] 56.) Madrid: Ministero de Educacion
        Nacional, 1963. 1 vol., illus.

> Copy at DLC (Wc). Contains elaborate indices and descriptions.

STOCKHOLM (Sweden). ALLMÄNNA KONST- OCH INDUSTRIUTSTÄLLNINGEN, 1897 [N. B.: *See also Section II under* CLAUDIUS, CARL.]

Literature

1425   "Musikinstrumente auf der nordischen Kunst- und Industrie-Ausstellung," *ZfI*
        17 (1896/97): 660, 669.

1426   "Musikinstrumenter paa Stockholmsutställningen," *Svensk Musik-tidning* 19
        (1897/98): 98-100.

STOCKHOLM (Sweden). MUSEUM CHRISTIAN HAMMER. *See Section II under* HAMMER, CHRISTIAN

STOCKHOLM (Sweden). MUSIKHISTORISKA MUSEET (J117, A390)

1427   Svanberg, Johannes. *Musikhistoriska Museets i Stockholm Instrumentsamling,
        År 1902.* [Stockholm: Stellans Staals Boktrykeri, 1902.] 34 pp., ca. 250 items.

> Copies at NN (NYp), DLC (Wc).

1428   Norlind, Tobias. "Musikhistoriska museet i Stockholm," *Svensk Tidskrift för
        Musikforskning* 2 (1920): 94-114, 307-8; 4 (1944): 58-62; 7 (1925): 159-62.
        Many illus.

STOCKHOLM (Sweden). MUSIKHISTORISKA MUSEET *continued*

1429 Norlind, Tobias. *En bok om musikinstrument* [deras utvecklingshistoria med särskild hänsyn till de i Musikhistoriska Museet, Stockholm. Med 189 illustrationer]. Stockholm: Klioförlaget, 1928. 102 pp.

   Cited from Miller*; not located.

1430 Eimsheimer, Ernst. "Musikmuseets instrumentsamlingar." In *Svenska musik-perspektiv. Minneskrift . . .* , pp. 115-26. Stockholm: Nordiska Musikforlaget, 1971.

1431 Karp, Cary. "Baroque Woodwinds in the Musikhistoriska Museet," *GSJ* 25 (1972): 9-96.

1432 Lund, Cajsa and Gunnar Larsson. *Klans i flinta och brons* [exhibition]. Stockholm: Musikmuseet, 1974. 39 pp.

   Abbreviated English ed. as *The Sound of Archeology.* 25 pp.

1433 Kjelstroem, Birgit. *Dragspel: am kett kaert och misskaent instrument . . . i samarbete med Musikmuseet, Stockholm.* [Stockholm] : Sohlmans, 1976. 172 pp., illus.

Literature

1434 "Hufvudstadens nyaste museum," *Idun; illustrered tidning,* vol. 13, no. 3 (1900?). illus.

1435 "Stockholms musikhistoriska museum och dess grundläggare," *Svensk Musik-tidning* 20 (1900): 81-82.

1436 "Musikhistoriska Museet i Stockholm," *Svensk Musiktidning* 22, no. 4 (1902): 28-29.

1437 "I Musikhistoriska museet, af en musikälskare," *Varia* 7 (1904): 466-72.

1438 Svanberg, Johannes. *Musikhistoriska museet, dess uppkonst, utveckling och syftemål.* Stockholm: the Museet, 1910. 15 pp.

   Copy at NN (NYp).

1439 Norlind, Tobias. "Musikhistoriska museet i Stockholm," *Musik* (Copenhagen) 5 (1921): 110-12.

1440 "Musikhistoriska museet i Stockholm 1899-1924," *Musik* (Copenhagen) 8 (1924): 159-62.

1441 Norlind, Tobias. "Nyförärv till Musikhistoriska Museet," *Svensk tidskrift för Musikforskning* 7 (1925): 159-62. illus.

1442   Norlind, Tobias. "Musikhistoriska Museet," *Vår sång* (1934), pp. 194, 228.

1443   Norlind, Tobias. *Systematik der Saiteninstrumente.* Stockholm: Fritzes k. Hofbuchhandlung, [1936].

>   Copies at NN (NYp), DLC (Wc).

1444   Norlind, Tobias. "Musikhistoriska museet och dess dyrgripar," *Nya Dagligt Allehanda* (May 3, 1939).

>   Cited from DaSML*.

1445   Väisänen, A. O. "Tukholman musiikihistoriallinen museo," *Musiikkitieto* 8 (1940): 14-15.

1446   "Musikhistoriska museet i Stockholm," *Musikern*, no. 3 (1951), p. 8.

1447   [Description of activities and productions], *IAMIC Newsletter* i (1973): 28-29.

STOCKHOLM (Sweden). NORDISKA MUSEET   (J118, A398)   [N.B.: Instruments now (1977) in Musikhistoriska Museet, according to Jenkins*.]

1448   Boivie, Hedvig. *Nordiska Museet. Musikavdelningen. Vägledning utarbetad af Hedvig Boivie.* Stockholm: [1912]. 18 pp.

>   Cited from Heyer*, *MGG*, DaSML*, etc.; not located in U. S.

Literature

1449   Rehnberg, Mats Erik Adolf. *Säckpipan i Sverige.* (Nordiska museets handlinger, 18.) Stockholm: 1943. 76 pp., illus.

>   Copies at NN (NYp), DLC (Wc).

1450   Söderberg, Bertil. *Les instruments de musique au Bas-Congo et dans les regions avoisinantes.* (Nordiska museet. Monograph series, Publication no. 3, 1956.) Stockholm: 1956. 284 pp., illus.

>   Copies at MiU (AAu), NNMM, TxU (AUSu), DLC (Wc).

STRASBOURG (France). INDUSTRIE- UND GEWERBE-AUSSTELLUNG, 1895

Literature

1451   "Die Musikinstrumenten-Industrie auf der Industrie- und Gewerbe-Ausstellung," *ZfI* 16 (1895/96): 29-31, 60-61, 87-88.

STRASBOURG (France). INDUSTRIE- UND GEWERBE-AUSSTELLUNG   *continued*

General

1452   *Katalog der Ausstellung von Kunst und Altertum in Elsass-Lothringen auf dem
. . . Orangerie-Gebäude 1. July - 15. Octbr. 1895.* Strassburg: J. H. E. Heitz,
1895. 160 pp.

  Cited from KaY*; not located; instruments?

1453   *Amtlicher Katalog. . . .*   Strassburg: Strassburger Druckerei und Verlagsanstalt,
1895. xxxvi, 70 pp.

  Cited from KaY*; not located; instruments?

STRÁŽNICI (Moravia). KRAJSKÉ STŘEDISKO LIDOVÉHO UMĚNI   (J31)

1454   Dobrovolný, František. *Lidové hudební nástroje ČSSR v stálé výstavě Krajského
střediska lidového umění ve Strážnici; průvodoe výstavou.* Ve Strážnici: Krajské
středisko lidového umění, 1963. 1 vol., unpaged. Mostly illus.

  Copy at DLC (Wc).

STUTTGART (Germany). STUTTGARTER HOFKAPELLE   [N.B.: The Hofkapelle
formed by Ludwig der Fromme von Württemberg, 1568-1593.]

1455   "Inventarium instrumentorum musicorum in anno 1589." A Ms. in Altere
Kirchenratsakten K.10.L.620, f.1, transcribed by Gustav Bossert in "Die
Hofkapelle unter Eberhard III, 1628-1657," *Württembergische Vierteljahrshefte
für Landesgeschichte* 20, Heft II (1911): 133-37.

1456   Bossert, Gustav. "Die Hofkapelle unter Johann Friedrich, 1608-1628," *Württembergische Vierteljahrshefte für Landesgeschichte* 20, Heft I (1911): 204-8.

  Describes instruments acquired 1608-1628.

STUTTGART (Germany). STAATLICHE ERFINDUNGS-AUSSTELLUNG, 1910

Literature

1457   "Staatliche Erfindungs-Ausstellung," *ZfI* 30 (1909/10): 19, 389, 493, 599.

STUTTGART (Germany). WÜRTTEMBURGISCHES ELEKTROTECHNIK UND KUNST-GEWERBE-AUSSTELLUNG, 1896

Literature

1458 "Bericht über die Musikinstrumente auf der Ausstellung für Elektrotchnik und Kunst-Gewerbe," *ZfI* 17 (1896/97): 29-32.

1459 "In der Stuttgarter Kunstgewerbe-Ausstellung," *Neue Musik-Zeitung* 17 (1896): 197-98, 247 (prizes).

STUTTGART (Germany). WÜRTTEMBURGISCHES LANDES- GEWERBE-AUSSTELLUNG, 1881

Literature

1460 Winternitz, R. "Bericht," *ZfI* 1 (1880/81): 308-9, 321-22, 338-40; 2 (1881/82): 26-27, 32.

1461 Laffert, Oscar. "Die . . . Ausstellung," *ZfI* 2 (1881/82): 56-57, 77-78.

STUTTGART (Germany). WÜRTTEMBURGISCHES LANDESGEWERBEMUSEUM (J65)

1462 Josten, Hanns H. *Die Sammlung der Musikinstrumente, im Auftrage der Museum-direktion bearb.* Stuttgart: E. Klett, 1928. 120 pp., 53 illus.
> Anhang: "Klaviermechanikensammlung von Carl A. Pfeiffer." Copy at DLC (Wc).

Literature

1463 [Comment about and descriptions of instruments given to the Museum by Carl Pfeiffer], *ZiMG* 3, no. 5 (1902): 206.
> See also **PFEIFFER**, no. **2244**, in Section II.

STYRIA (Austria). *See* KÄRNTEN (Austria)

SUFFOLK (U. K.). HENGRAVE HALL

1464 "Instrewments and Books of Musicke [from an inventory of 1603]." In Rokewode, John Gage. *History and Antiquities of Hengrave,* pp. 23-25. [s.p.], 1822. ca. 40 items.
> Copy at DLC (Wc). Collection formed by Sir Thomas Kytson.
> See also Baines, A. in *GSJ,* vol. 4 (1959).

SUMISWALD (Switzerland). SAMMLUNG DER MUSIKINSTRUMENTEN-FABRIK
(J127)

Literature

1465   Leutenegger, E. "Alte Musikinstrumente aus den Emmental," *Der Hochwächter,* vol. 11 (1955).

Cited from Jenkins*; no pagination given.

SUNDSVALL (Sweden). ETNOGRAFIA MUSEET

1466   Fryklund, Daniel. *Afrikanska musikinstrument i Sundsvalls läroverks etnografiska samlingar.* (Bil. till Redogörelse för Sundsvall Högre Allmänna Läroverket, 1914/15.) Sundsvall: 1915. 38 pp.

Cited from DaSML*, *MGG*, and elsewhere; not located in U. S.

SUSSEX (U. K.). EXPOSITION SUSSEX, 1968

1467   Oldham, Guy. *Catalogue of the Musical Instrument Exhibition.* Sussex: 1968. 10 pp., illus.

SWANSEA (Wales). PUBLIC LIBRARIES COMMITTEE

1468   *The Swansea Public Libraries Committee Presents "Music in Wales"; An Exhibition of Musical Instruments, Scores, and Manuscripts Illustrating the History of Welsh Music, at the Central Public Library, Swansea, September 17th to 22nd 1951. Catalogue.* [Swansea] : 1951. 40 pp.

Copy at DLC (Wc).

SYDENHAM (U. K.). CRYSTAL PALACE. *See* LONDON (U. K.). CRYSTAL PALACE

SYDŁOWIEC (Poland). MUZEUM LUDOWYCH INSTRUMENTOW MUZYCZNYCH
(J106)

Literature

1469   "Ein neues polnisches Museum der volkstümlichen Musikinstrumente," *Polish/Music/Polnische Music* 10, no. 3 (1975): 25-29. illus.

SYDNEY (Australia). AUSTRALIA MUSIC CENTRE

1470   *The Lutes with the Delicate Air.* [A catalogue, preface by James Murdoch. Sydney]: AMC, [1976]. [24] pp., illus.

SYDNEY (Australia). INTERNATIONAL EXHIBITION, 1879

Literature

1471   Moonen, L. "Les instruments de musique Oceaniens," *Echo musical* 12 (1880): 113-15.

1472   "Gli strumenti musical dell'Oceanie," *Gazzetta musicale di Milano* 35 (1880): 166.
Refers to Moonen article.

1473   "L'exposition internationale de Sydney," *Echo musical* 12 (1880): 150-51.
A list published after the *Music Trades Review* (not located).

General

1474   . . . *Official Catalogue of the British Section.* London: J. M. Johnson & Sons, 1879.
Class 311, Musical instruments, pp. 221-27, illus.
Copy at DLC (Wc).

1475   *Official Record of the International Exhibition.* Sydney: Thomas Richards, 1881.
"Reports of judges, and awards. Class 313, Musical Instruments," pp. 422-29. Copy at DLC (Wc).

TAIPING (Malaysia). PERAK STATE MUSEUM   (J110)

1476   Blacking, J. A. R. "Musical Instruments of the Malayan Aborigines. A Short Description of the Collections in the Perak Museum, Taiping, the Selangor Museum, Kuala Lumpur, and the Raffles Museum, Singapore," *Federation Museums Journal,* n.s. 1 & 2 (1954/55 [publ. 1956]): 35-52.

TALLINN (Estonia). TEATRI- MUUSIKAMUUSEUM   (J134)

Literature

1477   *Orelid ja osjapillid, pasunad ja parmupillid, muusikainstrumente Teatri- Muusik-amuuseumis Tallinn.* [Tallinn: 1972.] 77 pp., illus.
Copy at DLC (Wc).

TALLINN (Estonia). TEATRI- MUUSIKAMUUSEUM *continued*

Literature

1478   Ministerstvo kultury Estonskoi SSR. *Muzei teatra i muzyki.* [Putevoditel'. 2-e izd.] Tallinn: 1971. 23 pp., illus.

   Copy at DLC (Wc).

TEMPE, ARIZONA (USA). ARIZONA STATE UNIVERSITY. LAURA BOULTON COLLECTION   (L9).   *See Section II under* BOULTON, LAURA

TENRI (Japan). TENRI SANKOKAN   (J86)

1479   *Minzoku gakki. Folk Music Instruments, 1. Gen-mei gakki. Chordophones.* (Shiryo annai shiriizu; Handbook of the Tenri Sankokan collection, V.) Tenri: 1969. 32 pp., illus.

TEPLITZ (Czechoslovakia). INDUSTRIE- GEWERBE- UND ELEKTRISCHE- AUSSTELLUNG, 1884

Literature

1480   "Liste der Aussteller," *ZfI* 4 (1883/84): 382.

1481   "Officielle Liste der . . . Preise für Gruppe XIII," *ZfI* 4 (1883/84): 450, 452.

1482   "Die Tasteninstrumente auf der . . . Ausstellung," *ZfI* 4 (1883/84): 411-12, 423-24.

TEPLITZ (Czechoslovakia). NORDBÖHMISCHE INDUSTRIE- UND GEWERBE- AUSSTELLUNG, 1895

Literature

1483   "Die nordböhmische Industrie- und Gewerbeausstellung," *ZfI* 15 (1894/95): 827 (exhibitors), 900; 16 (1895/96): 36 (awards).

TERVUREN (Belgium). MUSÉE ROYAL DE L'AFRIQUE CENTRALE. *See also*
Liebrecht *under* **BRUSSELS. EXPOSITION INTERNATIONAL, 1897** [N. B.: Though
not all of the following constitute catalogues of the Musée's collections, in the usual
sense, they are studies of those collections and reflect the museum's holdings.]

1484 [Coart, E. and A. de Haulleville.] *Notes analytiques sur les collections
ethnographiques du . . . Tome I, Fasc. I: Les arts* [Instruments de musique.
Musique - chant - danse] . (Annales du Musée du Congo. Ethnographie et
anthropologie, Sér. III.) Bruxelles: En vente chez Spineux et cie, 1902.
2 vols. (vol. 2, pls.)

> Copy at NBuU-M (BUu).

1485 Boone, Olga. "Les xylophones du Congo Belge," *Annales du Musée du Congo.
Sér. in 4⁰, Sciences humaines,* no. 3 (1936), pp. 69-144.

1486 Boone, Olga. *Les tambours du Congo Belge et du Ruanda-Urandi.* (Annales du
Musée du Congo. Nouv. sér. in 4⁰, Sciences de l'homme. Ethnographie, vol. 1.)
Tervuren: 1951. 121 pp., illus.

> "Description de tambours conservés au Musée," pp. 3-46.
> Copy at DLC (Wc).

1487 Laurenty, Jean Sébastien. *Les cordophones du Congo Belge et du Ruanda-
Urundi.* (Annales du Musée du Congo. Nouv. sér. in 4⁰, Sciences humaines,
vol. 2.) Tervuren: 1960. 2 vols. (vol. 2, pls.)

> Copy at NBuU-M (BUu).

1488 Laurenty, Jean Sébastien. *Les sanza du Congo.* (Annales du Musée du Congo.
Nouv. sér. in 4⁰, Sciences humaines, vol. 3.) Tervuren: 1962. 2 vols. (vol. 2, pls.)

> Copy at NBuU-M (BUu).

1489 Laurenty, Jean Sébastien. *Les tambours à fente de l'Afrique centrale.* (Annales du
Musée du Congo. Nouv. sér. in 4⁰, Sciences humaines, vol. 6.) Tervuren: 1968.
2 vols. (vol. 2, pls.)

> Copy at NBuU-M (BUu).

Literature

1490 Laurenty, Jean Sébastien. "Notes sur les rhombes du Musée royal du Congo
Belge," *Africa-Tervuren* 5 (1959): 41-43.

> With a list of the museum's rhombes, p. 42.

1491 Brandily, Monique. *Instruments de musique et musiciens instrumentistes chez les
Teda du Tibesti.* (Musée royal de l'Afrique centrale. Annales. Sér. in 8⁰, Sciences
humaines, no. 82.) Tervuren: 1974. xii, 260 pp., illus.

TIFLIS (USSR). SAK'ART' WELOS MUSEUMI

1492   Arakishvili, Dmitrii Ignat'evich. *Opisanie i obmer narodnykh muzykal'nykh instrumentov.* Tbilisi: "Tekhnika da shrova," 1940. 69 pp., 43 pls.
Copy at NNMM.

TILBURG (Netherlands). VOLKENKUNDIG MUSEUM

1493   *Daar zit muziek in! Muziekinstrumenten Tentoongesteld, 22 Okt. 1972 to 1 Jan. 1973.* [n.p.], 1973. 19 pp., illus.
Copy at NL-DHgm.

TOKYO (Japan). JAPAN AUDIO FAIR

1494   Shinagawa, Serio and Dean Takeshi Nagasawa. *The Phonograph* [exhibition]. Tokyo: Stereo Sound, 1977. 86 pp., illus.

TOKYO (Japan). MUSASHINO ONGAKU DAIGAKU. GAKKI HAKUBUTSUKAN   (J87)

1495   Kikkawa, Eishi, Kazuo Yasuda, Shun'ichi Kikuchi and Kazumi Yahagi. *. . . Museum of Musical Instruments, Musashino Academia Musicae. . . .* [Tokyo]: 1967. [14] pp., mostly illus.
Copy at DLC (Wc).

1496   Kikuchi, Shun'ichi and Osamu Yamaguchi. *Catalogue. Museum of Musical Instruments. Musashino Academiae Musicae, on the Fortieth Anniversary of the Institute.* 2 vols. (vii, 108; 58 pp.). Tokyo: 1969, 1974. illus.
Duckles* 3:1624, text in Japanese and English, *vis-à-vis*.
Copies at CST (STu), NN (NYp).

Literature

1497   *Museum of Musical Instruments* [including some of those collected by Mr. Sahei Mizuno. Tokyo?: 1967?]. [22] pp., photos.
Copy at NL-DHgm.

TOLEDO, OHIO (USA). MUSEUM OF ART

1498   *Musical Instruments Through the Ages. [Exhibition] February 10 - March 30, 1952.* [Toledo?] : 1952. 11 pp. 102 items.

> Copy at NBuU-M (BUu). Most items were lent by the Cincinnati Art Museum from the Doane Collection, a few from the Stearns Collection at Michigan University.

TONGRES (Belgium). PROVINCIAL GALLO-ROMEINS MUSEUM (A49)

1499   *Volks muziek instrumenten uit de lage landen Provincial Gallo-Romeins.* Tongeren: [1972]. 19 pp., illus.

> Copy at CU (BEu).

TORONTO (Canada). CANADIAN NATIONAL EXHIBITION

1500   Todoruk, Ihor, ed. *Century of Sound* [exhibition]. Montreal: Studio artistique un deux trois limitée, 1977. 52 pp., illus.

TORONTO (Canada). ROYAL ONTARIO MUSEUM (L568)

1501   Cselenyi, Ladislav. *Musical Instruments in the Royal Ontario Museum.* [Toronto: 1971.] 96 pp., illus.

> Copy at DLC (Wc). Duckles* 3:1625, more than 100 items.

TRENTO (Italy)

Literature

1502   Lunelli, Renato and Riccardo Maroni. *Strumenti musicali nel Trentino.* (Voci della terra trentina, 6.) Trento: V. D. T. T., 1968. 128 pp., illus.

> Though this is neither a catalogue nor related to a specific collection, it deserves notice. See *Orgue,* no. 132 (October/December 1969), p. 165.

TRONDHEIM (Norway). RINGVE MUSEUM. BACHKE COLLECTION (J102)

1503   Kjeldsberg, Peter Aandreas. *Musikinstrumenter ved Ringve Museum. The Collection of Musical Instruments.* (Ringve Museums Skrifter, II.) Trondheim: the Museum, 1976. 92 pp., illus.

> See review by H. M. Brown, *Early Music* 4, no. 4 (1976): 473.

Literature

1504   Howes, Helen Claire. "A Museum Worth Listening To," *Christian Science Monitor* 63 (April 28, 1971): 15. Notes some 2,000 items.

1505   Kjeldsberg, Peter Andreas and Body Kjeldsberg. "A Museum of Music," *CIMCIM Newsletter* 5 (1977): 30-31.

TUCSON, ARIZONA (USA). ARIZONA PIONEERS' HISTORICAL SOCIETY. MUSEUM (L10)

1506   Haefer, J. Richard. *A Catalogue and History of the Musical Instrument Collection of the . . . Society.* Sells, Ariz.: Haefer, 1971. 71 pp., illus.

> A typescript available from the Museum according to *RILM**.

TUCSON, ARIZONA (USA). ARIZONA STATE MUSEUM (L11)

1507   Kaemblein, Wilma. "Yuma Dolls and Yuma Flutes in the . . . Museum," *The Kiva* 20, no. 2/3 (1955): 1-10. illus.

TURIN (Italy). ESPOSIZIONE GENERALE ITALIANA, 1884

Literature

1508   Stadler, Antonio. "Die Klaviere und sonstigen Musikinstrumente auf der nationalen Ausstellung in Turin," *ZfI* 5 (1884/85): 14, 16-19, 28-30, 59 and 61 (awards).

1509   "Die nationale Ausstellung in Turin," *ZfI* 4 (1883/84): 331-33 (exhibitors).

General

1510   *Catalogo degli oggetti esposti . . . con introduzione di Cesare Correnti.* Milano: Fratelli Dumolard, 1886- .

> Copy at DLC (Wc); not examined.

TURIN (Italy). ESPOSIZIONE INTERNAZIONALE D'ARTE DECORATIVA MODERNA, 1902

Literature

1511 "Modern ausgestattete Tasteninstrumente von G. Mola auf der Internationalen Ausstellung für moderne dekorative Kunst," *ZfI* 23 (1902/3): 5-6. illus.

1512 Pudor, Heinrich. "Erste internationale Ausstellung für moderne dekorative Kunst," *DIbZ,* vol. 3 (June 7, 1901/2).

TURIN (Italy). ESPOSIZIONE NAZIONALE DI TORINO, 1898

1513 Foschini, Gaetano F. "La musica all'Esposizione generale italiana di Torino: 1898," *RMI* 5 (1898): 786-836. illus.

Musical instruments, pp. 828-36.

Literature

1514 "Musikinstrumente auf der nationalen Ausstellung in Turin," *ZfI* 3 (1897/98): 747-48 (exhibitors).

General

1515 *Catalogo generale dell:esposizione. . . .* Torino: Roux e Frassati, 1898. 431 pp.; Appendice, *ibid.,* 1898. 41 pp.

Cited from PaG*; not located.

TURIN (Italy). MOSTRA INTERNAZIONALE, 1911

1516 [Die Musikinstrumenten-Industrie auf der . . .] , *ZfI* 31 (1910/11): 129, 649 and 687 (German exhibitors), 871, 898, 937-41 (exhibitors), 981, 1011, 1042 and 1051 (French exhibitors), 1323 and 1353 (jury); 32 (1911/12): 9-10, 15, 17, 19, 86, 200-201; 33 (1912/13): 399 ("Nachklänge" from *Leipziger Abendzeitung*), 1019, 1021; 34 (1913/14): 309-340 (awards).

Literature

1517 Honold, Eugen. "Die moderne Geigenbaukunst auf der Turiner Weltausstelling," *Allgemeine Musik-Zeitung* (Berlin) 38 (1911): 715-17.

1518 Zero, R. "Streiflichter von der internationalen Industrie- und Gewerbe-Ausstellung in Turin," *ZfI* 31 (1910/11): 858-59.

TURIN (Italy). MOSTRA INTERNAZIONALE, 1911 *continued*

General

1519   *Catalogo generale ufficiale dell'esposizione internazionale delle industrie e del lavoro,* Torino 1911. Torino: Pozzo, 1911. 692 pp.

> Musical instruments in Class 76, Group XIV.
> Cited from PaG*; not located.

TURIN (Italy). UNIVERSITÀ. ISTITUTO DI ANTROPOLOGIA. MUSEO

1520   Scotti, Pietro. "Gli strumenti musicali africani del Museo antropologico-etnografico dell'Istituto di Antropologia della R. Università di Torino." In *Atti della 40ª Riunione della Società Italiana per il progresso delle Scienze,* pp. ?. Torino: 1939.

> Copies at CtY (NHu), IaU (IOu), MiU (AAu), NcD (DMu).

UDINE (Italy). MUSEO CIVICO

1521   Fael, Vittorio. *Gli strumenti musicali del Civico Museo di Udine. Lettere tenuta nell'adunanza del 17 febbraio 1938 - XVI.* Udine: graf. Friulane, 1938. 22 pp., illu

> Offprint from *Accademia di scienze, lettere e arti di Udine,*
> *Atti,* ser. 6, vol. 4 (1937-38). Copy at NN (NYp).

ÚSTÍ NOD LABEM (Czechoslovakia). *See* AUSSIG (Austria)

VATICAN. *See* ROME (Italy)

VENICE (Italy). MUSEO CIVICO E RACCOLTA CORRER. *See Section II under* CONTARINI-CORRER COLLECTION

VERMILLION, SOUTH DAKOTA (USA). UNIVERSITY OF SOUTH DAKOTA. SHRINE TO MUSIC MUSEUM (L473)

1522   Larson, Andre Pierre. *A Catalog of the Double Reed Instruments in the Arne B. Larson Collection of Musical Instruments.* M. M. thesis, University of South Dakota, 1968. 102 pp., illus.

> See another catalogue of his private collection under
> **LARSON** in Section II.

1523 Larson, Andre Pierre. *Catalog of the Nineteenth-Century British Brass Instruments in the Arne B. Larson Collection.* . . . Ph.D. dissertation, University of West Virginia, 1974. vi, 158 pp.

Literature

1524 "Shrine to Music Museum to Open," *AMIS Newsletter* 4, no. 3 (1975): 4-5; 5, no. 1 (1976): [1] and 5. illus.

1525 [Report of annual American Musical Instrument Society meeting at the Shrine to Music Museum], *AMIS Newsletter* 5 (June 1976): 3-5. illus.

1526 "The Shrine to Music Museum Opens Gallery in November," *AMIS Newsletter* 8, no. 3 (1978): [1]. illus.

VERONA (Italy). BIBLIOTECA CAPITOLARE

1527 Puglisi, Filadelfio. "The Renaissance Flutes of the Biblioteca Capitolare of Verona: The Structure of a 'Pifaro'," *GSJ* 32 (1979): 24-37.

> Does not include instruments belonging to the Accademia Filarmonica which, until recently, were housed in the Biblioteca.

VERONA (Italy). GRAN GUARDIA

1528 [Camploy,   .] *Catalogue des instruments à cordes appartenant à l'héritage . . . et existant dans le Palazzo della Gran Guardia Vecchia de Verone.* Verona: [19--].

> Cited from Lambertini* who gives no imprint or collation; not located.

VERONA (Italy). SOCIETÀ ACCADEMIA FILARMONICA   (J84)

1529 Turrini, Giuseppe. *L'Accademia Filarmonica di Verona dalla fondazione al 1600.* (Atti dell'Accademia di Agricoltura, Scienze e Lettere di Verona, Ser. V, vol. 18, 1940.) Verona: Tip. Veronese, 1941. 349 pp., illus.

[N.B.: No. **1529** includes reprints of the following inventories:]

1530 "Inventario de tutte le robe patriculare Et Comune che si ritroua nella Casa di moliseo, adi 7 X bre 1543." *Ibid.,* pp. 25-27.

> Ms. is in the Society's archives.

VERONA (Italy). SOCIETÀ ACCADEMIA FILARMONICA *continued*

1531   "Inventario de le Robbe della Accademia in fontenelle [1543]." *Ibid.*, pp. 28-33.

1532   "Inventario dele robbe de la Compagnia [Reg. n. 116f, 69v-71r, 1544]." *Ibid.*, pp. 33-38.

1533   "Inventario de le robe che al presente si ritroua in la compagnia che son ali 25 marcio 1559 le qual robe sono de detta compagnia." *Ibid.*, pp. 134-36.

1534   "Libro degli'inventarij Delli beni De la / Academia filarmonica. Principiando / Da l'anno 1562 [Reg. n.12, 2v-6v]." *Ibid.*, pp. 87-95.

       "Annesso [1564]," p. 95.

1535   "Inventario De tutti li Beni Mobili di qual Sorte si uoglia Della Academia philharmonica fatto à di p⁰ Zugno 1585 Nella Casa ai Leoni [Reg. m.12, f.30-f.34]." *Ibid.*, pp. 185-90.

1536   "Inventario d'Instrumenti Musicali dell'Acad.ᵃ Filarm.ᶜᵃ [Reg. n.12A, ff.88ss., 1628]." *Ibid.*, pp. 199-200.

Literature

1537   Castellani, Marcello. "Two Late-Renaissance Transverse Flutes," *GSJ* 25 (1972): 72-79. illus.

       Discusses inventories of the Society's collection.

1538   Weber, Rainer and John Henry van der Meer. "Some Facts and Guesses Concerning 'doppioni'," *GSJ* 25 (1972): 22-29. With 4 pls.

VERSAILLES (France). BIBLIOTHÈQUE DE LA MUSIQUE DU ROI

1539   Marcuse, Sibyl. "The Instruments of the King's Library at Versailles," *GSJ*, no. 14 (March 1961), pp. 34-36.

       Original list [1780] in the Archives nationales, Ms. 0¹*3246.

Literature

1540   Tessier, André. "Un catalogue de la Bibliothèque de la musique du Roi," *Revue de musicologie* 15 (1931): 106-17.

       Comments only, no list, for which see Marcuse (above).

VERSAILLES (France). MUSÉE NATIONAL

1541   [Auer, Erwin P.] *Vienne à Versailles. Les grandes collections autrichiennes au Château de Versailles, 6 mai - octobre 1964.* [Paris] : Ministère d'état Affaires culturelles, [1964]. 162 pp., 227 pls. (including instruments).

> Materials from the Kunsthistorisches Museum, Vienna, the Musiksammlung of the Österreichische National-bibliothek, Vienna, and the Ferdinandeum in Innsbruck.
>
> "Saal VII & VIII [include instruments]," pp. 44-71, with 15 pls.
>
> Also includes about ten instruments from each of the Ambras, Catajo, and Gesellschaft der Musikfreunde collections.

VICTORIA (Australia). PUBLIC LIBRARY, MUSEUMS AND NATIONAL GALLERY.
See under MELBOURNE (Australia)

VIENNA

This section includes literature under the following entries:

Gesellschaft der Musikfreunde
Historisches Museum
Industrie-ausstellung, 1845
Internationale Ausstellung für Musik- und Theater-wesen, 1892
Jubiläums- Gewerbe-ausstellung, 1888
Jubiläums- Kunstausstellung, 1898
Kunsthistorisches Museum
     THE AMBRAS INVENTORIES
     Later inventories (1666 to 1920)
     THE ESTE INVENTORIES
     Literature Since 1920
Museum für Völkerkunde
Nationalbibliothek
Nieder-österreichische Gewerbe-ausstellung, 1880
Weltausstellung, 1873

VIENNA (Austria). GESELLSCHAFT DER MUSIKFREUNDE (J10, A34, BB35)
[N.B.: Began in 1812; first sizeable acquisition, the collection of Franz Xavier Glöggl. Also includes collections of Ludwig Gerber, Erzherzog Rudolf (acquired 1831), some of the Aloys Fuchs, Nicolaus Dumba and Johannes Brahms collections; see *Geschichte*, no. **1545**.]

1542   Nottebohm, Martin Gustav. *Katalog der Musikinstrumenten Sammlung des Museums der Gesellschaft der Musikfreunde, von G. Nottebohm.* Wien: [n.d.] .

> A "ghost". Cited by Schlesinger*, the work is unknown to the Gesellschaft itself (1977) and does not appear in Nottebohm's *Nachlass.*

1543   *Gebäude und Kunstsammlungen der Gesellschaft . . . und ihres Conservatoriums.* Wien: 1872.

> Cited from Boalch*, Lütg*, and Heyer*. "Musikalische Instrumente," pp. 12-20; not located in U. S.

1544   "Raum VI (Instrumente)." In Vienna. Internationale Ausstellung für Musik- und Theaterwesen, 1892. *Fach-Katalog der musik-historischen Abteilung von Deutschland und Österreich-Ungarn,* pp. 460-66. Wien: 1892. 96 items.

> See also no. **1557** below.

1545   Mandyczewski, Eusebius. "Musikinstrumente." In *Zusatz-band zur Geschichte der K. K. Gesellschaft der Musikfreunde in Wien: Sammlungen und Statuten,* pp. 154-85. Wien: Holzhausen, 1912. 335 items with descriptions.

> Duckles* 3:1627.

1546   Anderson Galleries, Inc., New York. . . . *Thirty-two Old String Instruments from the Collection of the Society of the Friends of Music, Vienna. To Be Sold . . . January Fifteenth [1921].* New York: The Anderson Galleries, 1921. 7 [1] pp. 32 lots.

> Anderson catalogue no. 1549. Copy at NN (NYp).

Literature

1547   "Wiens musikalische Kunstschätze," *Allgemeine musikalische Zeitung* 28 (1826): cols. 497-504, 513-23, 629-34 and Beylage VI (plate); 22 (1827): 65-71 [article continues but does not concern instruments] .

1548   Luithlen, V. "Haydn-Instrumente der Gesellschaft der Musikfreunde in Wien," *Österreichische Kunst* 3, no. 3/4 (1932): 40-43.

VIENNA (Austria). HISTORISCHES MUSEUM (J11, BB37)

Literature

1549 Andra, L. "Musikalisches aus den Wiener Museen. I. Das Museum der Stadt Wien," *Neue Musik-Zeitung* (Stuttgart) 31 (1910): 335-37. illus.

VIENNA (Austria). INDUSTRIE-AUSSTELLUNG, 1845

1550 Schmidt, August. "Industrie-Ausstellung der österreichischen Monarchie in musikalischer Beziehung," *Wiener allgemeine Musik-Zeitung* 5 (1845): 309, 313-14, 321-22, 325-26, 329-30, 333-34, 337-38, 341-42, 345-47, 349-51, 353-54.

VIENNA (Austria). INTERNATIONALE AUSSTELLUNG FÜR MUSIK- UND THEATER-WESEN, 1892

1551 Hipkins, Alfred J., Morris Steinert and Siegmund Schneider. *The International Exhibition for Music and the Drama, Vienna 1892.* Translated from the German ed. by Rosa Wohlmuth. Vienna: M. Perles, 1894. 339, [5] pp., pls. throughout.

> "The Musical Instruments in the Exhibition," by Oskar Fleischer, pp. [55]-75. "The Archduke Franz Ferdinand of Oesterreich-Este Collection," by Guido Adler, pp. 50-52. "The M. Steinert Collection of Keyboard Instruments," by M. Steinert, pp. 217-[24], with 4 plates. More illustrations of keyboard instruments in the exhibition are included in Steinert's article, "Classic Monochord to Modern Piano," pp. 225-59. (For catalogues of the complete Steinert collection, see Section II.)

1552 Hipkins, Alfred J., Morris Steinert and Siegmund Schneider. *The International Exhibition for Music and the Drama, Vienna 1892* [in German]. Wien: M. Perles, 1894. vi, 344 pp., 89 pls.

> "Die Musik-Instrumente in der Ausstellung," Tables XIII-XVII. "Die . . . Clavier-Baukunst," Tables XXXVII-LXX. "Die Instrumenten-Sammlung des Erzherzogs Franz Ferdinand von Oesterreich-Este," by Guido Adler, pp. 57-75. "Die Musik-Instrumente auf der Ausstellung," by Oskar Fleischer, pp. 225-50.

1553 *Illustrirter Führer durch die . . . Ausstellung . . . und Katalog der gewerblichen Special-Ausstellung.* Wien: 1892. viii, 278 pp., illus.

> Cited from Hirsch* (400); Marr* says 220 pp.; cites another of 36 pp., not verified. This not located in U. S.

VIENNA (Austria). INTERNATIONAL AUSSTELLUNG . . . *continued*

1554   Rainer, Louis. *Illustrirter Führer durch die Internationale Ausstellung.* . . .
Hrsg. von Louis Rainer. Wien: Wallishausser, 1892. 106 pp., illus.

> Copies at MB (Bp), DLC (Wc).

1555   Rainer, Louis. *Illustrirter Führer durch die Internationale Ausstellung.* . . .
2. Aufl. Wien: 1892; Leipzig: Literar. Anstalt A. Schulze, [1892]. 96 pp.

> Cited from KaY*; not located. Includes a catalogue
> of the exhibition.

1556   Kurka, Rudolf Wilhelm. "Internationale Ausstellung für Musik- und Theater-
wesen . . . Original Bericht," *ZfI* 12 (1891/92): 385-86, 411-12, 433-35, 457-
59, 485-87, 511-13, 539-41, 563-65, 592-94, 619-21, 647-49, 675-78, 703-7,
735-40; 13 (1892/93): 32-34, 85-87, 107-8, 131-33, 157-58, 181-83. illus.

[N. B.: The following catalogues are arranged alphabetically by country:]

1557   (Germany) Guido, Adler. *Fach-katalog der Musikhistorischen Abtheilung von
Deutschland und Oesterreich-Ungarn, nebst Anhang.* . . . Wien: Im Selbstverlag
der Ausstellungs-commission, 1892. xiv, 591 [4] pp.

> Includes instruments from the Catajo collection and the
> collection of the Gesellschaft der Musikfreunde (now in
> the Kunsthistorisches Museum), as well as the following:
> "Sammlung Erzherzog Franz Ferdinand von Österreich-
> Este," pp. 83-88, 121 items. "Sammlung Paul de Wit,"
> pp. 142-48, 79 items. "Königliche Slg. alterthümlicher
> Musikinstrumente zu Berlin," pp. 165-79. "Sammlung
> Baron Nathaniel von Rothschild," pp. 181-87, 56 items.
> "Sammlung Karl Zach," pp. 238-42, ca. 75 items. "Raum
> XIV, Instrumente," pp. 193-106 includes items from the
> collections of Paul de Wit, Graf Harrach (Vienna), and
> the Museum Francisco-Carolinum (Linz). Copies at
> CtY (NHu), IU (Uu), MiU (AAu), DLC (Wc).

1558   (Italy) Berwin, Adolfo. *Fach-katalog der abteilung des königreiches Italien.*
Verfasst und redigirt von cav. prof. Adolfo Berwin und dr. Robert Hirschfield.
Wien: [Druck von J. N. Vernay], 1892. vii, 294 pp.

> Instruments from the Museo Civico, Modena, pp. 193-94,
> according to Boalch*. Copies at CtY (NHu), ICN (Cn),
> IU (Uu), OCH (CIhc), DLC (Wc).

1559   (Poland) Nossig, Alfred. *Katalog der polnischen Abtheilung der . . . Ausstellung in Wien 1892.* Wien: 1892. ix, 81 pp.

Cited from BM* and Marr*; not examined.

1560   (Spain) Sanpere y Miquel, Salvador and Guillermo Roca. *Katalog der Ausstellung des königreiches Spanien. . . .* Wien: [Druck von J. N. Vernay], 1892. 95 pp.

Copies at ICN (Cn), IU (Uu), DLC (Wc); not examined.

1561   (U. K.) Hipkins, A. J. *Katalog der Ausstellung des königreiches Grossbritannien und Irland.* Translated by Berta Overbeck. Wien: [Druck von J. N. Vernay], 1892. 3, 47 pp.

Copy at NN (NYp); not examined.

1562   (U. K.) Broadwood, John, & sons, London. *List 69, 1892; Being the 169th Year Since the Establishment of the Firm. A Descriptive and Illustrated Catalogue of Pianofortes* [exhibited at the International Exhibition]. [London?: 1892.]

Cited from Marr*; not located.

1563   (USSR) *. . . Russland. Direction der kaiserlichen Hoftheater in St. Petersburg und Moskau. . . .* Wien: [Druck von J. N. Vernay], 1892. 84 pp.

Instruments? Copy at DLC (Wc); not examined.

Literature

1564   *Album der internationalen Ausstellung für Musik und Theaterwesen . . . Ausg. I.* Wien: M. Herzig, 1892. 15 colored pls.

NN (NYp) has, says 10 plates; KaY* says Ausg. II and III issued in lithograph.

1565   [Louis Ferdinand, Prince of Bavaria, 1859-1949.] "Der Besuch des hohen Protektors der deutschen Reichs-Abtheilung Sr. Kgl. Hoheit des Prinzen Ludwig von Bayern in der Theater- und Musik-Ausstellung zu Wien," *ZfI* 12 (1891/92): 591-92.

1566   Fleischer, Oskar. *Die Bedeutung der internationalen Musik- und Theater Ausstellung in Wien für Kunst und Wissenschaft der Musik.* Leipzig/Berlin: Verlag der Universal-Bibliothek für Musiklitteratur, 1894. 71 pp., illus.

Copy at NN (NYp).

1567   "Internationale Musik- und Theater-Ausstellung 1892 in Wien," *ZfI* 12 (1892/92): 51-53, 115, 168, 187, 201-2, 256-58, 292, 315, 371, 421, 439-40, 462, 469, 490, 516, 525, 569, 597-98, 625, 653-54, 681, 768-71; 13 (1892/93): 62, 245; 14 (1893/94): 169-70, 312.

1568   "Internationale Ausstellung für Musik- und Theaterwesen," *Neue Musik-Zeitung* 13 (1892): 103, 126, 136-37, 147-48, 159-60, 173, 199, 222-23.

VIENNA (Austria). INTERNATIONALE AUSSTELLUNG ... *continued*

1569 *Jugend-Führer. Anleitung zur Besichtigung der Ausstellung mit besonderer Rücksichtnahme auf die Jugend.* Wien: 1892. 44 pp.

Cited from BM*; not located.

1570 Thibouville-Lamy, M. J. "Offizieller Bericht über die Musikinstrumenten-Industrie auf der . . . ," *ZfI* 12 (1891/92): 15-17, 32, 66, 83, 97-99, 113, 127-28, 142, 165.

1571 Sittard, Josef. *Kritische Briefe über die Wiener Internationale Musik- und Theater-Ausstellung.* Hamburg: C. Boysen, 1892. 2, 88 pp.

Copy at DLC.

1572 "Verzeichnis der Austeller in der gewerblichen Abtheilung," *ZfI* 12 (1891/92): 469-73, 499-501, 525-26.

1573 Riemsdijk, J. C. M. van. "De internationale muziektentoonstelling te Weenen," *Vereeniging voor Nederlandsche Muziekgeschiedenis, Tijdschrift* 4 (1897): 97-109.

VIENNA (Austria). JUBILÄUMS- GEWERBE-AUSSTELLUNG, 1888

Literature

1574 Kurka, R. W. "Jubiläums- Gewerbe-Ausstellung. XVIII Gruppe: Bau musikalischer Instrumente," *ZfI* 9 (1888/89): 42-46.

General

1575 *Katalog der Jubiläums- Gewerbe-Ausstellung Wien 1888.* Hrsg. von der Ausstellungs-commission der Nieder-österr. Gewerbe-Vereins. Wien: [Hölder], 1888. vii, 374 pp.

Group 18, musical instruments. Cited from KaY*; not located.

VIENNA (Austria). JUBILÄUMS- KUNSTAUSSTELLUNG, 1898

Literature

1576 [Liste der Aussteller], *ZfI* 3 (1897/98): 636, 645.

1577 Schewitz, C. L. "Klavierinstrumente auf der Wiener . . . ," *ZfI* 3 (1897/98): 770-73.

General

1578 *Offizieller Katalog der Jubiläums-Ausstellung Wien.* Wien: A. Schulze, 1898. iii, 528 pp., illus.

Class 72, musical instruments. Cited from KaY*; not located.

VIENNA (Austria). KUNSTHISTORISCHES MUSEUM (J12-13) [N. B.: The literature about this collection is considerable and complex, and for a detailed history, the reader is directed to it. Some brief historical review is necessary, however, in order to explain the arrangement of items throughout this bibliography.

The Museum's two most famous groups of instruments—and those which served as its basis—are the well-known Ambras and Este collections, first inventoried in the sixteenth century. Later additions came from the Gesellschaft der Musikfreunde, the Baroness Clarice de Rothschild, the Stift Göttweig, the Oberösterreichisches Landesmuseum, some items purchased from the E. Fiala collection, and others.

The bibliography which follows is set out in two sections. The first covers the years to 1920 by which date the Ambras and Este collections had been joined and named the *Sammlung alter Musikinstrumente* and Schlosser's 1920 catalogue (no. **1609**) of the combined collections had been published. The second section includes catalogues and literature about the Museum since 1920. The first section itself is subdivided into two sections listing separately the inventories of the Ambras and Este groups.

The so-called **AMBRAS COLLECTION**, founded about 1570 by Ferdinand of Tirol, Archduke of Austria, was housed throughout most of its existence in two locations, Schloss Ambras and Schloss Ruhelust. Kaiser Franz I moved them together to Vienna in 1806. They were exhibited in the Belvedere from 1814 and from 1891 in the Kunsthistorisches Museum.

The **ESTE COLLECTION** was formed by the Marchese Pio Enea degli Obizzi (d. 1674) at "Il Catajo" near Padua where it remained until the last Count of Obizzi, Tommaso, died in 1805 (Pietro Selvatico says 1803 in his *Guida di Padova*, pp. 433-34. Padova: Sacchetto, 1869). The instruments then went to Duke Ercole III of Modena, later to the Este family. Some of the collection was shown at the Internationale Ausstellung in Vienna in 1892 (see catalogues **1551-52** and **1557**) and from 1904 to 1908 in the Palais Modern. It was later moved to the Neue Burg and joined there in 1916 by the **AMBRAS** instruments.

The group from the Gesellschaft der Musikfreunde was added in 1938 (a few items have since been returned to the Gesellschaft) and all of the instruments were housed in the Palais Pallavicini until after WWII when the integrated collection was returned to a reconstructed Neue Burg.

Complete citations for authorities referred to throughout the following section can be found under the numbers:]

    1604 Senn, Walter
    1609 Schlosser, Julius
    1619 Luithlen, Victor

VIENNA (Austria). KUNSTHISTORISCHES MUSEUM

THE AMBRAS INVENTORIES

Under Erzherzog Ferdinand II, von Tirol, 1564 to 1595

1579　(1596) "Regest 5556 [f. 228¹-232] 1596 Mai 30, Innsbruck. Inventari weilend der fürstlich durchlaucht erzherzog Ferdinanden zu Österreich . . . Ruelust [but cf. Senn, p. 166] . . . Musicalinstrument und püecher." Transcribed by Boeheim, Wendelin, "Urkunden und Regesten aus der k. k. Hofbibliothek," *Jahrbuch des kunsthistorischen Sammlungen* 7/II (1888): CCLVII-CCLVIII.

　　　　According to Senn, "Inventar A 18/1," Österreichische Nationalbibliothek.

1580　(1596) "Regest 5556 [f. 228¹-232] 1596 Mai 30, Innsbruck. Inventari weilend der fürstlich durchlaucht erzherzog Ferdinanden zu Österreich . . . [etc.] ." In Waldner, Franz. "Zwei Inventarien aus dem XVI. und XVII. Jahrhundert über hinterlassene Musikinstrumente und Musikalien am Innsbrucker Hofe," *Studien zur Musikwissenschaft* 4 (1916): 129-30.

　　　　See also Waldner's "Nachrichten über die Musikpflege am Hofe zu Innsbruck," *MfM* 36 (1904): 141-55.

1581　(1596) "Regest 5556 [f. 228¹-232] 1596 Mai 30, Innsbruck. Inventari weilend der fürstlich durchlaucht erzherzog Ferdinanden zu Österreich . . . [etc.] ." Reprinted by Schlosser, Julius. *Die Sammlung alter Musikinstrumente: beschreibendes Verzeichnis,* pp. 11-12. Wien: Schroll, 1920. Reprint ed. Hildesheim/New York: Olms, 1974.

1582　"Instrumente im Inventar von 1596." In Senn, pp. 166-71.

Under Erzherzog Maximilian, von Österreich, 1602 to 1618

1583　(1603) [Inventar A 40/10, Österreichische Nationalbibliothek.] In Senn, p. 341.

　　　　Notes its similarity to the 1596 inventory.

1584　(1613) [An inventory of 1613.]

　　　　According to Schlosser, p. 14, included by Anton Roschmann in a Ms. inventory of 1730. Luithlen, p. xix, says the 1730 Ms. is now in the Kunsthistorisches Museum, Sammlung für Plastik und Kunstgewerbe, Inv. Nr. 665. Not noted by Senn.

1585　(1615) [Inventar A 41/1, Österreichische Nationalbibliothek.]

　　　　Senn, p. 341, remarks that this and the 1621 inventory below contain but one entry more than that of 1596.

Under Erzherzog Leopold V, 1619 to 1632

1586   (1619) An inventory referred to by Senn, p. 334, passim, as the "Maximilian Inventar," and identified as "Leop[oldina]" 0/40.

1587   (1621) [Inventar A 4-/13, Österreichische Nationalbibliothek.] " . . . über obbemete Kunst- und Rüsst Camer, ain ordenliche und merere beschreib- und Benennung der Stuckh fürzunemen."

> Also included in Roschmann's 1730 Ms.; see no. **1584** above.
> See also Schlosser, p. 14; Senn, pp. 167, 334, 415 (note 2).

Under Erzherzog Ferdinand Karl, 1646 to 1662

1588   (1653? 1660?) These are dates given by Senn and Luithlen respectively for the purchase of a portion of the Ferrara collection of Antonio Goretti. Luigi Cittadella, however, in his *Notizie relative a Ferrara* (Ferrara: 1864), notes the sale to the "Principe d'Inspruck" between the dates 1614 and 1620 in his chronology. See Luithlen, p. xi, Senn, p. 334.

Under Erzherzog Siegmund Franz, 1662 to 1665

1589   (1663) [Inventar A 40/41.]

> Noted by Senn, but not otherwise identified.

1590   (1665) "Inventar der von Erzherzog Siegmund Franz hinterlassenen Musikalien, Innsbruck, 1665." Reprinted in Waldner, Franz. "Zwei Inventarien aus dem XVI. und XVII. Jahrhundert . . . ," *Studien zur Musikwissenschaft* 4 (1916): 130-33. Cf. **1547**.

> Waldner locates the original in the k. k. Statthalterei-archiv,
> "Leop." Lit. J. 40. Luithlen, in his 1966 catalogue of the
> Museum, locates it in the Landesregierungsarchiv, Innsbruck.

Later inventories (the court removed to Vienna, 1666)

1591   (1680) Senn notes, p. 341ff., but does not identify further.

1592   (1696) Senn notes, p. 341ff., but does not identify further.

1593   (1704) [Inventar A 20/27.]

> Noted by Senn, p. 341ff.

VIENNA (Austria). KUNSTHISTORISCHES MUSEUM

THE AMBRAS INVENTORIES *continued*

1594   (1725) "Ambraser Inventar von 1725."

> According to Luithlen, p. xix, who locates the original
> in the Haus-, Hof- und Staatsarchiv, Vienna. See also
> Senn, p. 341ff.

1595   (1730) [An inventory of this date in Ms. in the Kunsthistorisches Museum, according to Senn, p. 341ff. Schlosser ascribes to Anton Roschmann and indicates that it includes inventories of 1613 and 1621.] (See nos. **1584** and **1587** above.)

1596   (1741) Senn notes, p. 334, but does not further identify.

1597   (1768) Senn notes, p. 334, but does not further identify.

1598   (1788) [Ms. in the Kunsthistorisches Museum.] Reprinted in Primisser, Alois. *Die kaiserlich-königliche Ambraser-Sammlung,* pp. 216-19. Wien: 1819.

1599   (1806) [Inventar A 40/32, Österreichische Nationalbibliothek.]

> An inventory prepared by Alois Pfaundler von Sternberg which
> Schlosser, p. 14, calls a "neues summarisches Inventar."

1600   (1810) [Inventar A 41/19, 29, Österreichisches Nationalbibliothek.]

> Senn notes, p. 415, but does not further identify.

1601   (1855) "O. Musikalisches Instrumente (Kasten XVII und XVIII)." In Sacken, Eduard, Freiherr von. *Die k. k. Ambraser-Sammlung. Zweiter Teil: Die Kunst und Wunderkammern und die Bibliothek,* pp. 143-54. Wien: Wilhelm Braunmüller, 1855.

1602   (1891) Hajdecky, Alexander. "Musikinstrumente." In Ilg, Albert. *Führer durch die Sammlung der Kunstindustriellen Gegenstände der kunsthistorischen Sammlungen des allerhöchsten Kaiserhauses,* pp. 153-58. Wien: Im Selbstverlag der kunsthistorischen Sammlungen, 1891.

1603   (1908) Schlosser, Julius. *Die Kunst- und Wunderkammern der Spätrennaisance.* (Monographien des Kunstgewerbes . . . XI.) Leipzig: Klinkhardt & Biermann, 1908. 3, 146 pp., illus.

> Some of the items noted and illustrated are from the
> Ambras Collection. See especially pp. 52-57.

Literature

1604 Senn, Walter. *Musik und Theater am Hof zu Innsbruck; Geschichte der Hofkapelle vom 15. Jahrhundert bis . . . 1748.* Innsbruck: Österreichische Verlagsanstalt, 1954. xx, 447 pp.

> Includes a discussion of many of the inventories
> and their differences, pp. 166-71, 334-44.

1605 Luchner, Laurin. *Denkmal einer Renaissance-Fürsten. Versuch einer Rekonstruktion des Ambraser-Museums von 1583.* [Hrsg. von Kunsthistorisches Museum, Wien.] Wien: Schroll, [1958]. 143 pp., 21 pls.

1606 "Ein Schloss in Tirol: Ambras und seine Sammlungen. Aufnahmen Franco Cianetti," *DU-Atlantis; Kulturelle Monatsschrift,* vol. 26 (April 1966).

> Whole issue, various authors, including Otto Ulf's
> "Musik auf Schloss Ambras."

THE ESTE INVENTORIES

Under Marchese Pio Enea degli Obizzi, d. 1674

1607 [An unpublished, crude, but early inventory of the Obizzi collection prepared by Nobiluomo Santyan y Velasco, mentioned by Schlosser, p. 15, but not located.]

Under Franz Ferdinand, Erzherzog von Österreich-Este, 1863 to 1914

1608 "Raum VII. Sammlung Erzherzog Franz Ferdinand von Oesterreich-Este." In Adler, Guido. *Fach-katalog der Musikhistorischen Abtheilung von Deutschland und Oesterreich-Ungarn* (no. **1557** above), pp. 83-88. Wien: Im Selbstverlag der Ausstellungs-Commission, 1892. 121 items.

Literature Since 1920

1609 Schlosser, Julius. *Die Sammlung alter Musikinstrumente; beschreibendes Verzeichnis.* (Kunsthistorisches Museum in Wien. Publikationen aus den Sammlungen für Plastik und Kunstgewerbe . . . Bd. III.) Wien: A. Schroll & Co., 1920. 143 pp., 57 pls., 361 items.

> Copy at MB (Bp), MiU (AAu), PP (PHf), ViU (CHu),
> DLC (Wc).

1610 Corrigenda (to no. **1609**) by Schlosser in his "Randnoten zum Katalog des neuen Wiener Instrumentenmuseums," *ZfMW* 4 (1921): 162-68.

VIENNA (Austria). KUNSTHISTORISCHES MUSEUM

THE ESTE INVENTORIES *continued*

1611   Comments about the Museum and a review of the catalogue (no. **1609**) by
        Curt Sachs in his "Das neue Wiener Instrumenten-Museum," *AfMW* 3 (1921):
        128-34.

1612   Schlosser, Julius. *Die Sammlung alter Musikinstrumente; beschreibendes
        Verzeichnis. Nachdruck der Ausg. Wien 1920.* Hildesheim/New York: Olms,
        1974.

1613   Schlosser, Julius. *Kleiner Führer durch die Sammlung alter Musikinstrumente.*
        Wien: A. Schroll & Co., 1922. 37 pp., 16 pls., 271 items.

        Copy at DLC(Wc). LV&A* cites variant: 40 pp., 16 pls., 1925.

1614   Schlosser, Julius. *Kleiner Führer durch die Sammlung alter Musikinstrumente.*
        (Führer durch die Kunsthistorischen Sammlungen in Wien . . . 22.) Wien:
        Verlag der kunsthistorischen Sammlungen, 1933. 35 pp., 16 pls., 271 items.

        Most of the 1922 edition reprinted. Copy at DLC(Wc).

1615   Luithlen, Victor. *Führer durch die Sonderschau: Klaviere aus fünf Jahrhunderten.*
        Wien: Verlag der Museumsfreunde, 1939. 31 pp., viii pls.

        First combined exhibition of items from the Ambras,
        Este and Gesellschaft der Musikfreunde collections.

1616   Luithlen, Victor. *Führer durch die Sonderschau: Saiteninstrumente. Klaviere,
        Streichinstrumente, Zupfinstrumente. Verzeichnis. . . .* Wien: [Verlag der
        Verein der Museumsfreunde], 1941. 24 pp., xii pls.

1617   Luithlen, Victor. *Die Sammlung alter Musikinstrumente in der Neuen Burg zu
        Wien.* [Vienna?: 1953?] 3-9 pp., pls.

        From *Wort und Bild,* Folge 47/48, 1953. Copy at DLC(Wc).

1618   Luithlen, Victor. *Alte Musikinstrumente; die Sammlung des Kunsthistorischen
        Museum in der neuen Burg zu Wien.* (Phaidros Reihe) Wien: H. Bauer, [1954].
        28 pp., mostly illus.

        Copies at NN(NYp), DLC(Wc). Duckles* 3:1626,
        a visitor's guide.

1619   Luithlen, Victor and K. Wegerer. *Katalog der Sammlung alter Musikinstrumente.
        1. T. Saitenklaviere. . . .* (Führer durch das Kunsthistorische Museum, Nr. 14.)
        Wien: Kunsthistorisches Museum, 1966. 95 pp., 32 pls., 76 items.

        Copy at DLC (Wc). Duckles* 3:1629, first of 3 vols.
        Review by Friedrich Ernst in *Die Musikforschung*
        21 (1968): 506-7.

Literature

1620 Sachs, Curt. "Das neue Wiener Instrumenten-Museum," *AfMW* 3 (1921): 128- .
Mostly a review of Schlosser's catalogue (no. **1609**).

1621 Ungerer, I. D. "Die Wiener Instrumentensammlung," *Musica* 10 (1956): 429-31.
illus.

1622 Luithlen, Victor. "Musical Treasures of the Vienna Art Museum." In *Music,
Libraries and Instruments . . . Congress, 1959,* pp. 244-51. London: Hinrichsen,
1961.

1623 Luithlen, Victor. "Haydn-Erinnerungen in der Sammlung. . . ." In *Anthony van
Hoboken. Festschrift,* pp. 110-14. Mainz: Schott, 1962.

1624 Luithlen, Victor. "Die Entwicklungsreihe des Klaviers in der Sammlung alter
Musikinstrumente des Kunsthistorisches Museums in Wien." In *Colloquim
Restauratie-problemen van Antwerpse klavicembels,* pp. 49-52. Antwerp: 1971.

1625 Marvin, B. "Recorders and English Flutes in European Collections," *GSJ* 25
(1972): 30-57.
Many listed from the Kunsthistorisches Museum.

1626 Bazant, W. "In Wien sind diese Instrumente Gegenwart - die Sammlungen in der
Neuen Burg," *Instrumentenbau-Zeitschrift* 27 (1973): 383.

VIENNA (Austria). MUSEUM FÜR VÖLKERKUNDE (J13, BB37)

1627 Janata, Alfred. *Aussereuropäische Musikinstrumente.* [Katalog und Ausstellung:
Alfred Janata; Fotos: Edeltrud Mandl; Zeichnungen: Franka Becker. Wien:
1961.] 88 pp., illus., 654 items.
Copy at DLC (Wc). Duckles* 3:1630.

1628 Mais, Adolf. *Volksmusikinstrumente der Balkanländer.* [Ausstellung und]
Katalog Adolf Mais. (The Museum's Sonderausstellungsreihe "Aus der
Volkskultur der Ost- und Südostgebiete der ehemaligen Donaumonarchie," 1.)
Wien: Selbstverlag des Österreichischen Museums für Volkskunde, 1969. 51 pp.
Copy at DLC (Wc).

1629 Janata, Alfred. *Musikinstrumente der Völker. Aussereuropäische Musikinstrumente und Schallgeräte, Systematik und Themenbeispiele. Sammlungs-
katalog des Museums.* Katalog und Ausstellung, Alfred Janata. . . . Wien: Das
Museum, 1975. xvi, 320 pp., pls.

VIENNA (Austria). NATIONALBIBLIOTHEK (BB32). *See Vienne à Versailles under* **VERSAILLES (France). MUSÉE NATIONAL**

VIENNA (Austria). NIEDER-ÖSTERREICHISCHE GEWERBE-AUSSTELLUNG, 1880

Literature

1630   Stein, Otto. "Die Claviere auf der . . . Ausstellung," *ZfI* 1 (1880/81): 41-42.

General

1631   . . . *Katalog . . . Wien 1880*. Wien: [Hartleben], 1880. xxxvii, 222 pp.

Cited from KaY*; not located in U. S.

VIENNA (Austria). WELTAUSSTELLUNG, 1873

1632   Paul, Oskar. *Musikalische Instrumente*. Braunschweig: Vieweg und Sohn, 1874. 110 pp.

Copy at DLC (Wc). "Aus dem 'Amtlichen Berichte über die Wiener Weltausstellung . . . ,'" Bd. II, Heft 5. *Amtlicher Berichte*, 3 vols., 1874-77, located at MH, PBL, ICRL, MB, DLC.

1633   Schelle, Eduard. . . . *(Gruppe XV). Musikalische Instrumente*. (Officieller Ausstellungs-Bericht . . . unter Red. von K. T. Richter, no. 39.) Wien: k.k. Hof- und Staatsdruckerei, 1873. 90 pp.

Copy at DLC (Wc).

1634   Schebek, Edmund. *Die Cremoneser Instrumente auf der Wiener Weltausstellung in Jahre 1873*. Wien: 1874.

Cited from Torri*; not verified. Journal article?

1635   Gallay, Jules. "Instruments de musique. Instruments à archet." In France. Commission supérieure. *Rapports . . .* , vol. 3, pp. 311-22. Paris: Impr. nationale, 1875.

Copy at DLC (Wc).

1636   Gallay, Jules. "Les instruments à archet à l'Exposition universelle de Vienne en 1873," *Chronique musicale* 3ème année, Tome 10 (1875): 153-65.

1637   Lissajous, Jules Antoine. "Instruments à vent et autres appareils acoustiques." In France. Commission supérieure. *Rapports . . .* , vol. 3, pp. 322-29. Paris: Impr. nationale, 1875.

Copy at DLC (Wc).

Literature

1638 Bannelier, Charles. "Les instruments historiques à l'Exposition universelle de Vienne (1873)," *Revue et gazette musicale de Paris* 42 (1875): 283-84, 289-90.

1639 Coco Zanghi, Giuseppe. *Per l'Esposizione Universale del 1873 in Vienna: raguagli illustrativi di un antico violino.* Catania: 1873.

> Cited from Lambertini*; not located.

1640 "Exposition universelle de Vienne," *Echo musical* 4, no. 5 (1872): 1.

1641 "Special Programs for the Exhibition of Cremona Instruments at the Universal Exhibition in Vienna, 1873," *Musical World* 50 (1872): 567-68.

1642 "L'esposizione di violini cremonesi a Vienna," *Gazzetta musicale di Milano* 27 (1872): 35-36.

General

1643 "Istrumenti musicali . . . di Salvatore de Castrone Marchesi." In *Relazione dei giurati italiani . . . Fasc. I, Gruppo X, Istrumenti musicali,* pp. 47-63. Milano: Regia Stamperia, 1873.

> Copy at DLC (Wc).

1644 "Gruppe XV, Musikalische Instrumente." In *Amtlicher Katalog . . . Oesterreichs,* pp. 404-11. Wien: "Die Presse," 1873.

> Copy at DLC (Wc).

1645 Germany. Centralcommission für die Wiener Weltausstellung, 1873. *Amtlicher Katalog des. . . .* Berlin: Decker, 1873. xliv, 672 pp.

> Copy at ICU (Cu); not examined.

VILLINGEN I. BADEN (Germany). GEWERBE- UND INDUSTRIE-AUSSTELLUNG, 1907

Literature

1646 [Musikinstrumenten-Industrie auf der . . .], *ZfI* 27 (1906/7): 902 (exhibitors), 937, 939, 1072-73 (by Paul de Wit).

VLAARDINGEN (Netherlands). VISSERIJMUSEUM

1647 *Handleiding / katalogus bij de Tentoonstelling van uitheemse muziekinstrumenten van 22 juni tot 29 aug. 1975 in de muziekkammer van het Museum, op initiatief van de Culturele Raad. . . .* [n. p.], 1975. [12] pp., illus. (71 items)

> Voorword: Ton Stolk.

WARSAW (Poland). PANSTWOWA WYZEZA SZKOLA MUZYCZNA (J107)

1648   Dobrowolski, Andrzej. *Polskie instrumenty muzyczne. Katalog wystawy.* Warszawa: Centr. Handlowa Przemyslu Muz., 1966. 72 pp.

Literature

1649   Sobieska, Jadwiga. "Na marginesie wystawy 'Polskie instrumenty muzyczne'," *Muzyka; kwartalnik pozwiecony historii i teatri* 12 (1967): 81-87.

         Article includes citations to many journal and newspaper articles about the exhibition.

WASHINGTON, D. C. (USA). LIBRARY OF CONGRESS

1650   Smart, James R. and Jon Newsom. *"A Wonderful Invention;" A Brief History of the Phonograph from Tinfoil to the LP: An Exhibition in the Great Hall of the Library of Congress.* Washington, D. C.: Library of Congress, 1977. 40 pp., illus.

WASHINGTON, D. C. (USA). LIBRARY OF CONGRESS. DIVISION OF MUSIC

1651   Gilliam, Laura E. and William Lichtenwanger. *The Dayton C. Miller Flute Collection; A Checklist.* Washington, D. C.: 1961. vi, 115 pp., illus., 1593 items.

         Duckles* 3:1634.

Literature

1652   Wilkins, H. Blakiston. *The Stradivari Quartet of Stringed Instruments in the Library of Congress* [presented to the Library by Mrs. Matthew John Whittall]. Washington: U. S. Government Printing Office, 1936. 6 pp.; another issue, 1937. 7 pp.

1653   Orcutt, William Dana. *The Stradivari Memorial at Washington.* Washington: [1938]. 49 pp., illus. Reprint ed. New York: Da Capo, 1977.

WASHINGTON, D. C. (USA). MUSEUM OF HISTORY AND TECHNOLOGY (L104)

1654   Wilson, Thomas. *Prehistoric Art; Or the Origin of Art as Manifested in the Works of Prehistoric Man.* (U. S. National Museum, Annual Report, 1896, pp. 512-664.) Washington, D. C.: 1898. illus.

         "Much of the material [about instruments, pp. 512-664] was prepared by Mr. E. P. Upham." Copy at NPV (POvc).

1655   Krieger, Herbert W. *Material Culture of the People of Southeastern Panama, Based on Specimens in the United States National Museum.* (U. S. National Museum, Bulletin 134.) Washington, D. C.: Smithsonian Institution, 1926.
> "Music," pp. 115-28; instruments shown, pls. 6-8.

1656   Densmore, Frances. *Handbook of the Collection of Musical Instruments in the United States National Museum.* (U. S. National Museum, Bulletin 136.) Washington, D. C.: Government Printing Office, 1927. Reprint ed. New York: Da Capo, 1971. iii, 164 pp., 49 pls.
> Duckles* 3:1635.

1657   Smithsonian Institution. Division of Musical Instruments. *A Checklist of Keyboard Instruments at the Smithsonian Institution . . . Museum of History and Technology.* Washington, D. C.: Government Printing Office, 1967. v, 79 pp., 5 pls.
> Includes ca. 200 keyboard instruments from the Hugo Worch gift, 1914. Duckles* 3:1631.
> 2nd ed., 1975. 87 pp.

1658   Sheldon, Robert E. *Wind Instruments* [exhibition brochure]. Washington, D. C.: Division of Musical Instruments, Smithsonian Institution, 1968. [5] pp.

1659   Fesperman, John T. *Organs in Early America* [exhibition brochure]. Washington, D. C.: Division of Musical Instruments, Smithsonian Institution, 1968. [5] pp.

1660   Hoover, Cynthia A. *Harpsichords and Clavichords.* Washington, D. C.: Smithsonian Institution, 1969. 43 pp.
> Duckles* 3:1633.

1661   Odell, J. Scott. *Plucked Dulcimers; A Checklist of Appalachian Dulcimers and Similar Instruments in the Collections of the Division of Musical Instruments.* Washington, D. C.: 1971. 5 pp.
> Reproduced from typescript.

1662   Odell, J. Scott. *A Checklist of Banjos in the Collections of the Division of Musical Instruments.* Washington, D. C.: 1971. 4 pp.
> Reproduced from typescript. Rev. ed., 1973.

1663   Hoover, Cynthia A. *Music Machines—American Style; A Catalog of the Exhibition. With Introductory Notes by Erik Barnouw and Irving Kolodin.* Washington, D. C.: National Museum of History and Technology, 1971. 139 pp., illus.

1664   Hoover, Cynthia A. [*Idem,* with title:] *The History of Music Machines.* New York: Drake, 1975.

WASHINGTON, D. C. (USA). MUSEUM OF HISTORY . . . *continued*

1665   Smithsonian Institution. *A Checklist of Keyboard Instruments at the Smith-sonian Institution, Prepared by the Division of Musical Instruments.* 2nd ed. Washington, D. C.: Smithsonian Institution, 1975. vi, 87 pp., illus.

1666   Herman, Lloyd E. *The Harmonious Craft. American Musical Instruments, September 29, 1978 - August 5, 1979 . . .* [catalogue of the exhibition]. Washington, D. C., 1978. 7 folded pp., (88 items), illus.

Literature

1667   "National Museum Musical Collection," *Musical Leader and Concertgoer* (Chicago) 6, no. 12 (1903): 19.

1668   Watkins, C. Malcolm. "American Pianos of the Federal Republic in the United States National Museum," *Antiques* 59 (1951): 58-61.

1669   Fesperman, John. "Report from Washington: Music and Musical Instruments at the Smithsonian Institution," *Current Musicology* 6 (1968): 63-65.
        About the recently formed Division of Musical Instruments.

1670   "Plucked Strings in the Special Exhibition," *Town Tatler,* September 9, 1961.

1671   Hollis, Helen R. *Pianos in the . . . Institution.* (Smithsonian Studies in History and Technology, no. 27.) Washington, D. C.: 1973. iii, 47 pp., illus.

1672   Hollis, Helen R. and James M. Weaver. *Music Instruments of the Baroque and Early Classical Eras in the Smithsonian Institution. An Audio-Visual Presentation.* [Washington, D. C.: 1975?] 23 pp. booklet, 2 cassettes, 50 slides.

1673   Hollis, Helen R. *The Musical Instruments of Joseph Haydn.* (Smithsonian Institution Studies in History and Technology, no. 38.) Washington, D. C.: 1977. 33 pp., illus.
        Most of the instruments discussed from the Smithsonian.

1674   "Smithsonian Acquires Important Bowed Strings in 1978-79," *AMIS Newsletter* 8 (October 1979): 1-3. illus.
        Some items from the collection of Laurence Witten.

1675   "The Harmonious Craft. American Musical Instruments [exhibit prepared by Lloyd E. Herman and James Weaver]," *Guitar and Lute,* no. 8 (January 1979): p. 33. illus.

WEIMAR (Germany). HOFKAPELLE

1676   [Ms. D177, No. 19^e, Stüc, 15, Ernestinisches Gesamtarchiv.] "Ithem wass vonn Instrumentenn da seint, die meines gnedigan Fürsten undt Herrn seindt . . . 1570." Reprinted in Aber, Adolf. *Die Pflege der Musik unter den Wettinern und wettinischen Ernestinern . . . 1662,* p. 107. (Veröffentlichungen des Fürstlichen Institutes für Musikwissenschaftliche Forschung zu Bückeburg, IV. R., I. Bd.) Bückeburg/Leipzig: 1921.

1677   Drese, Adam. "Inventarium der musikalischen Instrumenta und anderer Singendten Sachen. Verzeugnus in kiesige Weimarische Capell gehörige instrumenta . . . 1662." Ms. A. 2047, Weimar Städtische historische Archiv, lvs. 117-20, and Ms. A. 2054, lvs. 58-63. Reprinted in Aber, Adolf. *Idem.,* pp. 150-51, [supplement], p. 152.

WEISSENFELS (Germany). VEREIN FÜR NATUR- UND ALTERTUMSKUNDE

Literature

1678   Werner, Arno. "Heimatliche Musikausstellungen," *ZiMG* 4 (1903): 605-8.

WIESBADEN (Germany). MUSIKHISTORISCHES MUSEUM HECKEL-BIEBRICH
(J66, A251). *See Section II under* HECKEL, WILHEM

WILLISAU (Switzerland). INDUSTRIE-AUSSTELLUNG, 1855

General

1679   *Katalog der Industrie-Ausstellung in Willisau, Kanton Luzern.* Willisau: Druck von Konrad Kneubühler, 1855. 262 pp.

"Saal Nr. V, Musikalische Instrumente," pp. 52-55.

WINDSOR CASTLE, BERKSHIRE (U. K.).   [N. B.: Forty-four instruments from the collection were exhibited by Carl Engel at the South Kensington Museum in 1872 and are included in his catalogue of that exhibition, q.v., under LONDON.]

WROCŁAW (Poland). GEWERBE- UND INDUSTRIE-AUSSTELLUNG, 1881

Literature

1680   "Gewerbe- und Industrie-Ausstellung zu Breslau 1881," *ZfI* 1 (1880/81): 289-90.

WROCŁAW (Poland). SCHLESISCHES MUSEUM FÜR KUNST-GEWERBE UND ALTERTÜMER

1681   Epstein, Peter and Ernst Schreyer. *Führer und Katalog zur Sammlung alter Musikinstrumente.* Breslau: Verlag des Museums, 1932. 63 pp., illus., (10 pls.).

> Copies at ICN (Cn), NN (NYp), PPULC (PHlc). Grove's* says the collection was mostly lost or dispersed and that surviving items were shown at the Poznan exhibition in 1949 and included in Szulc's catalogue, no. **1332**.

Literature

1682   [Notice of and comments about unusual and rare instruments] , *ZiMG* 2 (1900/1901): 54.

1683   Matzke, Hermann. "Alter Musikinstrumente in Schlesien. Zur Musikinstrumentenausstellung des 12. Deutschen Sängerbundesfestes," *ZfI* 57 (1936/37): 359-60, 382-83.

YORK (U. K.). CASTLE MUSEUM (J160, A116, BB108)   [N. B.: Includes part of the R. T. Richmond collection and all of the collection of J. L. Kirk.]

1684   Wood, G. Bernard. *Musical Instruments in York Castle Museum (with Photographs by the Author).* York: [ca. 1945]. 16 pp., 16 pls.

> Copy at NBuU-M (BUu).

ZAGREB (Yugoslavia). ETNOGRAFSKI MUSEJ (J162)

1685   Širola, B. and M. Gavazzi. *Muzikolski rad Etnografskog Museja u Zagreb* [catalogue] . (The Museum's Etnološka Biblioteka, 12.) Zagreb: 1931. 84 pp., illus.

> Cited from LV&A*.

Literature

1686   Širola, Božidar. *Fuckalice sviraljke od kore svježeg dreveta.* (The Museum's Etnološka Biblioteka, 15.) Zagreb: 1932. 38 pp., illus.; summary in German, pp. 36-37.

> Copy at DLC (Wc).

1687   Širola, Božidar. *Sopile i zurle.* (The Museum's Etnološka Biblioteka, 17.) Zagreb: 1932. 67 pp., illus.; summary in German, pp. 63-64.

> Copy at DLC (Wc).

ZAGREB (Yugoslavia). MUZEJ ZA UMJETNOST I OBRT (J162)

1688 *Automatofoni, muzicki automati* [exhibition catalogue]. [Zagreb: 1963.] 8 pp., illus.

>   Cited from LV&A*.

ZEITZ (Germany). FEST-VERSAMMLUNG DES PESTALOZZI- UND LEHRER-VEREINS DER PROVINZ SACHSEN, 1899

1689 Loebus, Carl. *Führer durch die Musikinstrumenten-Ausstellung.* [Zeitz?: 1899?]

>   Cited from article in *ZfI* (see following citation);
>   unable to verify or locate.

Literature

1690 Schlemüller, G. "Klavier-Ausstellung in Zeitz," *ZfI* 20 (1899/90): 30-31.

ZEITZ (Germany). GEWERBE- UND INDUSTRIE-AUSSTELLUNG, 1891

Literature

1691 "Die Gewerbe- und Industrie-Ausstellung in Zeitz," *ZfI* 12 (1891/92): 1-2.

ZITTAU (Germany). OBERLAUSITZER GEWERBE- UND INDUSTRIE-AUSSTELLUNG, 1902

Literature

1692 Menzel, Hans. "Die Musikinstrumente auf der . . . Ausstellung," *ZfI* 22 (1901/2): 933-36, 971-74, 1004. illus.

General

1693 *Amtlicher Katalog der . . . Ausstellung . . . zusammengestellt von Richard Kramer.* Zittau: [A. Graun], 1902. iv, 184 pp.

>   Cited from KaY*; not located.

ZÜRICH (Switzerland). MUSEUM BELLERIVE (J127, A430)

1694　*. . . Ausstellung Musikinstrumente, vom 10. Dezember 1916 bis zum 28. Januar 1917.* (Zürich. Kunstgewerbemuseum. Wegleitungen, 16.) [Zürich: 1916.] 48 pp., illus.

> "Alte Musikinstrumente," by Alicja Simon;
> "Der Instrumentenbau in der Schweiz," by
> Peter Fassbaender, pp. 33-37. The exhibit
> includes the historical collection of Hug & Co.
> which was given to the Museum in 1962.
> Copy at NN (NYp).

1695　Fehr, M. "Ausstellung von Musikinstrumenten in Züricher Kunstgewerbemuseum," *Schweizerische Musikzeitung und Sängerblatt* (1917), pp. 1-2.

1696　*Musikinstrumente. Juni - Festwochen 1962.* [Hrsg. von Alfred Altherr.] (The Museum's Wegleitungen, 247.) [Zürich: 1962.] 28 pp., chiefly illus.

> Copy at NN (NYp).

Literature

1697　Ruhoff, Martin. "'Alte Musikinstrumente'. Eine Ausstellung im Kunstgewerbe-Museum Zürich," *Schweizerische Musikzeitung* 102 (1962): 75.

1698　Hiestand-Schnellmann, Josef. "Die Sammlung alter Musikinstrumente in Kunstgewerbemuseum," *Glareana* 15, no. 3/4 (1966): 2-17.

1699　Hiestand-Schnellmann, Josef. "Die Ausstellung alter Musikinstrumente der Sammlung Hug in neugestalteten Vestibül der Tonhalle Zürich," *Glareana* 26, no. 3/4 (1977): 36-39.

ZÜRICH (Switzerland). SCHWEIZERISCHE LANDESAUSSTELLUNG, 1883

1700　Arnold, Gustav. *Musikalische Instrumente. Fachbericht über die Gruppe 33 der Schweizerischen Landesausstellung in Zürich, 1883.* Zürich: Orel, Füssli & Co., 1884. 48 pp.

> Cited from Nef*. Hirsch* says Luzern, 1883. Neither located.

Literature

1701　Kuhn-Kelly, J. "Gruppe musikalischer Instrumente auf der schweizerischen Landesausstellung," *ZfI* 3 (1882/83): 233-34.

1702　Laffert, Oscar. "Die schweizerische Landesausstellung," *ZfI* 3 (1882/83): 279-80, 282-84.

1703 R., D. "Verzeichnis der vom Preisgericht in Gruppe 33 entheilten Diplome auf der Landesausstellung," *ZfI* 3 (1882/83): 418-19.

1704 "Nachlese von . . . ," *ZfI* 4 (1883/84): 38, 40.

1705 "Die Musikinstrumente auf der Schweizerische Landesausstellung," *Signale für die musikalische Welt* 41, no. 50 (1883): 785-89.

1706 [Weber, Gustav.] "Gruppe 33 der Schweizerischen Landesausstellung. (Umfassend die Musikinstrumente)," *Schweizerische Musikzeitung* 23 (1883): 87-88.

General

1707 . . . *Bericht über die Verwaltung.* . . . Zürich: Füssli & Co., 1884. viii, 196, 146 pp., illus.

> Copy at DLC (Wc); not examined.

1708 Hardmeyer-Jenny, J. *Officieller Katalog der viertes . . . Catalogue officiel de la quatrième . . . Landesausstellungen.* 3. Aufl. Zürich: Füssli & Co., 1883. cxliii, 355 pp.

> "Gruppe 33: Musikalische Instrumente," pp. 269-72
> (nos. 4442-4500). [Foreword by Gustav Weber],
> pp. CXXII-CXXIV. Copy at DLC (Wc).

1709 Salvisberg, Paul. *Illustrirter Catalog der Kunstausstellung auf der schweizerischen Landesausstellung.* . . . Zürich: Füssli & Co., 1883. vi, 170 pp.

> Cited from KaY*; not examined.

ZÜRICH (Switzerland). SCHWEIZERISCHES LANDESMUSEUM (J127, BB109)

1710 Schumacher, Heinrich. *Bericht über die im Schweizerischen Landesmuseum befindlichen Musikinstrumente.* [Luzern: 1905.]

> A Ms., according to Heyer*.

1711 Geiser, Brigitte. "Die Zithern der Schweiz [Ausstellung. 21. Januar bis zum 6. April 1975]," *Glareana* 23 (1974): lvs. [42]-87.

> "Ausgestellten Zithern (32)," lvs. 78-86.

ZWICKAU (Germany). GEWERBE- UND INDUSTRIE-AUSSTELLUNG, 1906

Literature

1712 "Musikinstrumenten Industrie auf der . . . ," *ZfI* 26 (1905/6): 232, 1035 (exhibitors), 1128 (awards).

SECTION II

PRIVATE COLLECTIONS

*This section is divided into two parts, item nos. **1713-1787**, a series of auction and*
sale catalogues of collections whose owners cannot be identified.
These are set out in chronological order by date of sale.
*In the second part, beginning with item no. **1788**,*
the citations are arranged alphabetically by collector.
The phrase, "P&S Index*," used frequently throughout Section II refers to the following:
Alphabetical list of some of the principal sales of Literary Property Music
and Works of Art conducted by Messrs Puttick & Simpson,
191 Piccadilly, and 47 Leicester Square, 1846 to 1870.
This typescript, an index to owners of properties sold in P&S sale catalogues,
nos. 1-1208, was sent to the British Museum by J. H. Puttick in January of 1871.
Arranged alphabetically by the names of consignors, it includes
many whose names do not appear in the sale catalogues themselves.
When those names have been used as entries in this bibliography,
they are enclosed in square brackets.
Though the "index" is not without errors,
it is a colossal misfortune that we do not possess a similar index
for sales during the remaining hundred years of the firm's existence, 1870 to 1971.
It seems unlikely that we will ever have one.

PRIVATE COLLECTIONS
BY OWNER

Part I

Unnamed   12.17.1691

1713   *A Catalogue of Ancient and Modern Musick Books, Both Vocal and Instrumental
with Divers Treatises . . . and Several Musical Instruments . . . Will Be Sold at
Dewing's Coffee-House in Pope's-Head Alley . . . December the 17th, 1691.*
[London] : 1691. 16 pp.

> Title page misleading; no instruments. The stock of Henry
> Playford sold by his son John Playford. See Coral, Lenore.
> *Music in English Auction Sales, 1676-1750.* Dissertation,
> University of London, 1974. lvs. 53-55, 131-33.

Unnamed   8.9.1774

1714   van der Vinne, Vincent, auctioneer. *Catalogus van een fraaije party konstige en
plaisante schilderyen, door voorname meesters . . . Als meede fraaije speelinstrumenten, muzyk en rarietyten. Welke verkogt . . . den 9 augustus 1774. . . .*
Te Haerlem: 1774. 10 pp., 281 lots.

> Musical instruments, 16 lots, music scores, 70.
> Not examined; cited from Lugt*.

Unnamed   5.28.1789

1715   Greenwood, Mr. auctioneer. *A Catalogue of a Superb Assortment of Musical
Instruments, Consisting of Fine-Toned Harpsichords, Pianofortes, Organized
Ditto; Bass Viols, Cremona and Amati Violins. . . . A Variety of Other*

Unnamed   5.28.1789   *continued*

> *Instruments, Music and Books . . . Sold . . . the 28th of May, 1789. . . .*
> *To Be Viewed on Wednesday, and Catalogues Had. . . .* 6 pp., 62, 61 lots.
>> Instruments: last 61 lots. Copy at GB-Lcia.

"A Shopkeeper and Engraver in the City"   6.22-23.1791

1716   Greenwood, Mr., auctioneer. *A Catalogue of the Genuine Stock in Trade of . . . ,*
Gone into Another Line of Business: Consisting of Carnelians, Bloodstones,
Onyxes . . . &c. Show Glasses, Cabinets, a Variety of Musical Instruments in
Piano Fortes, Capital Violins, and a Superb Tenor by Amati, Drums, Harps &c.,
&c. . . . Sold . . . the 22d of June 1791, and Following Day. . . . To Be Viewed
on Monday, and Catalogues Had. (2d day's sale), 7 pp., 152 lots.
> Instruments: lots 81-118. Copy at GB-Lcia.

Unnamed   12.3-7.1792

1717   Roos, Gerbrand & Johannes Weege, firm. *Catalogus van een . . . schoone*
verzameling . . . boeken . . . nevens een groote en keurige verzameling Muziek
Werken en Instrumenten en fraaye Rariteiten . . . verkogt . . . 3 December 1792,
en volgende dagen, ten Huize van Johannes Weege . . . Te Amsterdam . . . 1792.
80, 66 pp., 4170 lots.
> "Catalogus van Muziek-Instrumenten, &c.," p. 1 in
> 2nd part (lots 1-18). Copy at NL-Apk (some n & p).

"An Amateur"   2.20.1795

1718   Christie, Mr., auctioneer. *A Catalogue of a Very Valuable Collection of Musical*
Instruments, Comprising a Capital Stainer Violin, an Amati Tenor, and Several
Amati, and Other Undoubted Cremona Violins, the Property of, and Collected
by an Amateur During a Long Residence in Italy . . . Sold . . . February the 20th,
1795. London: 1795. 4 pp., 20 lots.
> The 20 lots of instruments also include 5 Guarnerius items.

"A Gentleman"   5.9-11.1796

1719   Graham & Phillips, Messrs., firm. *A Catalogue of All the Genuine Elegant House-*
hold Furniture . . . Jewels. . . . Valuable Library of Select Books. . . . Musical
Instruments, an Undoubted Violin by Stainer, a Remarkably Fine-Toned Upright
Grand Piano Forte by Stodart, a Three-Barreled Hand Organ . . . Sold . . . May
the 9th, and Two Following Days. [London: 1796.] 24 pp., 115, 109, 96 lots.
> Instruments: "Second Day's Sale," p. 12, lots 1-10.
> Copy at GB-Lbl.

Unnamed   3.5-8.1803

1720   Gartman, H., W. Vermandel en Zoon, en J. W. Smit, firm. *Catalogus van een uitmuntende verzameling gekleurde en ongekleurde Tekeningen en Printen . . . Glasen . . . Laastelyk Muziek en muziek-instrumenten . . . verkocht . . . den 5, 7 en 8 Maart 1803, ten Huize van Bauer en van Leeuwen . . . Te Amsterdam . . . 1803.* 2, 48 pp., 1022 lots.

> Includes 63 musical instruments according to Lugt*; not examined. Copy at NL-Apk.

"A Gentleman"   12.5-6.1804

1721   King, Jr., Mr., auctioneer. *A Catalogue of a Small Library of Books, Musical Instruments and Music, of a Gentleman, Deceased. . . . The Music Comprises a Brilliant Toned Grand Piano Forte, by Broadwood, Cremona Violin, Ditto by Duke . . .* [etc.] *Sold . . . Dec, 5th, 1804, and Following Day. . . .* [London]: 1804. 14 pp., 244 lots.

> Includes 96 lots of music and musical instruments according to Lugt*; not examined. Copy at NL-Apk.

"An Amateur"   11.9-10.1810

1722   Christie, Mr., auctioneer. *Pictures, Fine Prints . . . Musical Instruments, &c. A Catalogue of a Valuable Collection of . . . Pictures* [etc.]. *Also . . . a Few Musical Instruments. A Capital and Fine-Toned Grand Piano Forte . . . the Property of . . . Sold November 9, 1810, and Following Day.* London: 1810. 11 pp.

> Instruments, p. 9 (lots 35-****50). Copy also at GB-Lva.

Unnamed   7.10-11.1823

1723   Musgrave, W. P., firm. *Vocal and Instrumental Music, Instruments, Treatises and Books. A Catalogue of an Extensive and Valuable Library of Vocal and Instrumental Music (To Be Disposed of under Peculiar Circumstances) . . . Likewise a Number of Excellent Violins, Particularly a Gualliani of the Finest Tone, Several Tenors, a Violoncello, Piano-Fortes* [etc.] *Sold July 10th, 1823, and Following Day. . . .* 16 pp., 258 lots.

> Instruments, lots 74-91. Copy at GB-Lbl; film copy at NBuU-M (BUu). Not a very interesting or well-described group:
>> Lot 77, "A Foreign ditto and ditto";
>> Lot 78, "A *fine* old ditto and ditto";
>> Lot 79, "A ditto ditto and ditto";
>> Lot 85, "A ditto and ditto, in a hair case."

Unnamed   5.1-2.1826

1724   Musgrave, W. P., firm. *A Catalogue of Vocal and Instrumental Music. . . .*
Square, Upright, Horizontal Grand Piano-Fortes, Pedal Harps, Violins, Tenors,
Violoncellos, Flutes and Flageolets, by the Most Esteemed Makers . . . Sold
. . . the 1st & 2nd of May, 1826. [London] : 1826. 21 pp., 259 lots.

> Instruments, lots 203-59. Copy at GB-Lbl;
> film copy at NBuU-M (BUu).

Unnamed   12.13.1826

1725   Musgrave, W. P., firm. *A Catalogue of a Choice Collection of Vocal & Instru-*
mental Music . . . Many Hundreds of Engraved Plates . . . a Large Consignment
of Roman Strings . . . Likewise, Violins, Tenors, Violoncellos, Flutes, Harps,
Piano Fortes . . . Sold . . . December 13th, 1826. [London] : 1826. 20 pp.,
290 lots.

> Instruments, lots 242-90; some purchased by Dragonetti.
> Copy at GB-Lbl; film copy at NBuU-M (BUu).

Unnamed   3.17.1827

1726   Musgrave, W. P., firm. *A Catalogue of a Very Extensive and Highly Valuable*
Collection of Vocal & Instrumental Music. . . . Also Piano Fortes, Harps,
Violins, Tenors, Violoncellos, Guitars, Flutes, Union Pipes . . . Sold . . . 17th
of March, 1827. . . . [London] : 1827. 31 pp., 426 lots.

> Instruments, lots 391-426. Copy at GB-Lbl;
> film copy at NBuU-M (BUu).

Unnamed   12.14.1827

1727   Musgrave, W. P., firm. *A Catalogue of a Choice Collection of Modern Vocal &*
Instrumental Music. . . . Three Cases of Roman Violin Strings, Together with
Violins, Violoncellos, Flutes, &c. . . . Sold . . . the 14th of December, 1827.
[London] : 1827. 10 pp., 134 lots.

> Instruments, lots 51-61, 125-34. Copy at GB-Lbl;
> film copy at NBuU-M (BUu).

Unnamed   1.29.1828

1728   Musgrave, W. P., firm. *A Catalogue of a Choice Collection of Modern Vocal & Instrumental Music, Comprising the Stock of a Bankrupt . . . Together with Violins, Violoncellos, Flutes, Guitars, Piano-Fortes, Double-Action Harp by Dizi, &c. . . . Sold . . . 29th of Jan., 1828, and 2 Following Days.* [London] : 1828.

     Instruments, lots 59-72. Copy at GB-Lbl.

Unnamed   3.18.1828

1729   Musgrave, W. P., firm. *A Catalogue. A Very Choice Collection of Ancient and Modern Vocal & Instrumental Music . . . Tenors, Flutes, Piano Fortes, &c. . . . Sold . . . 18th of March, 1828.* [London] : 1828. 12 pp., 131 lots.

     Instruments, lots 59-72. Copy at GB-Lbl;
     film copy at NBuU-M (BUu).

Unnamed   8.6.1829

1730   Musgrave, W. P., firm. *Music Books, Instruments, Paintings, Roman Strings, &c. A Catalogue of a Very Choice Collection of Modern Vocal & Instrumental Music, Violins, Flutes, Guitars, Harps, &c. A Double Set of Platt's Harmonic Glasses . . . Sold . . . 6th of August and Following Days. . . .* [London: n.d., prob. 1829.] 8 pp., 141 lots.

     Instruments, lots 70-80. Copy at GB-Lbl;
     film copy at NBuU-M (BUu).

Unnamed   4.26-27.1830

1731   Morise (C. P.); Bon (Peintre-Exp.). *Catalogue d'une collection unique d'une grande quantité de tableaux, peints sur verre . . . de plusiers mécaniques à musique, dont une très capitals; et de divers objets d'optique . . . vente 26-27 avril 1830 et jour suivant.* [Paris: 1830.] 23 pp., 196 lots.

     Mechanical instruments and their repertoire explained
     in "Avertissement." Copy at GB-Lbl.

Unnamed   11.22-24.1831

1732   Foster, Mr. Edward, auctioneer. *A Catalogue of All the Genuine Stock of Modern Furniture* [etc.] . . . . *Grand & Square Pianos by Broadwood. A Five-*

Unnamed   11.22-24.1831   *continued*

> *Barrel Organ . . . Sold 22d of November, 1831, and Two Following Days . . .*
> *by Direction of the Proprietor . . . Having Disposed of the Lease to Mr. Slater. . . .*
> [London] : 1831. 16 pp., 290 lots.
>
> > Instruments, lots 49, 51, 63-77, 80-84. Copy at GB-Lva.

"A Professional Gentleman Lately Deceased"   3.11.1835

1733   Mr. Watson, auctioneer. *A Catalogue of a Quantity of Vocal & Instrumental*
Music, by Modern Composers, a Fine Collection of Violins Tenors, &c., the
Property of . . . Sold by Auction . . . at the Mart . . . March the 11th, 1835.
8 pp., 171 lots.

> > Instruments, lots 95-131. Copy: compiler.

"Several Private Gentlemen"   6.24.1845

1734   Mr. Fletcher, auctioneer. *Catalogue of a Collection of Miscellaneous Music,*
Vocal and Instrumental . . . Also Numerous Musical Instruments (the Property
of Several Private Gentlemen) . . . Sold . . . June 24th, 1845. 8 pp., 184 lots.

> > Instruments, lots 119-84, not differentiated by owner.
> > Copy at GB-Ob (2591.d.3. [68]).

Unnamed   11.19.1847

1735   de Vries, J; A. Brondgeest; and C. F. Roos, firm. *Catalogus van allervoor-*
treffelijkste zuivere fijne Paarlen . . . eindelijk eenige muzijk-instrumenten en
muziekwerken . . . verkocht . . . den 19den November 1847. Amsterdam:
1847. 14 pp., 223 lots.

> > Instruments, p. 11 (16 lots). Copies at NL-DHrk and F-Pe.

"A Distinguished Professor" 12.17.1847. *See Part II under* **GAUNTLETT, HENRY JOHN**

Unnamed   11.12.1851

1736   Kelly, Mr., Musical Instrument Auctioneer. . . . *Will on Wednesday, Nov. 12th,*
1851 . . . Submit for Sale . . . Upwards of 40 New and Second-Hand Pianofortes

and Harps by the Most Celebrated Makers, Also Finger and Barrel Organs, Harmoniums [etc.] .

> Assembled from an advertisement in *Musical Times;* availability of a catalogue is noted, but catalogue not found.

Unnamed   2.11.1852

1737   Walker, Mr., Musical Instrument Auctioneer. . . . *Will, on Wednesday, February 11th* [1852] . . . *Submit for Sale . . . Upwards of 80 Pianofortes by the Most Celebrated Makers, Together with a Large Number of Other Instruments.* . . .

> Assembled from an advertisement in the *Musical Times;* availability of a catalogue is noted, but catalogue not found.

Unnamed   3.10.1852

1738   Kelly, Mr., Musical Instrument Auctioneer. . . . *Will, on Wednesday, March 10th* [1852] *Submit for Sale . . . Upwards of 70 Pianofortes, by the Most Celebrated Makers, Together with a Large Number of Other Musical Instruments.* . . .

> Assembled from an advertisement in the *Musical Times;* availability of catalogue is noted, but catalogue not found.

Unnamed   4.14.1852

1739   Kelly, Mr., Musical Instrument Auctioneer. . . . *Will on Wednesday, April 14th* [1852] . . . *Submit for Sale . . . Upwards of 60 Pianofortes . . . Together with a Large Number of Other Musical Instruments and the Genuine Stock of a Music Dealer Declining Business.* . . .

> Assembled from an advertisement in the *Musical Times;* availability of catalogue is noted, but catalogue not found.

"Late Distinguished Professor of the Violoncello [Markey?] "   1.29-30.1858

1740   Puttick & Simpson, firm. *Catalogue of the Very Important and Interesting Music Collections of a Distinguished Amateur, with Selections from Various Libraries. . . . Also Musical Instruments . . . Sold January 29st* [sic] *, and Following Day. . . .* [London] : 1858. 30 + 1 + [1] pp., 477 lots.

> Instruments (property of the late distinguished prof.), 391-477. Catalogue no. 526.

"Well-Known Amateur"   5.19-20.1862

1741   Puttick & Simpson, firm. *A Catalogue of a Large Collection of Valuable Music,
        Comprising Various Antiquarian Works . . . Also Numerous Musical Instruments
        . . . Valuable Violins, and Violoncellos from Several Private Collections . . . Sold
        . . . May 19th, and Following Day. . . .* London: 1862. 32 pp., 889 lots.

> Instruments, lots 734-889; "Property of a well-known
> amateur," lots 734-86; lot 780 is a Guarnerius, formerly
> Paganini's, before that Tartini's.

"A Distinguished Amateur"   4.8.1864.   *See Part II under* **ROWDEN, Rev. Dr.**

"A Distinguished Professor"   12.5-6.1865

1742   Puttick & Simpson, firm. *Catalogue of the Library of Music of the Society of
        British Musicians . . . Numerous Full Scores . . . Concerted Instrumental Works
        . . . Also Musical Instruments . . . Violins and Violoncellos, by Esteemed Cremona
        Makers . . . Sold December 5th, 1865, and Following Day.* 25 pp., 653 lots.

> Instruments, lots 570-653; "Property of a Distinguished
> Professor," 587-653 (and very fine). Catalogue no. 888.

Unnamed   4.18-19.1871

1743   Bom, G. Theod., firm. *Catalogus eener uitmuntende collectie . . . Zilverwerke,
        kunstwerken in ivoor . . . porcelein* [etc.] *. . . Instrumenten, uitmuntende violen,
        enz. enz. Verkooping . . . 19 April 1871 in Diligentia. . . .* Amsterdam: 1871.
        23 pp., 579 lots.

> Instruments, lots 553-71 (including a Strad, a Stainer,
> an Amati, etc.). Copies at NL-DHrk, NL-Apk, NL-Rbm.

Unnamed   1877

1744   Weishaupt, O. & Co., firm. *Instruments de musique anciens . . . en vente chez. . . .*
        Paris: 1877. 16 pp., 102 lots.

> Copy at NL-DHgm.

Unnamed 3.20.1878

1745 Puttick & Simpson, firm. *Catalogue of a Vast Assemblage of Musical Instruments ... Including 16 Pianofortes ... Violins, Tenors, and Violoncellos* [etc.] *... Sold ... March 20th, 1878.* 16 pp., 321 lots.

> Instruments, lots 1-239. Catalogue no. 1732.

"An Amateur" 5.24-25.1881

1746 Puttick & Simpson, firm. *Catalogue of a Very Extensive and Valuable Assemblage of Musical Instruments ... Pianofortes ... Organs & Harmoniums ... a Numerous Collection of Rare Cremona Violins, Tenors, and Violas, Chiefly the Property of an Amateur, and Procured from the Gillot, Goding, and Other Collections ... a Few Copyright Music Plates, the Property of the Late Richard Limpus ... Sold May 24th, 1881 and Following Day.* 14 pp., 392 lots.

> Instruments, lots 71-383; "Amateur's," 204-30.
> Catalogue no. 2023.

Unnamed 4.30-5.1.1883

1747 Escribe (C. P.). *Notice de beaux meubles modernes. ... Harpe, violons et pianos. ... Bronzes ... beaux rideaux ... 450 bouteilles de vins ... dont la vente ... 30 avril 1883.* Paris: 1883. 4 pp.

> Copy at P-Fe. Lugt* notes that lots are unnumbered;
> not examined.

Unnamed 2.19.1884

1748 Puttick & Simpson, firm. *Catalogue of a Valuable Assemblage of Musical Property, Including Full-Compass Pianofortes, Costly Grands by Broadwood, Kirkman, Erard. ... Harmoniums ... a Collection of Violins, Violas, and Violoncellos ... Double Basses. ... Also a Quantity of Music, Library of the Enfield Musical Society. ... Several Sets of Music Plates, with Copyrights & Stock of Same ... Sold February 19th, 1884.* 9 pp., 223 lots.

> Catalogue no. 2238.

Unnamed   6.4.1885

1749   Gand et Bernardel, frères. *Catalogue des objets de vitrine, boîtes, tabatières, curiosités diverses. . . . Instruments de musique, anciens et modernes, violons, altos, violoncelles, guitare, archets, par* [Guarnerius, Guadagnini, etc.]. *Partitions de musique . . . vente aura lieu Hôtel Drouot . . . 4 juin 1885. . . .* [Paris: 1885.] 19 pp., 155 lots.

        Instruments, 56 lots according to Lugt*; not examined.
        Copies at F-Paa and F-Pn.

Unnamed   3.5.1886

1750   Janssens, A. (Exp.). *Liquidation pour cause de départ. Vendredi 5 mars 1886 . . . vente publique de la collection d'instruments de musique anciens. Arsène Janssens, expert en la Salle Saint-Gudule.* [Bruxelles: Moens et fils], 1886. 16 pp., 154 lots.

        Copy at US-Rs. Sale is noted in *ZfI* 6 (1885/86): 203.

Unnamed   8.17.1887

1751   Puttick & Simpson, firm. *Catalogue of a Collection of Musical Instruments, Including Pianofortes, American Organs and Harmoniums, Italian and Other Violins, Tenors, Violoncellos and Double Basses. . . . Also the Library of Music, Chiefly for the Violoncello Belonging to the Late Alfred Kew. . . . Autograph Ms. of Ludwig van Beethoven, etc. . . . Sold August the 17th, 1887.* 9 pp., 207 lots.

        Instruments, lots 1-153. (Kew's library, lots 157-207;
        Mss., 191-207). Catalogue no. 2518.

"Een zeer geacht Pastoor"   3.26-27.1890

1752   Bom, H. G., firm. *Catalogus eener belangrijke Roomsch Katholieke bibliotheek, nagelaten door . . . eene kostbare verzameling plaatwerken . . . muziek en muziek-instrumenten . . . verkooping . . . 26 maart, en volgenden dag. . . .* Amsterdam: H. G. Bom, 1890. 39 pp., 744 lots.

        Instruments, lots 445-81. Copy at NL-Avb.

Unnamed

4.21.1890

1753　Mayer, J.-F & M. S. (Exp.); Duchesne (C. P.). *Catalogue de meubles anciens et modernes. Bronzes, porcelaines* [etc.]. *Instruments de musique. Violons anciens et modernes, violoncelle, piano droit, etc. . . . vente . . . 21 avril 1890. . . .* Paris: 1890. 8 pp., 92 lots.

> Instruments, 37 lots according to Lugt*; not examined.
> Copy at F-Paa.

"Un Amateur connu"

11.3.1890

1754　Muller, Frederik, & Cie. *Collection importante d'instruments à cordes, réunie par un amateur connu, mise aux enchères publiques à cause de départ. Réunie à deux pétites collections provenant de successions.* Amsterdam: [1890]. 16 pp., 120 lots.

> Instruments, lots 1-59 (a fine group). Copy at NL-Avb.

"A Lady"

12.6.1893

1755　Puttick & Simpson, firm. *Catalogue of a Valuable Collection of Ancient Musical Instruments, the Property of a Lady . . . Sold December the 6th, 1893, at Three o'Clock.* 8 pp., 71 lots.

> Catalogue no. 2972. The sale of the important musical
> instrument collections of Woolhouse and Cusins took
> place the same day (Catalogue no. 2971). See Part II
> under **WOOLHOUSE**. Second portion, see following item.

"A Lady"

3.21.1894

1756　Puttick & Simpson, firm. *Catalogue of the Remaining Portion of the Collection of Ancient Musical Instruments, the Property of a Lady . . . Sold March the 21st, 1894.* 11 pp., 113 lots.

> Catalogue no. 2989. See above, no. **1755**.

"A Gentleman"

3.24.1896

1757　Puttick & Simpson, firm. *Catalogue of Musical Instruments . . . Plus a Valuable and Scarce Collection of Antique Instruments, the Property of a Gentleman . . . Sold . . . March 24, 1896.* 14 pp., 349 lots.

> "Collection of antique instruments," lots 200-209.
> Catalogue no. 3138.

Unnamed   12.2.1896

1758   Puttick & Simpson, firm. *Catalogue of the Valuable Collection of Violins, Violas, Violoncellos, etc., Together with Interesting Specimens of the Spinet, Harpsichord, Clavichord, etc. from Various Private Sources . . . Sold . . . December the 2nd, 1896.* 15 pp., 91 lots.

> Catalogue no. 3191; copy also at US-Rs.

Literature:

1759   M., T. de [Trinita Dei Monti?]. "Messrs. Puttick and Simpson's Special Sale," *Violin Times* 4 (1896/97): 42-43.

1760   "Geigen-Auktion in London," *ZfI* 17 (1896/97): 273.

Unnamed   4.7.1899

1761   Christie, Manson & Woods, Messrs. *Catalogue of a Collection of Porcelain and Decorative Objects of. . . . Furniture, the Property of a Gentleman* [i.e., Sir Henry Bessemer] *. . . . Old Musical Instruments . . . Sold . . . April 7, 1899. . . .* London: 1899. 14 pp., 148 lots.

> Instruments, lots 50-74A, including antiques:
> pochette, piandura, lute, viol, vielles, manola, etc.
> Copy at GB-Lva.

Unnamed   1900

1762   Gläsel-Wiener, Moritz, firm. *Musikinstrumenten* [Katalog]. Markneukirchen: 1900. 126 pp., illus.

> Auction catalogue or manufacturer's? Cited from
> *ZiMG* 1 (1899/1900): 327; not examined.

Unnamed   12.19.1900

1763   Puttick & Simpson, firm. *Catalogue of Valuable Collection of Violins, Violas* [etc.] *. . . from Various Private Sources . . . Sold December 19th, 1900.* 16 pp., 138 lots.

> Catalogue no. 3496.

Literature

1764   "Streichinstrumenten-Versteigerung in London," *ZfI* 21 (1900/1901): 335.

"A Distinguished Professor"

12.19.1902

1765 Puttick & Simpson, firm. *Catalogue of a Valuable Collection of Violins, Violas, Violoncellos, Bows, Cases, etc., Including a Very Fine Example of Antonius Stradiuarius, the Property of a Distinguished Professor . . . Sold December 19th, 1902.* 13 pp., 105 lots.

> Catalogue no. 3686; copy also at US-Rs.

"A Lady"

·12.24-25.1903

1766 Puttick & Simpson, firm. *Catalogue of Valuable Musical Properties . . . Including Valuable Old Violins (Property of a Lady) . . . and the Extensive Library of Music Formed by the Late Sir George Armytage . . . Sold February 24th, 1903, and Following Day.* 27 pp., 590 lots.

> Instruments, lots 1-460D; Armytage's library, 462-590.
> Catalogue no. 3704.

Unnamed

12.16.1903

1767 Puttick & Simpson, firm. *Catalogue of a Valuable Collection of Violins, Violas, and Violoncellos . . . Sold . . . December 16th, 1903.* 12 pp., 96 lots.

> Catalogue no. 3784; copy also at US-Rs.

Literature

1768 "Geigen-Auktion in London . . . alter Geigen," *ZfI* 24 (1903/4): 299.

> Includes prices fetched and brief identifications.

"A Well-Known Collector" 5.20.1904. *See Part II under* **UHTOFF, L. E.**

Unnamed

12.5.1905

1769 Glendining, Messrs. [Catalogue of an auction sale of stringed instruments.] London: 1905. 12 pp., 145 lots.

> Before lot 1: "A violinist will be in attendance
> to try instruments for clients." Information from
> Mr. Robert Lewin; not examined.

Unnamed

11.22.1905

1770 Puttick & Simpson, firm. *Catalogue of a Valuable Collection of Violins, Violas, and Violoncellos, with the Bows and Cases . . . Sold November 22nd, 1905.* 15 pp., 105 lots.

Catalogue no. 3968.

Unnamed

12.10.1906

Literature

1771 Polonaski, E. [A note about Puttick & Simpson's sale of instruments, December 10th, 1906], *Violin Times* 14 (1907): 11.

P & S sale catalogue for 12/10/1906 not found; sale catalogues for December 12 and December 18, 1906 (nos. 4071 and 4072) both contained unremarkable collections of instruments.

Unnamed

2.25.1907

Literature

1772 Glendining, Messrs. [Remarks about a sale of interesting instruments, February 25, 1907], *Violin Times* 14 (1907): 54.

The catalogue not found.

Unnamed

6.19.1907

1773 Puttick & Simpson, firm. *Catalogue of a Valuable Collection of Violins, Violas, Violoncellos & Bows, Including the Violin . . . Known as "Le Mercure," the Property of Sir William B. Avery . . . Sold June 19th, 1907.* 19 pp., 122 lots.

Catalogue no. 4125.

Literature

1774 "Violins under the Hammer," *Violin Times* 14 (1907): 125-26, 141-42.

A very detailed listing, tantamount to a catalogue.

"A Well-Known Amateur, Deceased"

12.8.1909

1775 Puttick & Simpson, firm. *Catalogue of a Valuable Collection of Violins, Violas, and Violoncellos, with the Bows and Cases, Including . . . a Large Collection, the Property of. . . . Antique Instruments . . . Sold December 8th, 1909.* 20 pp., 155 lots.

Antique instruments, lots 142-55; Amateur's, 63-88.

Catalogue no. 4368.

Literature

1776   "Über die letzte Geigen-Auktion in London," *ZfI* 30 (1909/10): 416.

Repeats and comments upon opinions about the prices
in an article in *Le Menestrel.*

Unnamed   12.14.1910

1777   Puttick & Simpson, firm. *Catalogue of a Valuable Collection of Violins, Violas,
and Violoncellos, with the Bows and Cases* . . . [also antique instruments] . . .
Sold December 14th, 1910. 19 pp., 137 lots.

Catalogue no. 4484.

Literature

1778   "Geigen-Auktion in London," *ZfI* 31 (1910/11): 361, 390, 395.

Notes a large collection of old masterpieces from various
collections, some of them described in the article.

"A Gentleman"   2.28.1911

1779   Puttick & Simpson, firm. *Catalogue of Musical Instruments . . . Pianofortes . . .
Fine Old Italian Violins, Violas* [etc.], *Including a Collection, Property of a
Gentleman . . . Sold February 28th, 1911.* 13 pp., 271 lots.

Gentleman's instruments, lots 51-89. Catalogue no. 4508.

Literature

1780   "Geigenauktion in London," *ZfI* 31 (1910/11): 500.

Probably refers to the sale of February 28th. Very brief.

Unnamed   2.28.1911

Literature

1781   "Auktion alter Streichinstruments in Wien," *ZfI* 31 (1910/11): 557.

Refers to an auction by August Bittner, firm, February 28, 1911.

Unnamed   6.16.1911

1782   Puttick & Simpson, firm. *Catalogue of a Valuable Collection of Violins, Violas,
Violoncellos, with the Bows and Cases, Including a* [Strad, etc., properties of
various owners] . . . *Sold June 16th, 1911.* 19 pp., 131 lots, pls.

An excellent group of instruments. Catalogue no. 4549.

Unnamed 6.16.1911   *continued*

Literature

1783   "Streichinstrumenten-Auktion in London," *ZfI* 31 (1910/11): 1041-42.

A number of the group described; some prices noted.

Unnamed   11.11.1911

1784   Henkels, Stan V. (at the Auction Rooms of S. T. Freeman). *An Extraordinary Collection of Fine Old Cremona Violins. . . .* Philadelphia: Henkels, 1911. 3 pp.

Lots 271-286; a supplement to Henkels' catalogue
no. 1043. The properties in no. 1043 were mostly
those of Dr. Charles A. Oliver. Day of sale,
November 11, 1911. Copies at US-NYp, US-Aau.

Unnamed   12.4.1911

Literature

1785   "Versteigerung alter Streichinstrumente in Wien," *ZfI* 32 (1911/32): 247, 249, 363.

Refers to an auction by August Bittner, firm, in Maria
Theresien-Saale des "Dorotheums," Dec. 4, 1911;
Expert, Th. Jaura. Fifty-six items are described in the
article, and an auction catalogue is noted; not found.

Unnamed   11.13.1913

Literature

1786   "Auktion alter Saiteninstrumenten [by H. Lempertz, firm, Cologne, on Nov. 13, 1913]," *ZfI* 34 (1913/14): 179.

Lots no. 314-24 are noted especially for their quality.
The sale catalogue not located.

Unnamed   1916

1787   Casa Liquidora [firm?], Lisbon. *Leilão de antiquidades, objectos d'arte e objectos raros e de uma importante collecão de instrumentos musicaes antigos.* Lisbon: 1916.

Cited from Lambertini*; not located.

Part II

ABEL, KARL FRIEDRICH, composer, 1723-1787

1788   Greenwood, Mr., auctioneer. *A Catalogue of the Capital Collection of Manuscript and Other Music, an Exceeding Valuable and Fine-Toned Viol de Gamba, a Forte-Piano by Buntebart, a Violin, &c. . . . of Charles Frederick Abel . . . Musician to Her Majesty . . . Sold . . . 12th of December, 1787.* 8 pp., 92+101 lots.

> Instruments, lots 39-49* (Stainer, Granerius [sic],
> Schudi, etc.). Music Mss., lots 22-38, mostly Abel's.
> Photographic negative at US-NYfrick.

ADAMS, JOHN, of Blockheath

1789   Puttick & Simpson, firm. *Catalogue of a Very Fine Collection of Violins, Violas, and Violoncellos, Including the Collection Formed by the Late . . . Also Spanish Guitars . . . Sold . . . June 17th, 1908.* 18 pp., 116 lots; Adams', lots 52-70.

> Catalogue no. 4224; a "special" sale.

ADAMSON, Mr., music seller. *See under* CERUTTI, SIGNOR

ADOLPHUS FREDERICK, Duke of Cambridge, 1774-1858

1790   Puttick & Simpson, firm. *Catalogue of the Musical Collections of . . . the Duke of Cambridge, Including . . . Also Two Violins by Stradivarius, a Tenor by Amati . . . to Which Is Added, Another Musical Library and Numerous Valuable Musical Instruments . . . Sold . . . November 28, 1850.* 22 pp., 564 lots.

> Instruments, lots 489-564 (various properties,
> undifferentiated). Catalogue no. 185.

ALFONSO II, d'ESTE, 1533-1597

1791   "Inventario delli instrumenti [1598]." In Straeten, Edmond van der. *La musique aux Pays-Bas,* vol. 6, pp. 122-23. Bruxelles: Muquardt [etc.], 1867-88. Reprint ed. New York: Dover, 1969.

1792   "Inventario delli instrumenti [1598]." In Valdrighi, L. F. *Musurgiana,* no. 1, pp. 26-30. Modena: Soc. Tipogr. Soliani, 1879.

> Collection now in Ferrara, according to *MGG**.

ALLWOOD, F. W.; G. HERBERT; GEORGE JACOBI

1793　Puttick & Simpson, firm. *Catalogue of Valuable Musical Properties Including Pianofortes . . . Harmoniums . . . Violins, Violas* [etc.] , *Including Many Desirable Instruments, the Property of the Late F. W. Allwood . . . the Large Library of Music of the Late G. Herbert . . . the Instrumental Works of the Late George Jacobi . . . Sold . . . October 29th, 1907.* 19 pp., 383 lots.

Allwood's instruments, lots 178-91; Herbert's library, lots 244-98; Jacobi's works, lots 331-80. Catalogue no. 4154.

ALSAGER, THOMAS M.　*See under* BOSCAWEN, GEORGE HENRY

AMERMAN, J. L.

1794　*Catalogue of Musical Instruments.* [n.p., n.d.] [46] pp. of illus.

A Ms. catalogue at NNMM (US-NYmm).

AMERSFOORDT, JACOB PAULUS, 1817-1895

1795　Bom, G. Theod. & Zoon, firm. *Notitie van Teekeningen, Historie- en Topographische Prenten . . . Fraaie en kostbare oude Violens, violoncels en andere muziekinstrumenten, eenige muziek, enz., nagelaten door. . . . Publiek verkooping . . . 23 Maart 1886 en volgende dagen. . . .* Amsterdam: 1886. 46 pp., 929+A-S lots.

Instruments, p. 46, lots A-S. Copies at NL-Ak, NL-Apk, NL-Arb.

AMES, GEORGE ACLAND; RICHARD BENNETT, of Lever Hall, Lancashire

1796　Puttick & Simpson, firm. *Catalogue of the Valuable Collection of Violins, Violas, Violoncellos, etc., of the Late George Acland Ames . . . Richard Bennett . . . and Others . . . Sold April the 19th, 1893.* 12 pp., 54 lots.

Ames', lots 1-12 (fine); Bennett's, lots 45-54. Catalogue no. 2931. Priced copy also at NRU (Rs).

ANDERSON, G. F.; *and* "A GENTLEMAN"

1797   Puttick & Simpson, firm. *Catalogue of a Valuable Library of Music, the Property of a Gentleman . . . Also Musical Instruments . . . Sold . . . February 27, 1878.* 12 pp., 298 lots.

> Instruments, lots 229-98; Anderson's, 252-58, including four Amati's. Catalogue no. 1728.

ANDREOLI, CARLO, of Milan

1798   Puttick & Simpson, firm. *Catalogue of a Valuable Collection of Violins, Violas, Violoncellos and Double Basses, Including the Collection Formed by the Late Signor . . . Sold . . . December 18th* [-19th] *1912.* 19 pp., 146 lots.

> Andreoli's, lots 1-87 (first day's sale). Catalogue no. 4700.

APFELBAUM, FREDERICK; ARNOLD GINGRICH; PIERRE F. GOODRICH

1799   Sotheby Parke Bernet, firm. *Important Musical Instruments, the Property of Various Owners, Including Frederick Apfelbaum* [et al] . *Auction, Friday, October 29, 1976.* New York: 1976. 157 lots, lavishly illus.

> Sale no. 3914. A few lots each.

APLIN, A. E. *See under* MAC DONAGH, JAMES

APPLEBY, SAMUEL. *See under* DOUGLAS, ROBERT COOPER

ARMINGAUD (prob. JULES A., 1820-1900)

1800   Silvestre, Lasquin (Exp.); Chevallier (C. P.). *Collection de M. Armingaud. Instruments de musique . . . tableaux, dessins, aquarelles. . . . Vente . . . 25 avril 1900. Hotel Drouot. . . .* Paris: 1900. 8 pp., 98 lots.

> Instruments, 30 lots, according to Lugt*. Copy at F-Pn.

ARRIGONI, LUIGI

1801   Gandouin (Exp.); Quevremont (C. P.). *Collection de M. Luigi Arr*** de Milan. Instruments de musique anciens rares et curieux des XVe, XVIe et XVIIIe siècles. Ayant figure à l'Exposition nationale italienne (1881) dont la vente aura lieu Hôtel Drouot le 19 Dec. 1881.* Paris: 1881. 16 pp., 179 lots, (Instruments, 172).

   Copy at F-Pn (with prices fetched).

1802   Arrigoni, Luigi. *Organografia, ossia Descrizione degli istrumenti musicali antichi. Autografia e bibliografia musicale della collezione Arrigoni Luigi, bibliofilo antiquario in Milano.* Milano: [Stab. tip. F. Pagnoni], 1881. 3, 118 pp.

   Instruments, pp. 95-118, 172 items. ALS, pp. 1-56.
   Copy at DLC (Wc).

ASHFIELD, FREDERICK; A GENTLEMAN

1803   *A Catalogue of a Small but Very Curious Library of the Books and M.S.S. of Frederick Ashfield, Esq.; Who Lately Deceased in His Return from Italy; A Gentleman Eminently Distinguished for His Elegant Taste in Alchymy, Philosophy . . . and Musick. . . . With Several Compleat Setts of Concerto's, Solo's, and Sonata's by the Most Celebrated Italian Masters and Others, Together with a Fine Harpsichord by Couchet, Violins by Stratuarius, and Stainer . . . Sold . . . the 24th of This Instant March. . . . Next Door to the Golden Ball, Near St. James-House, Pall-Mall. . . .* [London: 1792.]

   Copy at GB-Lbl.

ASTOR, Lord, of Hever; Mrs. NORA DANDO; Miss CICELEY M. MAUNSELL; M. E. MEDLICOTT; et al

1804   Christie, Manson & Woods, Ltd. *Catalogue of Fine Miniatures and Musical Instruments, the Property of . . . Sold . . . November 12, 1963.* 32 pp., 150 lots, pls.

   Instruments, lots 1-31 (Gaglianos, Amati, Dodd bow, etc.).
   Astor's, lots 1-13 (4 theorbos, citterns, lutes, etc.).

AUSTIN, JOSEPH W.; A DISTINGUISHED PROFESSOR; AN AMATEUR, DECEASED

1805   Puttick & Simpson, firm. *Catalogue of Numerous and Valuable Musical Instruments, Including Twenty Pianofortes, by Broadwood . . . Violins and Violoncellos . . . Philosophical Apparatus . . . Sold . . . December 24, 1859.* 11 pp., 203 lots.

Instruments, lots 56-203; Amateur's, 107-13;
Professor's, 121-25; Austin's, 136-203. Residue
sold February 4-5, 1861; see under **SPINNEY, ROBERT.**
Copy also at HH.

BACHKE, VICTORIA *and* **CHRISTIAN**   [N. B.: Their collection the basis of that now in
TRONDHEIM, RINGVE MUSEUM, q.v., in Section I.]

BACON, JOHN

1806   White, Mr., auctioneer. *A Catalogue of the Collection of Music Books and
Instruments Which Will Be Sold by Auction by Mr. White . . . Westminster,
on Wednesday, June 26th, 1816.* [Westminster, 1816.] 8 pp., 157 lots.
Copy at DLC (Wc).

BALFOUR, Messrs. & Co.

1807   Puttick & Simpson, firm. *Catalogue of a Large Collection of Musical Instruments
. . . A Large and Valuable Collection of Violins, Including the Property of. . . .
A Very Fine Example of Antonio Stradivari . . . and Music . . . Sold . . . October
25th, 1902.* 18 pp., 405 lots.
Instruments, lots 1-364; Balfour's, lots 109-64.
Catalogue no. 3666.

BALFOUR, HENRY. *See Section I under* **OXFORD (U. K.). UNIVERSITY. PITT
RIVERS MUSEUM**

BAKER, THOMAS. *See under* **DUCHESNE, R.**

BANNISTER, J. COUSINS

1808   Puttick & Simpson, firm. *Catalogue of Valuable Musical Properties . . . Organs
. . . Harps, Violins, Violas, Violoncellos and Double Basses Belonging to the Late
. . . , and Others . . . Sold December 22nd, 1903.* 12 pp.
Instruments, lots 1-237; not differentiated.
Catalogue no. 3784.

BARDOUT, GASTON *and* **RENÉE.** *See Section I under* **NEUCHÂTEL (Switzerland).
MUSÉE D'ETHNOGRAPHIE**

[BARKER, G.]

1809 Christie, Manson & Woods, firm. *Catalogue of a Collection of Oriental, Dresden, Sevres & Chelsea Porcelain . . . the Property of a Gentleman Leaving His Residence. Also, of Twelve Capital Pianofortes by Middleton & Co. . . . Sold February 8, 1861.* 13 pp., 206 lots.

> "Capital pianofortes," lots 177-92; "Pianofortes by Broadwood, Erard [etc.]," lots 193-206.

BARNAART, JACOBUS

1810 [Lugt* notes a sale in Harlem, by Augustini, Dec. 7, 1763 containing 2017 lots of which 107 were musical instruments. The only location given by Lugt*, the Kupferstichkabinett in Dresden reports that the catalogue was destroyed in WWII.]

BARROW, WILLIAM

1811 "Instruments of the Masters," *The Listener* (January 12, 1939), pp. 100-101.

> In Llandudno, N. W. Most of the Barrow collection is listed.

BARRY, SMITH

1812 Christie, Mr., auctioneer. *A Catalogue of the . . . Library of (Chiefly M.S.) Music of the Late Hon. S. Barry, Dec., Also a Few Musical Instruments . . . Sold . . . June, 1803.* 11 pp.

> Copy also at NN (NYp).

BATE, PHILIP. *See Section I under* OXFORD (U. K.). UNIVERSITY. FACULTY OF MUSIC. BATE COLLECTION

BATES, EDWARD

1813 Puttick & Simpson, firm. *Catalogue of the . . . Musical Library of the Late Edward Bates, Esq., Comprising Many Works Formerly in the Possession of Joah Bates . . . Together With . . . Musical Instruments . . . To Be Sold . . . December 20th, 1867.* 20 pp., 481 lots.

> Instruments, lots 372-487. Catalogue no. 1023.
> In P & S Index* the collectors named are W. Bates and Joan [*sic*] Bates.

BATES, F. W., et al

1814 Puttick & Simpson, firm. *Catalogue of a Large Assemblage of Ancient and Modern Music . . . Including a Further Selection from the Library of. . . . Numerous Musical Instruments, Pianofortes, Organs . . . Violins and Violoncellos, Including the Collections of General Oliver and the Late F. W. Bates . . . Sold . . . June 28th and 29th, 1872.* 32 pp., 717 lots.

> Instruments, lots 572-717; Oliver's, lots 605-30; Bates', lots 631-717. Catalogue no. 1326.

1815 Puttick & Simpson, firm. *Catalogue of a Collection of Music, Including the Libraries of F. W. Bates, Esq., and R. Underwood, Esq. . . . Also Musical Instruments . . . Sold . . . July 25, 1872, and the Following Day.* 20 pp., 539 lots.

> Instruments, lots 434-539.

BATTISCOMBE, JAMES F.

1816 Puttick & Simpson, firm. *Catalogue of Grand and Cottage Pianofortes by Well-Known Makers . . . Including the Instruments of the Late . . . Sold . . . August 16th, 1904.* 10 pp.

> Catalogue no. 3855. Copy also at NN (NYp).

BAX, Mrs. BARBARA. *See under* WHITE, ERIC W.

BEADELL, WILLIAM. *See under* HICKSON, THOMAS *and* DOUGLAS, ROBERT COOPER

BEDOT-DIODATI, MAURICE [N.B.: According to Jenkins* 48 instruments from his collection went to STOCKHOLM. MUSIKHISTORISKA MUSEET in 1927. No sale catalogue found. See catalogues after 1927 under STOCKHOLM (Sweden), Section I.]

BEKE, LEENDERT van

1817 *Catalogus van zeer fraije ende rare Nederduitse boecken, als meede van uytnemende Partyen-Muzycq, Muzycq-Instrumenten, Prent-Konst . . . Nagelaten by Leendert van Beke, in zyn Castelein in 't Gemeen-Landshuys, van Delfland. Welke verkogt zullen werden . . . 20 February 1708. . . .* Deflt: Gedruckt by Adries Voorstad, 1708.

> "Catalogus van de Muzycq-Instrumente," pp. 14-15 (17 lots). Copy at NL-Apk (n & p).

BELLAMY, THOMAS LUDFORD. *See under* BINFIELD, of Reading

BENAVENTE, S. B.

1818   Bom, G. Theod. & Zoon. *Notitie eener uitgebreide en belangrijke verzameling Muziek voor Piano, Viool, Violoncel . . . Violen, Fluiten, Cithers en Blaas-instrumenten . . . Verkooping . . . van den Notaris L. H. J. Mirani . . . 23 tot . . . 25 Mei 1905.* Amsterdam: 1905. 31 pp., 875 lots.

Instruments, lots 782-875. Copy at NL-Arb (n & p).

BENNETT, JOHN HUDSON

1819   American Art Association - Anderson Galleries. *Seven Rare and Valuable Stringed Instruments, Including Two Stradivarius Violins and Two by Guarnerius del Gesu. The Collection of . . . Sold . . . February 5th. . . .* New York: 1932. 14 pp., 13 lots.

Sale no. 3949. Copies at NN (NYp), DLC (Wc).

BENNETT, RICHARD, of Lever Hall, Lancashire. *See under* AMES, JAMES ACKLAND

BENSON, J. W., of Bedfor

1820   Puttick & Simpson, firm. *Catalogue of Old Italian & Other Violins* [etc.], *Including the Stock of the Late . . . Sold . . . July 24th, 1924.* 12 pp., 304 lots.

Benson's stock, lots 151-220 (old instruments, not new).

BERENS, HENRY HULSE. *See under* TOMKIES, JAMES

BERLIN, JOHANN DANIEL, 1711-1787

1821   *Fortegnelse over adskillige Mathematiske og Musikalske Instrumenter, samt Bøger i adskillige Videnskaber, som først i tillkommende Aar 1788 blive ved Auction bortsolgte i afg. Overbrandmester Berlins Huus ker i Byen.* Trondheim: 1787. 30 pp.

Instruments, pp. 8-10 (50 lots). Copy at Oslo Universitets-biblioteket, with n & p.

BERNARD, JEAN

1822   De Vries, Jeronimo; Albertus Brondgeest; Engelberts & Roos. *Catalogus van eene verzameling fraaije schilderijen . . . teekeningen nagelaten door . . . benevens eene uitmuntende verzameling van voortreffelijke muzijk-instrumenten en muzijk-werken, (volgens afzonderlijke Catalogus) verkocht . . . 24 November 1834, en volgenden dagen. . . .* Amsterdam: 1834. 78 pp., 1732 + 43 lots.

> At end: "Catalogus van uitmuntende muzijk-instrumenten en muzijk-werken . . . 26sten November, 1834 . . . ,"
> pp. [75-78]. Instruments, p. 75 (17 lots). Copy at NL-Apk.

BERNOUILLI, WILHELM   (J125)

1823   Hiestand-Schnellmann, Joseph. "Die Bernouillische Blasinstrumentsammlung im Schloss Greifensee," *Glareana,* vol. 1, no. 6 (1952). 237 items.

1824   Bernouilli, Wilhelm. "Meine Sammlung historischer Blechblasinstrumente und Trommeln," *Brass Bulletin* 5/6 (1973): 85-92. 20 pls.

> Text in German, French and English.

Literature

1825   Nef, Walter. "Eine eigenartige Sammlung von Musikinstrumenten," *Basler Nachrichten,* no. 503 (November 26, 1964).

> Jenkins* cites; not verified.

BERRYMAN, DOUGLAS R.   *See Section I under* CORNWALL (U. K.). MUSEUM OF MECHANICAL MUSIC

BEUDEKER, C.

1826   Roos, de Vries & Engelbert, firm. *Catalogus van eene fraaije verzameling schilderijen . . . teekeningen . . . prenten* [etc.] *en muzijk-instrumenten volgens afzonderlijke notitien . . . verkocht . . . 30sten Mei 1855. . . .* Amsterdam: 1855. 44, 7, 3 pp., 507 + 108 + 43 lots.

> Instruments, last 3 pp., 30 lots. Copies at F-Pe, NL-Apk, NN (NYp).

BEVILACQUA, Count MARIA, d. 1593

1827   "L'inventario . . . Die 6 Augusti 1593." Reprinted in Bevilacqua, amico della musica," by Enrico Paganuzzi in Franzoni, Lanfranco. *Per una storia dell collezionismo: Verona: La galleria Bevilacqua*, pp. 145-46. (Saggi di cultura contemporanea, 90.) Verona/Milano: Edizioni di Comunita, [1970].

   Copy at MH (CAc).

1828   Castellani, Marcello. "A 1593 Veronese Inventory," *GSJ* 26 (1973): 15-24. 78 items.

BEVOIS MOUNT, Southampton

1829   Perkins & Sons, firm. *A Catalogue of the Important Sale of the Costly Equipment of the Above Mansion, Including a Valuable Collection of . . . Paintings . . . Statues; A Magnificent Collection of Musical Instruments, Including the Grand Prize Medal Organ by Walker . . . Several Very Valuable Pianofortes and Harmoniums . . .* [etc.] *Sold . . . June 7th 1869 and 3 Following Days. . . .* [Southampton: 1869.]   40 pp., 949 lots.

   Instruments, pp. 25-33, lots 637-46. For the self-acting organ and harmonium (lots 645-46) the catalogue lists dozens of pieces (by Handel, Bach, Haydn, etc.) each is equipped with "slides" to play. Copy at US-NYfrick.

BIEBER, E.

1830   Puttick & Simpson, firm. *Catalogue of Old Italian and Other Violins, Violas* [etc.] *. . . A Phonologist Player Pianoforte. . . . A Collection of Brass and Wood Wind Instruments, the Property of the Late . . . Sold . . . June 11th, 1925.* 9 pp., 190 lots.

   Bieber's, lots 156-77. Catalogue no. 6118.

[BINFIELD], of Reading (Thomas, d. 1840?); THOMAS LUDFORD BELLAMY

1831   Puttick & Simpson, firm. *Catalogue of an Extensive and Valuable Musical Library . . . and Musical Instruments, Including a Seraphine, by Gunter . . . Sold . . . Jan. 12th, and Following Day, 1847.* 19 pp., 411+ lots.

   Instruments, lots 341-96 (Binfield's?). Catalogue no. 13, Puttick & Simpson's Third music sale.

BIRÓ, LAJOS   [N.B.: Collection now in **BUDAPEST, ORSZÁGOS NÉPRAJZI MÚZEUM**, q.v., Section I.]

BLAKE, Sir PATRICK; FRANCISCO BIANCHI

1832   Mr. Phillips, auctioneer. *The Musical Compositions of the Late Celebrated Signior Francisco Bianchi; and the Valuable Musical Instruments and Music of the Late Sir Patrick Blake . . . Sold . . . the 25th Day of March, 1819. . . .* 12 pp., 148+ lots.

> Blake's instruments, lots 78-93+, 112-33.

BLES, DAVID JOSEPH, 1821-1899

1833   Muller, F. & Cie. *Atelier-David Bles, tableaux et études du maitre . . . vente publique aura lieu . . . 27-28 février . . . 1 mars. . . .* Amsterdam: 1900. 51 pp., 645 + 3 lots., illus.

> Instruments, lots 172-89, 544, 555, 621 (lots 172, 176, 177 in photo, pl. opposite p. 15). Copy at US-NYfrick.

[BLIGH, E.]; JAMES BAKER; WILLIAM CRAMER

1834   Puttick & Simpson, firm. *Catalogue of a Large Collection of Music, from Several Private Libraries, Including Those of the Late Rev. James Baker . . . the Late William Cramer . . . Also Musical Instruments* [property of Bligh?] *. . . Sold . . . April 30th, 1855.* 42 pp.

> Instruments, lots 1015-1105; An Amateur's [Bligh's?], 1033-68; A Distinguished Amateur, 1069-70 (a Strad and an Amati). Catalogue no. 405.

BOAG, Mrs. MARY ANN. *See under* **COCKBURN, D.**

BODDINGTON, HENRY

1835   *Catalogue of Musical Instruments Principally Illustrative of the History of the Pianoforte, the Property of H. Boddington, Formerly the Collection of J. Kendrick Payne.* Manchester: 1888. 42 pls., obl. F°.

> Copies at CtY (NHu), PU (PHu), NNC (NYcu).

BODDINGTON, HENRY   *continued*

1836 Puttick & Simpson, firm. *Catalogue of Antique Instruments, Including a Selection from the Collection of . . . Formerly the Property of Kendrick Payne* [sic] *. . . Sold . . . July 24th, 1901.* 9 pp., 92 lots. Boddington's, lots 80-92.

> Catalogue no. 3555.

Literature

1837 "Versteigerung von 92 alten Musikinstrumenten," *ZiMG* 2 (1900/1901): 409.

BODEL, CORNELIS ADRIAAN; CATHARINA SOPHIA BRAMER; J. MULLER; JAC. AUG. JOURDANY; A. I. LOHMANS; HENDRIK SWITSER; TJEERT ANDRINGA

1838 Buys . . . Loot, firm. *Catalogus van een . . . Inboedel . . . Orseleinen . . . Lijnwaden . . . Einkelgoederen . . . welluidende Pianofortes, Violen en verder Muzijk-Instrumenten . . . verkocht . . . 27e December 1827, en volgende dagen. . . .* Amsterdam: 1827. 186 pp., [587] lots.

> "Muziek-Instrumenten," pp. 25-27 (60 lots), including a "Viool, door Stratoarus," and lot 15, "1 Kanarieorgetje, speelt 8 aria's." Owners are not identified. Copy at NL-DHrk.

BOER, S. M. de

1839 de Vries, Brondgeest, Engelberts, en Roos, firm. *Catalogus van eene verzameling fraaije schilderijen . . . alsmede van eenige voortreffelijke muzijk-instrumenten, en van de meest gezochtste muzijkwerken . . . verkocht . . . 15^{den} April 1840. . . .* [Amsterdam: 1840.] [2], 19 pp., 142+52 lots.

> Instruments, p. 16, lots 1-8 (Strad, Amati, Chanot, etc.). Copies at F-Pe, NL-DHrk, US-NYfrick.

BONJOUR, ABEL

1840 Gand et Bernardel (Exp.); Escribe (C. P.). *Vente du . . . 5 Février 1887, Hôtel Drouot . . . Succession de M. Abel Bonjour. Neuf violoncelles de Stradivarius, Rugger, École Amati, Steininger. Quatuor de Gand et Bernardel frères, Archets de Tourte . . . Pianos et musique.* Paris: 1887. 15 pp., 116 lots.

> Copies at F-Pn, B-Bc.

Literature

1841 [Lengthy note about this sale of his cello and bow collection], *ZfI* (1887/88): 192.

BOOSEY & HAWKES (private collection). *See Section I under* **EDGWARE (U. K.).**
BOOSEY & HAWKES GROUP. MUSEUM

BOREHAM, W. W. *See under* **CARRODUS, JOHN TIPLADY**

BOSCAWEN, GEORGE HENRY, 3rd Earl of Falmouth

1842 Puttick & Simpson, firm. *Catalogue of the Important Musical Collections of the Earl of Falmouth, in Which Is Comprised the Musical Library of . . . T. M. Alsager. Together with Violins, Tenors & Violoncellos (etc.) . . . Which Will Be Sold by Auction May 26* [-28] *1853.* 43 pp., 873 + 3 lots.

> Boscawen's instruments, lots 721-87 + 3.
> Catalogue no. 325. Copy also at MB (Bp).

BOSSY, Dr. *See under* **VENUA, FRÉDÉRIC MARC ANTOINE**

BOULTON, LAURA. *See Section I under* **NEW YORK, NEW YORK (USA). CULTURAL CENTER**

BRAGANZA, MARIA BARBARA de. *See under* **MARIA BARBARA DE BRAGANZA**

[BREE, J. B. van]

1843 Roos, C. F.; G. de Vries; W. Engelberts, firm. *Catalogus van eene verzameling antiquiteiten, rariteiten . . . voorts eenige Muzijk-instrumenten en kasten . . . Welke verkocht . . . den 10den April 1862. . . .* Amsterdam: 1862. 16 pp.

> "Muzijk-instrumenten en Muzijkwerken . . . nagelaten
> door . . . J. B. van Bree," pp. 14-16 (13 instruments,
> 48 scores and books).

1844 Roos, C. F.; G. de Vries; W. Engelberts, firm. *Vervolg op den Catalogus der Muzijkwerken. . . .* 4 pp., 108 lots.

> Bound in copy at NL-Apk (n & p).

BRENOT, PAUL

1845   Chevallier, P., firm. *Objets d'art de la Chine et du Japan: porcelaines, bronzes
. . . [etc.] formant la collection de feu M. Paul Brenot. Vente . . .* [June 5-10,
1903. Paris?: 1903].

> *ZiMG* 4 (1902/3): 656 says it includes "kleine Sammlung
> japanischer Instrumente." Copy not located.

BREW, R. J., of Liverpool

1846   Puttick & Simpson, firm. *Catalogue of a Very Valuable Collection of Musical
Properties . . . Pianofortes and Harmoniums. . . . The Collection of Violins of
the Late R. J. Brew . . . Sold . . . July 31st, 1882.* 9 pp., 211 lots.

> Brew's instruments, lots 105-28. Catalogue no. 2120.

BRICQUEVILLE, EUGÈNE de

1847   Bricqueville, Eugène de. *Catalogue des instruments de musique composant la
collection formée par . . . 1887-1889.* Avignon: Seguin frères, [1889]. 22 pp.

> Cited from BN*; not located. Collection now at Versailles.

1848   Bricqueville, Eugène de. *Collection de Bricqueville à Versailles. Anciens instruments de musique.* Paris: D. Jouast, 1893. 32 pp.

> Copies at NN (NYp), MiU (AAu), DLC (Wc).

1849   Bricqueville, Eugène de. *Catalogue sommaire de la collection d'instruments de
musique anciens formée par le Cte. De Bricqueville.* Versailles: Cerf et Cie.,
1895. 18 pp.

> Copy at NBuU-M (BUu).

Literature

1850   Bricqueville, Eugène de. "Le songe d'un collectionneur. Dialogue des morts."
In his *Un coin de la curiosité. Le anciens instruments de musique.* Paris:
Librairie de l'art, [1894].

1851   Bricqueville, Eugène de. "Instruments de musique anciens," *Academie de
Vaucluse, Mémoires* 8 (1889): 71-80.

BRIDSON, J. R.; Mlle. GABRIELLE VAILLANT

1852 Puttick & Simpson, firm. *Catalogue of a Valuable Collection of Violins, Violas, Violoncellos, Double Basses and Antique Instruments, Including the Collections of the Late J. R. Bridson, Esq., & Mlle. Gabrielle Vaillant . . . Sold . . . July 4th, 1902.* 13 pp., 102 lots.

> Bridson's instruments, lots 39-62; Vaillant's, lot 69 only.
> Catalogue no. 3641. Copy also at NRU (Rs).

BRITTON, THOMAS, 1651-1714

1853 *A Catalogue of Extraordinary Musical Instruments. . . . Also Divers Valuable Compositions, Ancient and Modern, by the Best Masters in Europe . . . Being the Entire Collection of Mr. Thomas Britton of Clerkenwell, Small Coal-Man, Lately Deceased, Who at His Own Charge Kept Up So Excellent a Consort Forty Odd Years at His Dwelling-House, That the Best Masters Were at All Times Proud To Exert Themselves Therein . . . Are To Be Sold by Auction at Mr. Ward's House in Red Bull-Yard, in Clerkenwell . . . 1714.* Reprinted in Hawkins, Sir John. *A General History of the Science and Practice of Music,* vol. 2, pp. 792-93. London: Payne and Sons, 1776. 27 lots.

> For numerous reprints of the Hawkins' *History,* see Duckles*
> 3:103. See also King*, pp. 11-12.

1854 *A Catalogue of Extraordinary Musical Instruments. . . . Also Divers Valuable Compositions, Ancient and Modern, by the Best Masters in Europe . . . Being the Entire Collection of Mr. Thomas Britton of Clerkenwell, Small Coal-Man, Lately Deceased, Who at His Own Charge Kept Up So Excellent a Consort Forty Odd Years at His Dwelling-House, That the Best Masters Were at All Times Proud To Exert Themselves Therein . . . Are To Be Sold by Auction at Mr. Ward's House in Red Bull-Yard, in Clerkenwell . . . 1714.* [Reprinted after Hawkins by F. G. E.], *MT* 47 (1906): 533.

BROADWOOD, JOHN & SONS, firm. *See also under* LONDON. INTERNATIONAL EXHIBITION, 1862; LONDON. INTERNATIONAL INVENTIONS EXHIBITION, 1885; *and* LONDON. CRYSTAL PALACE. INTERNATIONAL LOAN EXHIBITION, 1900

1855 *Collection of Antique Instruments at John Broadwood & Sons, Ltd., Conduit St., Bond Street.* [London: 1903.] 8 pp.

> Cited from Heyer*, Boalch*, *MGG*, and Hirt*.

BROADWOOD, JOHN & SONS, firm   *continued*

1856   *The Broadwood Collection of Antique Instruments . . . On View at the Broadwood Galleries.* London: [J. Broadwood & Sons, 1910?]. 16 pp.

Cited from BM*.

1857   Sotheby Parke Bernet, firm. *Important Musical Instruments . . . Violins, Violas, Woodwind, Brasswind* [etc.] *Sold by Auction . . . 20th March 1980. . . .* 107 pp., 302 lots, illus.

Broadwood's lots, 292-302 (important pianos).

Literature

1858   "Eine Klavier-Ausstellung der Firma Broadwood & Sons in London," *ZfI* 21 (1900/1901): 647-50. Lavishly illus.

1859   "Broadwood's Pianoforte Exhibition [in their galleries]," *Musical Opinion* 24 (1900/1901): 506A.

1860   "Broadwoodiana [housewarming exhibition of old keyboard instruments]," *MT* 45 (1904): 378-79.

1861   "Eine Klavierhistorische Ausstellung," *ZfI* 24 (1903/4): 757-59. 22 items described.

BROOKE, JOHN, of Leicester

1862   Greenwood, Mr., auctioneer. *A Catalogue of a Genuine and Exceedingly Valuable Collection of Prints, Books of Prints, and a Well Chosen Library, Select Music . . . Musical Instruments, Particularly a Most Capital Violin by Stainer . . .* [etc.]. *Collected With Great Care and at a Considerable Expence . . . Sold . . . 1st March, 1796, and Three Following Days.* 20 pp., 448 lots.

Lugt* indicates 34 lots of instruments. Copy at GB-LCia.

BROWN, JOHN CROSBY. *See Section I under* **NEW YORK, NEW YORK (USA). METROPOLITAN MUSEUM OF ART**

BROWN, Mrs. MARY ELIZABETH (ADAMS). *See Section I under* **NEW YORK, NEW YORK (USA). METROPOLITAN MUSEUM OF ART**

BRUNT, M. W. *See Section I under* **JERSEY (Channel Islands). SOCIÉTÉ JERSIAISE**

[BRYANT, et al]

1863 Christie & Manson, Messrs. *A Catalogue of a Small but Choice Assemblage of Painted Greek Pottery from Vulci. . . . Two Double Basses, and Other Musical Instruments . . . Sold . . . May the 31st, 1833.* London: 1833. 10 pp., 132 lots.

Instruments, lots 31-45.

BRYDGES, JAMES, 1st Duke of Chandos, 1674-1744

1864 "Pepusch's Catalogue of Musical Instruments Belonging to His Grace, the Duke of Chandos, 1720." In Baker, Charles, Henry Collins, and Muriel I. Baker. *The Life and Circumstances of James Brydges . . .* , pp. 139-40. Oxford: Clarendon Press, 1949.

BÜLOW, HANS VON   [N.B.: His collection the basis of that at HAMBURG MUSEUM FÜR KUNST UND GEWERBE, q.v., Section I.]

BULL, OLE BORNEMANN

1865 Berenzi, Angelo. *Di alcuni strumenti fabbricati da Gasparo da Salo, posseduti da Ole Bull, da Dragonetti e dal sorelle Milanello.* Brescia: Fratelli Geroldi, 1906. 49 pp., illus.

Copy at CtY (NHu).

BULL, PERCY A. *See Section I under* LONDON (U. K.). HORNIMAN MUSEUM

BURGER, WILLI

1866 [Jenkins* notes an article in *Glareana*, vol. 19, no. 3/4 (1970).]

Unable to examine.

BUSCHMANN, GUSTAV ADOLF

1867 "Hundert Jahre des Harmoniumbaues und anderer Zungeninstrumente 1810-1910. Notizen aus den Buschmann-Archiv," *ZfI* 32 (1911/12): 1055.

See also *ZfI* 30 (1909/10): 996.

[CALLCOTT, WILLIAM HUTCHINS]

1868   Puttick & Simpson, firm. *A Catalogue of a Collection of Music . . . Also Musical Instruments . . . Properties of Amateurs . . . and the Remaining Manufactured Stock of the Minima Organ Company . . . Sold . . . June 13th and June 15th, 1863.* 27 pp., 724 lots.

> Instruments, lots 607-21, 626-724, undifferentiated.
> Catalogue no. 771.

CAMPION, FRANÇOIS

1869   "Vente après le dècés de M. Campion . . . consistant en épinettes, grande nombre de belles guitarres, de thuorbes et de luths et autres instruments [etc.]. Rue du Petit-Lion S. Saveur, à l'image S. Grégoire," *Les affiches de Paris et avis divers, 19 février 1748.*

> Noted by François Lesure in his introduction to Campion's
> *Nouvelles découvertes.* [Reprint] Genève: 1977.

CAPEL, JOHN

1870   Winstanley, Messrs. *A Catalogue of Nearly the Whole of the Excellent Furniture . . . and Other Articles of Taste, a Fine-Toned Finger Organ . . . Grand Pianoforte, by "Collard". . . . The Valuable Library of Music. . . . A Fine Copy of Marcello's Psalms . . . Sold . . . 26th of April, 1847 and Three Following Days.* [London]: 1847. 40 pp., 637 lots.

> Lugt* notes 93 lots of musical instruments; not examined.
> Copy at GB-Lbl.

CAPPS, R. H.

1871   Puttick & Simpson, firm. *Catalogue of Musical Instruments . . . Violins, Violas, Violoncellos, Including the Collection of the Late . . . of New Cross . . . and a Quantity of Music . . . Sold . . . April 26th, 1904.* 12 pp., 252 lots.

> Instruments, lots 1-223C; Capp's, 178-92, on the whole
> a not very interesting group. Catalogue no. 3824.

CARRERAS Y DAGAS, D. JUAN

1872   *Catalogo de la biblioteca musical y museo instrumental propriedad de D. Juan Carreras y Dagas. . . .* Barcelona: Manuel Miro, 1870. 70 pp.

> Cited from BrCA*; not examined.

CARRODUS, JOHN TIPLADY; E. J. STAINFORTH; W. W. BOREHAM; L. PARSONS; Mrs. FIELDING

1873 Puttick & Simpson, firm. *Catalogue of the Valuable Collection of Violins, Violas, Violoncellos, etc., the Properties of the Late J. T. Carrodus, E. J. Stainforth, W. W. Boreham, Hon. L. Parsons, Hon. Mrs. Fielding. . . . Bows and Cases . . . Sold . . . December the 10th, 1895.* 15 pp., 99 lots.

> Carrodus' instruments, lots 14-19; Boreham's, lots 68-75; Stainforth's, lots 20-34. Catalogue no. 3112. Copy also at NRU (Rs), priced.

Literature

1874 "Geigen-Auktion in London . . . an 10. Dezbr. 1895," *ZfI* 16 (1895/96): 307-8.

1875 "Messrs. Puttick & Simpson's Special Sale," *Violin Times* 3, no. 26 (1895): 35-36.

CARSE, ADAM. *See also Section I under* LONDON (U. K.). HORNIMAN MUSEUM

1876 *List of Wind Instruments in the Private Collection of Adam Carse.* [Gt. Missenden?: 193-.] [11] pp.

> Copies at CU (BEu) and ICN (Cn); CU (BEu) says: [Bucks, Eng., 19--?].

1877 *Detailed Catalogue of His Interesting Private Collection of Wind Instruments.* [s.p.] : Privately printed, [1934].

> Cited from *JbP** (1934); not located. Same as no. **1876**?

Literature

1878 "The 'Adam Carse' Collection of Wind Instruments," *GSJ* 2 (1949): 3-9. pl. I (between pp. 24 & 25)

CARTER, T. A.; F. W. NEWRICK; "A GENTLEMAN"

1879 Puttick & Simpson, firm. *Catalogue of Valuable Violins, Violas, and Violoncellos, the Property of the Late T. A. Carter [and] F. W. Newrick . . . and Various Sources. . . . Bows . . . Sold . . . June 26th, 1924.* 12 pp., 261 lots.

> Carter's instruments, lots 226-41; Newrick's, 242-61; the Gentleman's, 219-25. Catalogue no. 5996.

CASADESUS, HENRI. *See Section I under* **BOSTON, MASSACHUSETTS (USA). SYMPHONY ORCHESTRA**

CASIMIR I, Graf MORITZ. *See under* **SAYN-WITTGENSTEIN, CASIMIR, Graf von BERLEBURG**

CASAMORATA, L. F. *See Section I under* **FLORENCE (Italy). CONSERVATORIO DI MUSICA LUIGI CHERUBINI. MUSEO**

CASTELBARCO, CESARE, conte di, d. 1860

1880   Puttick & Simpson, firm. *Catalogue of the Superb Collection of Cremona Instruments of the Late Count Castelbarco, of Milan. . . . Five Violins by Stradivarius, Two Violins by Guarnerius, Four Violins by Nicolas and Andreas Amati, Violas by Stradivarius and Steiner, Two Violoncellos by Stradivarius, a Violoncello by Amati, Also, an Autograph Letter of Ant. Stradivarius . . . Sold . . . June 26th, 1862.* 5 pp., 31 lots.

   Catalogue no. 727. Copy also at NN (NYp).

CASTLE, ZILLAH *and* **RONALD** (J100)

   Literature

1881   Castle, R. "The Zillah and Ronald Castle Collection [in Wellington, New Zealand]," *GSJ* 13 (1960): 93-94.

CERUTTI, Signor; T. PYMAR; CLAYTON FREELING; JOSEPH GWILT; Mr. ADAMSON

1882   Puttick & Simpson, firm. *Catalogue of a . . . Collection of Music from Several Private Collections, Including Those of the Late Signor Cerutti, the Late T. Pymar . . . Clayton Freeling, Joseph Gwilt and Mr. Adamson, Music Seller. . . . Also Numerous and Important Musical Instruments from the Above Named and Other Collections . . . Sold . . . July 19, 1854, and Two Following Days.* 39 pp., 1113 lots.

   Instruments, lots 892-1113, undifferentiated.
   Catalogue no. 379.

CESARE D'ESTE, Duke of Modena, 1533-1628

1883   *Adi 18 decembre 1600 . . . instrumenti et altre robbe pertinente alla musicha, per farli condure a Modena al Ser^mo duca Cesare d'Este.* Ms. in the Archivio di stato, Modena. Reprinted in Straeten, Edmond van der. *La musique aux Pays-Bas,* vol. 6, pp. 117-18. Bruxelles: Muquardt [etc.], 1867-88. Reprint ed. New York: Dover, 1969.

1884   *Inventario degl'instromenti e libri grandi di musica che havea in custodia il gia. D. Nicolo* [1625]. Ms. reprinted in Straeten, Edmond van der. *La musique aux Pays-Bas,* vol. 6, p. 120.

1885   *Inventario degl'instromenti e libri grandi di musica che havea in custodia il gia. D. Nicolo* [1625]. Reprinted in Valdrighi, Luigi Francesco. *Musurgiana,* no. 11, (1884), pp. 68-71.

> Valdrighi's reprint includes music books.

CHALMERS, WILLIAM; "A LADY"

1886   Puttick & Simpson, firm. *Catalogue of Violins, Violas, and Violoncellos . . . Bows . . . Wind Instruments, etc., the Property of the Late . . .* [and] *a Lady . . . Sold . . . May 26th, 1938.* 10 pp., 164 lots.

> Chalmers instruments, lots 116-45.
> Catalogue no. 106 [2nd ser.].

CHRYSANDER, FRIEDRICH [N.B.: Collection now in HAMBURG, MUSEUM FÜR KUNST UND GEWERBE, q.v., Section I.]

CHICHESTER, J. H. R.; RICHARD RANDELL

1887   Puttick & Simpson, firm. *Catalogue of the Musical Library of J. H. R. Chichester, Esq., and . . . Mr. R. Randell (pupil of Handel) . . . Including . . . Musical Instruments . . . Sold . . . March 4, 1863, and the Following Day.* 29 pp., 615 lots.

> Instruments, lots 401-615; Chichester's, 420-51.
> Catalogue no. 753. Copy also at NN (NYp).

CHRISTIAN LUDWIG II, Herzog von Mecklenburg-Schwerin

1888   "Instrumentus musicus [a catalogue] (1778)." In Meyer, Clemens. *Geschichte der Mecklenburg-Schweriner Hofkapelle . . . ,* pp. 51-52. Schwerin i.M.: 1913.

CLAPISSON, LOUIS

1889   Pillet, Charles and Carle Delange (C.-P.). *Catalogue de la curieuse collection d'instruments de musique parmi lesquels une magnifique épinette du XVIe siècle . . . de feu M. Clapisson . . . Vente . . . Hotel Drouot . . . 12 mai 1866.* [Paris] : 1866. 24 pp., 163 lots.

> Copy at NL-DHgm. Clapisson was the first conservator of the instrument collection in the Paris Conservatoire.

CLARKE, H. S.

1890   Sotheby & Co., firm. *Catalogue of China, Furniture, Musical Instruments etc. . . . Sold by Auction . . . May 14th, 1936.* [London] : 1936. 47 pp.

> "Collection of Musical Boxes," pp. 19-24, lots 116-57.

CLAUDIUS, CARL   [N.B.: Heyer* cites a catalogue, *C. Claudius' Instrumentsamling, Malmö*, a listing of 65 instruments from the Claudius collection supposedly exhibited at the 1897 Allmänna Konst- och Industrie-utställningen in Stockholm. Not found. Nor do two general catalogues of the exhibition—the *Officiel berättelse* (2 vols., 1899-1900) and the *Konstafdelningen* (3. uppl., 1897)—mention the collection. See *"Literature"* about the exhibition in Section I.]

1891   *Katalog öfver C. Claudius' instrumentsamling utställda till förman för musik-historiska museet i Stockholm.* Malmö: Otto Krooks boktryckeri, 1901. 14 pp., 156 lots.

> "Pergament-Handskrifter," lots 150-56. Copy at NL-DHgm.

1892   Skjerne, Godtfred. *Carl Claudius' samling af gamle musikinstrumenter.* København: Levin & Munksgaard, 1931. 423 pp., illus., 799 items.

> Duckles* 3:1579 says 757 items; now administered by the University of Copenhagen. Copies at NN (NYp), MiU (AAu), DLC (Wc).

Literature

1893   Hetsche, Gustav. "Mellem Gamble instrumenter i Carl Claudius' Museum i Malmö," *Illustreret Tidende,* Nr. 49, Bind 43m (Copenhagen: 1902), pp. 774-76. Lavishly illus.

1894   Claudius, Carl. "Meine Sammlung von Musikinstrumente," *Der Kunstwanderer* 3, 2. Augustheft (1921): 96-97.

1895   "Om samlare av 'En samlare'," *Ur nitidens musikliv* 3, no. 2 (1922): 17-25.

CLEMENČIČ, RENE

Literature

1896 Clemenčič, Rene. *Old Musical Instruments.* New York: G. P. Putnam's Sons, [1968]. 120 pp. (about half, illus.)

> Issued in German as *Alte Musikinstrumente.* Stuttgart: Parkland, 1974. Seventeen plates show instruments from the author's collection; the rest are from various collections.

[CLIVE, Miss]

1897 Puttick & Simpson, firm. *Catalogue of a Small Musical Library and Several Valuable Music Instruments, Pianofortes. Barrel and Finger Organs, Harmonium by Alexandre, Violins and Violoncellos. . . . Also, a Portion of the Useful Stock of a Musical Instrument Maker, Deceased . . . Sold . . . September 13th, 1854.* 13 pp., 326 lots.

> Instruments, lots 162-87; stock of Phillips, the instrument maker, 188-263. Catalogue no. 384.

COBB, FRANCIS MARSDEN, of Margate

1898 Puttick & Simpson, firm. *Catalogue of Violins, Violas, Violoncellos and Double Basses. Bows, Guitars, Harp* [etc.], *the Property of the Late . . . Sold . . . October 4th, 1945.* 11 pp., 242 lots.

> All but lot no. 242 are Cobb's. Catalogue no. 719 [2nd ser.].

COCKBURN, D.; W. HOPWOOD; Mrs. MARY ANN BOAG; E. HODGES

1899 Puttick & Simpson, firm. *Catalogue of Music and Instruments, Including Sections from the Libraries of E. Hodges . . . and of Various Distinguished Amateurs; the Stock of Mrs. Boag, Musicseller . . . Stock of a Country Music Seller. . . . Twenty Pianofortes . . . Also (the Property of the Late W. Hopwood, D. Cockburn* [et al]*) Numerous Violins, Violoncellos, Superb Violoncello by Guarnerius . . . Sold . . . July 4th, 1864, and Following Day.* 33 pp., 866 lots.

> Instruments, lots 697-866; Cockburn's, 765-99; Boag's, 800-822; Hopwood's, 827-66. Catalogue no. 825. Copy also at NN (NYp): 966 lots; lots 841-966, fishing rods, guns, etc.

COCKS, ROBERT & Co.; et al

1900 Puttick & Simpson, firm. *Catalogue of Musical Instruments, Including a Portion of the Stock of. . . . Pianofortes . . . Harps . . . Violins etc. . . . Brass and Wood Wind Instruments . . . Sold . . . December 13th, 1898.* 16 pp., 385 lots.

> Instruments, lots 1-362. Catalogue no. 3347.

COCKS, W. H.

1901 Puttick & Simpson, firm. *Catalogue of Musical Instruments. . . . Pianofortes . . . Violins, Violas* [etc.], *Including the Property of the Late . . . and Music . . . Sold . . . September 29th, 1908.* 14 pp., 290 lots.

> Instruments, lots 1-227C; Cocks', 124-213.
> Catalogue no. 4242.

COLARD, HECTOR

1902 Le Roy, J. & A., frères. *Catalogue de tableaux anciens et modernes. . . . Tapisseries. . . . Instruments de musique composant la collection de feu. . . . Vente . . . 9 avril 1924. . . .* Bruxelles: 1924. 38 pp., 248 lots.

> Instruments, lots 200-248. Copy at NL-DHgm.

COLIZZI, J. H.; Dr. K[AUCLITZ]

1903 [Sale of collection by Scheurleer, at La Haye, November 14 and 28, 1808.] 2, 22pp., 833 + 3 lots.

> Information here from Lugt* who notes 67 lots
> of music, 206 lots of musical instruments. Missing
> at only known location, NL-DHrk.

COLT, C. F.

1904 Colt, C. F. *The Colt Clavier Collection, Silver Jubilee, 1944-1969. List.* Bethersden: 1969.

> Cited from Boalch* and others; not located or examined.

Literature

1905 Colt, C. F. "Restoration of Square Pianos," *GSJ* 14 (1961): 69-71.

> "List of the Collection," pp. 70-71.

CONDELL, [HENRY]; Mr. SHARPE

1906 Musgrave, Mr. W. P. *A Catalogue of the Well-Known Instruments, Late the Property of Mr. Condell . . . Amongst Which Are an Amati Violin . . . and the Matchless Tenor, Originally in the Possession of . . . Giardini. . . . Superior Violoncellos . . . One . . . by J. B. Rogerius, Till Recently in the Possession of the Duke of Marlborough . . . Flutes by Monzani. The Music Consists of . . . Works and Treatises, of the Most Distinguished Ancient and Modern Composers, Comprising the Collection of Mr. Sharpe of Knutsford . . . Sold . . . March 30, 1825.* 18 pp., 183 lots.

> Instruments, lots 75-87; an excellent group.
> Copy at GB-Lbl (n & p).

CONTARINI-CORRER COLLECTION   [N.B.: The collection was originally assembled by Marco Contarini (1631-1689), Procurator di San Marco, at Piazzola. Jacques Chassebras de Cramailles discussed the collection at Piazzola in the *Mercure galant,* February 1681 (the passage is quoted in Wiel, T., *I codici musicali contariniani,* p. xi. Venezia: 1888.). The instruments passed to Pietro Correr in Venice. In 1872 he placed them on sale, and Soranzo's catalogue of that date (no. **1908**, below) is truly a sale catalogue. Karl Bank listed the 121 instruments included by Soranzo in an article in the *Dresdner Journal* (no. 302), September 1872. Fürstenau, when he republished Soranzo's list (no. **1909**), says that as of 1874 they were not yet sold. Of the 121 items, most were acquired by the Musée of the Brussels Conservatoire, some by the Museo Civico in Venice, and a few by the Musée of the Paris Conservatoire.]

1907 Piccioli. *L'orologico del piacere che mostra l'ore del dilettevole soggiorno hauto dall'altezza serenissimo d'Ernesto Augusto Vescovo d'Osnabruc, dua di Bransuich, Luneburgo, ecc. Nel luoco di Piazzola di S. E. il Signor Marco Contarini, Procurator di S. Marco.* In Piazzola, Nel luoco delle Vergini, M.DC.LXXXV.

> According to Kinsky (*Randnoten*)*, this is a source about
> the instrument collection of Contarini. Not located.

1908 *Elenco degli strumenti musicali antichi da arco, fiato, pizzico e tasto, posseduti dal Nob. P. Correr di Venezia.* Venedig: Tipogr. Antonelli, 1872.

> According to Heyer*, an "Abschrift" after the autograph
> in the Musée of the Brussels Conservatoire prepared by
> Camillo Soranzo.

1909 Fürstenau, Moritz. "Eine Sammlung musikalischer Instrumente in Venedig," *MfM* 6 (1874): 103-7.

> Soranzo's "Elenco" (see above), pp. 105-7.

CONTARINI-CORRER COLLECTION   *continued*

1910   Venice. Museo civico e raccolta Correr. *Guida del Museo civico e raccolta Correr di Venezia.* Venezia: Tip. Emiliana, 1885. vi, 184 pp.

> "Strumenti musicali [41 items]," pp. 16-17 from the collections of Correr, Martinengo and the Istituto Esposti.

CONTI, Count

1911   Puttick & Simpson, firm. *Catalogue of a Valuable Collection of Violins, Violas, Violoncellos, Bows and Antique Instruments from Various Private Sources . . . Sold . . . December 17th, 1901.* 16 pp., 124 lots.

> Conti's instruments, lots 46-104.
> Catalogue no. 3584. Copy also at NRU (Rs).

COOK, HAROLD E. *See Section I under* LEWISBURG, PENNSYLVANIA (USA). BUCKNELL UNIVERSITY

COOKE, BENJAMIN

1912   Fletcher, Mr., auctioneer. *Catalogue of the Extensive, Rare, and Valuable Musical Library of the Late. . . . Numerous Full Scores. . . . Handel's Works. . . . Dr. Cooke's Manuscript Works. . . . Also the Musical Instruments . . . Sold August 5th, and . . . 6th, 1845. . . .* 18 pp., 450 lots.

> Instruments, lots 418-50; Cooke's, 418-36.
> Copy at NN (NYp).

COOKE, T.; JAMES ROBINSON

1913   Puttick & Simpson, firm. *Catalogue of the Stock of James Robinson . . . Dealer in Second-Hand Music . . . Comprising Above 100,000 Pieces of Classical and Popular Music. . . . Also Musical Instruments (Various Private Properties,) . . . Sold . . . November 11th, 1861, and Two Following Days.* 39 pp., 1345 lots.

> Instruments, lots 1204-1345; Cooke's, 1253-1345.
> Catalogue no. 699; copy also at NN (NYp).

COOPER, A. DAVIS. *See under* ROWE, Major

CORBETT, WILLIAM, d. 1748

1914 N. B.: An article, "Count Cozio di Salabue," *Violins and Violinists* 3 (1941): 104, notes that in 1724 Corbett advertised for sale "Stainer's Cremona violins and bases, with the four celebrated violins of Corelli, Gabbo, Torelli, and Nic. Cosimi." No information is given about the sale's success or about a sale catalogue. In 1748, the year of his death, he still had a collection which he had given to Gresham College [according to a note in *Violin Times* 2 (1895/96): 122] "for public exhibition, an arrangement which was not, unfortunately, carried out." Present whereabouts, unknown.

CORIN, PAUL (J157)

1915 *The Paul Corin Musical Collection; Souvenir Booklet.* St. Keyne Mill, Cornwall: [197-?]. ii, 16 pp., illus.

Copy at NBuU-M (BUu).

CORRER, PIETRO. *See under* CONTARINI-CORRER COLLECTION

CORSBY, GEORGE, of Prince St.

1916 Puttick & Simpson, firm. *Catalogue of the Extensive and Highly Valuable Stock of Musical Instruments of . . . Presenting the Largest and Most Interesting Assemblage of Cremona Instruments . . . Ever Offered for Sale at One Time . . . May 14th, 1863.* [London]: 1863. 15 pp., 385 lots.

Catalogue no. 764. Copy also at GB-Lva.

1917 Puttick & Simpson, firm. *Catalogue of a Collection of Miscellaneous Music . . . Scores . . . Scarce Music Treatises . . . Also Numerous and Valuable Musical Instruments . . . , Including a Portion of the Stock of Mr. G. Corsby . . . Sold June 26th, 1871, and Following Day. . . .* 21 pp., 637 lots.

Instruments, lots 442-637. Catalogue no. 1255.

1918 Foster, Messrs. *A Catalogue of the Collection of Splendid Old Cremona Violins and Tenors, Violoncellos and Double Basses of . . . Sold by Auction . . . the 22nd of January, 1874. . . .* [London]: 1874.

Copy at GB-Lva.

COSIMO III, Granduke of Tuscany, 1642-1723. *See Section I under* FLORENCE (Italy). CONSERVATORIO DI MUSICA LUIGI CHERUBINI. MUSEO; *also here under* FERDINAND, de Medici

COSPI, FERDINANDO, marchese di Petrioli

1919　Legati, Lorenzo. *Museo Cospiano annesso a quello del famoso U. Aldrovandi e donato alla sua patria dall'illustrissimo Signor Ferdinando Cospi . . . descrizione.* Bologna: 1677.

> Instruments, pp. 220-23. Schlosser* indicates that the collection was the basis of the Museo Civico, Bologna.

COSTA, MICHAEL, Sir. *See under* DUCHESNE, R.

COUSSEMAKER, EDMOND DE

1920　Olivier, F. J., firm. *Catalogue de la bibliothèque et des instruments de musique de feu Ch. Edm. H. de Coussemaker.* Bruxelles: 1877. iv, 208 pp.

> Sale date, April 17-20, 1877. Instruments, 36 lots, pp. 202-6. Copies at NN (NYp), DLC (Wc).

1921　Olivier, F. J., firm. *Catalogue de la bibliothèque et des instruments de musique de feu Ch. Edm. H. de Coussemaker. Reprint edition, with Introduction by A. Hyatt King.* (Auction catalogues of music, vol. 4.) Buren: Frits Knuf, 1977. iv, 152 pp.

COZIO DI SALABUE, IGNAZIO ALESSANDRO, Count. *See Section I under* CREMONA (Italy). MUSEO CIVICO

CRAMER, FRANCOIS

1922　McCalla, Mr., auctioneer. *A Catalogue of Classical Music, Valuable Instruments, Works of Art, &c., by Order of the Proprietor . . . Retiring from Public Life. . . . The Well-Known and Highly Valuable Violins, Tenors, Violoncellos, &c. . . . Small Library of Choice Books . . . Engravings . . . Sold by Auction by . . . July 23, and Following Day* [1844]. 16 pp., 69 lots.

> Instruments, lots 91A-101L, 293-303. Copy: compiler.

1923   Puttick & Simpson, firm. *Catalogue of the Valuable Violins by Cremona and Other Makers, the Property of . . . Sold . . . August 22nd, 1846.* 5 pp., 31 lots.

> Lots 13-31 are Cramer's. Catalogue no. 4, the firm's second sale. The catalogue is sometimes listed under the collector C. Raper. Lots 1-12 may be Raper's, but the catalogue does not mention him by name—nor does P & S's own Index*. Copy also at NN (NYp).

1924   Puttick & Simpson, firm. *Catalogue of a Choice and Extensive Musical Library, Chiefly the Collection of the Late . . . Together with Musical Instruments, Comprising the Final Portion of the Well-Known Collection of Violins of Mr. Francois Cramer, with Other Valuable Violins, Violoncellos, a Double Bass* [etc.] *. . . Sold March 9th,* [1847] *and Following Day. . . .* 18 pp., 459 lots.

> Instruments, lots 426-59. P & S Index* notes under both Cramer and G. Penson. Title page missing at GB-Lbl; inside, properties are not identified. Catalogue no. 18.

CRAMER, W.   *See under* **BAKER, JAMES**

CROSBY BROWN COLLECTION.   *See Section I under* **NEW YORK, NEW YORK (USA). METROPOLITAN MUSEUM OF ART**

CUBITT, W. D., Messrs., Son & Co.

1925   Puttick & Simpson, firm. *Catalogue of the Assemblage of Musical Instruments, Engraved Copper Plates of Various Publications, Printed Stock etc. of . . . Comprising about Thirty Grand & Cottage Pianofortes, by Broadwood, Erard,* [etc.] *. . . Harmoniums and American Organs, Harp . . . Violins, Violas and Violoncellos, from Various Private Collections. Wind Instruments, Banjoes, Guitars . . . 23 Kegs of Useful Black Paint . . . Sold . . . August 20th, 1886.* 2 + 12 pp., 296 lots.

> Instruments, lots 1-185. Catalogue no. 2441.

CUMMINGS, WILLIAM HAYMAN. *See also Section I under* **LONDON (U. K.). INTERNATIONAL LOAN EXHIBITION OF MUSICAL INSTRUMENTS, CRYSTAL PALACE, 1900**

1926   Puttick & Simpson, firm. *Catalogue of Musical Instruments, Including the Property of the Late W. H. Cummings . . . and from Various Sources . . . Sold . . . May 2nd, 1916.* 12 pp., 249 lots.

> Cummings' instruments, lots 178-203. Catalogue no. 5030.

CUSINS, Sir WILLIAM GEORGE. *See under* **WOOLHOUSE, W. S. B.**

DANCKERT, W. *See Section I under* **JENA (Germany). STAATSMUSEUM**

DANCOCKS, G. W.

1927   Puttick & Simpson, firm. *Catalogue of Musical Instruments, Including Properties of . . . G. W. Dancocks . . . Rev. Canon Beauchamp . . . John Sutcliffe [et al] . . . . Fine Old Italian and Other Violins . . . and Music . . . Sold . . . October 26th, 1915. . . .* 11 pp., 216 lots.

> Instruments, lots 1-201; Dancock's, 171-201.
> Dancock's library, 202-16. Other owners named,
> 1-4 lots each. Catalogue no. 4980.
>
> DLC (Wc) has a separate catalogue of six pages,
> lots 171-201 with a separate title page: *Catalogue of the Valuable Collection of Violins, Violas and Violoncellos Formed by the Late G. W. Dancocks . . . Sold . . . October 26th, 1915. . . . At the Conclusion of the Musical Instrument Sale and Before the Library of Music of the Above.*

1928   Puttick & Simpson, firm. *Catalogue of Musical Instruments . . . Pianofortes . . . Violins etc. . . . Antique Instruments, Including the Property of the Late . . . Sold . . . October 30th, 1915. . . .* 11 pp., 229 lots.

> Dancock's instruments, lots 141-155.

DANDELEU, JEAN BAPTISTE

1929 "Inventaire des instruments et livres de musique de feu le sieur Jean Baptiste Dandeleu, vivant premier commissaire ordinaire des monstres des gens de guerres du Roy, rétrouvez en la maison mortuaire d'Iceluy, à Bruxelles, avec les nombres d'iceux et le spécification de leurs auteurs, mis en marge, comme s'ensuit. . . ." In Straeten, Edmond van der. *La musique aux Pays-Bas,* vol. 1, pp. 31-37. Bruxelles: Muquardt [etc.], 1867-88. Reprint ed. New York: Dover, 1969.

> An inventory of 1667.

DANDO, JOSEPH HAYDN BOURNE. *See under* GOODHART, J. H.

DAVIS, J. LOYD

1930 Kansas City, Mo. (USA). Public Library. *Musical Instruments from the J. Loyd Davis Collection* [exhibition catalogue]. [Kansas City, Mo.: The Public Library, 1966.] [1], 5 pp., illus., 21 items.

DOANE, WILLIAM HOWARD (L394) [N.B.: Now at the Cincinnati Art Museum, the collection was included in the exhibition catalogue entered in Section I under **TOLEDO, OHIO (USA). MUSEUM OF ART**, q.v.]

DOLMETSCH, ARNOLD (J146)

1931 Puttick & Simpson, firm. *Catalogue of Musical Instruments . . . Pianofortes . . . Organs . . .* [string and wind] *Instruments. . . . Also the Fine Collection of Antique Instruments Formed by . . . and the Library of Music . . . Sold . . . October 29th, 1901, and Following Day.* 35 pp., 717 lots.

> Instruments, lots 1-485; Dolmetsch's instruments, 446-85; his library, 498-717. Catalogue no. 3565.

1932 Dolmetsch, J. *The Dolmetsch Collection of Instruments: Exhibition Catalogue, Compiled by J. Dolmetsch.* [Haslemere: Dolmetsch Foundation, 1972.] 8 pp.

> Typescript in the Victoria and Albert Museum.

DONALDSON, Sir GEORGE [N. B.: Two of Donaldson's collections (given in 1894 and 1900) are now in the **LONDON, ROYAL COLLEGE OF MUSIC**, q.v., in Section I.]

1933   Sotheby & Co., firm. *Catalogue of Valuable Embroideries and Textiles . . .*
[etc.] . *Musical Instruments, the Property of . . . Sir George Donaldson . . .*
J. A. Fuller-Maitland, Esq. . . . Mrs. Gordon Woodhouse . . . Sold . . . the 28th
of May, 1927. [London]: 1927.

> Instruments, pp. 8-10; Donaldson's, lots 24-31;
> Fuller-Maitland's, lots 34-39; Woodhouse's, lot 40.

DOORNE, J. VAN; ANTONI VAN HEURN

1934   van Os, Pieter, bookseller. *Catalogus van een zeer fraaye Bibliotheek . . . Boeken*
in alle Facultyten . . . Teekeningen, Prentwerken . . . Nagelaten door . . . van
Heurn. Voorts een meenigte Muziek-Werken en Instrumenten . . . nagelaten
door . . . van Doorne . . . verkogt . . . I. Maart 1762, en 7. volgende Daagen. . . .
's-Gravenhage: 1762. 271 pp.

> "Muziek Instrumenten," pp. 265-66 (29 lots—a Strad,
> several Stainers, an Amati, Techler, etc.). Copy at NL-Avb.

DOUGLAS, ROBERT COOPER; SAMUEL APPLEBY; WILLIAM BEADELL; AN AMATEUR, DECEASED

1935   Puttick & Simpson, firm. *Catalogue of a Large Collection of Musical Instruments*
. . . Pianofortes, Harmoniums and American Organs. . . . Violins, Violas, Violon-
cellos, and Double Basses, Comprising the Well-Known Collections Formed by the
Late Samuel Appleby, William Beadell, Robert Cooper Douglas, B. J. C. Pringle,
and Many Others. . . . Bows by Tourte [etc.] *Wind Instruments . . . Sold . . .*
June 24th [and] 27th, 1887. 18 pp., 441 lots.

> Douglas' instruments, lots 144-59c, 312-49; Appleby's,
> 56-65; Beadell's, 1-55 [cf. item no. 2066]; Pringle's,
> 91-92; Amateur's 185-294. Catalogue no. 2505.

DOWDING, WILLIAM

1936   Musgrave, W. P., auctioneer. *A Catalogue of the Entire Collection of Music,*
Instruments, and a Portion of the Library of Books, Late the Property of. . . .
Violins, a Tenor, and Violoncellos, Grand Piano Fortes . . . Sold . . . February
12th, 1823, and Following Day. . . . 14 pp., 262 lots.

Instruments, lots 43-58 (Dowding's?; not clearly identified).
Copy at GB-Lbl (1078.[6]).

DREXEL, JOSEPH [N. B.: His collection was given to the **NEW YORK, METROPOLITAN MUSEUM OF ART**, and though there appear to be no specific catalogues, see entries under "*Literature*" in Section I.]

DUCHESNE, R.; THOMAS PENRICE; W. S. PALMER; F. WACQUEY; Signor PATTI; T. BAKER

1937   Puttick & Simpson, firm. *Catalogue of the Valuable Collection of Violins, Violas, Violoncellos, etc., Including the Properties of the Late R. Duchesne . . . Thomas Penrice . . . W. S. Palmer . . . F. Wacquey. . . . Also the Properties of Signor Patti and Thomas Baker . . . Also . . . Sir Michael Costa, and a Small Collection of Antique Instruments . . . Sold . . . May 20th, 1898.* 20 pp., 156 lots.

> Lots 1-134, Patti and Baker; Autograph letters [etc.] of da Costa, 135-56; antique instruments, property of "An Amateur," 121-34; rest of lots not differentiated.

Literature

1938   "Geigen-Auktion in London," *ZfI* 18 (1897/98): 720, 729. A long notice about the sale.

DUMAS, J. H. P.

1939   Puttick & Simpson, firm. *Catalogue of a Valuable Collection of Musical Instruments . . . Pianofortes* [etc.] *, an Ancient Clavichord, Formerly in the Possession of John Sebastian Bach. Rare Italian Violins, Violas, Violoncellos, and Double Basses, Including the Collection of the Late . . . and . . . Music . . . Sold January 30th, 1906.* 14 pp., 316 lots.

> Instruments, lots 1-295A; Dumas', 92-142.
> Catalogue no. 3988.

DURAND-DUBOIS

1940   *Catalogue d'instruments de musique parmi lesquels en alto d'Antonius Stradivarius et un violon d'Antoine et Jérôme Amati . . . le vendredi 15 mars 1872.* Paris: [1872]. 8 pp.

> Copy at GB-Lbl (Hirsch 421.1) with some prices.

E**

1941   Fulgence (Exp.); Couturier (C.P.). *Catalogue des étoffes anciennes provenant de l'atelier de M. E**. Parements de Devants d'autel, Dalmatiques, Chasubles, Tapes en velours. . . . Instruments de musique et fanteuils . . . vente . . . 8 novembre 1875.* Paris: 1875. 8 pp., 86 lots.

Lugt* notes 20 lots of instruments; not examined.

EAMES, EDWARD A.

1942   *The Eames Collection of Musical Instruments* [exhibited under joint auspices of the Department of Music, University of British Columbia and the Centennial Museum. s. p.: 1972.]. 15 lvs.

Copy at NBuU-M (BUu).

EARL OF FALMOUTH. *See under* **BOSCAWEN, GEORGE HENRY**

EARL OF LIVERPOOL. *See under* **LEA, T.**

EAST INDIA COMPANY (from the Great Exhibition of 1851)

1943   Hoggart, Norton & Trist, Messrs. *A Catalogue of the Highly Important and By Far the Greater Portion of the Valuable and Interesting Collection As Exhibited by the Honourable The East-India Company . . . Representing Articles from . . . Bengal* [etc.] *. . . Sold . . . the 7th Day of June, 1852, and Four Following Days . . . the 28th of June, 1852, and Five Following Days. . . .* 7, 118 pp., 2128 lots.

Instruments, lots 1896-1939. Copy at GB-Lva.

EDELMANN, ALBERT (J122)

Literature

1944   Hiestand-Schnellmann, Joseph. "Die Musikinstrumentensammlung von Albert Edelmann," *Glareana* 12, no. 3/4 (1963): 4-6. 62 items.

312

EDWARDS, WILLIAM, of Spaulding

1945   Puttick & Simpson, firm. *Catalogue of a Collection of Ancient & Modern Music . . . Also Musical Instruments . . . Including the Collection of W. Edwards . . . Sold . . . April 29, 1875.* 12 pp., 278 lots.

> Instruments, lots 183-278; Edwards', 203-78.
> Copy also at NN (NYp).

EDWARDS, WILLIAM HENRY; THOMAS BAKER

1946   Puttick & Simpson, firm. *Catalogue of Grand and Cottage Piano-Fortes, Organs . . . Violins, Violas, Violoncellos and Double Basses, Including the Collection of the Late . . . Also a Library of Music . . . Collected by an Amateur . . . Sold . . . March the 30th, 1897.* 16 pp., 357 lots.

> Instruments, lots 1-266; Amateur's music, lots 267-357.
> Catalogue no. 3220.

EGGENBERG FAMILY

1947   Záloha, Jiří. "Českokrumlovský soupis hudebnin z počátku 18. století," *Hudebnı̌ věda* 6 (1969): 365-76.

> Reproduces an eighteenth-century inventory, 610 items,
> according to *RILM**.

EIKHGORN, A. F.

1948   *Polnaı̃a kollektsı̃a muzykal'nykh instrumentov narodov Tsentral'noı̆ Azii A. F. Eı̆khgorna (byvshego voennogo kapel'meistera v Tashkente). Katalog.* S.-Petersburg: Tip. ĨU. Shtaufa, 1885. 16 pp.

> Covers 38 instruments exhibited in the Muzee G. F.
> Pateka in Leningrad. Cited from Koltypina* and
> Emsheimer*; not examined.

ELEY, Mr.

1949   Watson, Mr. *A Catalogue of a Valuable Assemblage of Vocal & Instrumental Music, Comprising the Library of . . . , the Remainder of the Collection Formed by T. Greatorex. . . . Together with a Portion of the Library of John Sidney Hawkins. . . . Many of the Works Are from the Libraries of the Pretender and of The Margravine of Anspach. . . . Organs, Piano-Fortes . . . Together with the*

ELEY, Mr. *continued*

Violins, Tenors, and Violoncellos Belonging to the Late Mr. Eley . . . Sold . . .
June 26, 1832, and [four] *Following Days.* 30 pp., 636 lots.

> Instruments, lots 320-43, A-E, 430-36, 567-70.
> Copy at GB-Lbl (n & p).

ELLINGER, Miss DESIRÉE

1950 Puttick & Simpson, firm. *Catalogue of Old and Modern Violins, Violas, and Violoncellos. . . . Bows. . . . A Collection of Antique Wood Wind Instruments, the Property of . . . Sold . . . November 29th, 1934.* 12 pp., 232 lots.

> Ellinger's instruments, lots 202-32. Catalogue no. 7240.

ENGEL, CARL [N. B.: One hundred seven instruments from his own collection were included in the exhibition he prepared at the South Kensington Museum in 1872. The collection went partly to the Museum in 1875. A few were included in Puttick & Simpson sale of October 16, 1881 (catalogue no. 2047). His general and musical library was dispersed in Puttick & Simpson auctions of June 13 and July 7, 1881 and May 4, 1882.]

ERNST, FRITZ

1951 *Catalogue de la collection d'instruments anciens. . . .* Sièrne-Geneve: 1942.

> This brief citation from *Glareana*, no. 73; not verified.
> The collection is now in the **GENEVA, MUSÉE DES INSTRUMENTS ANCIENS DE MUSIQUE**, q.v., Section I.

1952 Nyon, Switzerland. Exposition, Trésors musicaux des collections suisses, 1949. *Trésors musicaux des collections suisses; exposition au Château de Nyon, juin 1949. Catalogue.* [Nyon: 1949.] 88 pp., illus.

> Part 2: Instruments de musique, the private collection
> of Fritz and Joachim Ernst, according to *MGG**.
> Copies at NN (NYp) and OrU (EUu); not examined.

Literature

1953 Gramm, J. " . . . une visité à la collection d'instruments anciens de M. Fritz Ernst in Sièrne," *Glareana*, vol. 3, no. 3 (1954).

1954 "Ginebra inaugura su museo de antiquos instrumentos de musica," *Ritmo* 31 (1961): 6-7. illus.

1955 Tappolet, Willy. "Eine Instrumentensammlung in Genf," *Musik-revy* 15 (1960): 277-78. illus.

[EUING, WILLIAM]

1956   Puttick & Simpson, firm. *Catalogue of a Collection of Music, a Portion of the Library of a Well-Known Professor . . . History and Theory of Music, with Interesting Ms. Notes. . . . Rare Autographs and MSS. Seventeen Letters of Kollmann Addressed to Dr. Callcott* [etc.] . *Unpublished Manuscripts of George Barker. . . . Musical Instruments. Pianofortes . . . Fine Violins and Violoncellos, Wind Instruments, etc. . . . Sold . . . May 29, 1876, and Following Day.* 37 pp., 650 lots.

> Instruments, lots 560-650 (Euing's?).

FALCOUNER, THOMAS, of Hampstead

1957   Puttick & Simpson, firm. *Catalogue of a Very Extensive Collection of Musical Instruments, Amongst Which Are Included 35 Pianofortes . . . Organs and Harmoniums . . . a Valuable Assemblage of Italian Violins, Violas, Violoncellos and Double Basses, Including Those of Thomas Falcouner . . . and Many Others from Private Sources . . . Sold June 22nd, 1880.* 13 pp., 316 lots.

> F's instruments, lots 189-201. Catalogue no. 1933.

FALMOUTH, Earl of. *See under* BOSCAWEN, EDWARD

FARMER, HENRY GEORGE. *See Section I under* GLASGOW (Scotland). KELVIN-GROVE ART GALLERY AND MUSEUM

FELIPE II, King of Spain, 1527-1598

1958   "Instrumentos de música [no. 1417-1531] ." In Beer, Rudolf. "Inventare aus dem Archivo del Palacio zu Madrid," *Jahrbuch des kunsthistorischen Sammlungen* 19, no. 2 (1898): CXXXII-CXXXVI.

1959   "Inventario real de los bienes que se Hallaran en esta Guardajoyas del rey Don Philipo Segundo, nuestro señor, que esta en gloria. Ano 1607." Reprinted in Straeten, Edmond van der. *La musique aux Pays-Bas,* vol. 8, pp. 298-312. Bruxelles: Muquardt [etc.] , 1867-88. Reprint ed. New York: Dover, 1969.

FERDINAND, de Medici, Prince of Tuscany, 1663-1713 [N.B.: The information presented here is drawn mainly from Gai* and Hammond (see full citations for each in Section I, nos. **497** and **498**, respectively). Prince Ferdinand (1663-1713) was responsible for most of the growth of the instrument collection at the Medici court, previously ruled by the Granduke Ferdinand I (1549-1609) and the Granduke Ferdinand II (1610-1670). Gai* lists numerous inventories of the collection spanning their reigns, and these are set out below; Hammond concentrates on the inventories from 1640 to 1669, and reprints them. In 1863 the collection was moved from the Pitti Palace to the Museo of the R. Conservatorio di Musica Luigi Cherubini; for literature after that date see nos. **494** and **505** in Section I. Correspondence about this transfer and a catalogue by Mariotti of that date (no. **494**) are reprinted by Gai*. Reprintings of other inventories are noted in the following.]

> **THE GUARDAROBA MEDICEO INVENTORIES** (in the Archivio di Stato Di Firenze) [N.B.: In chart form, Gai* has synthesized the instruments included in these inventories, and their numbers as shown in each successive inventory, under the title, "Quadro sintetico degli strumenti che appartenevano alla Corte Medicae dal 1640 al 1742," pp. 405.
>
> The final document reprinted by Hammond (fol. 99r) is "Totals of Instruments in Guardaroba," by type. The grand total, 200.]

1960　(1640: Guardaroba n. 664, fols. 85r-87v) "Adì primo Ottobre 1640: Inuentario Delle robe che sono nella Stanza degli Strumenti di S.A.S. Consegnati." Reprinted in Hammond (no. **498**), pp. 203-5.

1961　(1652: Guardaroba n. 664, fols. 89r-92v) "Inuentario della Strumenti, che sono nella Guardaroba di S.A. in Consegna del Sig.^{re} Bartolomeo Mazzanti riuisto, e rifatto questo dì 2 Agosto 1652." Reprinted in Hammond (no. **498**), pp. 205-7.

1962　(1654: Guardaroba n. 664, fols. 1v-45r) "Copia dell'Inuentario, è Rassegna di tutti li Strumenti che si ritrovono nella Stanza della Guardaroba della Musica in consegna al S. Bartolomeo Mazzanti. . . ." Reprinted in Hammond (no. **498**), pp. 207-13.

1963　(1669: Guardaroba n. 664, fols. 111r-112v) "Jhesus: Maria: 1669/Inuentario di tutti li Strumenti che si ritrouano nella Stanza della Guardaroba della Musica stati in consegna A' Bartolomeo Mazzanti in oggi Defunto, fatto questo dì 28 Agosto 1669." Reprinted in Hammond (no. **498**), pp. 213-15.

1964　(1669: Guardaroba n. 664, fols. 103v-112r) "Nella Riuisione fatta questo dì 28 Agosto 1669." Reprinted in Hammond (no. **498**), pp. 215-18.

> This inventory not cited by Gai*.

1965   (1670: Guardaroba n.822) "Copia dell'inventario e rassegna di tutti li strumenti ... della Guardaroba della musica in cosegna a Gio Batta Lasagnini, nuovo Guardaroba l'originale esistente nell Guardaroba Generale in Filza di giustificazioni a n.67 fatto il di 2 marzo 1670 ab incarnatione."

1966   (1694: Guardaroba n.1005) "Inventario di tutti li strumenti retrovati nella stanza deputata per detti che prima erano a cura di Gio Batta Lasagnini defunto, et oggi se n'e fatto il presente custode de' mesimi istrumenti."

1967   (1700, Guardaroba n.1117) "Inventario di diverse sorti d'instrumenti musicali in proprio del serenissimo Sig. Principe Ferdinando di Toscana." Reprinted in Gai, Vinicio. *Gli strumenti musicali della corte medicea,* pp. 6-22. Firenze: LICOSA, 1969.

1968   (1716, Guardaroba n.1241) "Inventario di tutti gli strumenti da Sonare di corde, e fiato, Pervenuti dall'Eredita del Ser.^{mo} Principe Ferdinando di G.M.^{a} consegnati di comandamento di S.A.R. a Bartolomeo Cristofori Custode dei med." Reprinted by Ferdinando Solti. In L. Puliti's *Cenni storici della vita del Serenissimo Ferdinando dei Medici,* Allegato D, pp. 101-7. (Estratto dagli Atti dell'Accademia del R. Istituto musicale di Firenze, 1874.) Firenze: 1874. 90 items.

1969   For comments on, and a list of, some of the keyboard instruments, see Russell, Raymond. *The Harpsichord and Clavichord,* p. 125. London: Faber & Faber, 1959.

1970   (1716, Guardaroba n.1306) [A copy of no. **1968**, according to Gai*.]

1971   (1732, Guardaroba n.1410) "Inventario di tutti gli strumenti da sonare di corde e fiato che esistono in questo Palazzo Vechio nelle due stanze nove poste al primo piano, a canto a quella che serve per udienza del Guardaroba maggiore; consegnati a Pietro Mazzetti novo custode, come per ordine di S.A.R., posto in Filza di giustificazioni a. . . . Stante la morte di Bartolomeo Cristofori già custode a prima."

1972   (1732-1765, Guardaroba n.1411) "Filza di ordini, e riceute de' debitori, fatta da Pietro Mazzetti custode delli strumenti."

FERDINAND II, von Tirol, Archduke of Austria, 1529-1595. *See Section I under* **VIENNA (Austria). KUNSTHISTORISCHES MUSEUM. AMBRAS COLLECTION**

FERDINAND II, Erzherzog von Innerösterreich, 1578-1637. *See under* **KARL von STEIERMARK, Erzherzog von Innerösterreich, 1540-1590**

FERDINAND KARL, Erzherzog von Österreich, 1628-1662. *See Section I under*
VIENNA (Austria). KUNSTHISTORISCHES MUSEUM. AMBRAS COLLECTION

FERNANDEZ BLANCO, ISAAC

Literature

1973 "Isaac Fernandez Blanco Collection," *Violins* 11 (1950): 100.

Housed in the Museo del Teatro, Buenos Aires.

FÉTIS, FRANCOIS JOSEPH

1974 *Catalogue des instruments de la collection Fétis.* A Ms. in the Musée of the
Brussels Conservatoire.

The collection (of 74 instruments, according to Lambertini*)
served as the basis for the Musée.

FIALA, ERICK (J15)

1975 Hiestand-Schnellmann, Joseph. "Alte Musikinstrumente aus den Besitz von
Dr. Fiala, Wien," *Glareana* 22 (1973): lvs. 33-49.

FIBICH

1976 Lavigne (Exp.) Charles Pillet (C. P.). *Catalogue de musique instrumentale. 21
violons & 1 violoncelle, archets de Tourte, etc. Livres modernes provenant de
la collection de M. Fibich, anciens violon de la chapelle de S. M. l'Empereur
de'Autriche . . . vente . . . Rue Drouot . . . 28 Mai 1868. . . .* Paris: Lavigne,
1868. 14 pp., 51 + 23 lots.

Instruments, final 23 lots. Copy at NL-DHgm.

FIELDING, The Hon. Mrs. *See under* **CARRODUS, JOHN TIPLADY**

FINCH, HENEAGE, 6th Earl of Aylesford, 1824-1871 (BM* says "4th Earl")

1977   Puttick & Simpson, firm. *Catalogue of a Collection of Music Including the Valuable Musical Library of the Late Earl of Aylesford, Comprising Rare Instrumental Works . . . Also Musical Instruments . . . Sold . . . August 25, 1873.* 23 pp., 430 lots.

>   Instruments (King* says "notable"), lots 387-430.
>   Copy also at NN (NYp).

FINZI, D. *See under* **ROWE, Major**

FISHER, bookseller of Brighton

1978   Leigh & Sotheby, firm. *A Catalogue of the Circulating Library of. . . . Likewise Twenty Fine-Toned Piano Fortes . . . Sold by Auction . . . October 3rd, 1805, and Five Following Days.* [London: 1805.] 39 pp.

>   Pianos, p. 29, lots 1375-94, include 9 Broadwoods.

FLAMENG, M. F. [N. B.: Hébert Rouget in the *Revue musicale* (Paris) 6 (1906): 58 notes the sale of Flameng's collection at the Hotel Drouot in this year. Catalogue not located.]

FLETCHER, BENTON. *See Section I under* **LONDON (U. K.). FENTON HOUSE, HAMPSTEAD**

FORKEL, JOHANN NIKOLAUS

1979   *Verzeichniss der von dem verstorbenen Doctor und Musikdirektor Forkel in Göttingen nachgelassenen Bücher und Musikalien welche den 10ten May 1819 und an den folgenden Tagen . . . in der Wohnung des Univ. Gerichts-Procur. und Notars Fr. Justus Schepeler an der Juedenstrasse in Göttingen meistbietend verkauft werden.* Göttingen, F. G. Huth, 1819. 200 pp.

>   "Musikalische und andere Instrumente," pp. 198-99
>   (15 lots). Copy: compiler.

FOUCQUES D'ERNONVILLE (of Abbeville)

1980   Gand et Bernardel (Exp.). [Vente apres décès de M . . .] *du juin 1881.*
Instruments des grands maitres italiens. Archets. Collection de musique.
Paris: 1881. 8 pp., 58 lots.

> Instruments, lots 1-19, 41-58. Copy at GB-Lbl
> (Hirsch 421 [10]) with some prices and marginal notes.
>   A notice of this sale of the owner's ancient
> instruments appears in *Le Menestrel.* A comment
> on this notice appears in *ZfI* 1 (1880/81): 286.
> Owner's name is given as Fouques d'Ermonville [sic].

FRANCOISE, JACQUES. *See Section I under* NEW YORK, NEW YORK (USA). LIBRARY AND MUSEUM OF THE PERFORMING ARTS, "Violins of France," 1971

FRANZ FERDINAND, Archduke of Austria, 1863-1914. *See Section I under* VIENNA (Austria). KUNSTHISTORISCHES MUSEUM. ESTE COLLECTION, *and under* VIENNA (Austria). INTERNATIONALE AUSSTELLUNG FÜR MUSIK- UND THEATERWESEN, 1892, *Fachkatalog . . . Deutschland-Ungarn*

FRASER, ARCHIBALD THOMAS FREDERICK

1981   Puttick & Simpson, firm. *Catalogue of a Varied Assemblage of Musical
Instruments . . . Including the Property of the Late . . . Sold . . . July 25th,
1884.* 8 pp., 176 lots.

> Fraser's instruments, lots 133-76. Catalogue no. 2282.

FREELING, CLAYTON. *See under* CERUTTI, Signor

FREEMAN, EDITH J. [N. B.: Though her collection is now in the Detroit Institute of Arts, catalogues of it appear in Section I under MINNEAPOLIS, MINNESOTA (USA). UNIVERSITY OF MINNESOTA. UNIVERSITY GALLERY.]

FRENCH, Col. P. T. *See Section I under* **DUBLIN (Ireland). ROYAL IRISH ACADEMY**

FRIEDRICH WILHELM DER GROSSE, 1640-1688. *See also under* **JOHANN GEORGE II**

1982 Rowe, Walter. "1667. Instrumenteninventar." Ms. in Kgl. Hausarchiv, Rep. XIX, Pers. Spec. Reprinted in Sachs, Curt. *Musik und Oper,* pp. 224-25. Berlin: Bard, 1910.

> The basis of the collection in the Brandenburgische Hofkapelle, Berlin.

FRISHMUTH, Mrs. William D.

Literature

1983 Haughom, Synnove. "Thomas Eakins' Portrait of Mrs. William D. Frishmuth, Collector,"*Antiques* 104 (1973): 836-39. illus.

> According to Haughom, Mrs. Frishmuth gave 1100 instruments to the Free Museum of Science and Art of the University of Pennsylvania, others to the Pennsylvania Museum and School of Industrial Art (later the Philadelphia Museum of Art), which later gave them back to the University of Pennsylvania. The University, in turn, finally donated parts of the collection to the Metropolitan Museum, to Yale University, and to the Smithsonian.

FROST, PERCIVAL

1984 Puttick & Simpson, firm. *Catalogue of a Valuable Collection of Violins, Violas, Violoncellos, etc., Including the Properties of the Late . . . Percival Frost . . . Dr. Fly Smith, Dr. Selle and Others . . . Will Be Sold . . . Friday, June 9th, 1899. . . .* 19 pp., 140 lots.

> Catalogue no. 3387; the last Puttick sale in the old Joshua Reynolds studio at 47, Leicester Square. See "Puttick's then, Phillips now," *The Strad* 90, no. 1069 (May 1979): 40-41.

1985 "Guaranteed Sale at Puttick & Simpson's," *Musical Opinion* 22 (1898/99): 708.

> An account of the June 9th sale that includes a long list of items sold with prices fetched.

FROST, PERCIVAL *continued*

1986   "The Last Sale of Valuable Violins in the Historical Room in Leicester Square," *The Strad* 111 (July 1899): 89-90 + photo.

> Also contains a list of items sold with prices fetched.
> The photo—of the sale and those in attendance—is
> reproduced in *The Strad* article, May 1979 (see no. **1984**).

FRYKLUND, LARS AXEL DANIEL

1987   *Collection Fryklund.* Hälsingborg: Schmidts boktr., 1929. 109 pp.

> A collection of ca. 800 items, according to *MGG**.
> Copies at MH (CAc), NjR (PRu).

1988   *Samlingen av musikinstrument paa Ystadutställningen 1936.* Hälsingborg: Aktiebolaget boktr., 1936. 7 pp.

> Cited from *BdMS*;* not located.

1989   *Att samla musikinstrument.* Hälsingborg: Aktiebolaget boktr., 1937. 18 pp.

> Cited from *BdMS** and DaSML*; not located.

1990   *Samlingen av musikinstrument i Hälsingborgs museum.* [Hälsingborg: Schmidts boktryckeri aktiebolaget, 1939.] 5-42 pp., illus.

> Offprint from *Kring kärnan,* Hälsingborgs museums
> aarskrift, 1939. *MGG** notes the same in a German
> translation, but it cannot be located.

1991   *Collection Fryklund 1949.* Hälsingborg: Aktiebolaget boktr., 1949. 50 pp., illus.

> Copy at NBuU-M (BUu).

Literature

1992   Nordberger, C. "Collection Fryklund - en unik sämling," *Slöjd och ton* 20 (1950): 38-40.

FUGGER, RAIMUND, d. j., 1528-1569

1993   (1566) "Verzeichniss Raymund Fugger's Musikkammer. 1566." Ms. in Haupstaatsarchiv, München, *Libri antiquitatum I,* fol. 170-73 under title, "Verzaichnuss Rayd. Fuggers Instrument vnd Musica." [Section on instruments] Reprinted in Stockbauer, Jacob. *Kunstbestrebungen am bayerischen Hof unter Herzog Albert V,* pp. [80]-84. (Quellenschrift für Kunstgeschichte und Kunsttechnik des Mittelalters, hrsg. von R. Eitelberger, vol. 8.) Wien: 1874. ca. 155 items.

> Copy at NBuU-M (BUu).

1994 (1566) "Verzeichniss Raymund Fugger's Musikkammer. 1566." Ms. in Haupstaatsarchiv, München, *Libri antiquitatum I,* fol. 170-73 [etc.]. [Section on instruments] Reprinted by Sandberger, Adolf. "Bemerkungen . . . zur Musikgeschichte der Städte Nürnberg und Augsburg," *Denkmäler der Tonkunst in Bayern* 5/1 (1904): L-LI.

1995 (1566) "Verzeichniss Raymund Fugger's Musikkammer. 1566." Ms. in Haupstaatsarchiv, München, *Libri antiquitatum I,* fol. 170-73 [with title: "VerZaichnus der Instrument Truhen, so der Bassani brueder gemacht haben, mit gar schönen vnd guetten Instrumenten"]. Reprinted in Wallner, Bertha Antonia. "Ein Instrumentenverzeichnis aus dem 16. Jahrhundert." In *Festschrift zum 50. Geburtstag Adolf Sandberger,* pp. 275-86. München: Zierfuss, 1918.

> *MGG** says original in the hand of R.'s son, H. J. Fugger.

1996 (1566) "Verzeichniss Raymund Fugger's Musikkammer. 1566." Ms. in Haupstaatsarchiv, München, *Libri antiquitatum I,* fol. 170-73 [with title: "Verzaichnuss d[er] Musica Kamer Lauten"]. Reprinted in Schaal, Richard. "Die Musikinstrumenten-Sammlung von Raimund Fugger d.j.," *AfMW* 21 (1964): 214-16. ca. 140 items .

1997 (1580) "Inventari der erkaufften von Her: Huldrich Fugger, gleichwol noch nit bezalten musica per fl. 4000 so, in 11. eingemachten vassen vnnd. 14. kisten, engepackt zue Brandenburg im Schloss ligt." Ms. in Archiv der Fürstl. und Gräfl. Fuggerschen Stiftungsadministration Augsburg 7, 2.

> Noted by Schaal (no. **1996**, p. 213).

Literature

1998 Schaal, Richard. "Die Musikbibliothek von Raimund Fugger d.j.," *Acta musicologica* 29 (1957): 126-37.

> Reproduces only the music lists, but notes the instrument collection.

1999 Pleijel, Bengt. "Musikvandring i Augsburg," *Musik revy* 15, no. 1 (1960): 13-15. illus.

GALE, ALBERT. *See Section I under* **LOS ANGELES, CALIFORNIA (USA). UNIVERSITY OF SOUTHERN CALIFORNIA. ALLAN HANCOCK MUSEUM**

GALLINI, NATALE. *See Section I under* **MILAN (Italy). MUSEO DI ANTICHI STRUMENTI MUSICALI**

GALOPIN, CAMILLE. *See Section I under* **GENEVA (Switzerland). MUSÉE D'ART ET D'HISTOIRE**

GALPIN, FRANCIS WILLIAM [N. B.: The first Galpin collection was purchased by William Lindsey and given to the Boston Museum of Fine Arts in 1917 in memory of his daughter, Leslie Lindsey Mason. Citations **220** and **224** refer to that collection. See also catalogues in Section I under **BOSTON, MASSACHUSETTS (USA). MUSEUM OF FINE ARTS.** For information about the second Galpin collection, see no. **2003.**]

2000   Galpin, Brian. "Canon Galpin's Check Lists," *GSJ* 25 (1972): 4-21.

> Presents the Canon's classed check list, a Ms.
> (before 1890) with annotations. Traces each item.

Literature

2001   Lynd, William. *A Popular Account of Ancient Musical Instruments and Their Development As Illustrated by Typical Examples in the Galpin Collection at Hatfield, Broad Oak, Essex.* London: J. Clarke & Co., [1897]. xii, 109 pp.

2002   Dotted Crochet. "Private Musical Collections. II. The Rev. F. W. Galpin's Musical Instruments," *MT* 47 (1906): 521-29.

2003   Galpin, Francis W. *Old English Instruments of Music; Their History and Character.* London: Metheun & Co., [1910]. xxv, 327 pp.

> According to Boalch* most of the instruments illustrated
> were from the Galpin collection. Subsequent editions:
> Chicago: McClurg, 1911; 3rd rev. ed., London: Metheun,
> [1932]; etc.; reprint of 1910 ed., St. Clair Shores:
> Scholarly Press, 1978.

2004   Kinsky, Georg. "Verkauf der Sammlung Galpin nach Amerika," *ZfI* 41 (1920/ 21): 1202, 1243.

2005   Puttick & Simpson, firm. *Catalogue of Antique String, Brass, Wood Wind and Keyboard Instruments, etc., the Property of the Late The Revd. Canon F. W. Galpin. Also Old and Modern Violins, Violas* [etc.] ... *Sold ... April 11th, 1946.* 7 pp., 122 lots.

> In Ms. on p. 1 of British Library copy: "Lots 1 to 46
> and lot 50 [all Galpin's properties] are withdrawn."
> Catalogue no. 767 [2nd ser.].

GAND, ERNEST

2006   Bernardel, Léon (Exp.); Julien Mallet (C. P.). *Collection Gand. . . . Vente aux enchères publiques, après le décès de M. Ernest Gand, d'une très belles collection d'instruments de musique. Violon et viole d'amour de Nicolas Lupot. . . . Hôtel Drouot . . . le mardi 22 mars 1904. . . .* [Paris: E. Moreau, 1904.] 8 pp., 141 lots.

> Until recently a troublesome fugitive. Grove's*
> and Vannes* place under Caressa! As Lugt* notes,
> Caressa was an apprentice to Gand et Bernardel,
> in Paris, but that seems little reason for the entry,
> especially since that E. Gand was, in fact, Eugène
> Gand, not Ernest. Those who have sought the
> work have looked for it under Caressa, under
> Eugène Gand, or under the firm name, and under
> those entries, even libraries in Paris and London
> were unable to verify its existence. A copy came
> to light, however, in one of the uncatalogued
> collections of early sale catalogues in the Sibley
> Library of the Eastman School of Music.
> "Collection Gand" was that of *Ernest* Gand.
> Later another copy was located at B-Bc.

GANTTER, LOUIS

2007   Puttick & Simpson, firm. *Catalogue of the Musical Library of. . . . Also Musical Instruments . . . Sold . . . Aug. 10, 1846.* 13 pp., 230 lots.

> Page 3 is headed: "Monday, August 12, 1846."
> Catalogue no. 3; Puttick & Simpson's first music
> sale. Copy also at NN (NYp). Instruments,
> lots 195-230 (Gantter's?).

GAST, GIDEON de

2008   Nijhoff, Paulus. *Catalogus van een groot (?) gebonden Boeken in all (?) en Talen Kerk en Schoolgoed . . . en fraaie Collectie Muzijk en Muzijk-Instrumenten . . . &c. alles nagelaten door Gideon de Gast, Boekverkoper te Arnhem waarachter een 2de Catalogus van Boeken, Muzijk en Muzijk Instrumenten, daar ander beste Clavicimbels, Bassen, Viool d'Amour en Anderen . . .* [7 April 1783, and following days]. Arnhem: 1783.

GAST, GIDEON de   *continued*

> Two vols. in 1 (178 pp.). Second "Catalogus" begins
> on p. 161. "Muziek," pp. 133-40 (180 lots);
> Instruments, p. 157 (lots 1-13; "Muziek," pp. 166-68
> (66 lots); Instruments, pp. 169-70 (24 lots).
>
> P. Nijhoff's first catalogue; see "Boekenveilungen
> van Paulus Nijhoff, 1783-1831," pp. [77]-106 in *De
> arnhemsche Boekverkoopers. . . .* 's-Gravenhage: 1934.
>
> Only known copy of the catalogue at NL-Avb has
> damaged title page.
>
> Lugt's* dating, April 8, 1783, is incorrect; first day
> of sale was April 7.

[GAUNTLETT, HENRY JOHN, 1805-1876]

2009 Puttick & Simpson, firm. *Catalogue of the Very Extensive, Rare and Valuable
Musical Library of a Distinguished Professor . . . and an Extraordinary Assemblage
of Stringed Instruments . . . Sold . . . December 17th, 1847, and Following Day.*
24 pp., 524 lots.

> Instruments of "A Gentleman" (Gauntlett?), lots 153-216.
> Gauntlett's name does not appear in catalogue, only in
> P & S Index*. Catalogue no. 51. Copy also at NN (NYp).

GEDON, LORENZ

2010 *Catalog der nachgelassenen Kunst-Sammlungen des Bildhauers und Architekten
Herrn Lorenz Gedon . . .* [with a Preface by Friedrich Schneider]. München:
1884. 15, 126 pp.

> His collection of old instruments was sold at auction June
> 17-21, 1884, and this catalogue may include that material.
> Neither this nor an auction catalogue located. A brief list
> of the instruments sold, however, appears in *ZfI* 4 (1883/
> 84): 346.

GERSON-KIWI, EDITH   (J76).   *See Section I under* JERUSALEM (Israel).   BEZALEL MUSEUM

GILLOTT, JOSEPH, of Birmingham   [N. B.: From a column in *Violin Times* 2 (1895/96): 122—Gillot owned about 500 stringed instruments, eventually lost his enthusiasm for collecting, and placed all but a few in lumber rooms in his manufacturing plant where they remained, neglected, until his death. "Then they were scattered among collectors. . . ." How they were scattered is not reported.

Some of the neglected instruments were exceedingly valuable; see Hill, W. H., A. F., and A. E. *Antonio Stradivari*. London: W. H. Hill & Sons, 1902; 2nd ed., London: Macmillan, 1909. Reprint ed. New York: Dover (1963), pp. 264, 274, 277, et passim.]

2011   Christie, Manson & Woods, firm. *Catalogue of the Renowned Collection of Ancient and Modern Pictures and Water-Colour Drawings of. . . . Catalogue of the Valuable Collection of Fine Old Italian Musical Instruments . . . Sold . . . April 29, 1872*. London: Wm. Clowes & Sons, [1872]. 81 pp.

> Instruments, pp. 73-81 (153 lots). Copy also at MdBP (BApi) with names of buyers and prices fetched. This sale included only the principal instruments, the lesser items probably disposed of by George Hart, the dealer and valuer at Probate [correspondence from Mr. Robert Lewin].

Literature

2012   "Sale of Stringed Instruments," *Musical World* 50 (1872): 289.

2013   Lewin, Robert. "Sotheby's May Sale [1979]," *The Strad* 90, no. 1069 (May, 1979): 45-47.

> Lewin includes comments about "The Gillott [sale which] with its massive offerings of top Cremonese may never be surpassed. . . ."

GINGRICH, ARNOLD

2014   Sotheby, Parke Bernet, firm. *Important Musical Instruments, the Property of Various Owners, Including Frederick Apfelbaum . . . Arnold Gingrich* [et al]. *Public Auction, Friday, October 29, 1976*. New York: 1976. 157 lots. Lavishly illus.

> Sale no. 3914.

Literature

2015   [Note about the sale of instruments from his estate.] In Kass, Philip. "An American First: Musical Instruments at the Tepper Galleries and the Sotheby Parke Bernet," *Journal of the Violin Society of America* 2, no. 4 (Fall 1976): 84-88.

G[LANDARZ], S[IGISMOND] G.

2016   Baubigny, (C.-P.). Gand et Bernardel (Exp.). *Vente apres décès de M. S. G. d'un trés-beau violon de Stradivarius; violons-violoncelle-archets. Hôtel Drouot . . . 14 février 1878.* 2 pp., 12 lots.

> Copy at GB-Lbl (Hirsch 421.7) with n & p.

GLEN, ROBERT. *See Section I under* GLASGOW (Scotland). KELVINGROVE ART GALLERY AND MUSEUM

GLÖGGL, FRANZ XAVER. *See Section I under* VIENNA (Austria). GESELLSCHAFT DER MUSIKFREUNDE

GLOVER, F. *See under* STEPHENSON, W.

GODING, JAMES

2017   Christie and Manson, Messrs. *Catalogue of the Valuable Collection of Pictures, Marbles, Bronzes. The Celebrated Musical Instruments . . . of the Late . . . Sold . . . February 18, 1857, and Following Days. . . .* 24 pp., 446* lots.

> Instruments, lots 371-446*. Magnificent!
> Seven items by Stradivarius, 5 Guarnerius,
> 2 Amati; bows formerly the property of,
> e.g., Paganini, Kreutzer, Tartini, Mozart.
> A note in *Violin Times* 2 (1895/96): 122—
> The collection when formed was the finest
> that existed. . . . After a few years, dispersed
> by the hammer of the auctioneer.

GÖPEL (prob. JOHANN ANDREAS, 1776-1823)

2018   *Verzeichnis der von dem verstorbenen academ. Musiklehrer, Organisten Göpel in Rostock nachgelassenen Musikalien, musikalischen Instrumente und Bücher, welche am 1sten Septbr. 1824 und folgenden Tagen . . . verkauft werden sollen durch den Auctions-Secretaire Uebele. . . .* Rostock: gedruckt bey Adlers Erben, 1824. 51 pp.

> II. Musikalische Instrumente, pp. 32-33 (48 lots).
> Copy: compiler.

GOODHART, J. H.; CHARLES KELVERY; J. H. B. DANDO; A. N. PAWLE

2019 Puttick & Simpson, firm. *Catalogue of a Valuable Collection of Violins, Violas, Violoncellos, & Bows, the Properties of J. H. Goodhart, Charles Kelvey, J. H. B. Dando, A. N. Pawle . . . Together with a Small Collection of Antique Instruments . . . Sold . . . November the 23rd, 1894.* 15 pp., 110 lots.

> Instruments: Kelvey's lots 9-25; Pawle's, 26-29; Dando's, 31-35; Goodhart's, 39-41; "Antique Instruments, the Property of the Late Prof. Wegener of Potsdam," 70-100. Copy at British Library: 14 pp., (100 lots only). Catalogue no. 3035. Copy also at NRU (Rs).

GORETTI, ANTONIO [N. B.: Collection purchased for Ambras, see Section I, no. **1588**.]

GORGA, EVAN. *See Section I under* ROME (Italy). R. ACCADEMIA NAZIONALE DI SANTA CECILIA *and* ROME (Italy). MOSTRA CECILIANO, 1953-1954

GORKE, MANFRED

2020 Leipzig. Musikbibliothek. *Katalog der Sammlung Manfred Gorke. Bachiana und andere Handschr. u. Drucke d. 18. u. frühen 19. Jh.* [bearb. von Hans Joachim Schulze]. (Bibliographisches veröffentlichungen der Musikbibliothek der Stadt Leipzig, 8.) Leipzig: 1977. 168 pp., illus.

GOSSELIN, HENRI

2021 Fievez, J. (Exp.). *Catalogue des instruments de musique anciens, antiquités & objets d'arts divers délaissés par M. Henri Gosselin . . . dont la vente publique en la Salle Sainte-Gudule . . . 12 février 1891. . . .* [Bruxelles: E. Lhoest] , 1891. 18 pp., 119 lots.

> Instruments, lots 1-50. Copies at NRU (Rs), B-Bc.

GOUFFÉ, A.

2022 Gand et Bernardel (Exp.). *Vente aux enchères publiques, par suite de décès d'une tres-belle contre-basse de Montagnana . . . Hotel Drouot . . . 29 novembre, 1875.* Paris: 1875. 3 pp., 29 lots.

> Copy at GB-Lbl (Hirsch).

GRAVE, HYACINTHE de. *See under* **FIERS, F.**

GULLEN, J. A.

2023 Bom, H. G. *Catalogus van de belangrijke en kostbare Bibliotheken, nagelaten door . . . Ds. P. Beets . . . A. F. de Boer . . .* [et al] *en J. A. Gullen, Organist te Amsterdam. . . . Muziek-instrumenten* [etc.] *Verkooping . . . 1 October 1901 en twaalf volgende Dagen. . . .* Amsterdam: 1901. 235 pp., 2647 + 985 lots.

> Musical items are Gullen's. Music, pp. 194-210
> (lots 147-374); Instruments, p. 210 (lots 375-404).
> Copy at NL-Avb.

GUNN, JOHN

2024 Musgrave, W. P., firm. *A Catalogue of the Select and Entire Musical Library of the Late . . . Likewise Excellent Flutes, Violins, Tenors, Violoncellos and Piano-Fortes, by the Most Approved Makers . . . Sold by Auction . . . June 1 & 2, 1824.* [London]: 1824. 22 pp., 257 lots.

> Instruments, lots 1-35. Film copy at NBuU-M (BUu).

GWILT, JOSEPH. *See under* **CERUTTI, Signor** *and* **NALDI, GIUSEPPE**

HACKETT, CHARLES DANVERS

2025 Puttick & Simpson, firm. *Catalogue of a Collection of . . . Music Including a Selection from the Library of . . . C. D. Hackett . . . with Plates and Copyrights. . . . Also Musical Instruments . . . Sold Feb. 23rd, 1859, and Two Following Days.* 29 pp., 762 lots.

> Instruments, lots 735-62 (Hackett's?).
> Catalogue no. 564. Copy also at NN (NYp).

HADDOCK, GEORGE

Literature

2026 "Versteigerung berühmter Geigen," *ZfI* 30 (1909/10): 749.

> Reported from the *Berliner Tageblatt.* Auction sale
> catalogue not located.

HADDOCK, Mrs. HILDA. *See under* **HAWES, W.**

HÄMMERLE, THEODOR

Literature

2027 Poller, Anton. "Die Streichinstrumenten-Sammlung von Hämmerle in Wien,"
ZfI 43 (1922/23): 667, 669.

HAL, FRANCOIS van

2028 Fievez, Joseph, firm. *Catalogue de la bibliothèque, gravures, musique et
instruments de musique provenant de la succession de feu M. Francois Van Hal
(La vente publique le 6 avril et trois jours suivants).* . . . Bruxelles: Fievez, 1900.

> Not examined. Noted in *ZiMG* 1900, p. 256.
> Copy at B-Bc.

HAMELSVELD, Y. van; J. MICHEL

2029 Gartman, van der Hey en Schmidt, firm. *Catalogus van twee Verzameling.* . . .
Boeken in alle Faculteiten. . . . *Eene collectie Teekeningen en Printen.* . . .
Muzyk en Muzykinstrumenten . . . nagelaten door . . . [October 5-10, 1812].
Te Amsterdam: 1812. 4, 109 pp., 3299 lots.

> "Muzyk-Instrumenten," p. 102 (20 lots).
> Copy at NL-Avb.

HAMMER, CHRISTIAN

2030 Heberle, J. M. (H. Lempertz' Söhne), firm. *Katalog der reichhaltigen und
ausgewählten Kunst-Sammlung des Museums Christian Hammer in Stockholm.
Serie II. Topfereien, Majoliken, Fayencen . . .* [etc.]. *Die Sammlung der
Musikinstrumente. Versteigerung zu Köln den 29. Mai bis 3. Juni 1893.* . . .
Köln: 1893. 132 pp., 1534 lots, gr. 4°

> "Musikinstrumente," pp. [117]-32 + 6 pls. showing
> all the instruments in the sale. Lots 1324-1534.
> Copies at NNMM (NYmm) and NL-Apk.

HAMMOND, E.

2031   Puttick & Simpson, firm. *Catalogue of Old Italian and Other Violins, Violas,* [etc.] , *Including the Collection of the Late . . . A Beckstein. . . . Pianola . . . Sold . . . October 18th, 1923.* 10 pp., 192 lots.

> Hammond's instruments, lots 139-63. Catalogue no. 5901.

HARDE, G. W.

2032   van Os. [An auction, February 14, 1763, at La Haye noted by Lugt* containing 8, 309 pp. and 5642 lots, 27 of which were musical instruments. The only location offered by Lugt*—the Kupferstichkabinett in Dresden—reports that their copy was destroyed in WWII.]

HARDING, GEORGE F.

2033   *Collection of Musical Instruments* [in the George F. Harding Museum] . [Chicago: 19--.]   2 typed lvs.

> Copy at NBuU-M (BUu).

Literature

2034   [A note about the Sotheby Parke Bernet auction of musical instruments in New York City, October 29, 1976 (see citation here under **GINGRICH**) that included keyboard items from the Harding Museum, lots 1-54 and lot 57.]   In Kass, Philip. "An American First: Musical Instruments at the Tepper Galleries and the Sotheby Parke Bernet," *Journal of the Violin Society of America* 2, no. 4 (Fall 1976): 84-88.

HARDING, ROSAMOND E. M.

2035   Puttick & Simpson, firm. *Catalogue of Old and Modern Violins, Violas, and Violoncellos . . . Bows, Antique Instruments, &cc., Including the Property of Miss Susan Luskington. . . . Miss Harding . . . Sold . . . March 25th, 1936.* 8 pp., 134 lots.

> Harding's instruments, lots 95-134; Luskington's, 79 only.
> Catalogue no. 7377.

2036   Sotheby & Co., firm. *Catalogue of Oriental Rugs and Carpets, the Property of Lady St. Vincent. . . . Musical Instruments, Including . . . Early Pianos and an English Spinet, 1726, the Property of . . . Sold . . . December 17th, 1954. . . .* [London]: 1954. 24 pp., 196 lots.

        Harding's instruments, lots 83-96.

HARPER, A. E. *See under* **PURRIER, V.**

HARPER, THOMAS

2037   Sotheby, Wilkinson & Hodge, firm. *Catalogue of Decorative Porcelain, Pottery* [etc.], *the Property of Mrs. Timmins. . . . A Collection of Trumpets, the Property of the Late Mr. Thomas Harper . . . Sold . . . 22nd of December, 1898, and Following Day.* London: 1898. 36 pp., 499 lots.

        Harper's trumpets, lots 372-85.

HART, GÜNTER

    Literature

2038   "Das Musikinstrumentensammlung von Pastor Hart in Oberg," *Glareana* 15, no. 2 (1966): lvs. 2-16. ca. 85 items.

HAWES, W.; Mrs. HILDA HADDOCK; J. E. SMITH

2039   Puttick & Simpson, firm. *Catalogue of Valuable Violins, Violas, and Violoncellos, Including The English Quartette . . . Property of J. E. Smith. . . . The First Portion of the Collection Formed by W. Hawes. . . . Bows . . . from the Haddock Collection . . . Sold . . . June 14th, 1928.* 14 pp., 187 lots.

        Haddock Collection, property of Mrs. Hilda Haddock, lots 153-70; "The Old English Quartette," lots 114-17; Hawes' instruments, lots 9-113. Catalogue no. 6496.

    Literature

2040   "Geigenversteigerung in London," *ZfI* 48 (1927/28): 1049.

        A cryptic list of items sold and prices fetched.

HAWKES, WILLIAM HENRY. *See Section I under* **EDGWARE (U. K.). BOOSEY & HAWKES GROUP. MUSEUM**

HAWKINS, JOHN SIDNEY

2041   Wheatley, Mr., auctioneer. *A Catalogue of a Large and Valuable Collection of Musical Instruments, the Property of . . . (Son of the Celebrated Writer . . .); Also an Exceedingly Curious Collection of Treatises on Music . . . Fourteen Fine-Toned Violoncellos . . . and Upwards of Twenty Violins and Tenors . . . Sold by Auction . . . the 26th Day of June, 1832.* 11 pp., 204 lots.

  Copy at GB-Lbl (S. C. W. 19 [4]).

HAWKSMOOR, NICHOLAS. *See under* MERCER, Hon. Col. JOHN

HAWLEY, ROYAL DE FOREST

2042   Lyon & Healy, firm. *Catalogue of Fine Violins: m d cccc i i i. Including the Very Celebrated Historic Violins Which Formed the Well-Known Hawley Collection.* [Chicago: c1903.] 140 pp., 20 pp. (illus.), 396 lots.

  Copy at NL-DHgm.

2043   Lyon & Healy, firm. *The Hawley Collection of Violins; With a History of Their Makers . . .* [etc.]. Chicago: Lyon & Healey, 1904. 105 pp., illus. (36 pls.).

  Introduction by Theodore Thomas. Copy at DLC (Wc).

HEATH

2044   Foster, Mr. Edw., auctioneer. *Greek Street, Soho Square. A Catalogue of the Household Furniture. Two Fine Cabinet Piano-Fortes, Music & Musical Instruments. A Fine-Toned Amati Violoncello, &c. . . . Part Removed from Wilton Place, Knightsbridge . . . Sold . . . the 28th of May, 1831. . . .* [London]: 1831. 12 pp., 259 + 14 lots.

  Copy at GB-Lva. Lugt* identifies collector as Heath.

HEATHCOTE, WILLIAM

2045   Robins, Mr. George, auctioneer. *A Catalogue of Lord Bute's Celebrated Mechanical Organ, with 64 Barrels, Set with Music from the Most Eminent Composers, It Has Besides a Finger Organ . . . Once the Property of the Earl of Shaftesbury . . . Also a Magnificent Finger Organ . . . from the Residence of William Heathcote . . . Sold . . . At His Great Room in Covent Garden . . . the 28th Day of April, 1835.* 3 pp., 2 lots.

  Copy: compiler.

HEATHER, WILLIAM, ca. 1563-1627

Literature

2046　Crum, Margaret. [Some discussion of Heather's books, music and musical instruments, given to Oxford University in 1627], *M & L* 48 (1967): 23-34.

HECKEL, WILHELM

2047　Groffy, Franz. *Musikhistorisches Museum Heckel-Biebrich, Abteilung Fagotte.* Wiesbaden-Biebrich: Wilhelm Heckel, 1968. 108 pp., illus.

　　　　Review by Karl Ventzke in *Das Musikinstrument* 17 (1968): 1008-10, and in *Glareana* 17, no. 2 (1968): lvs. 8-9.

Literature

2048　Altenburg, W. "Reinklingende Blechblasinstrumente und deren Herstellung durch W. Heckel in Biebrich," *ZfI* 23 (1902): 4.

HELLIER, SAMUEL

2049　"A Catalog of Musical Instruments [reprint of an early inventory, almost 200 years old]," *GSJ* 18 (1965): 5-6.

　　　　Collection was later owned by T. B. Shaw-Hellier; now in Warwick (U. K.) County Museum.

HEMETT, JACOB

2050　Christie, Mr., auctioneer. *A Catalogue of the Valuable and Extensive Library of Manuscript and Printed Music, Capital Cremona Violins, a Fine Toned Double Key'd Harpsichord by Kirkman, with Merlin's Stop, a Capital Pedal Harp . . . Sold . . . the 18th of June, 1791.* London: 1791. 4 pp., 87 lots.

　　　　Instruments, lots 1-29, 39-56, 76-87.

"HENRI, PRINCE" (i.e., Prins HENDRIK DER NEDERLANDEN, 1820-1879)

2051　*Catalogue de la collection du Musée renomme sous le nom de "Musée du Prince Henri." La vente . . . à la Haye, 19 Août 1889, dans l'Hotel Passage. . . .* La Haye: 1889. 58, 2 pp.

　　　　Group D, "Collection d'instruments," pp. 33-38 (45 lots). Copy at NL-Avb.

HENRY VIII, King of England, 1491-1547

2052 "The Musical Instruments of King Henry VIII. From an Inventory of the Guarderobes, etc., 1547 (Brit. Mus., Harl. 1419)." In Galpin, F. W. *Old English Instruments of Music,* pp. 292-300. 3rd ed. London: 1932.

2053 "The Musical Instruments of King Henry VIII." In Russell, Raymond. *The Harpsichord and Clavichord,* pp. 155-60. London: Faber, [1959]. 2nd rev. ed. London and New York: [1973].

HERRERA MATA, OSCAR. *See Section I under* **COSTA RICA. MUSEO ECCLESIASTICO**

HERRMANN, EMIL (L87) [N.B.: The collection is now at Yale University but may not be that described in these catalogues. The citations are from a European antiquariat's catalogue; the actual items not located though Mr. Herbert Goodkind, of Goodkind and Chapman, Violins, indicates that he has copies of the catalogues—in English. Not examined.]

2054 *Meistergeigen aus dem Besitz von Emil Herrmann.* Berlin: 1926/27. 46 lvs., illus.

2055 *Rare Violins. Meistergeigen.* Berlin: 1927/28. 58 lvs., illus.

Literature

2056 Wechsberg, Joseph. "Profile: Trustee in Fiddledale - Emil Herrmann (1888-1968)," *New Yorker* (October 17 & 24, 1953).

HESS, ALBERT G.

Literature

2057 "Eine Sammlung alter Musikinstrument in Amerika," *Hausmusik* (Kassel) (1952), pp. 86-87.

HEYER, WILHELM [N.B.: Heyer enlarged his basic collection by the third Leipzig collection of Paul De Wit (see "*Literature*" in this section); by most of the Museum of Baron Alessandro Kraus in Florence in 1908 (see catalogues, this section, nos. **2119-32**); by the piano collection of the firm Rudolf Ibach, Barmen; and by the collection of Ernst Praetorius. The museum opened in 1913 as the Musikhistorisches Museum Wilhelm Heyer (see no. **2061** below), with 2600 instruments. In 1926 it was bought by the State of Saxony, with help from F. Hinrichsen, and transferred from Cologne to the University at Leipzig (see catalogues under Leipzig in Section I, nos. **684-98**). In WWII it was in the Grassi-Museum and about forty percent destroyed. The Musikinstrumenten-Museum of the Karl-Marx-Universität was established in 1954 (see catalogues after that date in Section I). Other collections belonging to Heyer—not instruments—were sold in 1927 in four sales; catalogues by Henrici and Liepmannssohn. See *MGG**.]

2058   Kinsky, Georg. *Musikhistorisches Museum von Wilhelm Heyer in Cöln. Katalog von Georg Kinsky, Konservator des Museum.* Leipzig: Kommissions-Verlag von Breitkopf & Härtel, 1910-16. 4 vols., illus.

> Vol. 1, Keyboard instruments; vol. 2, Plectral
> and stringed instruments; vol. 3, never published
> (but see no. **2059** below); vol. 4, Musical autographs.
> Duckles 3:1592. Copies at NN (NYp), DLC (Wc), etc.

2059   Kinsky, Georg. *Kleiner Katalog der Sammlung alter Musikinstrumente, verfasst von Georg Kinsky.* Cöln: Breitkopf & Härtel, 1913. 250 pp.

> Contains entries for wind instruments which,
> presumably, would have been in the unpublished
> vol. 3. Copy at MiU (AAu).

Literature

2060   Lessmann, Otto. "Vom musikhistorischen Museum von Wilhelm Heyer in Cöln," *Allgemeine Musik-Zeitung* 38 (1911): 335-37; 40 (1913): 74-75.

2061   [Kinsky, Georg.] *Zur eröffnung des Musikhistorischen Museums von Wilhelm Heyer, Cöln, am 20. September 1913.* [Cöln: Druck von J. P. Bachem, 1913.] 36 pp., illus.

> I. Sammlung alter Musikinstrumente: pp. 8-18.
> An article with the same title appeared in *ZfI*
> 34 (1913/14): 29, 31 (Kinsky not mentioned).

2062   Frankenstein, L. "Ein musikhistorisches Museum," *Musikpädagogische Blätter* 36 (1913): 101-2.

2063   Kinsky, Georg. "Die Instrumentensammlung des musikhistorisches Museum in Köln," *Deutsche Musikerzeitung* 50, no. 1 (1925): 5-6.

2064   "Verkauf des musikhistorischen Museums von Wilh. Heyer in Köln nach Leipzig," *ZfI* 46 (1925/26): 879.

2065   Closson, Ernest. "Le Musée Heyer de Cologne cédé à Leipzig," *Revue musicale* 8 (July 1927): 64-66.

2066   Kahn, Joh. "Die Versteigerung des musikhistorischen Museums Heyer-Köln," *Allgemeine Musik-Zeitung* 54 (1927): 559.

HICKSON, THOMAS; WILLIAM BEADELL

2067   Puttick & Simpson, firm. *Catalogue of an Extensive and Valuable Collection of Musical Instruments, Including the Collection of the Late. . . . The Residue of the Beadell Collection . . . and Many Others . . . Sold . . . October 24th, 1887.* 13 pp., 346 lots.

> Hickson's instruments, lots 103-31 (not a very interesting group). Beadell collection items not identified. First sale of Beadell items, no. **1935**. Catalogue no. 2524.

HIESTAND-SCHNELLMANN, JOSEPH   (J123)

Literature

2068   "Ausstellung von Instrumenten aus der Sammlung Hiestand, Freienbach, im Instrumentenkabinett Paul R. Bänziger, Zürich," *Glareana,* vol. 3, no. 6 (1957). 26 items.

2069   "Die Musikinstrumentensammlung von Joseph Hiestand-Schnellmann," *Glareana* 11 (1962): lvs. 2-3.

HILL & SONS, firm. *See Section I under* OXFORD (U. K.). UNIVERSITY. ASHMOLEAN MUSEUM

HIPKINS, ALFRED JAMES

2070   Puttick & Simpson, firm. *Catalogue of the Valuable Property of Violins, Violas, Violoncellos, etc. . . . the Property of . . . Will Be Sold . . . December the 7th, 1897.* 15 pp., 112 lots.

> Hipkins' instruments, lots 36-112. The collection went to The Royal College of Music. Catalogue no. 3273. Copy also at NRU (Rs).

Literature

2071   "Messrs. Puttick and Simpson's Guaranteed Sale," *Violin Times* 5 (1896/97): 50.

> A long list.

HODGES, EDWARD. *See under* **COCKBURN, D.**

HOOF, HECTOR van

2072 van Herck, Eug.(Exp.); P. Thuysbaert (C.P.). *Catalogue d'une belle collection d'antiquités.... Meubles, coffres.... Instruments de musique...formant la collection de... dont la vente publique... 12 [-13] Décembre 1894....* Lokeren: 1894. 40 pp., 546 lots.

> Instruments, 32 lots, according to Lugt*; not examined.
> Copies at B-Gu, B-Bmr.

HOPWOOD, W. *See under* **COCKBURN, D.**

HORNIMAN, FREDERICK J. *See Section I under* **LONDON (U. K.). HORNIMAN MUSEUM AND LIBRARY**

HOTTINGER, HENRY

2073 *The Henry Hottinger Collection.* [n.p.]: R. Wurlitzer, 1967. 1 vol., unpaged, of pls.

> Thirty-four rare violins, thirteen of them Strads.
> Copy at DLC(Wc).

HOWARD, VINCENT

2074 Sotheby Parke Bernet, firm. *The Vincent Howard Collection of Bows... Sold ... 3rd May, 1979....* 34 pp., 71 lots, illus.

Literature

2075 Lewin, Robert. "Sotheby's May [1979] Sale," *The Strad* 90, no. 1069 (May 1979): 45-47.

HUG & CO., firm, Zürich   [N.B.: The private collection of historical instruments was exhibited in the Museum Bellerive in Zürich in 1916. Catalogue of that exhibit not found. Since 1962 the collection has been part of that museum, q.v., Section I.]

2076   *Catalogue of 452 Old Violins, Altos and Cellos. . . .* Zürich: Gebruder Hug & Co., [ca. 1925].

> Expert: E. Tenucci, according to Otto Haas
> antiquariat's catalogue no. 15, item 299.
> Not otherwise verified or located.

Literature

2077   Nef, Karl. "Eine historische Musikinstrumentensammlung in Zürich," *Schweizerische Musikzeitung*, vol. 49 (1909).

> Not located.

2078   Matzke, Hermann. "Das Züricher Musikinstrumenten-Museum," *ZfI* 57 (1936/37): 270-71.

HULSE, JOSEPH S.

2079   Puttick & Simpson, firm. *Catalogue of the Valuable Collection of Violins, Tenors, Violoncellos, Double Basses, etc. of . . . Sold . . . June 25th, 1883.* 8 pp., 107 lots.

> Catalogue no. 2187.

HUME, FREDERICK WILLIAM; HARLINGTON JONES; R. H. CAPPS

2080   Puttick & Simpson, firm. *Catalogue of Musical Instruments . . . Violins, Violas [etc.] . . . the Property of the Late . . . Sold . . . July 26th, 1904.* 12 pp., 253 lots.

> Hume's instruments, lots 103-26; Jones', 127-34;
> Capp's, 151-56A. Catalogue no. 3852.

HURGRONJE, CHRISTIAAN SNOUCK. *See Section I under* **LEYDEN (Netherlands). RIJKSMUSEEN VOOR VOLKENKUNDE**

HUTCHINSON, JOHN; FREDERICK HALLIDAY

2081   Puttick & Simpson, firm. *Catalogue of Musical Instruments . . . Pianofortes . . .*
Harmoniums and Organs . . . Violins, Violas, & Violoncellos . . . the Property of
Sir Frederick Halliday; Also a Collection of Modern Violins . . . the Property
of the Late J. Hutchinson, Esq., of Barnsley, and a Few Lots of Music . . . Sold
July the 24th, 1894. 14 pp., 391 lots.

> Instruments, lots 1-312; Hutchinson's, 157-222;
> Halliday's, 69-70.

Literature

2082   Trinita D[ei] M[onti]. "The Hutchinson Sale . . . [on July 24th, 1894, at
Puttick & Simpson]," *Violin Times* 1 (1893/94): 148-49.

> A good description of about 50 lots.

IBACH, RUDOLF. *See under* HEYER, WILHELM

ISABEL I, la Catolico, Queen of Spain, 1451-1504

2083   "Inventario instrumental de Isabel la Catolica. 1503." Ms. in Spain, Archivo
general de Simancas, Patronato real, leg. no. 3. Extracts in Pedrell, F. *Emporio*
cientifico e historico de Organografia, pp. 91-92. Barcelona: Juan Gili, 1901.

> Copy at NBuU-M. See also Straeten*,
> vol. 7, pp. 199-211.

ISTITUTO ESPOSTI. *See under* CONTARINI-CORRER COLLECTION

IVEAGH, EDWARD CECIL GUINNESS, 1st EARL

2084   *Catalogue of the Iveagh Bequest.* London & Harrow: [1930]. 31 pp.

> Instruments? Not examined.

JAFFRAY, FRED

Literature

2085   Schmidt, Georg. "Versteigerung der Sammlung altitalienischer Meisterinstrumenten
aus dem Nachlass von Fred Jaffray in Melbourne," *ZfI* 50 (1929/30): 776, 778, 780.

JAMES, W. R., of Heathfield

2086   Puttick & Simpson, firm. *Catalogue of an Extensive and Valuable Collection of Musical Instruments . . . Pianofortes . . . Organs, Harmoniums . . . a Number of Valuable Violins, Violas* [etc.], *Including the Collection of the Late. . . . Also Brass and Wood Wind Instruments . . . Sold . . . February 23rd, 1886.* 8 pp., 226 lots.

James' instruments, lots 59-72. Catalogue no. 2392.

JAMESON, Dr., of Cheltenham

2087   Musgrave, W. P., firm. *A Catalogue of the Musical Library and Instruments of the Late. . . . Violins, Tenors, Violoncellos, Flutes, & Flageolets, Bugles, Bassoon, &c. . . . Square, Cabinet, Celestina, and Upright Grand Piano-Fortes by Clementi & Co., Stodart, Wilkinson, &c. . . . Sold June 7, 1825.* [London] : 1825. 14 pp., 154 lots.

Instruments, lots 105-47. Copy at GB-LBl. Film copy at NBuU-M (BUu).

JANSEN, WILLI   (J96)

Literature

2088   "Fagott-Sammlung Willi Jansen, Loosdrecht," *Glareana,* vol. 8, no. 3 (1959). "Nachtrag," *Glareana,* vol. 11, no. 1 (1962).

JANSSEN, CURT. *See Section I under* **CLAREMONT, CALIFORNIA (USA).** **CLAREMONT GRADUATE SCHOOL. JANSSEN COLLECTION**

JENKINSON, CHARLES CECIL, 3rd Earl of Liverpool, 1784-1851. *See under* **LEA, T.**

JIMÉNEZ BORJA, ARTURO. *See Section I under* **LIMA (Peru). MUSEO DE LA CULTURA PERUANA. COLLECION ARTURO JIMÉNEZ BORJA**

JOHANN FRIEDRICH, Herzog, 1585-1628. *See Section I under* **STUTTGART (Germany). STUTTGARTER HOFKAPELLE**

JOHANN GEORG II, Kurfürsten von Sachsen. *See Section I under* **DRESDEN (Germany). K. SÄCHSISCHE MUSIK-KAPELLE**

JOHANN GEORGE II, Fürst von Brandenburg, 1571-1598. *See also under* **FRIEDRICH WILHELM DER GROSSE**

2089　"Instrumenteninventar 1582." Ms. in Kgl. Hausarchiv, Rep. XIX, Pers. Spec. Reprinted in Sachs, Curt. *Musik und Oper,* pp. 205-7. Berlin: Bard, 1910.

JONES, G. N.; "A DISTINGUISHED PROFESSOR"

2090　Puttick & Simpson, firm. *Catalogue of a Large and Interesting Assemblage of Music and Instruments, Including the Collection of . . . G. N. Jones . . . Sold . . . Nov. 28, 1857.* 16 pp., 372 lots.

> Instruments, lots 301-72; Jones', 333-72; those of "A Distinguished Professor of the Violoncello," 308-32. Catalogue no. 516. Copy also at NN (NYp).

JONES, W. H. HAMMOND

2091　Puttick & Simpson, firm. *Catalogue of the Valuable Collection of Violins, Violas, Violoncellos, etc., Including the Property of the Late . . . and a Few Antique Instruments . . . Sold . . . Saturday, December 10th, 1898.* 14 pp., 112 lots.

> Catalogue no. 3346. Copy also at NRU (Rs).

JOYCE, J. W., of Beckington; CIPRIANI POTTER

2092　Puttick & Simpson, firm. *Catalogue of a Most Important and Extensive Assemblage of Musical Instruments . . . Forty Pianofortes . . . Organs. . . . Valuable Italian and Other Violins, Violins* [sic] *Violoncellos and Double Basses; Including the Collection of the Late J. W. Joyce . . . Sold November 22, 1881.* 9 pp., 229 lots.

> Instruments, lots 1-216; Joyce's, 117-27; Property of the late Cipriani Potter, lots 136-216.

KARL von Neisse, Erzherzog von Habsburg, Bischof von Breslau und Brixen, d. 1624

2093　"Inventarium oder verzaichnus aller posidifn, regaln, fliegeln oder clavizimbeln und andern instrumenten, von pfeifen und seidenwerkh, sowoll aller und jeder bücher, gross und khlein, gescriebener und gedruckter, Lateinisch und Wälschen concerten, so ihr hochfürstliche durchlaucht hochseeligster gedechtnus alhiero in der Neiss in ihrer erherzoglichen capellen verlassen, wie volget: . . . Item von

KARL von Neisse, Erzherzog von Habsburg *continued*

alten und neuen authoribus allerlai pücher von motetten, messen . . . so alle von dem Antonio Cifra mit einem ordentlichen inventario eingeantwortt, welches inventari verlohren und jetzigem capellmaister Stephano Bernardo nichts eingeantwortet auch sich nichts darumb wil annemben." Reprinted in *Jahrbuch des kunsthistorischen Sammlungen des Kaiserhauses* 33 (1915): LXXVI-LXXVII. An inventory of 1625.

KARL von Steiermark, Erzherzog von Innerösterreich, 1540-1590

2094   (1577) "Verzaichnus Irer Frl. Dur: etc. Instrumenten, Trometten vnnd Gesanng Püecher, auch was darzue gehörig, so ich durch Merten Camerlannder den vierten Juni im aiebenundsiebenzigisten Jar, auch aines Thayls hernach, höchsternenter Irer Frl: Drht: Öbristen Musico Siman Gatto einantwortten vnd übergeben hab lassen." Ms. in Vienna, Haus-, Hof- und Staats-archiv. Hofakten des Ministeriums des Innern, I C 4, Kart. 7, fols. 20-21. Reprinted in Federhofer, Helmut. *Musikpflege und Musiker am Grazer Habsburgerhof der Erzherzöge Karl und Ferdinand von Innerösterreich (1564-1619)*, pp. 281-82. Mainz: B. Schotts Söhne, [1967]. 189 items.

2095   (1590) "Inventari aller und jeder varnus, so nach gottseeligen absterben weilen des . . . herrn Caroln. . . . Volgen instrumenten und saitenspil." Ms. in Vienna, Haus-, Hof- und Staats-archiv. Hofakten des Ministeriums des Inner, I C 4 Kart. 8, fols. 69-75. Reprinted in *Jahrbuch des allerhöchsten Kaiserhauses* 7 (1888): xvii.

2096   (1590) "Inventari aller und jeder varnus, so nach gottseeligen absterben weilen des . . . herrn Caroln. . . . Volgen instrumenten und saitenspil." Ms. in Vienna, Haus-, Hof- und Staats-archiv. Hofakten des Ministeriums des Inner, I C 4 Kart. 8, fols. 69-75. Reprinted in Federhofer, Helmut. *Musikpflege und Musiker am Grazer Habsburgerhof . . .*, pp. 283-85. Mainz: B. Schotts Söhne, [1967].

2097   (1590) "Inventari aller und jeder varnus, so nach gottseeligen absterben weilen des . . . herrn Caroln. . . . Volgen instrumenten und saitenspil." Ms. in Vienna, Haus-, Hof- und Staats-archiv. Hofakten des Ministeriums des Inner, I C 4 Kart. 8, fols. 69-75. Reprinted in Schlosser, Julius. *Die Sammlung alter Musikinstrumente . . . (1518)*, pp. 19-20. Wien: Schroll, 1920. Reprint ed. Hildesheim: Olms, 1974.

Literature

2098   Wallner, Bertha Antonia. *Musikalische Denkmäler der Steinsätzkunst des 16. und 17. Jahrhunderts*. München: Lentner, 1912. viii, 546 pp.; see especially p. 76.

KASTON, HENRYK. *See Section I under* **NEW YORK, NEW YORK (USA). LIBRARY AND MUSEUM OF THE PERFORMING ARTS**

KAUDERN, WALTER

Literature

2099 *Musical Instruments in Celebes.* (Ethnographical Studies in Celebes; Results of the Author's Expedition, 1917-1920, vol. 3.) [Göteborg: Elanders Bok. Aktiebolaget, 1927.] xiii, 322 pp., illus.

> Most of the instruments discussed and illustrated are, apparently, part of the author's collection. Copies at MiU (AAu), DLC (Wc), etc.

KAYSER, CARL GANGOLF

2100 Löscher, firm. *Auctions-Katalog der Sammlung aus dem Nachlasse des Architekten. . . . Glas, Porzellan, Majolika, Steinzeug . . . Versteigerung 18. März und die folgenden Tage. . . .* Wien: 1896. 44 pp., illus., 1613 lots.

> Instruments, lots 1023-43. Copies at NL-DHrk, A-Wal, D-brd-Mbn.

KEAT, D.

2101 Puttick & Simpson, firm. *Catalogue of Old Italian and Other Violins* [etc.] . *Brass and Wood Wind Instruments, Including the Property of the Late . . . Sold . . . October 23rd, 1925.* 10 pp., 210 lots.

> Keat's instruments, lots 177-210. Catalogue no. 6153. First sale.

2102 Puttick & Simpson, firm. *Catalogue of Old Italian and Other Violins* [etc.] *. . . the Property of Benedetti Valvona, J. George Moss, and D. K. (2nd portion) . . . Sold . . . November 26th, 1925.* 10 pp., 175 lots.

> Keat's instruments, lots 155-75; Valvona and Moss properties, a few lots each. Catalogue no. 6168. Second portion.

2103 Puttick & Simpson, firm. *Catalogue of Old Italian and Other Violins* [etc.] . *Brass and Wood Wind Instruments, Property of D. Keat* [3rd portion] *. . . Sold . . . January 21st, 1926.* 11 pp., 238 lots.

> Keat's instruments, lots 186-238.

KEIL, ALFREDO　[N. B.: For articles and catalogues of the collection after 1915, see Section I under **LISBON (Portugal). CONSERVATORIO NACIONAL.**]

2104　[Keil, Alfredo.] *Breve noticia dos instrumentos de música antigos e modernos do Colleção Keil.* Lisbon: Typ. do Annuario Commercial, 1904.

>　　Lambertini* notes 400 items; not examined.
>　　Copy at P-Ln.

2105　Lambertini, Michel'angelo. *Primeiro nucleo de um museu instrumental em Lisboa; catalogo sommario.* [Lisboa?]: 1914. 147 pp., illus.

>　　Copies at CU (BEu), IaU (IOu), DLC (Wc),
>　　NBuU-M (BUu).

Literature

2106　Keil, Alfredo. *Colleções e museus de arte em Lisboa.* Lisboa: Livraria Ferreira & Oliveira, 1905. 54 pp.

>　　Copy at NBuU-M (BUu).

2107　Lambertini, Michel'angelo. *As colleções d'instrumentos musicos.* Lisboa: Typ. do Annuario Commercial, 1913. 22 pp.

2108　Lambertini, Michel'angelo. *O museu instrumental e as minhas relações com o Estado.* Lisboa: Typ. do Annuario Commercial, 1913.

>　　Copy at P-Ln.

KELVEY, CHARLES. *See under* **GOODHART, J. H.**

KENNEDY, T[HOMAS?]

2109　Puttick & Simpson, firm. *Catalogue of Musical Instruments, the Well-Known Stock of Mr. T. Kennedy. . . . Upwards of Fifty Violins, Twelve Tenor Violins, Thirty-Five Violoncellos . . .* [etc.] *of Mr. Kennedy's Manufacture. Also Several . . . Formerly in the Possession of Signor Dragonetti . . . Sold . . . May 18, 1849.* 8 pp., 176 lots.

>　　All instruments manufactured by K. Catalogue no. 117.

2110　Puttick & Simpson, firm. *Catalogue of the Very Extensive, Rare and Valuable Musical Library of a Distinguished Professor* [W. Ayrton] *. . . Also the Musical Instruments, Including Some Choice Old Violins . . . a Further Portion of the Stock of Mr. T. Kennedy . . . of Upwards of One Hundred Violins, Tenors* [etc.] *. . . Sold . . . June 23, 1849, and Two Following Days.* 40 pp., 867 lots.

>　　Kennedy's instruments, lots 750-867.

2111 Puttick & Simpson, firm. *Catalogue of an Interesting Collection of Miscellaneous Music, Operas, Oratorios* [etc.] *and Numerous Very Important Musical Instruments, Including . . . a Superb Violin by Stradiuarius, (Probably the Finest in the Country), a Magnificent Violoncello, by Stradiuarius, from the Late Lord Falmouth's Collection, Other Violins and Violoncellos . . . Harps . . . Musical Boxes . . . Sold . . . June 23, 1859.* 14 pp., 304 lots.

> Instruments, lots 161-304, include the Strad "believed to be the most perfect example known," bought by Bligh for 249 guineas. This sale (and that Strad) are noted in Goodkind's* list! Catalogue no. 584.

2112 Puttick & Simpson, firm. *Catalogue of a Large and Varied Collection of Music, Including the Musical Library of . . . R. J. S. Stevens. . . . Also Numerous Musical Instruments, Including the Stock of the Late. . . . Upwards of One Hundred Violins and Tenors, One Hundred Violoncellos, Nineteen Fine Double Basses* [etc.] *Sold . . . March 27th, 1872, and Following Day.* 23 pp., 708 lots.

> Kennedy's instruments, lots 448-708. Catalogue no. 1202. Copy also at NN (NYp).

KENNEY, PLUNKETT

2113 Phillips, Mr., auctioneer. *A Catalogue of a Small Collection of Cabinet Pictures. . . . Valuable Old Italian Violins and Miscellaneous Property, the Property of. . . . Also a Magnificent and Powerful Finger and Barrel Organ . . . Sold . . . the 31st Day of May, 1858. . . .* [London]: 1858. 10 pp., 172 + 8 lots.

> Instruments, lots 35-56 and 135. Copy also at GB-Lva.

KERN, WILLY E. (J121)

2114 [An untitled, photocopied list of 73 bows, including a number of Tourtes, Dodds, Tubbs and Vuillaumes. . . . Bern: 197-?]

> Copy at NBuU-M (BUu).

KETTERINGHAM, T. *See under* STEPHENSON, W.

KEY, L. L. *See Section I under* BIRMINGHAM (U. K.). SCHOOL OF MUSIC

KING, RALPH GORDON NOEL MILBANKE, 2nd Earl of Lovelace. *See under*
LOVELACE

KIRBY, PERCIVAL ROBSON

2115   Kirby, Percival R. *The Musical Instruments of the Native Races of South Africa.*
London: Oxford University Press, 1934.

2116   Kirby, Percival R. *The Musical Instruments of the Native Races of South Africa.*
2nd ed. Johannesburg: Witwatersrand University Press, 1965. xxiii, 293 pp.,
73 pls.

> Not catalogues, but discussed are some 300-plus
> instruments from Kirby's collection, now in the
> Africana Museum in Johannesburg.

Literature

2117   Kirby, Percival Robson. "My Museum of Musical Instruments," *SAMAB. South
African Museums Assoc.-Suid Afrikaanse Museums Assos. Bulletin* 4, no. 1
(1947): 7-13. illus.

KIRK, J. L. *See Section I under* **YORK (U. K.). CASTLE MUSEUM**

KOEN?

2118   *Catalogus excellentissimorum librorum. Onder dez. een partye muzykboeken
en muzyk-instrumenten. Naargelassen door Ger. Koen, J. v. B. en K. v. V.*
's-Gravenhage: van Thol, 1741.

> Cited from Bobillier*; not otherwise verified or located.

KÖRNER, THEODOR. *See Section I under* **DRESDEN (Germany). KÖRNER-MUSEUM**

KOUSSEVITZKY, SERGE. *See under* **JERUSALEM (Israel). BEZALEL MUSEUM**

KRAUS, ALESSANDRO [N. B.: After the collector's death about 500 items were dispersed, most to the Musikhistorisches Museum Wilhelm Heyer in Cologne (see elsewhere in this section), some eventually to the Conservatorio di musica L. Cherubini in Florence.]

2119 Kraus, Alessandro. *Musée Kraus à Florence. Catalogue des instruments de musique anciens et modernes du Musée Kraus.* Firenze: Tip. dell'Arte della Stampa, 1878. 30 pp.

> Introductory note is signed: Alexandre Kraus, Alexandre Kraus, fils. Copies at ICN (Cn) and MiU (AAu).

2120 Kraus, Alessandro, figlio. *La musique au Japon . . . 85 figures en photographie réprésentant les instruments japonais du Musée Kraus à Florence.* Firenze: Imp. de l'arte della Stampa, 1878. 83 pp., 9 mounted photos.

> Copies at CtY (NHu). NN (NYp), DLC (Wc).

2121 Kraus, Alessandro, figlio. *La musique au Japon . . . 85 figures en photographie réprésentant les instruments japonais du Musée Kraus à Florence.* 2nd ed. Firenze: Imp. de l'arte della Stampa, 1879.

> Copies at MiU (AAu), NN (NYp), etc.

2122 Kraus, Alessandro, figlio. *La musique au Japon . . . 85 figures en photographie réprésentant les instruments japonais du Musée Kraus à Florence.* 3rd ed. Firenze: Imp. de l'arte della Stampa, 1880.

> Copies at MiU (AAu) and NNMM (NYmm).

2123 Kraus, Alessandro, figlio. "Collezione etnografico-musicale Kraus in Firenze," *Archivio per l'antropologia e la etnologia,* 31 (1901): 275-97.

2124 [Kraus, Alessandro, figlio.] *Catalogo della collezione etnografico-musicale Kraus in Firenze. Sezione istrumenti musicali.* Firenze: Tip. di S. Landi, 1901. 29 pp., 21 mounted photos.

> Schles* dates 1878; obviously incorrect. Copy at DLC (Wc). Brief inventory of 1,076 items, pp. 7-29.

Literature

2125 "Una collezione di strumenti musicali all'esposizione di Parigi," *Gazzetta musicale di Milano* 33 (1878): 198.

2126 "La collection d'instruments de Mm. Kraus, à l'Exposition universelle," *Echo musical* 10, no. 11 (1878): 3-4.

2127 M[ahillon], V. C. "Le musée Kraus de Florence," *Echo musical* 10, no. 13 (1878): 2.

2128 "Un concert historique à Florence," *Echo musical* 12 (1880): 78-79.

KRAUS, ALESSANDRO   *continued*

2129   Kraus, Alessandro, figlio. "Gli strumenti musicali degli Ostiacchi," *Archivio per l'antropologia e l'etnologia* 11 (1881): 249-54. 1 pl.

2130   "Das Museum Kraus in Florenz," *ZfI* 4 (1883/84): 70, 79.

"... ein Verzeichnis der höchst werthvollen Instrumenten."

2131   *The Kraus ethnographie-psychologie* [sic] *Musical Collection in Florence.* [Florence: 1901.] 37 pp.

Cited from the catalogue of NNMM (NYmm); not examined.

2132   Kraus, Alessandro, figlio. *Etnografia musicale; appunti sulla musica dei popoli nordici. 3 tavole illustrative di strumenti della collezione Kraus.* ... Firenze: Tip. di S. Landi, 1907. 43, 12 pp.

Published separately from the *Archivio per l'antropologia e la etnologia* 37 (1907): 47-87. Copies at NN (NYp) and DLC (Wc).

KURFÜRSTEN VON SACHSEN. *See Section I under* **DRESDEN (Germany).** **K. SÄCHSISCHE MUSIK-KAPELLE**

KYTSON, Sir THOMAS. *See Section I under* **SUFFOLK (U. K.). HENGRAVE HALL**

LACHMANN, ERICH   (L41)

2133   *Catalogue of the Erich Lachmann Collection of Historical Musical Instruments.* ... Los Angeles, Calif.: [193-]. 12 pp.

2134   Lachmann, Erich. *Erich Lachmann Collection of Historical Stringed Musical Instruments.* ... [1st ed.] Los Angeles, Calif.: Allan Hancock Foundation, University of Southern California, 1950. 53 pp., illus., 42 items.

Duckles* 3:1595.

LAFFAGE, ANTONIN. *See Section I under* **ROME (Italy). SOCIETA NAZIONALE "DANTE ALIGHIERI"**

LAMAS, ANTONIO. *See Section I under* **LISBON (Portugal). CONSERVATORIO NACIONAL**

LANDOLCI, E.

2135 Fievez, Jos., firm. *Catalogue des instruments de musique anciens, armes & antiquités, dont la vente publique . . . 17 février 1891 et jour suivant. . . .* [Brussels: Impr. E. Lhoest], 1891. 19 pp., 143+ lots.

> Copy at B-Bcm.

Literature

2136 [A note about the sale in the Saale Ste.-Gudule, Brussels, with a description of some lots], *ZfI* 11 (1890/91): 211, 239.

LANGE, J. P.

2137 de Vries, Roos, & Brondgeest, firm. *Catalogus van eene uitgebreide verzameling schilderijn . . . van . . : alsmede eene belangrijke verzameling . . . muzijk-instrumenten en muzijk-werken . . . verkocht . . . 10den September 1850 . . . door. . . .* [Amsterdam]: 1850. [2], 42, [3] pp., 833 lots.

> "Notitie van musijk-instrumenten en muzijk-werken . . . ," [3] pp. at end, lots 1-42. Instruments, lots 1-26. Copies at NL-Avb, NL-Apk, NL-DHrk, US-NYfrick, F-Pn.

LARSON, ARNE B. *See also citations in Section I under* VERMILLION, SOUTH DAKOTA (USA)

Literature

2138 Stoeckman, D. S. "From Thunder Boom to Lyric Art (the Arne B. Larson 'Shrine to Music')," *School Musician* 33 (June-July 1972): 38-39.

2139 Waltner, Willard and Elma. "Professor Larson's Bible Instruments," *Journal of Church Music* 15 (1973): 2-5. Many illus.

LAURENT, C.

2140 Puttick & Simpson, firm. *Catalogue of a Large and Valuable Assemblage of Musical Properties, Comprising . . . Pianofortes by Broadwood, Collard & Collard, Evans* [etc.] *from the Stock of the Well-Known Manufacturer Mr. C. Laurent . . . Also a Library of Music . . . Sold . . . June 30, 1876.* 21 pp., 468 lots.

> Laurent's instruments, lots 352-86. Catalogue no. [1606].

LAURENT, C. *continued*

2141 Puttick & Simpson, firm. *Catalogue of the Valuable . . . Musical Library of Miss Elizabeth Masson . . . Also of Several Valuable Copyrights. . . . Musical Instruments . . . Pianofortes, about Fifty Harmoniums, Including a Selection from the Stock of Mr. C. Laurent . . . Similar . . . to the Well Known Exhibition Instruments, Manufactured by Mr. Laurent for the Late Mr. Charles Kelly. . . . Collection of Choice Violins and Violoncellos by Stradivarius, the Amatis, and Other Cremona Masters . . . Sold . . . July 31, 1876.* 17 pp., 379 lots.

    Instruments, lots 258-379; Laurent's, 266-306.
    Catalogue no. 1612. Copy also at NN (NYp).

LAW, JAMES H., of Glasgow

2142 Puttick & Simpson, firm. *Catalogue of Old Italian and Other Violins, Violas, Violoncellos* [etc.] *. . . Including the Property of the Late . . . Sold . . . March 7th, 1929.* 9 pp., 172 lots.

    Law's instruments, lots 97-138. Catalogue no. 6585.

LAZARUS, HENRY. *See under* **ROWE, Major**

LEA, T.

2143 Puttick & Simpson, firm. *Catalogue of a Valuable Collection of Music, Including the* [Library] *of the Late Sir Henry R. Bishop . . . the Musical Library of a Distinguished Amateur . . . Also . . . Musical Instruments . . . Sold . . . June 14, 1855, and the Two Following Days.* 36 pp., 877 lots.

    Instruments, lots 700-877; Lea's, 732-788; the
    Earl of Liverpool's [i.e., Charles Cecil Jenkinson],
    789-99; A Band Master's, 827-42. Catalogue no.
    413. Copy also at NN (NYp).

LE COMTE, EUGÈNE [N. B.: No catalogue located though in *Revue musicale*, vol. 6, 1906, Hébert Rouget notes a "vente d'instruments de musique anciens" belonging to Le Comte.]

LEEUWARDEN, J. van. *See under* **MERKMAN, Vve P.**

LEEUWEN BOOMKAMP, CAREL van

2144 *The Carel van Leeuwen Boomkamp Collection of Musical Instruments. Descriptive Catalogue by C. van Leeuwen Boomkamp & J. H. van der Meer.* Amsterdam: Knuf, 1971 [1972]. 190 pp., illus.

> Duckles* 3:1576, "112 items described and illustrated in photos." The collection went to the Gemeentemuseum in The Hague. Catalogue reviewed by A. Baines, *GSJ* 25 (1972): 134-35.

Literature

2145 Paap, W. "De verzameling oude muziekinstrumenten van Carel van Leeuwen Boomkamp," *Mens en melodie* 14 (1959): 386-89.

2146 Paap, W. "De muziekinstrumentenverzameling van Carel van Leeuwen Boomkamp," *Mens en melodie* 27 (1972): 43-47. illus.

2147 Paap, W. "The Carel van Leeuwen Boomkamp Collection of Musical Instruments," *Sonorum speculum* 56 (1974): 36-44. illus.

> English translation of no. **2146.**

LEICESTER, Sir PETER

2148 Halcrow, E. M. *Sir Peter Leicester. Charges to the Grand Jury at Quarter Sessions.* Manchester: 1953.

> A list of his musical instruments, pp. 151-52, according to King*. Not examined.

LEOPOLD V, Erzherzog, 1586-1682. *See Section I under* VIENNA (Austria). KUNSTHISTORISCHES MUSEUM. AMBRAS AND RUHELUST INVENTORIES

LERY, Baron de

2149 *Catalogue des anciens instruments de musique . . . composant l'ancienne collection de M. le Baron de Lery et dont la vente aux enchères publiques aura lieu Hôtel Drouot . . . 14 [-16] juin, 1910. . . .* [Paris: C. Berger], 1910. 44 pp., 12 pls., 491 lots.

> Copy at NN (NYp).

LEWES HOUSE COLLECTION. *See under* WARREN, E. P.

LEWIS (WILLIAM) AND SON, Chicago

2150   *The Lewis Collection: Works of the Makers of the Seventeenth, Eighteenth, and Nineteenth Centuries.* Chicago: W. Lewis, 1947.

Copy at DLC (Wc).

LIVERPOOL, 3rd Earl of (i.e., JENKINSON, CHARLES CECIL, 1784-1851). *See under* LEA, T.

LLOYD, THOMAS EDWARD [et al]

2151   Puttick & Simpson, firm. *Catalogue of a Valuable Collection of Violins, Violas* [etc.] *Including the Properties of the Late Thomas Edward Lloyd* [and others] *. . . Sold . . . June 10th, 1910.* 20 pp., 145 lots.

Lloyd's instruments, lots 53-76. Catalogue no. 4432.

LOBECK, OTTO   [N.B.: According to Jenkins*, 318 of his instruments were given in 1956 to the Basle, Universität, Historisches Museum.]

Literature

2152   Mang, W. "Neuordnung einer schweizerischen Instrumentensammlung," *ZfI* 56 (1935/36): 185-86.

An exhibition in the Musik Schola Cantorum Basiliensis of about 350 items. The article says a catalogue was to be published, but it was not found.

2153   Walter, M. "Die Musikinstrumentensammlung Otto Lobeck," *Schweizerische musikpädagogische Blätter* 27 (1938): 370-72.

LOUIS FERDINAND, Prince of Bavaria, 1859-1949 [N.B.: His collection was exhibited at the INTERNATIONALE AUSSTELLUNG FÜR MUSIK- UND THEATERWESEN, 1892. *See Section I under* VIENNA, no. 1565.]

LOUP

2154   Gand et Bernardel, firm. *Catalogue de la collection, instruments de musique anciens rares et curieux des XVIIe XVIIIe et XIXe siecles. Tableaux, dessins* [etc.] *dont la vente. . . . Hotel Drouot . . . 28* [-30] *Mai 1888.* [Paris] : 1888. 27 pp., 303 lots.

> Instruments, lots 1-293. Copy at B-Bcm.

LOVELACE, [2d] Earl of (i.e., Ralph Gordon Noel Milbanke King, 2d Earl of Lovelace)

2155   Puttick & Simpson, firm. *Catalogue of a Valuable Collection of Violins, Violas, Violoncellos & Bows, Including the Property of the . . . Earl of Lovelace, Deceased . . . Sold . . . December 10th, 1908.* 15 pp., 108 lots.

> The Earl's instruments, lots 61-69 (and very good).
> Catalogue no. 4265.

LUDWIG III, der Fromme von Württemberg, 1554-1594. *See Section I under* STUTTGART (Germany). STUTTGARTER HOFKAPELLE

LUDWIG, Prinz von Bayern, 1859-1949. *See* LOUIS FERDINAND, Prince of Bavaria

M***

2156   Pingeon, G. (Exp.); Gazagne, L. (C. P.). *Vente de M***, de Lyon. Meubles anciens. . . . Armes, instruments de musique, bibelots . . . 12* [-14] *décembre 1888.* Lyon: [Impr. Mougin-Rusand], 1888. 31 pp., 4 pls., 125 lots.

> Copy at F-Pn.

M. . .

2157   Vatelot, E. (Exp.); Ader, Picard et Tajan (C. P.). *Très importante ensemble d'instruments de musique . . . dont la vente . . . Hôtel Drouot . . . 4 décembre 1974. . . .* Paris: 1974. [16] pp., 149 lots (more items).

> Copy at NL-DHgm.

MAC DONAGH, JAMES

2158 Puttick & Simpson, firm. *Catalogue of Old Italian and Other Violons, Violas, and Violoncellos. . . . Bows . . . the Property of the Late A. E. Aplin* [et al] *. . . . Collections of Wood Wind Instruments, Property of the Late James Mac Donagh . . . Sold . . . December 14th, 1933.* 9 pp., 159 lots.

> Aplin's instruments, lots 100-112; Mac Donagh's,
> 136-59. Catalogue no. 7137.

MAC GILLIVRAY, JAMES

2159 Sotheby Parke Bernet, firm. *The James McGillivray Collection of Woodwind Instruments . . . Sold by Auction . . . 8th November 1979.* London: 1979. 26 pp., 71 lots, illus.

MACKAY, J.; WILLIAM HOWARD (of Sheffield)

2160 Puttick & Simpson, firm. *Catalogue of a Valuable Collection of Violins, Violoncellos and Bows, Including a Portion of the Collection Formed by the Late . . . Sold . . . June 24th, 1903.* 16 pp., 146 lots.

> Mackay's instruments are not identified, but
> those the "property of the late William Howard
> of Sheffield" are, lots 140-46. Catalogue no. 3741.

2161 Puttick & Simpson, firm. *Catalogue of Musical Instruments . . . Including the Remaining Portion of the Collection of the Late . . . Small Library of Music . . . Sold . . . June 30th, 1903.* 16 pp., 352 lots.

> Instruments, lots 1-286; Mackay's, 103-34.
> Catalogue no. 3743.

MACRORY, EDMUND

2162 Puttick & Simpson, firm. *Catalogue of a Valuable Collection of Violins, Violas, Violoncellos & Bows . . . Including Property of the Late . . . Sold the 22nd November, 1905.* 15 pp., 104 lots.

> Macrory's instruments, 3 lots only (no. 50-53),
> though they are a Strad, a Guarnerius, and a Dodd bow.
> Catalogue no. 3968. Copy also at NRU (Rs).

MAHILLON, VICTOR *and* **JOSEPH.** *See* Kufferath, no. **322**, *in Section I under* **BRUSSELS (Belgium). EXPOSITION NATIONALE, 1880**

MANGOLD, KARL, and family

2163 Hiestand-Schnellmann, Joseph. "Ausstellung alter Musikinstrumente in Zollikon (Sammlung Mangold)," *Glareana* 13, no. 3/4 (1964): lvs. 6-12. 75 items.

MANSKOPF, NICOLAS. *See Section I under* **FRANKFURT a. M. (Germany). STADT-UND UNIVERSITÄTS-BIBLIOTHEK**

MARIA BARBARA DE BRAGANZA, Queen of Spain, d. 1758

2164 "Inventory of Queen Maria Barbara's Instruments [Madrid. Palacio. Ms. VII E 4 305, fol. 228r-231r]." In Kirkpatrick, Ralph. *Domenico Scarlatti*, p. 361. Princeton, N.J.: Princeton University Press, 1953.

An inventory of 1756.

MARIA DE AUSTRIA, Regent of the Netherlands, 1505-1558

2165 Patie, Rogier. "Cargo de vihuelas, e sacabuches, e pífanos, e cornetas, e otras cosas desta calidad [ca. 1560]." Ms. in Spain, Archivo general de Simancas. Contaduria mayor, leg. 1017, fol. 162ss. Reprinted by Straeten, Edmond van der. *La musique aux Pays-Bas,* vol 7, pp. 439-45. Bruxelles: Muquardt [etc.], 1867-88. Reprint ed. New York: Dover, 1969.

2166 Patie, Rogier. "Cargo de vihuelas, e sacabuches, e pifanos, e cornetas, e otras cosas desta calidad [ca. 1560]." Ms. in Spain, Archivo general de Simancas. Contaduria mayor, leg. 1017, fol. 162ss. Reprinted by Anglés, Higinio. *La musica en la corte de Carlos V,* pp. 11-13. (Monumentos de la música española, 2^1.) Barcelona: 1944.

MARR, ROBERT A. *See under* **EDINBURGH (Scotland). INTERNATIONAL EXPOSITION, 1886**

MARSHALL, J. HERBERT

2167   Puttick & Simpson, firm. *Catalogue of a Large and Varied Assemblage of Musical Instruments . . . Several Collections of Violins, Violas, Violoncellos, and Double Basses . . . Including That of J. Herbert Marshall . . . Sold . . . June 24th, 1884.* 12 pp., 337 lots.

> Instruments, lots 1-273; Marshall's, 82-98 (an unusually fine collection). Catalogue no. 2272.

MARTIN, FRANK, of Lewisham

2168   Puttick & Simpson, firm. *Catalogue of Musical Instruments, Including the Collection Formed by the Late . . . Pianofortes . . . Harps . . . Violins, Violas* [etc.] *. . . Sold . . . July 30th, 1918.* 18 pp., 438 lots.

> Martin's instruments, lots 193-221. Catalogue no. 5263.

MARTIN, JOHANNES HENRICUS

2169   de Hart, A. H. *Catalogus van eenen zeer netten en zindelijken Inboedel, Bestande in: Eenige uitmuntende schilderijen. . . . Muzijk instrumenten, waaronder eenige uitmuntende italiaansche en andere violen en violen celle, muzijk werken, boeken. . . . Alles nagelaten door . . . verkocht worden ten overstaan van. . . . Schultz van Haegen en Struyk . . . 8 April 1828 . . . en volgende dagen.* Dordrecht, bij H. Volkersz, 1828. 44 pp., 609 lots.

> Instruments, pp. 5-7 (35 lots). Copy at NL-Avb.

MAUCOTEL, CHARLES

2170   Puttick & Simpson, firm. *Catalogue of a Small and Select Musical Library . . . Also an Important Assemblage of Musical Instruments, Being the Stock of Mr. Maucotel, of Rupert Street . . . Sold . . . August 28th, 1860.* 21 pp., 554 lots.

> Instruments, lots 201-401; 402-554 are sundries and parts of instruments. In Harrison Horblit's collection, the date "28th" has been struck through by hand, renumbered "3rd". Catalogue no. 643.

MAULOZ

2171   Pillet, Charles, auctioneer. *Notice des instruments de musique et archets . . . dont la vente aura lieu . . . 29 novembre 1875. . . .* [Paris: 1875.] 4 pp.

        Copy at GB-Lbl (Hirsch 421.2).

MAXIMILIAN II, Erzherzog von Österreich, 1558-1618. *See Section I under* VIENNA (Austria). KUNSTHISTORISCHES MUSEUM. AMBRAS AND RUHELUST INVENTORIES

MAXWELL, Sir PETER BENTON *and* J. WILLIAMS, of Walsall

2172   Puttick & Simpson, firm. *Catalogue of the Valuable Collection of Violins, Violas, Violoncellos . . . Property of the Late Sir Peter Benton Maxwell . . . and J. Williams . . . Sold . . . June the 30th, 1893.* 14 pp., 66 lots.

        Properties are not differentiated. Catalogue no. 2951.

[MAY, Rev. G.]

2173   Puttick & Simpson, firm. *Catalogue of a Valuable Collection of Music in All Classes, Treatises* [etc.] *. . . . The Musical Instruments Include a Sweet-Toned Chamber Organ, Pianofortes, Violins, Violoncellos, Concertinas, &c. . . . Sold . . . February 6th* [1852]. 11 pp., 259 lots.

        Instruments, lots 223-59. Catalogue no. 246.

MAYER, JOHANN, of Munich

2174   Helbing, Hugo, firm. *Katalog der Antiquitäten und Kunstsammlungen des Herrn. . . . Rüstungen und Rüstungs-theile, Waffen. . . . Musik-instrumente* [etc.]. *Auction . . . den 10. April 1899 und folgende Tage.* München: Knorr & Hirth, 1899. 45 pp., 1102 lots.

        Instruments, lots 556-610. Copies at NL-DHrk, F-Paa, B-Bmr.

MAYER VON MAYERFELS, CARL EDLER

2175 Förster, Carl, firm. *Catalog der ausgezeichneten und berühmten Kunst- und culturhistorischen Sammlung aus dem Nachlasse des . . . auf Schloss Meersburg am Bodensee. I. Abth. . . . musikalischen Instrumenten, Gläsern* [etc.] . . . . München: vom 16. August 1883. 71 pp., 3 pls., 1986 lots.

> Instruments (for an orchestra?), lots 1550-1700.
> Förster'sche Kunst-Auction no. 28. Copies at
> NL-DHrk, D-brd-Mbn.

MEE, JOSEPH; J. KEEGAN (stock); [Rev. FULLER]

2176 Puttick & Simpson, firm. *Catalogue of a Large Collection of Music, Including the Stock in Trade of Mr. J. Keegan . . . Engraved Music Plates . . . the Musical Instruments, Including Several Piano Fortes . . . Harps, a Consignment from Parma of Twenty Violins by Cremona Makers, Other Violins and Violoncellos of High Quality . . . Double Basses, Tenors, the Property of the Late Joseph Mee . . . and Many Other Valuable Lots . . . Sold . . . March 5th, 1852.* 20 pp., 589 lots.

> Instruments: Mee's, lots 544-89; property of an
> Italian family, lots 524-43.

MENGELBERG, J. W.

2177 Mak van Waay, S. J., firm. *Catalogus van de Kunstveiling 109, bestaande uit de nalatenschap van wijlen Prof. Dr. J. W. Mengelberg. . . . Openbare verkoping . . . 25 Maart 1952, en volgenden Dagen. . . .* Amsterdam: "Kunstveilingen S. J. Mak van Waay," 1952. 94 pp., pls., 1608 lots.

> Instruments, lots 874-1018. Copy at NL-DHgm;
> prices fetched in Ms.

MERCER, Hon. Col. JOHN; NICHOLAS HAWKSMOOR

2178 Lambe, Aaron, auctioneer. *A Catalogue of the Household Furniture and Effects of the . . . and . . . Both Deceased. . . . Curious Collection of Musical Instruments, As Base Viols, Cremona Violins, Flutes, Harpsichords, Spinets, a Chamber Organ Which Plays with a Barrel* [etc.]. *To Be Sold by Auction at Mr. Lambe's, Facing the King's-Arms Tavern in Pall-Mall . . . the 15th Instant* [of April] *and the Six Following Days. . . .* [London: 1740.] 31 pp.

"Musical Instruments and Books of Musick," pp. 13-14
(32 lots, many more items). Instruments, lots 1-17.
Copy at GB-LBL.
Reprinted in *Sales Catalogues of Eminent Persons,*
edited by A. N. L. Munby, vol. 4, *Architects,* pp. 45-77.

Literature

2179 Downes, Kerry. [On Hawksmoor's sale catalogue], *Burlington Magazine* 45
(1953): 332-35.

MERKMAN, Vve P. (née J. van LEEUWARDEN)

2180 Van der Vinne, Vincent, firm. *Catalogus van een extra fraai kabinetje konstigen
plaisante schilderyen . . . prenten en tekeningen . . . speelinstrumenten. Fraaije
muziek, tuincieraaden en rarietyten. Alles nagelaten door . . . I. van Leeuwarden
. . . verkogt . . . 21 September 1773. . . . Te Haerlem. . . . 22 pp., 490 lots.*
Lugt* notes 26 instruments, 120 "livres musique";
not examined. Copy at F-Pe.

MEYER, ANDRÉ (J43)

2181 Bridgman, Nanie and Francois Lesure, eds. *Collection musicale. Manuscrits
autographes, musique imprimée et manuscrite; ouvrages théoriques . . .
instruments de musique.* Abbeville: F. Paillart, [1961]. 118 pp., 292 pls.
Supplement. Abbeville: F. Paillart, [1963]. [16] pp.
Instruments, 13 unnumbered lots. Copies at
MB (Bp), DLC (Wc), etc.

MICKLEBURGH LTD., firm (J138)

2182 *A Catalogue of the European Wind Musical Instruments in the Collection of
. . . at Stokes Croft, Bristol.* 3rd ed. Edinburgh: 1972. 10 lvs.
A typescript copy in the Victoria & Albert Museum.

MILES, FLOYD C.

Literature

2183 Richards, J. H. "Reed Organs in Floyd C. Miles Collection of Musical
Instruments," *Diapason* 63, no. 11 (1972): 1, 6. illus.
See also a Letter to the Editor 64, no. 1 (1972): 2.

MILLER, DAYTON C. (L20) [N. B.: Collection went to the Library of Congress in 1941. For literature after that date, see Section I under **WASHINGTON, D. C.**]

Literature

2184   Wynn, James. "The Flute. Illustrated with Photographs of the Collection of Prof. Dayton C. Miller," *Musical Quarterly* 15 (1929): 469-74.

MOECK, HERMANN, firm [N. B.: The collection was purchased by the government of Lower Saxony for the Göttingen, Universität, Musikwissenschaftliches Institut in 1964. About 1020 instruments, according to Jenkins*.]

Literature

2185   "Grösste private Musikinstrumenten-Sammlung in Europa," *Musikhandel* 13, no. 1 (1962): 30.

2186   Sievers, Heinrich and Gerhard Thebs. "Bemühungen um die Sammlung Moeck," *Instrumentenbau-Zeitschrift* 17 (1962/63): 318-21.

MOLINI, AUGUSTO

2187   Anderson Galleries, New York, firm. *Sixty-Seven Old and Rare Violins, Violas & Violoncellos by the World's Most Famous Makers, the Remarkable Collection of. . . . To Be Sold . . . May Twenty-Fifth.* New York: the Galleries, 1924. 22 pp., 69 lots.

   Copy at DLC (Wc).

MONTAGU, JEREMY (J152)

2188   *Musical Instruments of the World. Sheffield Festival Exhibition, 1967. Mappin Art Gallery, Sheffield.* [Sheffield] : 1967. 44 pp.

   Items mainly from Montagu's private collection.

2189   *Musical Instruments of the World. Sheffield Festival Exhibition, 1967. Mappin Art Gallery, Sheffield. Second Edition.* [Grinnel, Iowa] : Grinnel College, 1970. ii, 58 pp., 900 items.

MOORE, SAMPSON

2190   Puttick & Simpson, firm. *Catalogue of a Collection of . . . Music, Including a Selection from the Library of . . . C. D. Hackett . . . with Plates and Copyrights. . . . A Large Collection of Musical Instruments. . . . Fine Violins and Violoncellos . . . Including the Collection of the Late Sampson Moore . . . of Liverpool and Those of a Well-Known Amateur (dec.) . . . Sold . . . May 31st, 1875, and Two Following Days.* 32 pp., 1569 lots.

>   Instruments, lots 1409-1569; Moore's, 1454-1569.
>   Catalogue no. 564. Copy also at NN (NYp).

MORITZ, Landgraf zu Hessen, 1592-1627

2191   Heugel, Johann. "Instrumenta so die Musicanten undt Trumpter vnterhanden, Meinem G. F. vnd Hern zustendig [1573]." Reprinted in Zulauf, Ernst. *Beiträge zur Geschichte der Landgräflich-Hessischen Hofkapelle zu Cassel,* p. 34. Cassel: 1902.

2192   Heugel, Johann. "Instrumenta so die Musicanten undt Trumpter vnterhanden, Meinem G. F. vnd Hern zustendig [1573]." Translated in Baines, Anthony. "Two Cassel Inventories," *GSJ* 4 (1951): 31-32.

2193   Otto, Georg. "Inventarium aller Musikalischen Instrumenten, So uf bevelch unsers G. F. undt Herrn, Herrn Moritz Landtgraf zu Hessen etc: den 24ten Februarij ao. 1613 durch Georgium Ottorem Cappelmeister, Johannem Eckelium, undt Christophorum Cornett Seindt inventiret worden etc. wie folget." Reprinted in Zulauf, Ernst. *Beiträge zur Geschichte der Landgräflich-Hessischen Hofkapelle zu Cassel,* pp. 115-18. Cassel: 1902.

2194   Otto, Georg. "Inventarium aller Musikalischen Instrumenten, So uf bevelch unsers G. F. undt Herrn, Herrn Moritz Landtgraf zu Hessen etc: den 24ten Februarij ao. 1613 durch Georgium Ottorem Cappelmeister, Johannem Eckelium, undt Christophorum Cornett Seindt inventiret worden etc. wie folget." Translated in Baines, Anthony. "Two Cassel Inventories," *GSJ* 4 (1951): 32-34.

2195   Ende, Hans von. "Verzeichnis aller unsers G. F. undt Herrn musikalische Positif undt Instrumenten alkier im fürstlichen Hausse Cassell." Reprinted in Zulauf, Ernst. *Ibid.,* p. 118.

2196   "Marpurgische Instrumente." Reprinted in Zulauf, Ernst. *Ibid.,* pp. 118-19.

MORITZ, Landgraf zu Hessen, 1592-1627 *continued*

2197 "Inventarium aller Musicalischen Sachen, vffgericht den 22ten januarij 1638."
Reprinted in Zulauf, Ernst. *Ibid.*, pp. 133-36.

> Baines (see above) calls this "practically a restatement
> of [the inventory] of 1613."

Literature

2198 Engelbrecht, Christoph. "Die Hofkapelle des Landgrafen Carl von Hessen-Kassel.
I. 1663-1700," *Zeitschrift des Vereins für Hessische Geschichte und Landeskunde*
68 (1957): 141-73.

MORSE, R.

2199 Christie, Mr., auctioneer. *A Catalogue of the Very Capital Musical Instruments,
Plate, and . . . Old Wines of . . . , Well-Known for His Taste. . . . The Instruments
Consist of a Capital Violoncello by Stradivarius . . . a Famous Violoncello by
Guarnerius; and Others by Forster . . . Sold . . . June the 17th, 1816. . . .* London:
1816. 8 pp., 120, 53 lots.

> "Capital Music Instruments," lots 92-120.

MOSCHELES, IGNACE

2200 Puttick & Simpson, firm. *Catalogue of an Extensive . . . Collection of Music,
Including the Greater Portion of the Library of I. Moscheles. . . . Musical
Instruments, Including a Powerful Finger Organ . . . Pianofortes . . . Harps . . .
Violins and Violoncellos [etc.] . . . Sold . . . July 23rd, 1847, and Following Day.*
23 pp., 617 lots.

> Instruments, lots 561-611 (Moscheles'?). Catalogue no. 36.

MUMMERY, ALICE (J145)

2201 *The Mummery Collection.* [Hailsham: n.d.] 17 lvs.

> Photocopy of typescript at NBuU-M (BUu).

MYERS, ARNOLD (J143)

2202   *A List of Brass Musical Instruments in the Collection of Arnold Myers.* Edinburgh: 1973. 4 lvs.

A typescript at GB-Lva.

NALDI, GIUSEPPE

2203   Oxenham, Mr., auctioneer. *A Catalogue of the Excellent Household Furniture . . . [etc.]; A Brilliant-Toned Six-Octave Grand Pianoforte, a Square Ditto, and a Composer's Library Table, with Pianoforte, All by Messrs. Broadwood's; A Cremona Violin, a Celebrated Violoncello . . . Sold . . . 14th of February, 1821, and Three Following Days.* [London]: 1821. 38 pp.

Instruments scattered throughout. Film copy at NBuU-M (BUu).

2204   Musgrave, W. P., auctioneer. *A Catalogue of a Very Choice Collection of Modern Instrumental Music by the Most Eminent Masters . . . Violins, Tenors, and Violoncello by Amati . . . Property of Joseph Gwilt, Also . . . Portion of the Late Signor Naldi's Collection . . . Superior Violin and Tenor by Gaspar di Sala, Square and Cabinet Piano-Fortes, Harp by Erat . . . Sold . . . 10th July. . . .* [London: 1828?] 15 pp., 165 lots.

Instruments, lots 121-38 (owners not identified).
Film copy at NBuU-M (BUu).

NEPVEU, JACOB, *and* [A. Halm]

2205   de Vries, Brondgeest, Engelberts, en Roos, firm. *Catalogus van eene verzameling zeer fraaije schilderijen . . . eindelijk een antal uitmuntende muzijk-instrumente, waarlij een prachtig, aangenaam en wellnidend speel- en uurwerk, losse muzijk enz. . . . verkocht . . . 3ten April 1837 en volgende dagen. . . .* [Amsterdam: 1837.] 64 pp., 864 + 25 lots.

Instruments, pp. 56-58 (30 lots). Buyers include Praetorius, Hagedorn. Lugt* indicates Halm's properties included, but that name does not appear in the catalogue. Copy at US-NYfrick.

NETTLEFOLD, ARCHIBALD, of Kent

2206   Puttick & Simpson, firm. *Catalogue of the Collection of Antique and Other Brass and Wood Wind Instruments etc., Formed by the Late . . . Sold . . . April 25th, 1946.* 10 pp., 228 lots.

All Nettlefold's. Catalogue no. 770 [2nd ser.].

NEUBAUER, FREDERICK

2207 Christie, Mr. *Catalogue of Three Pair of Superb French Plates . . . of an Ambassador. . . . Also, Fifteen Harpsichords, with Double and Single Keys. . . . The Stock in Trade of Frederick Neubauer, Harpsichord Maker, Together with a Variety of . . . Article, the Property of a Gentleman, Deceased . . . Sold . . . March 11, 1772, and Following Day.* 11 pp., 181 lots.

> Instruments, 32 lots, according to Lugt*; not examined. Copy at GB-Lcia.

NEUPERT, MUSIKHISTORISCHES MUSEUM [N.B.: From 1927 to 1942 in Nuremberg; from 1942 to 1968 in Bamberg. In 1968 acquired by the Germanisches Nationalmuseum in Nuremberg (see catalogues in Section I).]

2208 "Klaviergeschichtliche Sammlung J. C. Neupert, Bamberg-Nürnberg." In Frankfurt a.M. Internationale Ausstellung, 'Musik im Leben der Völker,' 1927. *Katalog, von K. Meyer,* pp. 32-35. Frankfurt a.M.: 1927. ca. 65 items.

2209 Nuremberg. Musikhistorisches Museum Neupert. *Das musikhistorische Museum Neupert . . . Führer* [von Hanns Neupert]. [Nürnberg: 1938.] 33 pp., 20 pls.

Literature

2210 "Die historische Klavierausstellung der Firma J. C. Neupert in der 'Norrishalle' zu Nürnberg," *ZfI* 48 (1927/28): 66.

2211 "Das musikhistorische Museum Neupert in Nürnberg," *Der Auftakt* (Prague) 11 (1931): 63.

2212 "Eine wertvolle Bereicherung des musikhistorisches Museums Neupert - Nürnberg," *ZfI* 58 (1937/38): 177-78.

> See also same volume, pp. 257-58, 290.

2213 Wittkowski, Josef. "Kommt ohne Instrumente nit! Von Instrumentsammlungen in Franken," *Unser Bayern* (Munich) 3, no. 12 (1954): 92-93.

2214 Niessing, Paul. "Het Neupert-Museum te Bamberg," *Mens en Melodie* 19 (1964): 208-9. illus.

[N.B.: In the following "*General*" works, many of the references and most of the illustrations relate to instruments in the Neupert collection.]

General

2215 Neupert, Hanns. *Vom Musikstab zum modernen Klavier.* Bamberg: Neupert, 1925.

> 2nd ed., Bamberg: Neupert [c1926]; 3rd ed., Berlin: Krause, 1952.

2216   Neupert, Hanns. *Das Klavichord.* Kassel: Bärenreiter-Verlag, [1948] . 70 pp.
2nd ed., Kassel: Bärenreiter-Verlag, 1956.

2217   Neupert, Hanns. *Das Cembalo.* . . . Kassel: Bärenreiter-Verlag, 1933.
2nd ed., *ibid.*, 1951; 3rd ed., *ibid.*, 1956; 4th ed., *ibid.*, 1966.

2218   Neupert, Hanns. *Harpsichord Manual* . . . *English Translation*[from the 3rd German ed., by F. E. Kirby] . Kassel: Bärenreiter-Verlag, 1960.

> Translation of *Das Cembalo.* 2nd ed. [from the 4th German] , Kassel: 1968.

2219   Neupert, Hanns. *The Clavichord.* English translation by Ann P. P. Feldberg. Kassel: Bärenreiter-Verlag, [1965] .

> Translated from the 2nd German ed., 1956.

NEWRICK, F. W. *See under* CARTER, T. A.

NICHOLSON, J. W.

2220   Puttick & Simpson, firm. *Catalogue of the J. W. Nicholson Collection of Violins, Violas and Violoncellos, Including* . . . *Bows* . . . *Sold* . . . *January 26th, 1933.* 8 pp., 94 lots.

> Catalogue no. 7046.

OBIZZI, PIO ENEA DEGLI, Marchese. *See Section I under* VIENNA (Austria). KUNSTHISTORISCHES MUSEUM

O'BRIEN, Admiral

2221   Puttick & Simpson, firm. *Catalogue of an Interesting and Valuable Collection of Music* . . . *Also Musical Instruments. Costly Euterpeon* . . . *Musical Box* . . . *Choice Violins and Violoncellos* . . . *and the Valuable Instruments of the Late Admiral O'Brien* . . . *Sold December 19th, 1866, and Following Day.* 20 pp., 422 lots.

> Instruments, lots 346-422; O'Brien's, 392-408. The bidding on the Euterpeon was apparently not too brisk for it turns up in several subsequent P & S auctions: mentioned by name in sale no. 965 (January 11-12, 1867); also in sale no. 1004 (August 8-10, 1867); no. 1013 (November 18-19, 1867); in the sale (February 28, 1870); as "self-acting" Euterpeon; in sale no. 1345 (October 28, 1872); and again by name in sale 1380 (March 21, 1873). This catalogue no. 961.

OBRIST, Alois. *See Section I under* **EISENACH (Germany). BACHMUSEUM**

OLIPHANT, A. L.

2222 Puttick & Simpson, firm. *Catalogue of a Valuable Collection of Violins, Violas, Violoncellos, Guitars and Antique Instruments, Including the Properties of the Late A. L. Oliphant . . . J. D. de la Perelle . . . Lady Westbury, and a Distinguished Amateur . . . Sold . . . December 12th, 1904.* 15 pp., 111 lots.

Oliphant's instruments, lots 50-61; other properties of no great interest. Catalogue no. 3880.

OLIVER, General. *See under* **BATES, F. W.**

ORSI, ROMEO, firm

2223 "Il professore Romeo Orsi e la sua fabbrica d'istrumenti musicali," *Ars et labor* 61 (1906): 997-1002. illus.

With photos of the permanent "esposizione."

OTRIDGE, JOHN. *See under* **PARKER, H. M.**

OTTOBONI, PIETRO, Cardinal, 1667-1740

2224 "Cardinal Ottoboni's Instruments [Rome. Archivio di Stato. Atti del notaio Ang. Ant. de Caesaris, 5 marzo 1740, prat. 1838, f. 88b, 125v, 134rv, 175v, 182rv, 298v, 698v, 704rv, 723r]." In Kirkpatrick, Ralph. *Domenico Scarlatti,* p. 360. Princeton, N. J.: Princeton University Press, 1953.

PAGANINI, NICOLO

2225 *Catalogo della collezione Nicolo Paganini, per l'Esposizione di Torino, 1898.* Parma: Tip. G. Donati, 1898. 29 pp.

Cited from Pag*; not examined.

2226 Foschini, Gaetano. "La musica all'Esposizione Generale Italiana di Torino," *RMI* 5 (1898): 828-31.

2227   "Die Versteigerung von Paganini's Nachlass," *ZfI* 30 (1909/10): 453, 494, 505.

> Lists items sold, with buyers' names, at a sale January 24,
> 1910. Altogether 233 lots. Sale catalogue not located.

2228   "List of Instruments in Paganini's Possession at the Time of His Death." In
Courcy, G. I. C. de. *Paganini, the Genoese*, vol. 2, pp. 388-91. Norman: University
of Oklahoma Press, [1957].

> Footnote, p. 295, vol. 2: "Paganini's collection of
> instruments remained for some time in the possession
> of his heirs. A few were exhibited at the General
> Italian Exposition in Turin in 1898. His bow, the
> Rugeri cello, a little violin and bow, and a guitar and
> mandolin . . . were auctioned in Florence on January
> 24, 1910."

PALMER, W. S. *See under* **DUCHESNE, R.**

PARK, GEORGE C.

Literature

2229   Doring, Ernest N., Jr. "The Park Collection of Old Violins," *The Violinist* 21
(1917): 328.

PARKER, Dr. *See Section I under* **LANCASHIRE (England). CHORLEY PUBLIC LIBRARY**

PARKER, H. M.; JOHN OTRIDGE

2230   Puttick & Simpson, firm. *Catalogue of the Stock of Music . . . and Selections from
Several Private Libraries. . . . Musical Instruments . . . Violins and Violoncellos . . .
Well Known Violin by Stadiuarius the Property of an Amateur . . . Sold . . . April
24, 1854, and Two Following Days.* 34 pp., 853 lots.

> Instruments, lots 479-576; Parker's, 527-46; Otridge's,
> 547-76. Catalogue no. 364; copy also at NN (NYp).

PARSONS, Hon. L. *See under* **CARRODUS, JOHN TIPLADY**

PARTELLO, DWIGHT J.

2231   Abell, A. M. "The Partello Collection of Violins," *Musical Courier* 58, no. 21 (May 26, 1909): 5-6; 58, no. 21 (June 2, 1909): 5-7. Many illus.

>   " . . . it is the only great violin collection in the world."
>   It was indeed an excellent collection containing some 22
>   violins, 2 violas, 2 cellos, 31 bows, 17 of which were Tourte.

2232   Abell, A. M. "The Partello Collection of Violins," *The Violinist* 23, no. 1 (July 1918): 271-79. Many illus.

>   Most of the collection is shown.

2233   "Die berühmte 'Partello-Collection' alter Meistergeigen," *ZfI* 42 (1921/22): 202-3 (with a list of the instruments); 43 (1922/23): 267, 364; 44 (1923/24): 129.

Literature

2234   "The Partello Collection," *The Violinist* 2, no. 10 (June 1902): 5.

PASQUALINI, GIOACCHINO. *See Section I under* ROME (Italy). ACCADEMIA NAZIONALE DI SANTA CECILIA

PASSALACQUA, JOSEPH

2235   *Catalogue raisonné et historique des antiquités découvertes en Egypt. . . .* Paris: Galerie d'antiquités égyptiennes, 1826. xv, 303 pp.

>   "Instruments de musique, etc.," pp. 30-31, 156-57.
>   Copies at NIC (Iu), ICU (Cu), etc.

PATTI, Signor. *See under* DUCHESNE, R.

PAWLE, A. N. *See under* GOODHART, J. H.

PAYNE, E. J.; WILLIAM WEBSTER; THOMAS LINTOLT; J. B. COOKE; WILLIAM COCHRANE

2236   Puttick & Simpson, firm. *Catalogue of a Valuable Collection of Violins . . . Bows and Antique Instruments, the Property of the Late William Webster . . . E. J. Payne . . . Thomas Lintolt . . . J. B. Cooke . . . William Cochrane . . . the Rev. Clementi-Smith . . . Sold . . . May 17th, 1905.* 21 pp., 155 lots.

> Payne's instruments, lots 87-102; other properties,
> 1-2 lots each. Catalogue no. 3926.

PAYNE, JAMES HENRY

2237   Puttick & Simpson, firm. *Catalogue of Musical Instruments, Including the Property of the Late . . . Old Italian and Other Violins* [etc.] *. . . Sold . . . July 31st, 1906.* 13 pp., 306 lots.

> Payne's instruments, lots 101-74 (but spelled "Paine"
> within the catalogue). Catalogue no. 4043.

PELZER, GIULIA; Mme. SIDNEY PRATTON; GEORGE PIDDOUX

2238   Sotheby & Co., firm. *Catalogue of Ceramics, Glass, Armour and Weapons, Musical Instruments . . . the Property of Mme. Giulia Pelzer and Mme. Sidney Pratton . . . Musical Boxes the Property of George Piddoux . . . Sold . . . the 15th of December. . . .* [London] : 1928.

> Pelzer and Pratton guitars, pp. 27-29, lots 191-211;
> Piddoux musical boxes, pp. 21-26, lots 142-88.

PENRICE, THOMAS. *See under* DUCHESNE, R.

PERERA, P. R., of Manchester

2239   Puttick & Simpson, firm. *Catalogue of the Celebrated Collection of Cremona Violins and Violoncellos . . . Including a Superb Quartette of Instruments of Stradivarius, Together with the Bows of Tourte, Dodd . . . Also a . . . Perfect Violoncello by Nicholas Amati . . . Sold . . . May 29, 1877.* 8 pp., 42 lots.

> The Quartette bought by Hart for 280 pounds.
> Catalogue no. 1670.

PERERA, P. R. *continued*

2240   Puttick & Simpson, firm. *Catalogue of a Large Assemblage of Valuable Musical Instruments . . . 20 Pianofortes . . . Also Rare Cremona Violins from the "Perera" and Other Collections. . . . 4,000 Pieces of Musical Sheet Music . . . Sold . . . March 23rd, 1880.* 9 pp., 187 lots.

> Instruments, lots 38-187. Catalogue no. 1907.

PERKINS, FREDERICK

2241   Puttick & Simpson, firm. *Catalogue of a Valuable Collection of Music, Including the Libraries of Frederick Perkins . . . Dr. Edward Rigby. . . . Musical Instruments . . . Sold . . . July 17th, 1861, and Two Following Days.* 40 pp., 872 lots.

> Instruments, lots 662-872; Perkins', lots 771-90.
> Catalogue no. 689; copy also at NN (NYp).

PERY, EDMUND SEXTON

2242   Puttick & Simpson, firm. *Catalogue of the Valuable Musical Library of Charles Edward Horsley. . . . Also Musical Instruments . . . Sold . . . April 16, and the Following Day [1862].* 25 pp., 601 lots.

> Instruments, lots 430-601; Pery's, 516-40; A Gentleman's,
> 541-56. Catalogue no. 716; copy also at NN (NYp).

PETERSON, FREDERICK

2243   Walpole Galleries, New York. *Musical Instruments Collected by . . . Sold at Auction . . . February 16, 1923.* New York: 1923. 21 pp., 180 lots.

> Instruments, lots 129-59. Catalogue no. 268;
> copy also at NN (NYp).

PFEIFFER, CARL, firm. *See also Section I under* **STUTTGART (Germany). WÜRTTEM-BURGISCHES LANDESGEWERBEMUSEUM**

Literature

2244   "Eine Führung durch die Carl A. Pfeifferische Musikinstrumentsammlung," *ZfI* 43 (1922/23): 267, 269.

PHILIP II, King of Spain. *See* **FELIPE II, King of Spain**

PIDDOUX, GEORGE. *See under* **PELZER, GIULIA**

PIKE, H. W.

2245   Puttick & Simpson, firm. *Catalogue of Violins, Violas, and Violoncellos . . . the Property of the Late . . .* [and] *a Gentleman Deceased . . . Sold . . . May 12th, 1938.* 9 pp., 131 lots.

        Catalogue no. 102 [2nd ser.].

PILLSBURY, D. S. *See Section I under* **DEARBORN, MICHIGAN (USA). HENRY FORD MUSEUM**

PLATTER, FELIX

Literature

2246   [Brief list of the instruments in his collection.] In Nef, Karl. "Die Musik in Basel," *SiMG* 10 (1908/9): 544.

PLATTNER, LOUIS

2247   van der Meer & Verbruggen, firm. *Catalogue d'une collection nombreuse et très-précieuse d'instruments de musique, archets, cordes et articles différents, laissée par feu . . . vente . . . 19 juin 1843 et jours suivants.* Rotterdam: 1843. 59 pp., 1927 lots.

        Instruments, total of 1311 lots. Copy at NN (NYp).

PLEY, ADOLPH (Luthier)

2248   Fievez, Joseph (Exp.). *Catalogue de instruments de musique, anciens et modernes . . .* [etc.] *dont la vente publique . . . 19 novembre 1906 et jour suivant . . . Salle Sainte-Gudule . . . à Bruxelles.* 30 pp., 470 lots.

        Instruments, lots 1-300, 323-31.

POMEROY, J. VINER, of Clifton, Bristol

2249   Puttick & Simpson, firm. *Catalogue of a Valuable Collection of Violins, Violas, Violoncellos and Double Basses, Including the Property of . . . Sold . . . June 19th, 1900.* 16 pp., 110 lots.

> Catalogue no. 3459; copy also at NRU (Rs).

POTHONIER, de, *and* "A LATE PROFESSOR"

2250   Puttick & Simpson, firm. *Catalogue of a Valuable Assemblage of Musical Properties, Including . . . Pianofortes. . . . Valuable Italian Violins, Including the Collection of Mons. de Portonier* [sic] *. . . Sold March 22, 1881.* 14 pp., 349 lots.

> Instruments, lots 1-166; Pothonier's (or Portonier's),
> 52-67; those of "A Late Professor," 167-283.
> Catalogue no. 2003.

POTTER, CIPRIANI. *See under* JOYCE, J.

PRATTON, Mrs. SIDNEY. *See under* PELZER, GIULIA

PRESTIA FLUTE COLLECTION. *See Section I under* MADISON, WISCONSIN (USA). UNIVERSITY. SCHOOL OF MUSIC

PRIEGER, ERICH

2251   Lempertz, M., firm. *Musiksammlung Nachlass Dr. Erich Prieger. I. Musikbibliothek. II. Praktische Musik aller Art. Alte Musikinstrumente . . . Versteigerung 7.-10. Nov. 1922.* Bonn: 1922. [4], 86 pp., 2327 lots.

> "Alte Musikinstrumente," lots 2319-24. Copy at DLC (Wc).

PURRIER, V.; A. E. HARPER; A. SCHREIBER

2252   Puttick & Simpson, firm. *Catalogue of the Valuable Collection of Violins,*
Violas, Violoncellos, etc., Including the Property of the Late V. Purrier . . .
A. E. Harper . . . A. Schreiber . . . Sold . . . June 17th, 1897. 15 pp., 106 lots.

Catalogue no. 3247; copy also at NRU (Rs).

Literature

2253   "Messrs. Puttick & Simpson's Guaranteed Sale," *Violin Times* 5 (1896/97): 166-67.

A long list, with prices fetched. Summary of the same
article is in *ZfI* 17 (1896/97): 766.

PYMAR, T. *See under* CERUTTI, Signor

PYNE, J. KENDRICK. *See under* BODDINGTON, HENRY

R . . .

2254   Charpentier, Marcel (C.P.). *Succession de Monsieur R . . . et appartenant à divers.*
Beaux livres . . . gravures anciens . . . instruments de musique anciens . . . par
Gagliano, Amati, Bernardel, père, etc. . . . vente à Paris . . . [June 17] *1964.*
[2], 5 pp., 120 lots.

Instruments, lots 31-41-bis.

RAPER, C. *See note under* CRAMER, FRANCOIS

READE, CHARLES

2255   Puttick & Simpson, firm. *Catalogue of a Large Collection of Musical Properties,*
Including . . . Pianofortes . . . Wood Wind Instruments . . . Also . . . Cremona and
Other Violins, Violas, & Violoncellos, Including Amongst Others, Those of the
Late . . . Sold May 19th, 1885. 10 pp., 255 lots.

Instruments, lots 1-185; Reade's, 63-185.
Catalogue no. 2338.

REGIBO, ABEL

2256 *Catalogue d'une bibliothèque musicale et d'une collection d'antiquités ... dont la vente publique ... Septembre 1897.* Renaix: 1897.

> Cited by Heyer*, Boalch*, and Hirt*, who says
> 117 lots of instruments are included, pp. 89-95.
> Not located or examined.

RENDALL, GEOFFREY. *See Section I under* **EDINBURGH (Scotland). UNIVERSITY**

RICHMOND, R. T. *See Section I under* **YORK (U. K.). CASTLE MUSEUM**

RIDLEY, EDWARD ALEXANDER KEANE. *See Section I under* **LUTON (U. K.). PUBLIC MUSEUM**

RIEMEYER, ALBERT. *See Section I under* **BASEL (Switzerland). UNIVERSITÄT. HISTORISCHES MUSEUM**

RIPON, EDMUND. *See Section I under* **BOSTON, MASSACHUSETTS (USA). MUSEUM OF FINE ARTS**

ROBINSON, JOHN, of York

2257 Puttick & Simpson, firm. *Catalogue of Very Important, Interesting and Valuable Musical Property ... Also ... Musical Instruments, Including the Property of ... Sold ... June 16* [and 18], *1857. ...* 34 pp., 816 lots.

> Instruments, lots 642-816; Robinson's, 652-74.
> Catalogue no. 496.

ROBSON, PHILIP A.; EDMUND VALLOCK

2258 Puttick & Simpson, firm. *Catalogue of a Large Collection of Musical Instruments ... Italian Violins, Including the Property of ... Violas, Violoncellos and Double Basses ... Sold ... December 19th, 1905.* 14 pp., 319 lots.

> Instruments, lots 1-307; Vallock's, 219-33; Robson's
> not identified. Catalogue no. 3979.

ROSE, ALGERNON SIDNEY

2259   "A Private Collection of African Instruments," *ZiMG* 6 (1904/5): 60-66.

ROSSINI

2260   Mannheim (Exp.); Pillet (C. P.). *Catalogue des objets d'art et de curiosité . . . instruments de musique . . . dépendant de la succession Rossini . . . vente . . . 12 et 13 mars 1869.* Paris: 1869. 20 pp., 210 lots.
>   Instruments (decorative), lots 156-65.
>   Copies at F-Paa, F-Pe, US-NYfrick (priced).

ROTHSCHILD, Baron NATHANIEL VON

2261   "Raum XIII. Sammlung Baron Nathaniel von Rothschild. I. Musikalische Instrumente." In Vienna. Internationale Ausstellung für Musik- und Theater- wesen, 1892. *Fach-katalog der musikhistorischen Abtheilung von Deutschland und Oesterreich-Ungarn,* pp. 181-88. Wien: 1892. Total of 117 items, 56 of them instruments.

ROWE, Major; A. DAVIS COOPER; GEORGE STANISTREET; D. FINZI

2262   Puttick & Simpson, firm. *Catalogue of the Valuable Collection of Violins, Violas, Violoncellos, etc., the Properties of Major Rowe, the Late A. Davis Cooper, Esq., George Stanistreet, Esq., D. Finzi, Esq. . . . Together with the Collection of Clarionets Belonging to H. Lazarus, Esq. . . . Sold . . . June the 19th, 1895.*
>   Lowe's instruments, lots 1-45; Cooper's, 46-87
>   and 107-8; Lazarus', 88-106. Catalogue no. 3084;
>   copy also at NRU (Rs).

Literature

2263   "Ein Streichinstrumenten-Versteigerung in London," *ZfI* 15 (1894/95): 763-64.

ROYAL ARTILLERY BAND

2264 Puttick & Simpson, firm. *Catalogue of a Collection of Music in All Classes . . .
the Stock of a Foreign Publishing House . . . Also Musical Instruments . . . Sold
September 2nd, 1863, and Following Day.* 28 pp., 839 lots.

> Instruments, lots 735-839; "Wind Instruments from
> the Band of the Royal Artillery," 815-39.

RÜCK COLLECTION [N. B.: The collection was begun by Wilhelm Rück, continued by
his sons Ulrich and Hans (d. 1940). Part housed at Erlangen, Universität (see no. **492**
in Section I). Ulrich died in 1962 and the collection was acquired by the Germanisches
Nationalmuseum in Nuremberg in 1963 (see Section I).]

RUSHWORTH & DREAPER, LTD. [N. B.: Citations of various catalogues of this
collection—since 1967 in the Merseyside County Museums in Liverpool—abound, but
there appear to be only two catalogues with a host of variants depending upon the
number of illustrations and the amount of advertising included.]

2265 *The Rushworth & Dreaper Collection of Antique Musical Instruments and
Historical Manuscripts.* Liverpool: Rushworth & Dreaper, Ltd., [192-?].

> Variants: [192-?], 12 lvs. at NN (NYp)
> [n.d., 192-?], 16 pp., Mummery Antiquariat catalogue
> [192-?], 23 pp., at MB (Bp)
> 1927, 42 pp. in yet another Mummery catalogue

2266 *Catalogue of the Rushworth & Dreaper Permanent Collection of Antique
Musical Instruments.* Liverpool: Rushworth & Dreaper, 1932. 24 pp.

> This citation from Miller* and Hirt*. NBuU-M (BUu)
> has [194-?], 12 pp., illus. The Liverpool City Library
> has several from the 1940's and 1950's that are essentially
> the same catalogue with different advertising, according
> to Mr. Ralph Malbon, Liverpool City Librarian.

RUSSELL, RAYMOND. *See Section I under* **EDINBURGH (Scotland). UNIVERSITY**
[N. B.: A few other items from the Russell collection were sold at auction by Sotheby &
Co. (London) in their sales of June 29, 1956 and May 9, 1958.]

S* * *, Baron I. de

2267 Mannheim, Charles. *Catalogue de faiences italiennes des fabriques . . . armes anciennes . . . objets en fer; bijoux; instruments de musique . . . en partie de la collection de M. Baron I. de S. . . . vente . . . 12 mars 1877.* Paris?: 1877. 18 pp., 120 lots.

> Lugt* says that it includes 20 musical instruments.
> Copies at F-Paa, F-Pe, GB-Lng; not examined.

SALE, JOHN; P. TAYLOR

2268 Musgrave, Mr. W. P., auctioneer. *A Catalogue of the Libraries of . . . (Both Deceased) . . . Ancient and Modern Vocal and Instrumental Music, Valuable Treatises . . . Violins, Tenors, Flutes* [etc.] *. . . Sold . . . the 12th and 13th of May, 1828.* 20 pp., 291 lots.

> Instruments, lots 56-62, 239-41; owner not identified.
> Copy at GB-Lbl (7897.d.13.[17]).

SALMREIFFERSCHEID, Monseigneur le Compte de

2269 *Catalogue raisonné des diverses curiosités du cabinet de . . . évêque de Tournay, composé d'une nombreuse collection d'histoire naturelle, de tableaux, d'estampes, de divers instruments et pièces de musique de différens maitres. . . .* A. Tournay: Impr. de Romain Varles, 1771.

> Cited from Gaspari*; not otherwise located.

SALOMONS, J. B.

2270 Puttick & Simpson, firm. *Catalogue of a Valuable Collection of Violins, Violas, Violoncellos and Double Basses, Including the Property of the Late . . . Sold . . . December 20th, 1899.* 16 pp., 124 lots.

> Lots 69-74 were gifts to Salomons from Dragonetti.
> Catalogue no. 3422; copy also at NRU (Rs), 113 lots only.

SALZ, ANSLEY K. *See Section I under* BERKELEY, CALIFORNIA (USA). UNIVERSITY OF CALIFORNIA. DEPARTMENT OF MUSIC

SAMARY, GEORGES

2271   Gand et Bernardel, firm. Chevallier (C.P.). *Catalogue des instruments de musique . . . composant la collection de . . . vente . . . 15 mars 1887 à Paris. . . .* Paris: 1887. 34 pp., 219 lots.

> At the Hôtel Drouot. See note in *ZfI* 7 (1886/87): 231 and 243. Also mentioned in *Menestrel* 53 (1886/87): 118. Copies at NRU (Rs), B-Bc.

SARGENT, Mrs. WINTHROP. *See Section I under* BOSTON, MASSACHUSETTS (USA). NEW ENGLAND CONSERVATORY OF MUSIC

SAVOYE

2272   Gand et Bernardel, firm (Chevallier, C. P.). *Catalogue des instruments de musique anciens, rares et curieux des XVe, XVIe, et XVIIIe siècles. La collection de M. Savoye dont la vente aura lieu . . . Hôtel Drouot . . . 15 mai 1882.* [Paris: Pillet & Dumoulin, 1882.] 22 pp., 214 lots.

> Bricq* says sold in 1887, Lambertini* 1880, and Weckerlin* 1862! Copies at NRU (Rs), B-Bc.

SAVOYE, LÉON

2273   *Catalogue des anciens instruments de musique; clavecins et orgues . . . harpes . . . instruments à archets . . . vielles . . . composant l'ancienne collection Léon Savoye . . . vente . . . aura lieu Hôtel Drouot . . . 13 juin 1924.* [Paris: 1924.] 19 pp., illus.

2274   "Une vente d'instruments de musique anciens," *M & I* 10 (1924): 615-17. Many illus.

SAVOYE, RENÉ

2275   *Catalogue des instruments de musique de la collection Savoye. Liste numérique et désignation des instruments.*

> Ms. dated 1910 in the Heyer* collection including 756 items, according to Boalch*.

SAX, ADOLPHE

2276 Carré, Gustave (C. P.). *Catalogue du Musée instrumental de M. Adolphe Sax. Collection unique d'instruments de musique. De tous temps et de tous pays dont la vente . . . 13 novembre 1877.* Paris: V. es Renou, Maulde et Cock, 1877. 40 pp., 467 lots.

Arranged by nationality. Copies at NL-DHgm, B-Bc.

SAYN-WITTGENSTEIN, CASIMIR, Graf von Berleburg

2277 "Inventarium sämmtlicher Mobiliare, aufgenommen nach Ableben des Grafen Casimir 1741. . . . In der musicalischen Instrumenten- und Musicalien-Cammer, wobey Herr Forst- Secretarius Gernand mit gewesen und die Instrumenta angezeiget." In Domp, Joachim. *Studien zur Geschichte der Musik an westfälischen Adelshöfen im 18. Jahrhunderts,* pp. 68-69. Regensburg: Pustet, 1934.

Another brief catalogue, dated 1750, *ibid.,* p. 13.

SCHEURLEER, DANIEL FRANCOIS   [N. B.: The nucleus of the present collections in the Hague, Gemeentemuseum.]

2278 *Catalogus der musiekbibliotheek en der verzameling van musiekinstrumenten van D. F. Scheurleer.* 's-Gravenhage: M. Nijhoff, 1885. 5, 290 pp., illus.

Instruments, pp. 241-58. Copy at DLC (Wc).

2279 Schilderkundig Genootschap Pulchri Studio. *Catalogus der tentoonstelling van muziekinstrumenten, prenten, photografiën en boeken daarop betrekking hebbende. October-November 1893.* Den Haag: 1893. 64 pp.

Copy at NL-DHgm.

2280 *Oude muziek-instrumenten, en prenten en Fotografieën naar Schilderijen en Teekeningen, waarop Instrumenten voorkomen. . . .* Rotterdam: Mouton & co., 1898. 121 pp.

Copy at NNMM (NYmm).

2281 *Catalogus van oude muziekinstrumenten en prenten en fotografiën naar schilderijen en teekeningen waarop instrumenten voorkomen.* Haarlem: [Den Haag: Mouton & Co.], 1898.

In the list of Scheurleer's works in the Festschrift. *Gedenkboek aangeboden aan Dr. D. F. Scheurleer op zijn 70sten verjaardag* . . . 1925, this and no. **2278**, are noted as separate items. No copy located.

SCHEURLEER, DANIEL FRANCOIS *continued*

2282 *Eene Wooninge, in de welcke ghesien worden veelderhande gheschriften, boeken, printen ende musicaale instrumenten.* ['s-Graven-Haghe: 1913.] 2 pp., 36 pls.

>   Photos of Scheurleer's collections in his home at
>   The Hague. Copy at NBuU-M (BUu).

2283 Balfoort, Dirk J. *Eigenartige Musikinstrumente. Berechtigte Uebersetzung aus dem Holländischen von Felix Augustin. Abbildungen . . . nach Instrumenten aus dem Museum Scheurleer im Haag.* (De Muziek, Band IV.) Haag: 1932. 100 pp., 26 illus.

Literature

2284 [Sigma, D. F., i.e., Scheurleer.] "Musea voor muziekinstrumenten," *De Nederlandsche Spectator* (1881), p. 119.

2285 Sanders, Paul F. "Het museum Scheurleer," *Muziek* 2 (1928): 312-19. illus.

2286 Beynum, Bertha van. "Klavierinstrumenten in het Museum Scheurleer," *Muziek* 5, no. 3 (1931): 104-13. With 6 pls.

2287 Andre. "Het Museum Scheurleer," *Symphonia* (Hilversum) 15 (1932): 108-9. illus.

>   Apparently appeared also in *Caecilia,* vol. 89 (1933).

2288 H., W. "Van het museum Scheurleer en van een voorgenomen belangwekkende Tentoonstelling," *Symphonia* (Hilversum) 14 (1931): 142.

2289 Zuiden, D. S. van. "Onze Haagsche Musea. VIII. Het Muziekhistorische museum Scheurleer, Carnegielaan," *Haagsche Gids* 3, no. 9 (September 1931): 204-7. illus.

SCHLEY, C. B.

Literature

2290 Freeman, J. C. "A Collection of Bergonzis," *The Violinist* 22, no. 6 (June 1918): 233-35. illus.

SCHOLZ, JANOS. *See Section I under* NEW YORK, NEW YORK (USA). LIBRARY AND MUSEUM OF THE PERFORMING ARTS

SCHORER, DANIEL

2291 van de Zande, Jeroen, firm. *Catalogus van de voortreffelyke versameling van
... boeken. . . . Een fraay cabinet schilderyen, een orgel, schepen, muziecq-
instrumenten . . . verkogt . . . den 15 April 1771 en volgende dagen. . . .* Te
Middleburg . . . 1771. 2, 82 pp., 2698 lots.

> Instruments, pp. 78-80 (38 lots). Copy at NL-Avb.

SCHREIBER, A. *See under* PURRIER, V.

SCHREINZER, KARL

Literature

2292 Skeaping, Kenneth. "The Karl Schreinzer Collection of Violin Fittings." In
Music Libraries and Instruments. Congress . . . Cambridge, 1959, pp. 251-53.
London: Hinrichsen, 1961.

SCHUMACHER, HEINRICH

2293 *Katalog zu der Ausstellung von Musikinstrumente früherer Zeiten. Aus den
Sammlung H. Schumacher.* Luzern: 1888.

> MGG*, Grove's*, Boalch*, Heyer* and others all cite,
> but only copies in the Heyer collection and at the
> Gesellschaft der Freunde alter Musikinstrumente have
> been located. It may be Ms.

2294 [*Sammlung H. Schumacher. Handgeschriebener Katalog.* Luzern: 1900.]

> Noted in the catalogue of materials in the Gesellschaft
> der Freunde alter Musikinstrumente (see GFaM* in
> Sources). Boalch* says the collection was offered for
> sale in 1909, finally dispersed in 1923. Now part of the
> **RICHARD WAGNER-MUSEUM** in **LUCERNE**, q.v., in Section I.

SELCH, FREDERICK. *See Section I under* FREDERICKSBURG, VIRGINIA (USA). MARY WASHINGTON COLLEGE

SELHOF, NICOLAS

2295 *Catalogue d'une très belle bibliothèque de livres curieux et rares, en toutes*
sortes de facultez et langues . . . auquel suit le catalogue d'une partie très
considerable de livres de musique . . . ainsi qu'une collection de toutes sortes
d'instruments deslaissez par feu M. Nicolas Selhof, libraire, lesquels seront
vendus publiquement aux plus offrants mercredi 30 mai 1759 et jours
suivants, dans la maison de la veuve d'Adrien Moetjens, libraire, dans
Hofstraat. A la Haye: chez la veuve d'Adrien Moetjens, 1759. 260 pp.,
2,945 lots.

> Instruments, pp. 250-60, 210 lots. After imprint:
> "Ou l'on distribue le catalogue. Pour lequel deux
> sols pour les pauvres."

2296 *Catalogue d'une très belle bibliothèque de livres curieux et rares, en toutes*
sortes de facultez et langues . . . [etc.] . [Reprint ed.] , with an introduction
by A. Hyatt King. (Auction catalogues of music, 1.) Amsterdam: Frits Knuf,
1973. xii, 264 pp.

Literature

2297 Becker, Georg. [An article about Selhof's collection] , *Le Guide musical*
(June 24, 1878).

> Not located in U. S.

2298 [A lengthy discussion of the 1759 catalogue and its important musical contents] ,
Bouwsteenen, III: 114-17.

SELLE, Dr. *See under* FROST, PERCIVAL

SETTALA, MANFREDO

2299 Terzago, Paolo Maria. *Musaeum Septalianum Manfredi Septalae patritii medio-*
lanensis industrioso labore constructum. . . . Dertonae: Typis Filiorum qd. Elisei
Violae, 1664. 324 pp.

> Instruments described, pp. 285-89.

2300 Terzago, Paolo Maria. [With title:] "Mvsaevm Septalianvm. Musica instrumenta.
Capvt vltimvm." In Vienna. Kunsthistorisches Museum. *Die Sammlung . . .*
von Julius Schlosser, pp. 17-19. Wien: 1920. Reprint ed. Hildesheim/New York:
Olms, 1974.

2301 Scarabelli, Pietro Francesco. *Museo ò Galeria adunata dal sapere e dallo studio del Sig. Canonico Manfredo Settala nobile milanese. Descritta in Latino dal Sig. Dott. Fis. Coll. Paolo Maria Terzago et hora in Italiano dal Sig. Pietro Francesco Scarabelli, dottor fisico di Voghera.* . . . In Tortona: Per li Figliuoli del qd. Eliseo Viola, 1666. 408 pp.

> Instruments, pp. 363-68.

Literature

2302 Byrne, Maurice. "Instruments by Claude Rafi in the Collection of Manfredo Settala," *GSJ* 18 (1965): 126-27.

SEVERYN, JACOBA JONNA, HEMRAN HAESEBROEK, ANNA ABELEVEN, HENRY LOUIS LE NORMANT, DANIEL ABELEVEN, FRANZ MAURITZ SMIT JOLLES, JOHAN FRIEDRICH ANDREAE, JOSEPH VAN JACOB BUENO DE MESQUITA, JOSEPH MESQUITA, Jr.

2303 Mercker, J. D. [and many others], auctioneers. *Catalogus van eenen . . . kostbaren . . . inboedel . . . paarlen . . . diamanten . . . gesteenten . . . horologien.* . . . *Negeh exrta welluidende piano-fortes . . . door van der Does, M. en P. Meijer.* . . . *Muzijk- als andere Instrumenten . . . verkocht . . . 23 October 1827, en vele volgende dagen.* . . . Amsterdam: 1827. 64, 10 pp., 1216 + 3 lots.

> Collation above from Lugt* is incorrect. Only known
> copy at NL-DHrk is paged 1-64, 201-10, intervening
> pages missing.
>   Citation here makes the best of an enormously
> complicated title page.
>   "Muzyk, draaibank en andere instrumenten, enz.,"
> pp. 48-49, lots 1-27.

[SEVILLA, DON FREDERIC de, Marquis de Negron]

2304 Van Herck fils & Melle Eva Krug; Eugene Brassine (Notaire). *Ville d'Anvers. Catalogue d'antiquités et objets d'art. Magnifiques montres en or et argent ciselé.* . . . *Instruments de musique . . . vente . . . 20 avril 1891 et jours suivants.* . . . Anvers: 1891. 73 pp., 959 lots.

> Instruments, lots 86-101. Copies at B-Gu, F-Paa, MB (Bp).

SEYMOUR, J.; E. W. WHINFIELD

2305   Puttick & Simpson, firm. *Catalogue of Musical Instruments . . . Pianofortes, Harmoniums and Organs. . . . Old Italian and Other Violins* [etc.] *and Music, the Property of. . . . Orchestral Music, Full Scores* [etc.] *Sold . . . June 26th, 1900.* 15 pp., 283 lots.

> Seymour's instrument collection, lots 81-100.
> Catalogue no. 3462.

SHAW-HELLIER COLLECTIONS. *See* HELLIER, SAMUEL *and also* Day's catalogue

of the Royal Military Exhibition, London, 1890 in *Section I*, no. **871**

SHIELDS, R. R. *See under* SPINKE, SAMUEL

SIDNEY, RICHARD CHASE

2306   Mr. Fletcher, auctioneer. *A Catalogue of the Extensive and Valuable Musical Collections of the Late George Cooper, Ernest August Kellner . . . Valuable Scores, Printed and MS of the Works of the Great Masters . . . Together with the Musical Instruments, Comprising the Well Known Cremona Violins of the Late Richard Chase Sidney, at Leicester House, Jersey . . . Sold . . . Dec. 9th, 1844, and Three Following Days. . . .* 31 pp., 863 lots.

> Instruments, lots 591-643e. Copy at GB-Ob
> (2591.d.3* [48]).

SIEGMUND FRANZ, Archduke of Austria, 1630-1665. *See Section I under* VIENNA
(Austria). KUNSTHISTORISCHES MUSEUM. AMBRAS COLLECTION, especially no. **1590**

SIKES, of Gloucester

2307   Puttick & Simpson, firm. *Catalogue of a Collection of Music . . . Glees and Other Vocal Music, Modern Operas . . . Theoretical and Preceptive Works* [property of T. Turner?] *Also the Musical Instruments . . . Harps . . . Musical Boxes . . . Flutinas, Accordeons . . . Guitars, Violins, Tenors, and Violoncellos by Amata* [sic] , *Stradiuarius, Guarnerius, Steiner* [sic] *. . . Sold . . . February 4th, 1851.* 12 pp., 290 lots.

> Instruments, including "the collection of violins,
> tenors and violoncellos of the late Mr. Sikes,"
> lots 221-90. Catalogue no. 194.

SIMON AUGUST, Graf und Edler zur Lippe-Detmold

2308 Kittel, J. F. "Verzeichniss derer, in der Musicalien Kammer des Hoch Reichs Gräfl. Schlosses zu Dtm. befindlichen Instrumenten und Musicalien, geführt von Concertmaster I. F. Kittel 1780." In Domp, Joachim. *Studien zur Geschichte der Musik an westfälischen Adelshöfen im 18. Jahrhunderts,* pp. 45-51. (Freiburger Studien zur Musikwissenschaft, 1.) Regensburg: Pustet, 1934.

SIMONETTI, ATTILIO, Chevalier

2309 Capobianchi, Vincenzo, firm. *Catalogue des objets d'art et de haute curiosité, composant la collection de . . . vente . . . à Rome . . . 16 avril 1883 et jours suivants.* . . . Roma: Impr. A. Befani, 1883. 163 pp., 8 pls. (Italian ed.); 16, 240 pp. (French ed.), 1282 lots.

       Copies at F-Pe, GB-Lva.

SIMPSON, ALEXANDER. *See Section I under* DUNDEE (Scotland). CENTRAL MUSEUM

SKINNER, BELLE

2310 Kinkeldey, Otto. *The Belle Skinner Collection of Musical Instruments; A Descriptive Catalogue Compiled for the Collector's Brother, William Skinner, by Otto Kinkeldey.* Holyoke, Mass.: 1932.

       In NN (NYp) is a microfilm of Kinkeldey's holograph, type-script and corrected page proof. Credit to Kinkeldey, however, was omitted from the published catalogue, 1933 (below).

2311 *The Belle Skinner Collection of Old Musical Instruments, Holyoke, Massachusetts. A Descriptive Catalogue Compiled under the Direction of William Skinner.* [Philadelphia, New York, etc.: Beck Engraving Co.] , 1933. xi, 210 pp., illus.

       Duckles* 3:1593, 89 items; on loan to Yale University since 1959. See note to no. **2310**, above.

SMITH, ERIC PENDRELL

2312 Puttick & Simpson, firm. *Catalogue of Old and Modern Violins, Violas and Violoncellos . . . Bows . . . . Balalaikas and Domras, &c., Including the Property of the Late . . . Sold . . . July 25th, 1935.* 7 pp., 118 lots.

       Smith's instruments, lots 84-96G. Catalogue no. 7319.

SMITH, FLY. *See under* **FROST, PERCIVAL**

SMITH, JAMES GORDON

2313   Sotheby, Wilkinson & Hodge, firm. *Catalogue of Old and Rare Musical Instruments, Arms, Guns* [etc.] . . . *Sold* . . . *Tuesday the 15th of July 1873.* [London]: 1873.

> Stringed instruments, pp. 12-14, lots 153-94.
> Wind instruments, pp. 15-16, lots 195-232.

SNETHLAGE, E. HEINRICH

2314   "Musikinstrumente der indianer des Guaporégebietes," *Bässler-archiv* 10 (1939): 3-38.

> Bolivian instruments collected by the author.

SNOECK, CÉSAR CHARLES [N. B.: At least three of the collections put together by Snoeck were separately catalogued. Instruments in the first went to the Staatliche akademische Hochschule in Berlin (catalogue dated 1894). The second group (in the 1903 catalogue) went to the Brussels Conservatoire. Closson (in *ZiMG* 11 [1909/10] article) says a third collection was sold to Baron de Stackelberg, director of the St. Petersburg Imperial Chapel at about the same time that the group went to the Brussels Conservatoire. The collection sold to the Général Baron numbered 363 items but Closson says neither the second nor the third collection matched the quality of the first.]

2315   *Catalogue de la collection d'instruments de musique anciens ou curieux formée par C. C. Snoeck.* Gand: J. Vuylsteke, 1894. v, 216 pp., illus.

> According to Lambertini*, 1145 items. Collection sold
> to Berlin Hochschule (see Section I, nos.**127-77**, and
> especially nos. **141** and **143**). Copy at DLC (Wc).

2316   *Catalogue de la collection d'instruments de musique flamands et néerlandais formée par C. C. Snoeck.* Gand: Impr. I. Vanderpoorten, 1903. 65 pp., 437 items.

> Collection sold to Brussels Conservatoire (see Section I,
> nos. **250-302**, and especially no. **281**). Copy at DLC (Wc).

2317   Meerens, Charles. *Catalogue de la collection de lutherie néerlandaise formée par C. C. Snoeck.* Gand: Impr. Vanderpoorten, 1903.

> Cited only in the *Annuaire* (1904, p. 176) of the Brussels
> Conservatoire. Otherwise unable to verify.

Literature

2318   [Notice of his death and the sale of his first collection, with descriptions of some important items], *ZiMG* 1 (1899): 31.

2319   Lyr, R. *Un grand Renaisien . . . Cesar Snoeck, musicologue et collectionneur d'instruments anciens.* Renaix: 1952. 30 pp.

Copy at NL-DHgm.

SNOUCK HURGRONJE. *See under* HURGRONJE, CHRISTIAAN SNOUCK

SOUTHGATE, G. L., of Lee

2320   Puttick & Simpson, firm. *Catalogue of Musical Instruments, Including the Collection Formed by the Late Dr. G. L. Southgate . . . Sold . . . May 1st, 1917.* 11 pp., 226 lots.

Southgate's instruments, lots 125-57. Catalogue no. 5123.

[SOUTHGATE, J. W.: ? BOYS; ? COLNAGHI; J. BOHN; et al]

2321   Southgate, Mr. . . . *Catalogue of the Valuable Property of a Gentleman (Removed from the Country) Including a Valuable Library of Books . . . Engravings . . . Collection of Music . . . [etc.] Sold . . . December 16th, 1839, and Six Following Days. . . .* 50, 6, 3 pp. 1658 + 11 lots.

Instruments, lots 1280-1443. Copy at GB-Lbl.

SOWINSKI, HANS

2322   "Steirische Volksmusikinstrumente," *Das Joanneum* 3 (1940): 188-202.

Entered also as no. **577**, q.v. Most of the instruments illustrated are from Sowinski's collection, loaned (as of 1940) to the Joanneum.

SPINKE, SAMUEL; R. R. SHIELDS

2323   Puttick & Simpson, firm. *Catalogue of Valuable Musical Property . . . Violins, Violas, Violoncellos, Double Basses, Including Many Desirable Examples the Property of Samuel Spinke, of East Dulwich, of the Late R. R. Shields of Manchester . . . and a Library of Music . . . Sold October 27th, 1903, and Following Day.* 20 pp., 442 lots.

> Instruments, lots 1-378; Spinke's, 126-140A; Shields', 212-63. Catalogue no. 3767.

SPINNEY, ROBERT

2324   Puttick & Simpson, firm. *Catalogue of a Collection of Music, Including the Library of the Late. . . . Musical Instruments . . . a Few Brass Instruments . . . Also Twenty Pianofortes by the Best Modern Makers . . . Sold . . . February 4th, 1861, and Following Day. . . .* 35 pp., 821 lots.

> Instruments, lots 657-821; Spinney's, 726-46; property of Dr. Austin, of Cork, 766-72. Catalogue no. 663; copy also at NN (NYp).

STAINFORTH, E. J. *See under* CARRODUS, JOHN TIPLADY

STANISTREET, GEORGE. *See under* ROWE, Major

STANLEY, JOHN

2325   Christie, Mr., auctioneer. *A Catalogue of All the Capital Musical Instruments, Extensive and Valuable Collection of Manuscript, and Other Music . . . Late the Property of . . . Sold . . . 24th of June, 1786.* [London] : 1786. 4 pp.

> Instruments, lots 75-92. Film copy at NBuU-M (BUu).

STEARNS, FREDERICK. *See Section I under* ANN ARBOR, MICHIGAN (USA). UNIVERSITY OF MICHIGAN. STEARNS COLLECTION OF MUSICAL INSTRUMENTS

STEHLING, R. A., of Warwick Gardens

2326   Puttick & Simpson, firm. *Catalogue of Musical Instruments . . . Including the Collection of the Late . . . Also a Quantity of Music . . . Sold April 29th, 1902.* 14 pp., 419 lots.

> Stehling's properties not identified. Catalogue no. 3622.

STEINERT, MORRIS (J87) [N. B.: Part of his collection was shown at the International Exposition in Vienna in 1892 and at the World's Columbian Exposition in Chicago in 1893 (see no. **2328** below). Marr* says another account of his participation in Vienna appears in *Musik und Theaterzeitung* for August, 1892 (see also Section I, no. **1551**). A number of items from the collection were given to Yale University in 1900. Some of Morris' instruments went to his son Albert's collection at the Rhode Island School of Design (now on loan to Yale).]

2327   *The M. Steinert Collection of Keyed and Stringed Instruments. With Various Treatises on the History of These Instruments. . . .* New York: Charles F. Tretbar, [1893]. 170 pp., illus., 82 items.

> Copies at DLC (Wc) and NNMM (NYmm).

2328   *. . . Catalogue of the M. Steinert Collection of Keyed and Stringed Instruments . . . Exhibited as a Loan Collection at the World's Columbian Exposition* [Chicago, 1893] *by Its Proprietor M. Steinert* [and the] *International Exposition for Music and Theatre, Vienna, 1892.* [New Haven, Conn.: Press of Tuttle, Morehouse & Taylor, 1893.] 30 pp., illus.

> Copies at NN (NYp) and NNMM (NYmm).

Literature

2329   "Eine Musikinstrumenten-Sammlung in Amerika zum Verkauf," *ZfI* 30 (1909/10): 80, 89.

STEPHENSON, W.; W. KETTERINGHAM; F. GLOVER; RICHARD BENNETT

2330   Puttick & Simpson, firm. *Catalogue of the Valuable Collection of Violins, Violas, Violoncellos, etc., the Properties of the Late W. Stephenson . . . W. Ketteringham . . . F. Glover. . . . Also from the Collection of Richard Bennett. . . . Bows and Cases; Also Valuable Autograph Scores, Letters, &c. . . . Sold . . . April the 19th, 1894.* 15 pp., 83 lots.

> Properties not differentiated. Catalogue no. 2994;
> copy also at NRU (Rs).

STEPHENSON, W.; W. KETTERINGHAM; F. GLOVER; RICHARD BENNETT *continued*

Literature

2331   Trinita Dei Monti. "The Sale of Guaranteed Violins [on April 19, 1894]," *Violin Times* 1 (1893/94): 102-3.

2332   "Geigen-Versteigerung in London," *ZfI* 14 (1893/94): 576-77.

A long article, some descriptions, prices fetched and buyers noted.

STEVENS, RICHARD JOHN SAMUEL. *See under* KENNEDY, THOMAS

STEWARD, of Wolverhampton

2333   Puttick & Simpson, firm. *Catalogue of a Large and Valuable Assemblage of Musical Instruments . . . Pianofortes . . . Harmoniums* [etc.] *Including the Celebrated Collection of Instruments, Chiefly by . . . di Salo, Formed by the Late Mr. Steward . . . Sold November 23, 1880.* 10 pp., 258 lots.

Steward's instruments, lots 94-120. Catalogue no. 1965.

STOBART, J. M., of Wandsworth Common

2334   Puttick & Simpson, firm. *Catalogue of Musical Instruments, Including the Property of the Late J. M. Stobart . . . Wandsworth Common; the Stock of Messrs. Sarle & Son . . . Collection of Violins, Violas, Violoncellos and Double Basses . . . Pianofortes . . . Harps . . . etc., & a Quantity of Music . . . Sold March 31st, 1903, and Following Day.* 21 pp., 469 lots.

Instruments, lots 1-429; Stobart's not identified;
Sarle's, 403-29. Catalogue no. 3716.

STOKOE, Dr.

2335   Puttick & Simpson, firm. *Catalogue of Several Important Musical Properties, Amongst Which are I. The Copyright Works of the Late Thomas Moore in Original Mss. and Engraved Plates. . . . II. The Very Interesting Literary and Musical Collections of Richard Clark. . . . V. A Miscellaneous Collection of Musical Instruments, Various Properties . . . Sold . . . June 25* [27 and 28], *1853.* 42 pp., 676 [i.e., 680] lots.

Instruments, lots 616-80; Stokoe's, 636-80.
Catalogue no. 329; copy also at NN (NYp).

STONE, WILLIAM HENRY; JAMES SMYTH, Bandmaster; HAROLD THOMAS

2336 Puttick & Simpson, firm. *Catalogue of a Large and Interesting Assemblage of Musical Property, Including the Collections of . . . Pianofortes . . . Harmoniums. . . . Cremona and Other Violins, Violas, Violoncellos & Double Basses . . . Brass & Wood Wind Instruments. . . . Library of Music, Comprising a Large Number of Full Scores* [etc.] *Sold November 24th* [1885], *and Following Day. . . .* 12, 20 pp., 357, 453 lots.

> Instruments, 1st day, lots 1-300. Catalogue no. 2369.

SULLIVAN, Sir ARTHUR SEYMOUR; ROBERT SUTHERLAND; ALFRED WAY; R. WALDY

2337 Puttick & Simpson, firm. *Catalogue of a Valuable Collection of Violins, Violas, Violoncellos, Guitars and Antique Instruments, Including the Properties of the Late Sir Arthur Sullivan, Robert Sutherland, Alfred Way, and R. Waldy . . . Sold . . . May 22nd, 1901.* 18 pp., 139 lots.

> Sullivan's instruments, lots 35-50; Sutherland's, 52-61; Way's, 79-83. Catalogue no. 3542; copies also at NRU (Rs) and NN (NYp).

Literature

2338 [Sale noted and a number of instruments described], *ZiMG* 2 (1900/1901): 358.

2339 "Puttick & Simpson's Guaranteed Sale," *Musical Opinion* 24 (1900/1901): 650.

> A list of some lots sold with prices fetched.

SUTHERLAND, ROBERT. *See under* SULLIVAN, Sir ARTHUR SEYMOUR

TAGORE, SOURINDA MOHUN [N. B.: His collection is now in the ROYAL COLLEGE OF MUSIC in LONDON, q.v., Section I. No list of the collection which he donated to the College in 1894 has been found. Some 98 other instruments were given by him to the Brussels Conservatoire, still others to the Indian Museum in Calcutta.]

TAPARELLI, MASSIMO. *See under* AZEGLIO, MASSIMO TAPARELLI, marchese di

TAPHOUSE, THOMAS WILLIAM

2340   *Catalogue of Musical Instruments in the Collection of. . . .* [n.p., n.d.]   104 lvs.,
5 photos.

> Ms. in NNMM (NYmm).

2341   Sotheby, Wilkinson & Hodge, firm. *Catalogue of the Collection of the Late . . .
Sold . . . 7th Day of June, 1905. . . .* [London] : 1905.   11 pp., 125 lots
(all instruments).

Literature

2342   [A note about the forthcoming sale of Taphouse's instruments on June 6 [sic]
1905] , *MT* 46 (1905): 408.

2343   Dotted Crochet. "The Musical Library of . . . ," *MT* 45 (1904): 629-36. illus.

> With notes about and photos of the instrument collection.

TARISIO, LUIGI

Literature

2344   "Tarisio, the Violin Collector," *The Violinist* 2, no. 10 (June 1902): 6.

> See also Hill, W. H., A. F. and A. E. *Antonio Stradivari,*
> pp. 134, 206, 263, 270-71. New York: Dover, [1963].

TAYLOR, EDWARD

2345   Puttick & Simpson, firm. *Catalogue of the Musical Library and Musical Instruments
of the Late . . . Sold . . . Dec. 3, 1863, and Two Following Days.*   69 pp., 1208 lots.

> Instruments, lots 1149-1208. Catalogue no. 789;
> copy also at DLC (Wc).

TAYLOR, P.   *See under* SALE, JOHN

TEALE, JAMES MASSINGBERD, of Doncaster, deceased

2346   Puttick & Simpson, firm. *Valuable Musical Instruments . . . Pianofortes . . . Organs
and Harmoniums. Violins, Tenors* [etc.] , *the Collection of. . . . Also Several Important
Autograph Manuscripts . . . Sold . . . November the 23rd, 1886.*   12 pp., 311 lots.

> Instruments, lots 1-284; Teale's not differentiated.
> Catalogue no. 2454.

TERBY, JOSEPH

2347   *Catalogue de la belle collection de violons italiens, archets de Tourte . . . vente . . . 17 juillet 1879.* [Louvain] : 1879. 14 pp.

> Mainly literature about and for the violin; at the end, lots 1-6 and A-O are actual instruments.

TOMKIES, JAMES

2348   Puttick & Simpson, firm. *Catalogue of the Valuable Collection of Violins, Violas, Violoncellos, etc., the Properties of the Late James Tomkies . . . Henry Hulse Berens . . . Sold . . . June the 19th, 1896.* 15 pp., 103 lots.

> Separate properties not identified. Catalogue no. 3160; copy also at NRU (Rs).

2349   Puttick & Simpson, firm. *Catalogue of Musical Instruments, Comprising Piano-fortes, Violins, Violas, Violoncellos, and Double Basses (Including the Property of the Late . . .) and Sheet Music . . . Sold June the 30th, 1896.* 14 pp., 400 lots.

> Instruments, lots 1-370; Tomkies', 94-110A. Catalogue no. 3164.

TORCY, THEODORE, Count de

2350   Baubigny, [C.-P.] . *Vente volontaire par suite de décès . . . de instruments de musique, notamment violon de Stradivarius . . . le mardi 16 avril 1878. . . .* Paris: 1878. 3 pp.

> Copy at GB-Lbl (Hirsch 421.8) with Ms. prices.

TROMBETTA

2351   Aulard, Paul (C.P.); Chardon et fils (Exp.). *Vente aux encheres publiques . . . après décès de M. Trombetta, Professeur de Musique. . . . Rue et Hotel Drouot . . . 9 mai 1899 . . . de 10 violons, altos, violes et violoncelles de Stradivarius, Gaspard da Solo* [sic] *, Gand et Bernardel* [etc.] *. 20 Archets de Voirin, Pageot et autres. . . . Quantité de livres sur la musique et partitions. . . .* Paris: 1899. 8 pp.

> Instruments, lots 1-35. Copy at NRU (Rs).

TUERLINCKX, CORNEILLE JEAN JOSEPH

2352   van Melckebeke (Notaire). *Instruments de musique, provenant de la fabrique renommée de J.-J.-A. Tuerlinckx à Malines. . . . Belles collections de musique, livres, minéraux, coquillages, fossiles, etc. Dont la vente . . . en la mortuaire de Monsieur C.-J.-J. Tuerlinckx-Dochez . . . 6 mai: Instruments . . . 7 mai: Collection de musique. . . .* Malines: Impr. van Velsen, [n.d., ca. 185-] .

   Copy at B-Bc.

TURNER, G. A. W. *See under* WILLSHAW, R.

TURNER, Sir G.; OSBORNE PAGE

2353   Christie, Mr., auctioneer. *A Catalogue of a Very Valuable and Curious Selection of Article of Virtu, and Miscellaneous Curiosities . . . Plate . . . Marbles and Bronzes. . . . An Extremely Valuable Assortment of Musical Instruments, Among Which Are . . . Amati Violoncello, a Guarnerius . . . Sold June 29th and Three Following Days.* London: 1824. 20 pp., 142 lots.

   Instruments, lots 98-139.

TURNER, THOMAS; STANLEY W. SLOANE; G. T. BRIDGEWATER

2354   Puttick & Simpson, firm. *Catalogue of an Unusually Extensive and Valuable Assemblage of Musical Instruments, Comprising Upwards of Thirty Pianofortes and Harps . . . Also Numerous Violins and Violoncellos of the Highest Quality . . . Including Examples Formerly in the Possession of the Late W. Sloan Stanley . . . G. T. Bridgewater . . . Thomas Turner, with Others from the Collection of Amateurs of Distinction . . . Sold . . . June 30th, 1860.* 30 pp., 632 lots.

   Sloane's, lots 141-42; Bridgewater's, 143-49; Turner's, 154-79. Catalogue no. 635.

VAILLANT, GABRIELLE. *See under* BRIDSON, J. R.

VALDRIGHI, LUIGI FRANCESCO [N. B.: Most of his collection went to the Civico Museo in Modena. Some items were included in the International Exhibition, London, 1862, and in the Mostra Internazionale di Musica, 1888, in Bologna. See *"Literature"* in Section I under **LONDON (England)** and **BOLOGNA (Italy)**.]

2355 "(Collezione strumentistica) [and] Corollarii IV. Collezione Valdrighi." In his *Nomecheliurgografia antica e moderna*, pp. 292-93 and his *Aggiunta*, pp. [31]-43. Modena: 1884 and 1888. Reprint ed. (combined). Bologna: Forni, 1967. 93 items.

VALLOCK, EDMUND. *See under* **ROBSON, PHILIP A.**

VAN RAALTE, CHARLES, of Brownsea Castle

2356 Fox and Sons, firm. *Catalogue of the Contents of the Mansion, Including . . . Valuable Collection of Musical Instruments Formed by the Late C. Van Raalte, Esq. . . .* [which will be sold by] *Messrs. Fox and Sons . . . June 21, 1927.* [Bournemouth: 1927.] 206 lots.

> Instruments, pp. [94]-123, illus.
> "A descriptive inventory of the musical instruments at Brownsea Castle was recently prepared by the Revd. Canon Francis W. Galpin . . . [and] the details [are] given in the following lots. . . . Canon Galpin states in a Foreword to his catalogue. . . ." That catalogue not located, perhaps extant only in Ms. Film copy of Fox and Sons' catalogue at NBuU-M (BUu).

VECLA, EMMA. *See Section I under* **MILAN (Italy). MUSEO NAZIONALE DELLA SCIENZE E DELLA TECNICA**

VENUA, FRÉDÉRIC MARC ANTOINE, b. 1788

2357 Puttick & Simpson, firm. *Catalogue of an Extensive and Valuable Collection of Music, Including the Library of . . . , and the Library of a Well-Known Professor. . . . Works of Ancient and Modern Composers . . .* [etc.]. *Musical Instruments, Capital Modern Pianofortes. . . . Cremona Violins, Violoncellos. . . . Wood and Brass Wind Instruments of the Best Makers . . . Sold . . . April 12th, 1865.* 32 pp., 716 lots.

> Instruments, lots 574-716; Dr. Bossy's, 610-37; Venua's, 638-72. Catalogue no. 858; copy also at NN (NYp).

VIDAL, LOUIS ANTOINE

2358   Lavigne (Exp.); Charles Pillet (C. P.). *Catalogue de la collection musicale et des instruments de musique, provenant du cabinet de feu M. Vidal, ancien premier violon de la chapelle de Charles X et de Louis-Philippe . . . vente . . . Hotel Drouot . . . 6 février 1868. . . .* Paris: 1868. 14 pp., 102, 23 lots.

   Instruments, last 23 lots. Copy at NL-DHgm.

VIGEUR, A.; JOHN RENÉ PAYNE

2359   Puttick & Simpson, firm. *Catalogue of Grand and Cottage Pianofortes . . . Harps . . . Violins* [etc.] *Property of the Late . . . and a Small Library of Music . . . Sold January 31st, 1905, and Following Day.* 18 pp., 362 lots.

   Instruments, lots 1-315; Vigeur's, 83-91; Payne's, 92-92A. Catalogue no. 3895.

VUILLAUME, JEAN BAPTISTE

2360   Gand et Bernardel (Exp.); Alégatière (C. P.). *Vente après décès de M. . . . Catalogue composant sa collection de violons, violoncelles, contre-basses et instruments anciens. . . . Autographes, gravures, musique, livres, etc. Dont la vente . . . 21 et 22 Mai 1880.* Paris: 1880. 8 pp., 164 lots.

   Instruments, 150 lots. Copy at F-Pn.

W***, M. V. de, of Lille

2361   *Collection de M. V. de W***, de Lille. 2 Violons Stradivarius. Altos, violons, violoncelles italiens et française. Dont la vente par suite de décès aura lieu Hôtel Drouot . . . 26 février 1897.* [Paris?] : 1897.

   Cited from Lambertini*; not verified or located.

WACQUEY, F. *See under* DUCHESNE, R.

WAGNER, EDUARD. *See Section I under* LEIPZIG (Germany). MUSEUM FÜR VÖLKERKUNDE

WALDY, R. *See under* SULLIVAN, Sir ARTHUR SEYMOUR

WALLACE, W. VINCENT

2362   Puttick & Simpson, firm. *Catalogue of a Collection of Miscellaneous Music from Several Private Libraries, Including . . . Mr. Charles Lucas* [and others] *. . . Also . . . Musical Instruments . . . Sold . . . June 30, 1869, and the Following Day.* 33 pp., 987 lots.

> Instruments, lots 887-987; Wallace's, 917-40; C. Boose's, 941-44. Catalogue no. 1137; copy also at NN (NYp).

WALTON, WILLIAM, of Preston

2363   Puttick & Simpson, firm. *Catalogue of Old and Modern Violins, Violas and Violoncellos . . . Bows etc., the Property of the Late Miss Marian Hirtsfield . . . the Late Mr. William Walton . . . Sold . . . November 24th, 1938.* 8 pp., 132 lots.

> Walton's instruments, lots 71-99 (Hirtsfield, 2 lots only). Catalogue no. 151 [2nd ser.].

WANAMAKER, RODMAN

Literature

2364   "Wurlitzer Buys Wanamaker Old Violin Collection," *Music Trade Review* 8 (November 1929): 45.

> A collection of 65 instruments and bows.

2365   "$3,000,000 Worth of Rare Old Violins: Purchase of Wanamaker Collection Gives Wurlitzer Virtual Monopoly on Rare Stringed Instruments in the U. S.," *Music Trade Review* 8 (December 1929): 17, 31.

> Collection purchased by Thaddeus Rich from Wanamaker, resold to Wurlitzer.

2366   Schmidt, Georg. "Die Meistergeigensammlung von Wanamaker," *Das Orchester* 7, no. 12 (1930): 141.

> *ZfMW*-schau* says "Wanaker"!

2367   Schmidt, Georg. "Der Verkauf der berühmten Meistergeigensammlung von Rodman Wanamaker in Philadelphia; nach amerikanischen Zeitungsberichten erläutert . . . ," *Zeitschrift für Musik* 97, no. 4 (April 1930): 270-71.

2368   "Verkauf der berühmten Wanamaker-Kollektion alter Meistergeigen," *ZfI* 50 (1929/30): 210; and 418-20 by Georg Schmidt which describes items, names buyers and notes prices fetched.

WARREN, E. P.

2369   Puttick & Simpson, firm. *Catalogue of Valuable Violins, Violas, and Violoncellos. . . . Bows . . . Viola d'amours, Viol da gambas . . . Early Spinets, and Other Antique Instruments . . . Property of William Ellis . . . Mrs. Esmund Pittman . . . the Lewes House Collection Formed by the Late E. P. Warren . . .* [et al] *. . . Sold October 31st, 1929.* 15 pp., 199 lots.

> Lewes House Collection, lots 170-97 (old instruments); other properties, 1-2 lots each. Catalogue no. 6663.

WATSON, HENRY. *See Section I under* MANCHESTER (U.K.). ROYAL MANCHESTER COLLEGE OF MUSIC

WATSON, JAMES R.

2370   Puttick & Simpson, firm. *Catalogue of Musical Instruments . . . Including a Collection of Over One Hundred Instruments . . . the Property of James R. Watson . . .* [at one time] *the Stock of Messrs. Dan Godfrey Sons . . . Sold October 25th, 1898.* 24 pp., 590 lots.

> Watson's instruments, lots 403-97. Catalogue no. 3335.

WATT, JAMES

2371   Hampson, Walter. "Mr. James Watt's Collection of Violins," *Violin Times* 5 (1896/97): 57-59, 78-79, 117-19.

WAUTERS, EMILE

Literature

2372   Briggs, Ernest L. "A Collection of Musical Instruments," *The Violinist* 20, no. 12 (1916): 521-24, 531. illus.

WAY, A. *See under* SULLIVAN, Sir ARTHUR SEYMOUR

WEBB, GRAHAM. *See Section I under* CORNWALL (U.K.). CORNWALL MUSEUM OF MECHANICAL MUSIC

WEBB, JOHN (of Paris)

2373   Christie & Manson, Messrs., auctioneers. *Catalogue of the Collection of Violins, Printed Music, &c. of . . . Deceased . . . Sold by Auction . . . at Their Great Room . . . February 1, 1849.* 8 pp., 177 lots.

> Instruments (violins), lots 111-46. Copy: compiler.

WEISS-STAUFFACHER, HEINRICH

2374   *Mechanische Musikinstrumente und Musikautomaten: beschreibender Katalog der Seewener Privatsammlung, hrsg. von Heinrich Weiss-Stauffacher und Rudolf Bruhin. . . .* Seewen SO: [the author; Auslfg., Pratteln: Interbook Productions, G. Kloos, 1975]. 248 pp., illus., ca. 300 items.

2375   *Mechanische Musikinstrumente und Musikautomaten: beschreibender Katalog der Seewener Privatsammlung, hrsg. von Heinrich Weiss-Stafufacher und Rudolf Bruhin. . . .* [In French as] *Automates et instruments de musique mecaniques.* Fribourg: office du Livre, 1976.

Literature

2376   Bruhin, Rudolf. "Eine Musik-Automaten-Sammlung in Schwarzbubenland," *Metallwerke AG Dornach, Haus-Zeitung* 17, no. 3 (1968): 15-19. illus.

2377   "Verzeichnis der mechanische Musikinstrumente in der Sammlung H. Weiss-Stauffacher, Seewen/SO [a checklist]," *Glareana,* vol. 20, no. 3/4 (1971).

WESLAKE, J.

2378   Puttick & Simpson, firm. *Catalogue of Musical Instruments . . . Including the Property of the Late . . . and a Library of Music . . . Sold October the 26th, 1897.* 17 pp., 387 lots.

> Instruments, lots 1-339; Weslake's not identified.
> Catalogue no. 3262.

WHITE, RICHARD GRANT

2379   Bangs & Co. *Catalogue of the Library of . . . , Engravings, Oil Paintings, and Musical Instruments. . . .* New York: Bangs & Co., 1885. 201 pp., 2057 + 20 lots.

> Copies at NN (NYp), MiU (Aau).

WHITTAKER, JOSHUA [or JOHN?]

2380   Puttick & Simpson, firm. *Catalogue of Musical Instruments ... Pianofortes ... Harps ... Violins, etc., Including the Collection Formed by the Late John* [sic] *Whittaker ... Sold March 27th, 1900, and Following Day.* 18 pp., 424 lots.

> "Property of Joshua [sic] Whittaker," lots 103-24.
> Catalogue no. 3438.

WHITTALL, GERTRUDE CLARK, FOUNDATION. *See Section I under* WASHINGTON, D. C. (USA). LIBRARY OF CONGRESS

WHITTINGHAM, ALFRED

2381   Puttick & Simpson, firm. *Catalogue of the Large Stock of Ancient and Modern Music, and the ... Musical Library of a Gentleman. ... Also Numerous and Valuable Musical Instruments ... Important Violins and Violoncellos, Brass and Wood Wind Instruments ... Sold ... November 23, 1870, and 3 Following Days.* 69 pp., 1840 lots.

> Instruments, lots 1642-1840 (Whittingham's?).
> Catalogue no. 1218.

WILKINSON, NORMAN; Lady KATHLEEN PILKINGTON

2382   Sotheby & Co., firm. *Catalogue of Valuable Porcelain and Pottery and Works of Art ... [etc.]. Musical Instruments the Property of Norman Wilkinson and Lady Kathleen Pilkington ... Sold ... 6th of July, 1934.* [London]: 1934.

> Musical instruments, pp. 17-18, lots 85-97A.

WILLIAMS, J.

2383   Puttick & Simpson, firm. *Catalogue of Old and Modern Violins, Violas, Violoncellos ... Bows ... Including the Property of the Late ... Sold June 10th, 1937.* 10 pp., 175 lots.

> Williams', lots 82-157 (includes some books).
> Catalogue no. 16 [2nd ser.].

WILLIAMS, J., of Walsall. *See under* **MAXWELL, Sir PETER BENTON**

[WILLMOTT, Miss G. A.]

2384   Sotheby & Co., firm. *Catalogue of Valuable Chinese Porcelain . . .* [etc.]. *A Selected Portion of the Well-Known Collection of Musical Instruments, the Property of . . . Sold . . . 5th of April, 1935.* [London] : 1935.
Musical instruments, pp. 10-15, lots 36-71.

WILLMS, WOLFGANG

2385   "Die Flötensammlung von Dr. med. Wolfgang Willms in Aachen-Laurensburg," *Glareana*, vol. 16, no. 3/4 (1967). iv, 27 pp., illus., 247 items.

WILLSHAW, R.

2386   Puttick & Simpson, firm. *Catalogue of Musical Instruments . . . Organs . . . Harps . . . Violins, etc. . . .* [a Strad] *the Property of G. A. W. Turner . . . Valuable Instruments, the Property of the Late William Cochrane . . . the Stock of Instruments* [of the late] *R. Willshaw . . . Brass and Wood Wind Instruments, Including* [those] *of H. M. S. Gibraltar . . . Sold June 28th, 1904, and Following Day.* 20 pp., 393 lots.
Instruments, lots 1-373; Willshaw's, 206-343;
H. M. S. Gibraltar's, 362-74; Turner's Strad, 119;
Cochrane's, 117-18. Catalogue no. 3845; copy
also at NRU (Rs) (379 lots only).

WILSON, Sir GIFFIN

2387   Puttick & Simpson, firm. *Catalogue of a Valuable Collection of Music, Including the Library of the Late . . . Also Violins, Violoncellos, Pianofortes, &c. . . . Sold . . . 23 March, 1849.* 14 pp., 953 lots.
Instruments. lots 244-75 (Wilson's?).
Catalogue no. 109; copy also at NN (NYp).

WIT, PAUL de [N. B.: Two of the collections of instruments formed by Paul de Wit went to the Musikinstrumenten-Museum of the Staatliches Institut für Musikforschung in Berlin—240 items in 1888, 280 items in 1890. No separate catalogues have been identified for those groups, but the items are covered in Fleischer's 1892 catalogue of the **MUSIKINSTRUMENTEN-MUSEUM**, q.v., Section I. The third collection brought together by Wit became part of the HEYER group which ultimately formed the basis of the Musikinstrumentenmuseum in the Universität, Leipzig.

Wit also founded and edited for many years the extraordinary journal, the *Zeitschrift für Instrumentenbau,* which contained in its 63 volumes much of the literature cited throughout this bibliography. A relatively scarce periodical, complete sets apparently do not exist (according to Fellinger's* union catalogue). For years it was thought that the only complete set in the United States was owned by (curiously enough) the U.S. Weather Bureau in Washington, D.C., but that attribution in the *Union List of Serials* is an error; the Bureau's siglum should have been entered, instead, under the title *Zeitschrift für Instrumentenkunde.* Fortunately, the Library of Congress, the Sibley Music Library, and the New York Public Library all possess long runs, and though none is a complete set, the runs, together, span all 63 volumes, 1880/81 through 1942/43. The Zentralantiquariat der DDR in Leipzig has recently announced a reprint of the set, but at close to $900.00 (U.S.) for the first ten volumes (all available at present), the increase in the number of libraries owning sets may be very modest.]

2388   "Sammlung Paul de Wit." In Vienna. Internationale Ausstellung für Musik- und Theater-wesen, 1892. *Fachkatalog . . . Deutschland und Österreich-Ungarn,* pp. 142-48. Wien: 1892. 79 items.

2389   "Raum XXVI. Kolossalgruppe Paul de Wit." *Ibid.,* pp. 409-12.

2390   Kurka, R. W. "Paul de Wit's Colossalgruppe 'Allegorie der Tonkunst' auf der Internationalen Ausstellung für Musik- und Theater-wesen in Wien, 1892," *ZfI* 12 (1891/92): 438-39. With "colossal" illus. between 444 and 445.

2391   Wit, Paul de. *Perlen aus der Instrumenten-Sammlung von Paul de Wit in Leipzig.* Leipzig: [author, 1892]. 14 pp., 16 colored pls., Obl. F°, ca. 190 items shown.

     Also issued with English text. Copy at NN (NYp); not examined.

2392   Wit, Paul de. *Kurzgefasster Katalog aller im musikhistorischen Museum von Paul de Wit vorhandenen Musikinstrumente, Gemälde und anderen Merkwürdigkeiten, die auf Musik oder Musik-instrumente bezug haben.* Leipzig: 1893.

     Cited from Scheurleer*; not located.

2393   Wit, Paul de. *Katalog des musikhistorischen Museums von Paul de Wit Leipzig. . . . Mit zahlreichen Abbildungen nach photographischen Originalaufnahmen.* Leipzig: P. de Wit, 1903. 207 pp., illus., 1,181 numbers, 771 instruments.

     Copy at DLC (Wc).

Literature

2394   Anger, Walter. "Die Viola da gamba des Vincenzo Ruggeri in der Sammlung des Herrn Paul de Wit," *ZfI* 6 (1885/86): 262-64.

2395   Simon, Paul. "Ein Besuch im Museum de Wit," *ZfI* 7 (1886/87): 249-50.

2396   "Die Rupf- und Streich-Instrumente im Museum de Wit in Leipzig," *ZfI* 7 (1886/87): 331-32, 346-48.

2397   "König Albert in musikhistorischen Museum von Paul de Wit," *ZfI* 13 (1892/93) 395-96.

2398   Eichhorn, Hermann. "Grade Zinken und Jägertrompete in musikhistorischen Museum von Paul de Wit," *ZfI* 15 (1894/95): 813-15, 838-42, 867-69. illus.

2399   "Die Entwicklung des Musikinstrumentenmacher-Gewerbes in Leipzig, unter Berücksichtigung der im musikhistorischen Museum von Paul de Wit noch vorhandenen Instrumente," *ZfI* 16 (1895/96): 172-74, 202-5, 229-30.

2400   Altenburg, Wilhelm. "Ueber einige Holzblasinstrumente mit Doppelzungenblatt in dem de Wit'schen Musikhistorischen Museum," *ZfI* 3 (1897/98): 519-21, 543-46. illus., ca. 15 items.

2401   Schurig, E. "Ein Kapitel aus der Geschichte der Trommel in Sachsen. Historische Skizze . . . ergänzt durch Abbildungen . . . in musikhistor. Museum von Paul de Wit," *ZfI* 20 (1899/1900): 286-89. illus.

2402   "Paul de Wits historische Ausstellung auf dem VI. Internationalen Gitarristentage in München," *ZfI* 24 (1903/4): 995-99. Many illus., 48 items.
   See also pp. 780-81, 939, 1039 for brief notices.

2403   "Historische Trommeln," *ZfI* 25 (1904/5): 317-18. illus.

2404   "Zwei Konzertinstrumente vergangener Zeiten aus dem Nachlass von Paul de Wit," *ZfI* 46 (1925/26): 1080-81. illus.

2405   Kinsky, Georg. "Paul de Wit [Nachruf]," *ZfMW* 8 (1925/26): 254-55.

2406   "Paul de Wit und sein Instrumentenmuseum," *ZfI* 57 (1936/37): 98.

WITHERS, GEORGE

2407   Puttick & Simpson, firm. *Catalogue of the Valuable Collection of Old & Modern Italian, French, English and Other Violins, Violas, and Violoncellos. The George Withers Collection of English Stringed Instruments. The Reference Library of Books on the Violin . . . Portraits . . . Paganini Relics . . . Autograph Letters, &c. . . . Sold May 12th, 1932, and Following Day.* 20 pp., 386 lots.

> Many plates, not common to P & S sale catalogues.
> Withers' collection of English violins and violas,
> lots 178-212; antique instruments, 339-76; Paganini
> letters, 271-76. Catalogue no. 6971.

WITSEN, JONAS

2408   Oosterwyk, Johannes, Boekverkooper. *Catalogus van uystekende konstige en plaisante schilderijen van groote en voorname meesters. En uytmuntende speel-instrumente, benevens een schoone inboel . . . nagelaten. . . . Verkogt werden . . . 23. Maart, 1717. . . .* T'Amsterdam: 1717. [7] pp., 139 lots.

> "Volgen nu de uytmuntende speel-instrumenten," p. 7
> (14 lots, but many more items, e.g., lot 3: "10 fioolen,
> waar onder verscheyde Cremonese, die uytmuntend zyn").
> Copy at NL-DHgm.

WITTEN, LAURENCE C., II   [N. B.: Lichtenwanger directory (L in list of secondary sources) notes a catalogue of an exhibit at Rockefeller University in New York City that included selections from the Witten collection, 1968. Not located.]

WITVOGEL, GERARD FREDERIK

2409   Rampen, Arent, auctioneer (?). *Catalogus Van een uitmuntende verzameling van een groote extra fraije gedrukte Partye Exemplaren van nieuw Musicq; Van de beroemste Meesters, Benevens De fyne kopere gesnedene Platen Van dien compleet . . . nagelaten door . . . , organist van den Luthersche Nieuwe Kerk t'Amsterdam, dewelke verkogt zullen werden 13 october 1746.* Amsterdam: By Arent Rampen, 1746. 28 pp.

> Instruments, p. 28, 12 lots. Copy at NL-DHgm.

Literature

2410   "De nalatenschap van G. F. Witvogel, 1746," *Tijdschrift der Vereeniging voor Noordnederlands Muziekgeschiedenis* 9 (1909-14): 245-49.

WOOLHOUSE, WESLEY S. B.; Sir WILLIAM GEORGE CUSINS

2411 Puttick & Simpson, firm. *Catalogue of the Valuable Collection of Violins, Violas, Violoncellos, etc., the Property of the Late W. S. B. Woolhouse . . . and the Late Sir William Cusins, Master of The Queen's Music . . . and Two Valuable Autograph Scores by Mozart and Spohr . . . Sold December the 6th, 1893.* 13 pp., 68 lots.

> Catalogue no. 2971; copy also at NRU (Rs).

Literature

2412 [Sale noted], *Violin Times* 1 (1893/94): 36-37.

2413 "Streichinstrumenten-Versteigerung in London," *ZfI* 14 (1893/94): 233.

> Notes 68 lots; gives prices fetched for some items.

WORNUM, ROBERT, of Wigmore Street

2414 White, Mr., auctioneer. *Capital Violoncellos, Tenors, Violins, Grand Piano-Fortes, &c. A Catalogue of Musical Instruments . . . the Property of. . . . A Very Capital Violoncello by Amati, a Do. by Guarnerius, and Two Other Violoncellos. A Violin by Stainer and Twenty Other Violins. Also a Small Collection of Music . . . Sold . . . July 20th, 1816.* 4 pp., 106 lots.

> Instruments, lots 52-106. Copies at GB-LBl, DLC (Wc) (Julian Marshall's copy).

X*** (="Amateur distingué")

2415 Carlier, Victor (C.P.). *Catalogue d'une jolie collection de tableaux anciens, la plupart de bons maitres Flamands, Hollandais, Italiens, Francais et d'objets de curiosité . . . provenant du cabinet de feu . . . vente . . . 18 et 19, 1850. . . .* Lille: 1850. 8, 3 pp., 149 + 31 + 61 lots.

> Thirty-four of the lots are musical instruments according to Lugt*; not examined. Copy at F-Pn.

ZACH, KARL

2416 "Glaskasten IX: Instrumenten Sammlung Karl Zach." In Vienna. Internationale Austellung für Musik- und Theater-Wesen, 1892. *Fach-Katalog . . . Deutschland und Österreich-Ungarn,* pp. 238-40. Wien: 1892.

ZIMMERMAN, JOSEF   (J57)

2417   *Von Zinken, Flöten und Schalmeien. Katalog einer Sammlung historischer Holzblasinstrumente.* [Vorwort: Alfred Berner.] [Birkesdorf-Düren: Druck Z. Bezani, 1967.] 125 pp., illus.

> Review in *GSJ*, vol. 23 (1970).

ZWEERS, H. A. J.; J. A. FRENTROP

2418   Bom, G. Theod. & Zoon, firm. *Catalogus eener uitgebreide en belangrijke verzameling Muziek. Oude italiaansche violen, alten, violoncels en fluiten . . . nagelaten door . . . H. A. Zweers, Muziekhandelaar, te Amsterdam en J. A. Frentrop, Muziekhandelaar, te 's Hage . . . 21 . . . 22 maart 1887.* Amsterdam: 1887. 26 pp., 668 lots.

> Instruments, lots 644-68 (an interesting group).
> Copy at NL-Avb (n & p).

APPENDIXES

Some Early Inventories, To 1825

Expositions and Exhibitions, 1818-1978

APPENDIX A
SOME EARLY INVENTORIES, TO 1825

Only the earliest inventory of each collection is listed here.
For a number of them
—e.g., the collections at Ambras and at Verona, and that of Ferdinand de Medici—
many later ones exist and are cited in the bibliography.

Date	Collection of /in	Item Nos.
1503	Isabel I, la Catolico	2083
1543	Verona. Società accademia filarmonica	1530-31
1547	Henry VIII, King of England	2052-53
1560	Maria de Austria, Regent of the Netherlands	2165-66
1566	Fugger, Raimund, d.j.	1993-96
1577	Karl von Steiermark, Erzherzog von Innerösterreich	2094
1582	Johann George II, Fürst von Brandenburg	2089
1589	Ludwig der Fromme von Württemberg	1455
1593	Dresden. K. Sächsische Musik-Kapelle	443
	Bevilacqua, Count Maria	1827-28
1596	Nonesuch Castle	1111
	Ambras Sammlung unter Erzherzog Ferdinand II, von Tirol	1579-82
1598	Alfonso II, d'Este	1791-92
1600	Cesare d'Este, Duke of Modena	1883
1602	Madrid. Palacio Nacional	937
1603	Kytson, Sir Thomas (of Hengrave Hall)	1464
1607	Felipe II, King of Spain	1959
1625	Karl von Neisse, Erzherzog von Habsburg	2093

Date	Collection of /in	Item Nos.
1640	Ferdinand, de Medici, Prince of Tuscany	1960
1664	Settala, Manfredo	2299-300
1667	Dandeleu, Jean Baptiste	1929
	Friedrich Wilhelm der Grosse	1982
167-?	Ruhelust collection under Pio Enea degli Obizzi	1607
1682	Meran. Pfarrkirche St. Nikolaus	974
1691	Sale at Dewing's Coffee-House	1713
1706	Osek, Czechoslovakia	1147-48
1714	Britton, Thomas	1853-54
1720	Göttweig, Austria. Benedictine Abbey	575
1740?	Rudolstadt. Hof-Kapelle	1386-87
1740	Mercer, Col. John and Nicholas Hawksmoor	2178
1741	Koen	2118
	Sayn-Wittgenstein, Casimir, Graf von Berleburg	2277
1747	Stiftes Kremsmünster	657
1748	Campion, François	1869
1756	Maria Barbara de Braganza, Queen of Spain	2164
1759	Selhof, Nicolas	2295-96
1763	Barnaart, Jacobus	1810
	Harde, G. W.	2032
ca. 1765	Hellier, Samuel	2049
1771	Salmreifferscheid, le Compte de	2269
1772	Neubauer, Frederick	2207
1773	Leeuwarden, J. van	2180
	Köthen. Hofkapelle	650-51
1774	Sale by van der Vinne	1714
1780	Simon August, Graf und Edler zur Lippe-Detmold	2308
	Versailles. Bibliothèque de la musique du roi	1539
1786	Stanley, John	2325
1789	Sale by Greenwood	1715
1791	"A Shopkeeper and Engraver in the City"	1716
1792	Ashfield, Frederick	1803
	Sale by Roos, Gerbrand & Weege	1717
1795	"An Amateur"	1718
1796	"A Gentleman"	1719
	Brooke, John	1862
1803	Barry, Smith	1812
	Sale by Gartman, Vermandel, Smit	1720
1804	"A Gentleman"	1721
1808	Colizzi, J. H.	1903
1810	"An Amateur"	1722

Date	Collection of/in	Item Nos.
1816	Bacon, John	**1806**
1819	Forkel, Johann Nikolaus	**1979**
1821	Naldi, Giuseppe	**2203**
1823-29	Eight anonymous sales by Mr. Musgrave	**1723-30**
1824	Göpel, Johann Andreas	**2018**
	Gunn, John	**2024**
1825	Jameson, Dr.	**2087**

APPENDIX B

EXPOSITIONS AND EXHIBITIONS, 1818-1978

Date	Place	Name or Title	Item Nos.
1818	Paris	Exposition des produits de l'industrie française	**1187**
1823	Paris	Exposition des produits de l'industrie française	**1188**
1824	Bern	Industrie-Ausstellung	**1932**
1827	Paris	Exposition des produits de l'industrie française	**1189-90**
1830	Brussels	Exposition des produits de l'industrie nationale	**305-6**
1834	Paris	Exposition des produits de l'industrie française	**1192-95**
1835	Brussels	Exposition des produits de l'industrie nationale	**307**
1839	Paris	Exposition des produits de l'industrie française	**1196-200**
1841	Brussels	Exposition des produits de l'industrie belge	**308**
1844	Berlin	Allgemeine deutsche Gewerbe-Ausstellung	**98-99**
	Paris	Exposition des produits de l'industrie française	**1201-4**
1845	Vienna	Industrie-Ausstellung	**1550**
1847	Linz	Industrie- und Gewerbs-Produktion Ausstellung	**727**
1848	Berlin	Industrie-Ausstellung	**198**
1849	Paris	Exposition des produits de l'industrie française	**1208-9**
1851	London	Great Exhibition of the Works of Industry of All Nations	**775-90, 875**
1853-54	New York	Exhibition of the Industry of All Nations	**1066**
1854	Munich	Allgemeine deutsche Industrie-Ausstellung	**1019-20**
1855	Paris	Exposition universelle	**1218-27**
	Willisau	Industrie-Ausstellung	**1679**
1856	Boston	Massachusetts Charitable Mechanic Association Exhibition [the 8th]	**219**
1857	Berlin	Schweizerische Industrieausstellung	**199**
1861	Florence	Esposizione italiana	**506**

Date	Place	Name or Title	Item Nos.
1862	London	International Exhibition	802-15
1867	Paris	Exposition universelle	1229-47
1872	London	International Exhibition	816
	London	Special Exhibition of Ancient Musical Instruments	877-79, 881
1873	Vienna	Weltausstellung	1632-45
1875	Santiago	Exposición internacional	1410
1876	Philadelphia	Centennial Exhibition	1323-25
	Florence	Esposizione storica nelle onoranze a Bartolomeo Cristofori	507-8
1878	Paris	Exposition universelle	1248-61, 2005-6
1879	Sydney	International Exhibition	1471-75
1880	Brussels	Exposition nationale	320-22
	Melbourne	International Exhibition	963-66
	Düsseldorf	Kunst- und Gewerbe-Ausstellung	466
	Vienna	Nieder-Österreichische Gewerbe-Ausstellung	1630-31
1881	Frankfurt a.M.	Allgemeine deutsche Patent- und Musterschutz-Ausstellung	515-16
	Kolberg	Allgemeine Gewerbe- und Industrie-Ausstellung	652
	Milan	Esposizione industriale nazionale	978, 980-87, 1770
	Paris	Exposition internationale d'électricité	1213
	Halle	Gewerbe- und Industrie-Ausstellung	613-15
	Wrocław	Gewerbe- und Industrie-Ausstellung	1680
	Detmold	Lippische Gewerbe-Ausstellung	433
	Stuttgart	Württemburgisches Landes- Gewerbe-Ausstellung	1460-61
1882	Nuremburg	Bayerische Landes- Industrie- Gewerbe- und Kunst-Ausstellung	1113-14
	Leipzig	" . . . historische und ethnologische Ausstellung musikalischer Instrumente"	668
	Moscow	Vserossiiskaīa vystavka	1016
1883	Amsterdam	Colonial Exhibition	7-17
	Boston	Foreign Exhibition	214-15
	London	Furniture Trades Exhibition	769-71
	Calcutta	International Exhibition	353-55
	Amsterdam	Internationale Koloniale en Uitvoerhandel-Tentoonstelling	7-17
	Zürich	Schweizerische Landesausstellung	1700-1709
1884	Turin	Esposizione generale italiana	1508-10
	Teplitz	Industrie- Gewerbe- und Elektrische-Ausstellung	1480-82
	London	International Exhibition	817-19
1885	Budapest	Budapesti országos általános kiállitas	328-30

Date	Place	Name or Title	Item Nos.
	Antwerp	Exposition universelle	36-41
	London	International Inventions Exhibition	820-30
	Görlitz	Niederschlesische Gewerbe- und Industrie-Ausstellung	566-68
1886	London	Colonial and Indian Exhibition	754-55
	Edinburgh	International Exhibition [of Industry, Science and Art]	472-75
	Liverpool	International Exposition	740
	Berlin	Jubiläums-Ausstellung	117-20
	Altenburg	Landesausstellung	4
	Augsburg	Schwäbische Kreisausstellung	60-61
1887	Freiburg i.B.	Oberrheinische Gewerbeausstellung	537-38
1888	Lucerne	Ausstellung von Musikinstrumente früherer Zeiten	2293
	Melbourne	Centennial International Exhibition	967-70
	Munich	Deutsch-nationale Kunstgewerbe-Ausstellung	1029-31
	Barcelona	Exposición universel	71-74
	Brussels	Exposition rétrospective d'art industriel	323-25
	Vienna	Jubiläums- Gewerbe-Ausstellung	1574-75
	Bologna	Mostra internazionale di musica	210-12
	Berlin	Nationale Gewerbe-Ausstellung	126
	Copenhagen	Nordiske Industri-, Landbrugs- og Kunstidstilling	402-3
1889	London	Cremona Society Exhibition	756
	Paris	Exposition universelle	1262-74
	Hamburg	Gewerbe- und Industrie-Ausstellung	618-21
1890	London	Royal Military Exhibition	871-72
1891	Prague	Allgemeine Landesausstellung	1333-34
	London	German Exhibition	772-74
	Zeitz	Gewerbe- und Industrie-Ausstellung	1691
1892	London	"First Musical Art Exhibition"	859
	Vienna	Internationale Ausstellung für Musik- und Theaterwesen	127-28, 1551-73
1893	Belém	Exposição industrial	91
	Antwerp	Exposition universelle	42-43
	Aussig	Gewerbe-, Industrie- und Landwirtschaft-Ausstellung	64
	Erfurt	Thüringer Gewerbe- und Industrie-Ausstellung	490-91
	Innsbruck	Tiroler Landesausstellung	638
	Chicago	World's Columbian Exposition	360-71, 2152
1894	Lyons	Expositions universelle et colonial	922-23
	L'vov	Galizischen Landesausstellung	921

Date	Place	Name or Title	Item Nos.
1895	Lübeck	Deutsch-nordische Handels- und Industrie-Ausstellung	910-11
	Strasbourg	Industrie- und Gewerbe-Ausstellung	1451-53
	Amsterdam	Internationale Tentoonstelling van Hotel-och Reizewezen	18
	London	Music Trades Exhibition	844-48
	Teplitz	Nordböhmische Industrie- und Gewerbe-Ausstellung	1483
1896	Nuremburg	Bayerische Landes- Industrie- Gewerbe- und Kunst-Ausstellung	1116-18
	Paris	Exposition internationale du théâtre et de la musique	1217
	Geneva	Exposition nationale suisse	544-45
	Berlin	Gewerbe-Ausstellung	105-11
	Budapest	Milleniumi kiállitás	341
	Dresden	Sächsischen Handwerk- und Kunst-Gewerbe Ausstellung	448
	Nizhni-Novgorod	Vserossiiskaĭa vystavka	1108-10
	Stuttgart	Württemburghisches Elektrotechnik und Kunst-Gewerbe-Ausstellung	1458-59
1897	Stockholm	Allmänna konst- och industriutställningen	1425-26
	Brussels	Exposition internationale	310-14
	Markneukirchen	Gewerbe- und Industrie-Ausstellung	955
	London	Music Trades Exhibition	849-50
	Leipzig	Sächsisch- Thüringische Industrie- und Gewerbe-Ausstellung	680-83
	London	Victorian Era Exhibition	903
1898	Berlin	Allgemeine Musik-Ausstellung	100-101
	Turin	Esposizione nazionale di Torino	1513-15
	Vienna	Jubiläums- Kunstausstellung	1576-77
	Holborn	Music Trades Exhibition	631
	London	Music Trades Exhibition	851
	Most	Nordwestböhmische Ausstellung für deutsche Industrie, Gewerbe und Landwirtschaft	1017
1899	Dublin	Feis Ceoil	450
	Zeitz	Fest-Versammlung des Pestalozzi- und Lehrer-Vereins der Provinz Sachsen	1689-90
	Leningrad	[Industrial Exposition]	711
	Bremen	Nordwestdeutschen Gewerbe- und Industrie-Ausstellung	235-36
1900	London	Broadwood's Pianoforte Exhibition	1858-61

Date	Place	Name or Title	Item Nos.
	Paris	Exposition universelle internationale	**1275-1300**
	London	International Loan Exhibition of Musical Instruments	**831-38, 1801-2**
	Amsterdam	Tentoonstelling van Muziek-instrumenten, boeken, muziekwerken der Nederlanders	**19**
1901	Berlin	Bach-Ausstellung	**102**
	Glasgow	International Exhibition	**563**
	Manchester	Music Trades Exhibition	**944-45**
1902	London	American Exhibition, Crystal Palace	**741-42**
	Frankfurt a.M.	English Coronation Exhibition	**533**
	Turin	Esposizione internazionale d'arte decorativa moderna	**1511-12**
	Boston	Historical Musical Exhibition	**216-18**
	Berlin	Industrie-Ausstellung für Gast- und Haus-Wirtschaft, Kochkunst, Erfindungen und Neuheiten	**115**
	Düsseldorf	Industrie- und Gewerbe-Ausstellung	**459-65**
	Liegnitz	Kunst- und Kunstgewerbe-Ausstellung	**722**
	Zittau	Oberlausitzer Gewerbe- und Industrie-Ausstellung	**1692-93**
	Leningrad	[Exhibition]	**705-7**
1903	Aussig	Allgemeine deutsche Ausstellung für Gewerbe, Industrie und Landwirtschaft	**65**
	London	International Pianoforte and Music Trades Exhibition	**839-40**
	Manchester	Music Trades Exhibition	**946-47**
	New York	"The Musical Instruments of the Incas"	**1062-63**
1904	St. Louis	Louisiana Purchase Exposition	**1392-95**
	London	International Pianoforte and Music Trades Exhibition	**841**
	London	Loan Exhibition of the Worshipful Company of Musicians	**852-57**
	Manchester	Music Trades Exhibition	**948**
1905	Liège	Exposition universelle et internationale	**719-20**
	St. Albans	English Church History	**1390**
	London	International Pianoforte and Music Trades Exhibition	**842**
	Manchester	Music Trades Exhibition	**949**
	Görlitz	Niederschlesische Gewerbe- und Industrie-Ausstellung	**569**
1906	London	Austrian Exhibition	**743**
	Nuremburg	Bayerische Jubiläums- Landes- Industrie- Gewerbe- Kunstausstellung	**1119-23**

Date	Place	Name or Title	Item Nos.
	Reichenberg i.B.	Deutsch-böhmische Ausstellung	1357-59
	Dresden	Deutsche Kunstgewerbe-Ausstellung	436-38
	Milan	Esposizione internazionale	988-92
	Zwickau	Gewerbe- und Industrie-Ausstellung	1712
	Berlin	Musik-Fachausstellung	121-24
1907	Coefeld	Dutch East Indian Art Exhibition	378
	Villingen	Gewerbe- und Industrie-Ausstellung	1646
	Leningrad	Pervaía vserossiiskaía vystavka muzykal'nykh instrumentov	712
1908	Munich	Münchener Jahres-Ausstellung	1045-46
	Nancy	Exposition internationale de l'est de la France	1051
	Leipzig	Musikfachausstellung	672
	Rotterdam	Tentoonstelling van muziekinstrumenten	1383-85
1910	Munich	Ausstellung von Meisterwerken muhammedanischer Kunst	1024-25
	Brussels	Exposition de l'art belge au XVIe siècle	303-4
	Brussels	Exposition internationale	315-19
	Munich	Musikfachausstellung	1047
	Rotterdam	Tentoonstelling van muziekinstrumenten	1385
	Stuttgart	Staatliche Erfindungs-Ausstellung	1457
1911	London	International Pianoforte and Music Trades Exhibition	843
	Dresden	Internationale Hygiene-Ausstellung	440-41
	Turin	Mostra internazionale	1516-19
1912	Paris	"La musique, la danse"	1315
	Paris	Salon	1315
1913	London	British Music Exhibition	749-52
	Ghent	Exposition universelle et internationale	555
	Leipzig	Internationale Bau-Fach-Ausstellung	665-67
	London	Olympia Exhibition	749-52
1914	Malmö	Baltiska Utstallning	940-43
	Paris	L'Exposition Pleyel	1304
	Berlin	Schweizerische Landesausstellung	200-202
1917	Zürich	Ausstellung Musikinstrumente	1694
1919	Paris	Foire [11th]	1301
	Lyons	Foire de Lyon	924
1920	Lyons	Foire de Lyon	925
	Schönbach	Musikinstrumentenbau-Ausstellung	1415
1921	Lyons	Foire de Lyon	926
1922	Rio de Janeiro	Exposição do centenario do Brasil	1361-62
	Brussels	Foire commerciale	326

Date	Place	Name or Title	Item Nos.
	Berlin	Musik-Fachausstellung [3rd]	125
	Leipzig	Mustermesse	673
1923	Paris	Exposition de physique et de T. S. F.	1186
	Paris	Foire [13th]	1302
	Leipzig	Mustermesse	674
	Paris	Salon de la musique	1316
1924	Paris	Foire [14th]	1303
	Paris	Salon de la musique [2nd]	1317
1925	Hamburg	Ausstellung musikgeschichtlicher Drucke, Handschriften und alter Musikinstrumente	622
	Paris	Exposition du travail	1210
	Paris	Exposition internationale des arts décoratifs et industriels modernes	1214-16
	Brussels	Foire commerciale	327
	Lyons	Foire de Lyon	927
	Paris	Salon de la musique [3rd]	1318
1926	Paris	Salon de la musique [4th]	1319
	Philadelphia	Sesquicentennial International Exposition	1328
1927	Munich	"Das Bayerische Handwerk"	1022-23
	Geneva	Exposition internationale de la musique	540-43
	Frankfurt a.M.	Internationale Ausstellung, Musik im Leben der Völker	522-28, 2063, 2065
	Paris	Salon de la musique [5th]	1320
1929	Barcelona	Exposición internacional	68-70
	Leipzig	Musikinstrumenten-Messe	675
	Paris	Salon de la musique [7th]	1321
1930	Antwerp	Exposition internationale [coloniale, maritime et de l'art flamand]	33-35
	Berlin	Grosse deutsche Funkausstellung und Phonoschau	112-13
1932	Berlin	Grosse deutsche Funkausstellung und Phonoschau	114
	Amsterdam	Internationale Ausstellung "Klank en Beeld"	6
1934	Paris	Exposition de la musique française	1185
1936	London	First Annual Piano Exhibition	768
	Leipzig	Musikinstrumenten-Messe	676
	Hälsingborg	Ystadutställningen	1988
1937	Budapest	Budapesti országos általános kiállitas	331
	Cremona	Esposizione di liuteria antica	406-10
	Paris	Exposition internationale	1211-12
	Leipzig	Musikinstrumenten-Messe	677
1938	Berlin	Internationale Handwerksausstellung	116
	Leipzig	Musikinstrumenten-Messe	678-79

Date	Place	Name or Title	Item Nos.
	Vienna	"Klaviere aus fünf Jahrhunderten"	1615
1946	Baltimore	"Musical Instruments and Their Portrayal in Art"	66
1949	Mittenwald	Deutsche Musikinstrumentenmesse	1004
	Florence	Esposizione nazionale dei conservatori musicale e delle musicale delle biblioteche Palazzo Davanzati	503-4
	Cremona	International Exhibition of Violin Playing	425
	Nyon	Trésors musicaux des collections suisses	1952
1950	The Hague	Bach en zijn Tijdgenoten, 1685-1750	586
	Mittenwald	Deutsche Musikinstrumentenmesse und Musikwoche	1005
	Leeds	Leeds Musical Festival	661-63
	Schiedam	Oud-Hollandse Meesters der Vioolbouw	1413-14
1951	Munich	Ausstellung alte Musik	1021
	Düsseldorf	Deutsche Musikmesse [3rd]	456-58
	Lima	"Exposición de instrumentos musicales peruanos"	724
	London	Festival of Britain	764-67
	The Hague	Internationale Tentoonstelling van moderne Blaasinstrumenten	597
	Providence	"Keyboard and Strings; Early Instruments and Performers"	1354
	Swansea	"Music in Wales"	1468
1952	Toledo	"Musical Instruments Through the Ages"	1498
	Berlin	"Musik exotischer Völker"	185
1953	Rome	Mostra Corelliana	1369-70
1954	Schwetzingen	Alte Musikinstrumente	1416
	Liège	Concours International de quatuor à cordes	717-18
1955	Amsterdam	String Instruments of the Low Countries	5
1957	London	"Private Musicke"	870
1958	Leeds	"An Exhibition of Master Violins . . . "	662
	Minneapolis	"Music and Art"	1003
1959	Cambridge(U.K.)	"Loan Exhibition of Musical Instruments"	356-57
	The Hague	"Het Muzikale hart van Nieuw-Guinea"	588
	Augsburg	"Musik und Musiker der Fuggerzeit"	62
1961	Vienna	"Aussereuropäische Musikinstrumente"	1627
	Lisbon	Exposição internacional de instrumentos antigos	737-38
	Madrid	Instrumentos musicales del Antiguo Perú	935
	Havana	Instrumentos y atributos folklóricos cubanos	630
	Haarlem	Tentoonstelling Nederlandse Orgelpracht	581
1962	Zürich	"Alte Musikinstrumente"	1696-97

Date	Place	Name or Title	Item Nos.
1963	Zagreb	"Automatofoni, muziki automati"	**1688**
	Jerusalem	"East and West in Music"	**644-45**
	Isola Belli	Esposizione violini stradivari	**640**
	Strážnici	"Lidové hudební nástroje"	**1454**
	Modena	Mostra di antichi strumenti musicali	**1009**
	Rome	"Mostra di strumenti musicali"	**1364**
	Edinburgh	Music and Dance in Indian Art	**471**
	Delhi	"Folk Musical Instruments of Rajasthan"	**432**
1964	Luanda	"Exposição etnográfica de instrumentos musicais"	**906**
	Versailles	"Vienne à Versailles"	**1541**
	Brussels	"Presence de Bruxelles"	**291**
1965	Berlin	"Klingende Saiten"	**186**
	Rome	"Mostra di strumenti musicali dell'Estremo Oriente"	**1375**
1966	Rome	"Mostra di strumenti musicali del '600 e '700"	**1376**
	Warsaw	"Polskie instrumenty muzyczne"	**1648-49**
1967	Ghent	Festival van Vlaanderen	**556**
	Sheffield	Sheffield Festival Exhibition	**2048**
	Berlin	"Trommeln und Trompeten"	**187**
1968	Edinburgh	Edinburgh International Festival	**476**
	Bruges	Festival van Vlaanderen	**240**
	Arnhem	"Luister van het Orgel"	**55**
	Eindhoven	"Een wereld vol muziekinstrumenten"	**481**
	Washington	"Organs in Early America"	**1659**
	Sussex	Exposition Sussex	**1467**
	Bloomington	"Traditional Music of the World"	**205**
	Washington	"Wind Instruments"	**1658**
1969	Copenhagen	"Classical Indian Musical Instruments	**385**
	Mexico City	Esposición internacional de instrumentos musicales	**975**
	Brunswick	"Geigenbau in Braunschweig. 125 Jahre Werkstatt Rautmann"	**247**
	Paris	Instruments de musique des XVIème et XVIIème siècles, Hôtel de Sully	**262**
	Basel	"Klangzauber"	**78**
	Vienna	"Volksmusikinstrumente der Balkanländer"	**1628**
	Eindhoven	"Van speeldos tot Cassettofoon"	**482**
1970	Liège	Festival de Liège ("Univers du pianoforte")	**721**
1971	Haifa	Music in the Ancient World	**609-12**
	Brussels	"Europalia 1971"	**263**
	Washington	"Music Machines-American Style"	**1663**
	Copenhagen	"Ocarina: den lille gås"	**394**
	Copenhagen	"Traek og Tryk, Pust og Sug"	**386**

Date	Place	Name or Title	Item Nos.
	New York	"Violins of France"	**1067**
1972	Augsburg	"Musikinstrumentenbau in Bayern bis 1800"	**1142**
	Grindelwald	"Das Alphorn in der Schweiz"	**579**
	Haslemere	"The Dolmetsch Collection of Instruments"	**1932**
	Vancouver	"The Eames Collection of Musical Instruments"	**1942**
	Copenhagen	"From Bone Pipe and Cattle to Fiddle and Psaltery"	**387**
	Château de Boleil & Château de Laarne	"Instruments de musique des XVIe et XVIIIe siècles"	**264-65**
	New York	"Musical Instruments of World Cultures"	**1064-65**
	Besançon	La vie musicale à Anvers au siècle de Granvelle	**203**
1973	London	"Eighteenth Century Musical Instruments, France and Britain"	**890-97**
	Tilburg	"Daar zit muziek in!"	**1493**
	Brig	"Das Hackbrett in der Schweiz"	**238**
1974	Berlin	Tönender Ton	**184**
	London	"Exhibition by Contemporary Craftsmen"	**744-45**
	Antwerp	Festival van Vlaanderen	**53, 262**
	Stockholm	"Klans i flinta och brons"	**1432**
	Paris	"Un moment de perfection de l'art français"	**1305**
	The Hague	Wereldmuziekconcours Kerkrade	**593**
	London	"Where the Wind Blows"	**867**
	Zürich	"Die Zithern in der Schweiz"	**1711**
1975	New York	"Collectors' Choice"	**1068-69**
	London	"Exhibition of Early Music"	**868**
	Vienna	"Musikinstrumente der Völker"	**1629**
	Vlaardingen	Tentoonstelling van uitheemse muziekinstrumenten	**1647**
	London	Retford Centenary Exhibition	**858**
1976	London	"Music and Musical Instruments in the World of Islam"	**798**
1977	Haifa	"Music in Ancient Israel"	**611**
	Zürich	"Alte Musikinstrumente der Sammlung Hug"	**1699**
	Toronto	Canadian National Exhibition	**1500**
	Paris	"Musique d'Asie"	**1313**
	London	Exhibition of Early Musical Instruments	**758-59**
	Berkeley	"Musical Instruments, East and West"	**97**
	Edinburgh	"Phonographs and Gramophones"	**478**
	Washington	"A Wonderful Invention"	**1650**
1978	Bennebrook	"Van Psalterium tot Piano"	**94**
	Washington	"The Harmonious Craft"	**1666, 1670, 1675**

INDEXES

General Index

Auctioneers, Antiquarians, and Firms

GENERAL INDEX

Item numbers are printed in boldface type; page numbers in italics.

Exposition universelle et colonial (Lyons, 1894) **922-23**

Exposition universelle et internationale (Ghent, 1913) **555**

Exposition universelle et internationale (Liege, 1905) **719-20**

Exposition universelle internationale (Paris, 1900) **1275-1300**

Fachschule für Musikinstrumenten-macher (Markneukirchen) **958**

Fachschule für Musikinstrumentener-zeugung (Kraslice) **656**

Fael, Vittorio **1521**

Fage, Juste Adrien Lenoir de la **1224**

Falcouner, Thomas **1957**

Falk, Marguerite **294**

Falle, Raymond **642**

Falmouth, Lord **2111**

Fara, Giulio **1322**

Farmer, Henry George **559-62, 716**

Fassbaender, Peter **1694**

Faure **307**

Fecit, Pietro **1241**

Fedeli, Vito **496**

Federhofer, Helmut **647, 974, 2094, 2096**

Fedtke, Traugott **164**

Fehr, M. **1695**

Feil, Arnold **1416**

Feis Ceoil (Dublin) **450**

Feldberg, Ann P. P. **2219**

Felipe II, King of Spain **1958-59**

Fenton House (London) **760-63**

Ferdinand I, Granduke (1549-1609) *316*

Ferdinand II, Erzherzog von Inner-österreich (1578-1637) **2094-98**

Ferdinand II, Granduke (1610-1670) *316*

Ferdinand II, von Tirol, Erzherzog von Österreich (1529-1595) **1579-82**

Ferdinand Karl, Erzherzog von Österreich (1628-1662) **1588**; *245*

Ferdinand de Medici, Prince of Tuscany (1663-1713) **1960-72**

Ferdinandeum (Innsbruck) **1541**

Fernald, Helen Elizabeth **1327**

Fernandez Blanco, Isaac **1973**

Fesperman, John T. **1659, 1669**

Festival de Liège (1970) **721**

Festival of Britain Exhibition (London, 1951) **764-67**

Festival van Vlaanderen, 1967 (Ghent) **556**

Festival van Vlaanderen, 1968 (Bruges) **240**

Festival van Vlaanderen, 1974 (Antwerp) **53**

Fest-Versammlung des Pestalozzi- und Lehrer-Vereins der Provinz Sachsen (Zeitz, 1899) **1689-90**

Fétis, Francois Joseph **785, 1218, 1230-32, 1974**

Fett, Harry Per **1150**

Fiala, Erick **1975**

Fibich **1976**

Fielding, Hon. Mrs. **1873-75**

Fievez, J., firm **2248**

Finch, Heneage, 6th Earl of Aylesford **1977**

Findeïsen, Nicolas **700, 1109**

Finsch, Otto **514**

Finzi, D. **2262-63**

First Annual Piano Exhibition (London, 1936) **768**

"First Musical Art Exhibition" (London, 1892) **859**

Fischhof, Joseph **784**

Fisher [bookseller of Brighton] **1978**

Fitze, Walter H. **112**

Fitzpatrick, Horace **575**

Flachat-Mony, Christophe Stéphane **1195**

Flachet, Stéphane. *See* Flachat-Mony

Flameng, M. F. *319*

461

AUCTIONEERS, ANTIQUARIANS, AND FIRMS
CONNECTED WITH SALES CITED IN SECTION II

Adler, Picard et Tajan **2157**
Anderson Galleries **1819, 2187**
Augustini **1810**
Aulard, Paul **2351**
Bangs & Co. **2379**
Baubigny **2016, 2350**
Bernardel, Léon **2006**
Bittner, August **1781, 1785**
Bom, G. Theod. **1743, 1795, 1818, 2418**
Bom, H. G. **1752, 2023**
Bon **1731**
Buys . . . Loot **1838**
Capobianchi, Vincenzo **2309**
Carlier, Victor **2415**
Carré, Gustave **2276**
Casa Liquidora **1787**
Chardon et fils **2351**
Charpentier, Marcel **2254**
Chevallier, P. **1845, 2272**
Christie, Mr. **1718, 1722, 1812, 2050,**
  2199, 2207, 2325, 2353
Christie & Manson, Messrs. **1863,**
  2017, 2373
Christie, Manson & Woods **1804,**
  1809, 2011-12
Delange, Carle **1889**

Escribe **1747**
Fievez, Jos. **2021, 2028, 2135-36, 2248**
Fletcher,Mr. **1734, 1912, 2306**
Förster, Carl **2175**
Foster, Edw. **2044**
Foster, Messrs. **1732, 1918**
Fox and Sons **2356**
Fulgence **1941**
Gand et Bernardel **1749, 1840-41,**
  1980, 2016, 2022, 2154, 2271, 2360
Gandouin **1801**
Gartman, van der Hey en Schmidt **2029**
Gartman, Vermandel, Smit **1720**
Gazagne, L. **2156**
Gläsel-Wiener, Moritz **1762**
Glendining, Mr. **1769, 1772**
Graham & Phillips, Messrs. **1719**
Greenwood, Mr. **1715-16, 1788, 1862**
de Hart, A. H. **2169**
Heberle, J. M. (H. Lempertz' Söhne)
  2030
Helbing, Hugo **2174**
Henkels, Stan V. **1784**
van Herck, Eug. **2072**
van Herck, Eug. & Eva Krug **2304**
Hoggart, Norton & Trist, Messrs. **1943**